2014

THE **NEW** ANCHOR STEP-BY-STEP ENCYCLOPAEDIA OF

Needlecraft

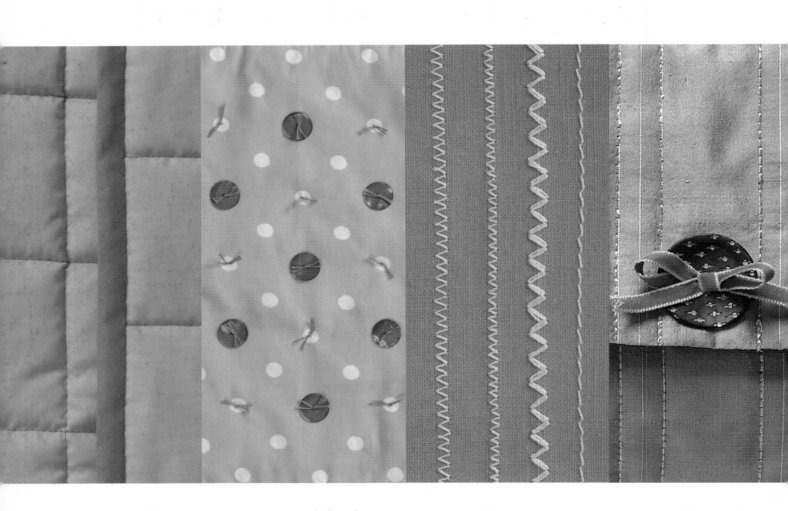

THE **NEW** ANCHOR STEP-BY-STEP ENCYCLOPAEDIA OF
Needlecraft

PATCHWORK · EMBROIDERY · QUILTING

SEWING · KNITTING · CROCHET · APPLIQUÉ

CARROLL & BROWN PUBLISHERS LIMITED

First published in 2007 in the United Kingdom by

Carroll & Brown Publishers Limited
20 Lonsdale Road
London NW6 6RD

Illustrations and compilation © Carroll & Brown Limited 2007

A CIP catalogue record for this book is available from the British Library.

ISBN 978-1-904760-59-7

10987654321

Reproduced by Universal Graphics Pte Ltd, Singapore
Printed and bound by Star Standard Pte Ltd, Singapore

CONTENTS

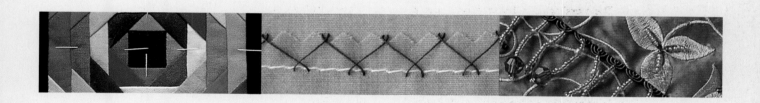

INTRODUCTION

There is something especially satisfying about making an article by hand, and we hope this book will provide you with hours of inspiration and enjoyment. From the moment you embark on a new project, you will find tremendous pleasure in selecting quality materials, choosing a design that reflects your taste, and creating a piece that is uniquely yours.

In this book, we provide step-by-step instructions for learning how to knit, crochet, embroider – by machine and hand – quilt, appliqué and sew. Each of these crafts has been around for generations, but all find honest uses on the contemporary scene. The techniques and patterns offered in the following pages represent the ingenuity of early needlecrafters, but the garments, accessories and household items you'll see featured in the book are far from old-fashioned. The crafts may be ancient, but the effects you can achieve after learning a few basics are timeless. All it takes is a little time and a little imagination.

For each craft, *The New Anchor Step-by-Step Encyclopaedia of Needlecraft* describes and illustrates the necessary materials and equipment, gives comprehensive how-to techniques, and provides extensive stitch and pattern glossaries. In addition, the book offers an enticing selection of beautifully designed garments and accessories for you to make for yourself, your home and your family and friends.

After you've entered the world of needlecrafts, you will find that the natural world around you – leaves, flowers, colours – will jump out as inspiration for your next project. After you've knitted your first sweater, stitched your first patchwork quilt or sewn your first pair of curtains, patterns, fabrics and textures will strike you in completely new ways. For instance, you may glance at a pale green leaf, and suddenly see it as the perfect pattern for a knitted sweater or an embroidery motif. Someone once described needlework as painting with a needle and we couldn't agree more!

The New Anchor Step-by-Step Encyclopaedia of Needlecraft gives each reader the confidence to create new items or to personalize the projects that appear in its pages. You will find items that can be worn, used in your home, or given as gifts, and the illustrated, step-by-step instructions and techniques give you all the information you need to start and, more importantly, finish these projects. Sweaters, hats and gloves; cushions, quilts and curtains; scarves, bags and boxes – the book contains over 50 fabulous items to show off your skills.

Each technique in *The New Anchor Step-by-Step Encyclopaedia of Needlecraft* is presented in full-colour photographs that let you follow the action every step of the way. And the photographs are so vivid, you can almost feel the texture of the yarn. It's like having an expert at your elbow. In the stitch and pattern glossaries, the large-size colour samples are so bold that it is easy to see each individual stitch – a boon for beginners as well as experienced needleworkers.

By referring to the all-colour project index, you have the opportunity to select something exciting to create and you'll have a guide to how your finished item should look. Most importantly, the majority of the projects are shown step-by-step so the margin for mistakes is extremely low.

In addition to the satisfaction of learning new skills, it is our wish that *The New Anchor Step-by-Step Encyclopaedia of Needlecraft* will open your eyes to appreciate the skill involved in the making of the needlecrafts found in stately homes and museums. We sincerely hope that you will use this book as a stepping stone to new skills and new interests – and to create heirlooms for the future.

BEADED ESPADRILLES

Plain cotton espadrilles are set to dazzle with the addition of sequins and beads in a heart-shaped motif.

FUNKY FLOWERS

Crochet a whole bunch in different colourways, to make the perfect finishing touch for lapels, hats, sweaters, chokers and wristbands.

QUILTED BELT

Create a simple silk belt then dress it up with appliqués cut from patterned fabric. Add a few beads for extra sparkle.

STRIPY FINGERLESS GLOVES

Snuggly and warm, these are great when you want to keep cozy but need your fingers free, say for some knitting! They are made on double-pointed needles, so you knit in a circle and won't have any seams to sew together.

BOLSTER CUSHION

Ideal for brightening up your living room, this sausage-shaped pillow is easy to sew and makes use of a bolster form. Accessorise your sofa by placing one at each end. A choice of two closings are given – ribbon tied, as shown here, or an elasticated version using cord.

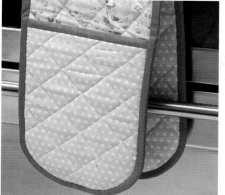

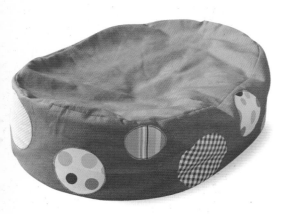

p.258

PEEK-A-BOO CUSHION COVER

This is an easy project for learning to crochet between the stitches. The stitch creates holes through which you can see the cushion. You start with a purchased cushion pad in a solid, bright colour. The corners of the cover can be trimmed with pompoms if you like.

p.304

MINI BEANBAG

This comfy cushion is just the job for children that like to sprawl about on the floor when watching TV. Once sewn, the cushion is filled with polybeads so it takes on the shape of whomever is sitting on it, and supports him or her in complete comfort. If you have a dog or cat, you could make one for your pet.

p.249

COTTON CABLE BACKPACK

This hands-free carryall knits up fast and the cotton denim yarn makes it hard-wearing as well. A bold cable pattern adds interest to the front side of the bag, which is just two rectangles joined together with a cord threaded through the top.

p.272

BOTTLE BAG

Make that gift of champagne or wine even more festive by creating a carrier bag with a couched design of vine leaves and grapes. The lining should help keep the contents cool, if necessary. Knotted leather ties make it easy to carry.

p.292

BABY'S QUILTED COVERLET

Welcome a new baby with this soft, cozy coverlet hand quilted with clouds. The clouds are dotted randomly across the fabric and it is up to you how many you have. The shapes are easy to sew if you are new to quilting. A soft fabric such as brushed cotton makes the coverlet even more cosy.

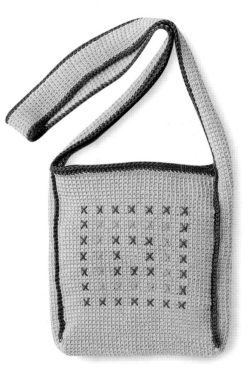

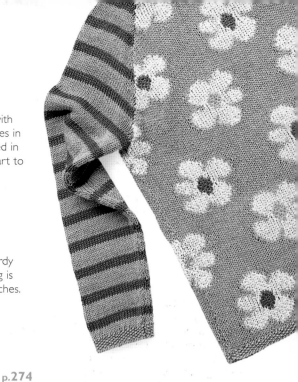

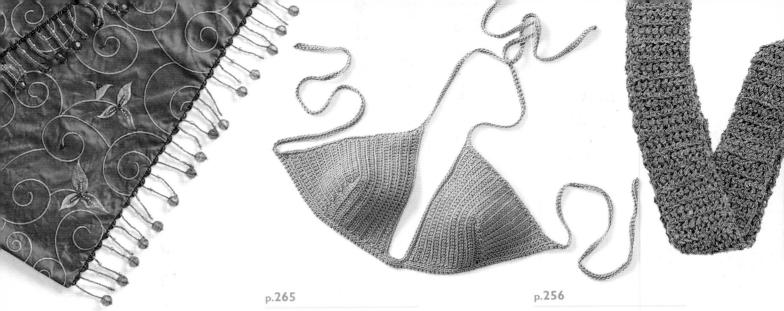

p.265

BIKINI TOP

This cotton string top can be paired with shorts, jeans or a sarong. It is made using just a few simple crochet stitches. The straps are made with a long string of chain stitches with double crochet added to each one for more strength.

p.256

SIMPLE SASH BELT

Practice your basic crochet skills by making this simple belt to wear with jeans, a dress – virtually anything. You can dress it up with a fantastic selection of beads and trimmings.

p.278

BEADED EVENING WRAP

A decoratively patterned piece of silk is transformed into a glamorous wrap by the addition of glass beads and a beaded fringe, which catches the light beautifully.

p.291

BUTTERFLY TOP

Any simple top can be dressed up by applying a lace motif embroidered in the shape of a butterfly and adding a scattering of twinkling sequins.

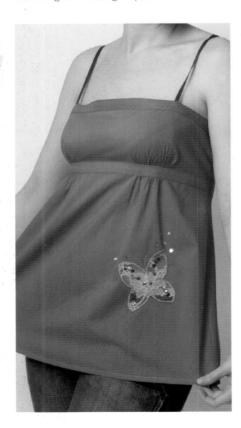

p.298

BEACH ROLL

This handy summertime accessory will make idling by the pool or shore even more enjoyable. Made to fold down or roll up in a flash, it has a shoulder strap for hands-free carrying. Its integral pillow and towel lining are the perfect surfaces from which to bask in the rays of the sun.

p.268

GRANNY SQUARE VEST

A perennial favourite, this crocheted top is pieced together from individual squares, opening up many possibilities for combining colours. See below for a matching top for a trendy pooch.

p.268

DOG COAT

Crocheted granny squares can be used to make a pooch poncho. You can adjust the number of squares to make one that will fit your dog, then add straps to fasten under his tummy and around his chest.

p.251

SLOUCH SOCKS

Great for keeping warm at home on a cold winter's day, these are knitted in a chenille-style chunky cotton on a set of double-pointed needles.

p.252

EMBROIDERED CUSHION

This pretty knitted cushion is made up of two blocks of blue and lavender. Beautiful embroidery using 4-ply yarn and colourful pompoms make it extra decorative.

p.296

DUFFEL BAG

This simple, roomy bag is the perfect all-arounder. As well as storing toys, it is ideal for a day out at the beach or pool. The bag is closed by cord threaded through the top hem. For a child-pleasing effect, there's a border of appliquéd animals.

p.273

EMBROIDERED HAND TOWEL

A plain terrycloth hand towel is given a border of crisp white cotton fabric decorated with lines of machine stitching.

p.281

CRAZY PATCHWORK PENNANTS

Great for hanging across a bedroom or in a dorm or even outdoors for festive occasions, these fabric pennants are an economical way to use leftover material. They are applied in a free-style overlapping design to a foundation fabric and edged with zig-zag stitch.

p.257

BUCKET HATS

These summer hats are comfortable, colourful, fun and are perfect for keeping the sun off delicate skin. They are also very quick and easy to crochet. Instructions are given for adult and baby sizes.

p.286

PICNIC BASKET COVER

Top a simple wicker basket with a neat cover that not only looks good but also will keep insects off the contents. Spotted furnishing fabric is tied to a backing with large contrasting buttons and embroidery floss. A striped ribbon secures it to the basket.

p.276

RECIPE BOOK COVER

Turn your recipe book into an heirloom by hand embroidering appropriate motifs on a chequered fabric. The cover can be adjusted to suit any size book.

p.279

COUCHED VELVET SCARF

Embroidery can add richness to a fabric and enables you to experiment with different design motifs. Here, simple flowers in a shade that echoes the satin backing are scattered over the toning raised grid to add textural interest to a shimmering velvet scarf.

p.285

QUILTED CLUTCH BAG

A simple but stylish envelope-style bag can be created from striped silk ornamented by stitching with metallic thread along stripes of different widths. A decorative button and silk ribbon trim provides the finishing touch.

p.259

ZIGZAG SCARF

This brightly coloured crochet scarf concertinas around the neck to produce a warm, snuggly covering.

p.293

SIMPLE CUSHIONS

It's so easy to make your own cushion covers, and these feature simple overlapped openings at the back. They can be removed for cleaning.

p.280

SMOCKED BANGLE BAG

Partly smocked silk fabric can be hung from bamboo handles to create an eye-catching bag that's great for special occasions.

p.267

LACY CAMISOLE

This crocheted camisole has a timeless quality, with its lacy stitch, tiny pearl buttons and slim straps. Pair it with jeans for a trendy, casual look or with dressy skirts or trousers for evening wear.

p.288

PATCHWORK SHOPPER

Plain and patterned fabric rectangles are sewn together to produce a contempory classic. An appliquéd seagull is a fun decorative touch, which can be outlined with embroidery floss and finished with a tiny button or bead. Cord makes an easy to fit and attractive adjustable handle.

p.254

BIG LOVE THROW

Have a heart and make someone you love this gorgeous throw. Made up of knitted squares, half worked in one colourway and half worked in another, each has a plump heart at its centre. Hot, bright colours have been used here, but pick shades that match your home and mood.

p.262

STRIPY POUCH

This mini bag is made from hand-dyed cotton yarn, and is the perfect size to hold a few essentials — mobile phone, keys and purse.

p.302

ROLL-UP SHADE

Perfect for a small window or glass-panelled door, this simple roll-up shade hangs flat against the wall when you want it down, but then is easily rolled up and tied in place when you want to let the light in. The shade hangs from a wooden batten, secured above the window, so you will need to do a bit of basic DIY as part of this project.

p.263

BEADED BAG

Crocheted cotton is embellished with iridescent glass beads, which are threaded onto the yarn and worked into the stitches as they are formed. The top has a fluted, double layer picot edge threaded with cord.

p.250

RIBBON-TIED CARDIGAN

This cotton cover-up is ideal for dressing up a simple evening outfit or worn as a lightweight top on warmer evenings. It is knitted in trinity stitch, a raised pattern, which gives it an interesting texture.

p.284

PET CUSHION

Paving stone patchwork blocks made up of plain colours and an animal print are turned into a cover for a super cushion on which any pet would be delighted to relax.

p.277

RIBBON BORDERED SKIRT

Easy to apply silk and velvet ribbons are combined with lines of decorative stitching and appliqué motifs to transform a plain skirt into something more special.

TECHNIQUES

WITHIN THIS SECTION, YOU WILL FIND all the techniques
necessary to master the most popular needlecrafts.

Each chapter covers a different craft, and within each chapter, you
are first acquainted with the required materials and supplies and
then led step-by-step from the initial stages through to advanced
techniques. You'll be in no doubt about what to do as each stage
is comprehensively illustrated by photographs and accompanied
by clear, non-technical text. Most chapters, too, contain extensive
stitch glossaries, which can help you to personalise your creations.

The techniques within the various sections will enable you to not
only create the projects contained in the book successfully but
also to attempt those found in magazines and other publications.
Fashions may change, but the techniques found within are the
tools that ensure mastery of the different crafts and will enable
you to create wonderful things to wear, decorate your home and
give as gifts.

CONTENTS

KNITTING

HAND KNITTING IS A WONDERFUL WAY to create truly
individual clothes and accessories for your family and home. The
wide choice of fibres and huge selection of colours available – from
natural, soft-coloured wools and shimmering silks, to hard-wearing
acrylics and polyesters or combination yarns – give you the
versatility to make fabulous one-off pieces.

Knitting was practised as far back as Biblical times, long before
Irish or Fair Isle fishermen were bundling up in warm, hardwearing
sweaters. Over the years the basic stitches have been combined
into complicated texture and colour patterns, many of which
were used to identify a particular village or area.

As each generation rediscovers the satisfaction of hand-knitting,
and with the increasingly wide range of yarns and patterns
available, there's now even more reason to become adept at this
stimulating and creative art, and in the following pages you will
find a wealth of information and inspiration to get
you started.

CONTENTS

EQUIPMENT & YARNS

STARTING A KNITTING project requires little more than enthusiasm, yarn, and a pair of standard straight knitting needles. These are made of aluminium, plastic, wood or bamboo and come in a range of sizes. For large pieces, and for knitting in the round, circular needles are useful, while gloves call for double-pointed needles. A few simple accessories are helpful.

TYPES OF NEEDLES

Special needles are used for cables, or for knitting in the round.

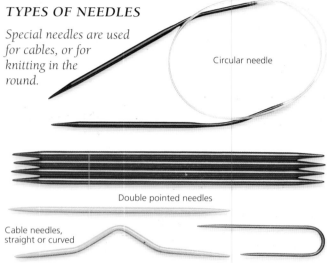

Circular needle

Double pointed needles

Cable needles, straight or curved

KNITTING NEEDLE SIZES

Equivalent knitting needle sizes:

US	Metric (mm)
14	2
13	2 1/4
12	2 3/4
11	3
10	3 1/4
9	3 3/4
8	4
7	4 1/2
6	5
5	5 1/2
4	6
3	6 1/2
2	7
1	7 1/2
0	8
00	9
000	10

OTHER USEFUL EQUIPMENT

These will help you hold or count your stitches, mark your place, or handle colours separately. Long pins and a blunt-pointed tapestry needle are needed for seams.

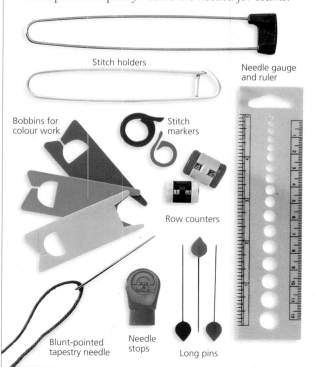

Stitch holders

Needle gauge and ruler

Bobbins for colour work

Stitch markers

Row counters

Blunt-pointed tapestry needle

Needle stops

Long pins

YARN WEIGHT AND PLY

Yarns come in a range of standard weights, and the most popular knitting yarns relate approximately to one another: double knitting is twice the weight of 4-ply, with Aran being roughly equal to three strands of 4-ply. Chunky is approximately equal to four strands of 4-ply or two strands of double knitting.

   The term ply refers to the number of strands which, when twisted together, make up the yarn, i.e. 2-, 3- and 4-ply are made up of that number of strands. Ply does not accurately define the weight – a thicker yarn may have fewer strands than a thinner one.

YARN CONTENT

Popular knitting yarns come in natural or synthetic materials. Natural yarns can be of animal or vegetable fibres, the former include wool, mohair, angora, cashmere, alpaca, and silk, while vegetable fibres produce cotton or linen yarns. Synthetic yarns include polyesters and acrylics; these are easier to wash and can be worn by people sensitive to wool. Yarns are often made of blends of two different types of fibre – mohair and nylon, or wool and silk are popular combinations.

Chunky

Aran

Novelty yarns

2-ply

4-ply

Chenille

Double knitting

BUYING YARN

Knitting yarns are most often sold in ready-to-use balls.
   Some yarns are sold in hanks or cones which are best wound into balls before use.

SHADE CARDS

Popular yarns usually come in a wide range of colours.

CASTING ON

THE FIRST STEP in knitting any article is to place the required number of stitches on the needles – this is called casting on. These stitches will form one edge of the finished article, usually the bottom. If you want the edge to be even, it is important that the stitches all be the same size. It is also necessary for the stitches to be moderately loose so you can easily work them off the needle. We recommend the one-needle cast on method for beginners, as it is easy to master, but if your resulting stitches are too snug on the needle, try the two-needle cast on. The first stitch in both methods is formed by making a slip knot.

Making a slip knot

About 15cm (6 in) from the yarn end, make a loop and insert needle under the short length (*left*). Draw thread through loop and pull both ends to tighten the knot on the needle (*right*).

ONE-NEEDLE CAST-ON EDGE

This should be made at a measured distance from the end of the yarn. Allow 2.5cm (1 in) per stitch for heavyweight yarn and 12mm (¹/₂ in) per stitch for lightweight. For example, start 25cm (10 in) from the slip knot to cast on 10 stitches in double knitting. The cast-on stitches will form a firm, yet elastic, foundation for all subsequent stitches, which is suitable for all patterns except those with a delicate edge.

TWO-NEEDLE CAST-ON EDGE

With this method, each new stitch is formed as a knit stitch (see page 26) and transferred to the left needle. If you work through the loop fronts on the first row, it produces a soft, loose edge, suitable for fine lace stitches. If you work through the loop backs on the first row, a firmer edge will be produced. Casting on with this method is useful when increasing stitches at one side (see page 30) or when completing a buttonhole (see page 65).

LEFT-HANDED KNITTERS

Reverse the instructions for left and right hands if you are left-handed. To cast on, hold the needle in your left hand and manipulate the working yarn with your right hand. When knitting, hold the needle carrying the stitches in your right hand and insert the left needle through the stitches. If you like, place this book in front of a mirror to follow the correct hand positions.

One-needle cast on

Hold the yarn in the fingers of your left hand

1 Allowing sufficient yarn for the number of stitches you want to cast on, form the slip knot; hold the needle in the right hand. Using the ring and little fingers of your left hand, hold the strands of yarn securely.

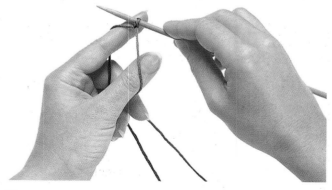

2 Slip your left forefinger and thumb between the strands so that the strand from the skein is at the back, and the working yarn is at the front.

Keep the yarn taught with your left thumb

3 Bring your left thumb up and spread your other fingers still holding on to the yarn ends.

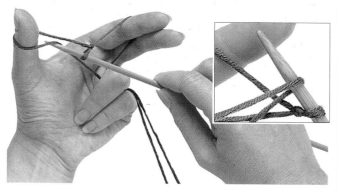

4 Take the needle under the yarn held across your thumb (*left*) and then up to the yarn on your left forefinger (*right*).

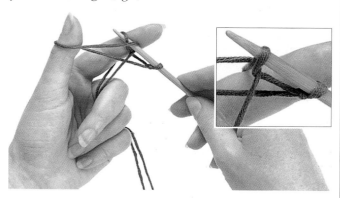

5 Putting the point of the needle behind the yarn on your left forefinger (*left*), draw the needle and yarn through the loop on your thumb to make the stitch (*right*).

6 Let the loop slip from your thumb and pull both ends to secure the new stitch. Repeat steps 1 to 6 for each required stitch.

Two-needle cast on

1 Make the slip knot and hold the needle in your left hand. Insert right needle through front of loop and pass the working yarn under and over its tip.

2 Draw yarn through the slip knot to form a new stitch.

3 Leaving the slip knot on the left needle, place the new stitch next to it.

4 Insert needle through front of loop of new stitch and pass the working yarn under and over its tip. Continue to form a new stitch as in steps 2 and 3 above.

Soft edge
Knit through the front of the stitch on the first row.

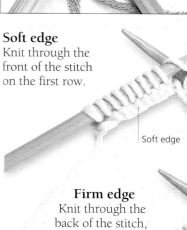

Soft edge

Firm edge
Knit through the back of the stitch, crossing the yarn.

Firm edge

KNIT & PURL STITCHES

KNIT AND PURL are the two fundamental stitches which most people recognize as plain knitting. Although these stitches are basic, they can be used in endless combinations to create any desired effect, whether you are knitting the simplest scarf or the most elaborate sweater. The knit stitch forms a flat, vertical loop on the fabric face; the purl stitch forms a horizontal semicircle. The simplest knitted pieces are worked in garter stitch, where every row is knitted; both sides look identical. Knitting and purling alternate rows produces stocking stitch – with a smooth knitted side and pebbly purled one.

The knit side of stocking stitch is smooth and flat

The reverse shows all the ridges of the purl stitches

STOCKING STITCH

This basic and versatile knitting pattern produces work that tends to curl if not blocked (see page 71). It stretches more widthwise than from top to bottom. The knit side is generally used as the right side.

REVERSE STOCKING STITCH

This is knitted in the same way as stocking stitch, but with the purl side used as the right side. It is often used as a background for cables and other raised patterns.

Reverse stocking stitch, with its purl stitches, can be used as a right side

The back shows the plain, smooth texture of the knit stitches

GARTER STITCH

This stitch is most commonly formed by knitting every row, but the same effect is achieved by purling every row. The work formed stays flat and firm, resists curling, and is good for borders, buttonhole bands, and edgings. It has a loose structure with "give" in both directions.

Knitting every row produces work that is identical on both sides, with ridges and furrows

KNIT STITCH USING RIGHT HAND

In this method, use your right hand to draw the yarn around the right needle. The amount of yarn released with each stitch is controlled by wrapping the working yarn between your two end fingers. Your left hand propels the knitting forward while your right hand makes the stitch – raising the thread, placing it over the needle, and pulling it through the loop.

KNIT STITCH USING LEFT HAND

In this method, often found to be faster than holding yarn in your right hand, you use the forefinger of your left hand to keep the yarn under tension and to scoop the yarn onto the right needle. The amount of yarn released is controlled partly by your last two fingers, and partly by your forefinger. Hold your left hand up slightly to help keep the yarn taut.

The forefinger keeps the yarn taught

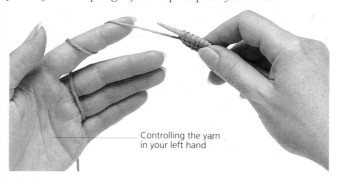

Controlling the yarn in your left hand

1 Hold the needle with cast-on stitches in your left hand. Take yarn around the little finger of your right hand, under the next 2 fingers, and over the top of your forefinger.

1 Hold the needle with the cast-on stitches in your right hand. Wrap the yarn over your left forefinger, let it fall across the palm and take up the slack between the last 2 fingers.

2 Keeping the yarn behind the work, hold the 2nd needle in your right hand and insert it into the front of the first stitch.

2 With work in left hand, extend your forefinger, pulling the yarn behind the needle. Using your thumb and middle finger, push the first stitch toward tip and insert right needle into front of stitch.

3 With your right forefinger, take the yarn forward under and over the point of the right needle.

3 Twist the right needle and pull the tip under the working yarn to draw loop onto the right needle.

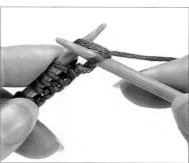

4 Draw yarn through the loop and push the resulting stitch toward the tip of the left needle so you can slip it onto your right needle.

The first stitch is formed on the right needle

4 If necessary, hold the loop with your right forefinger while you pull it down through the stitch. Pull the new stitch onto the right needle.

PURL STITCH USING RIGHT HAND

The movements here are opposite those for knit stitch. The needle is put into the front of the stitch, then the yarn, which is held in the front, is thrown over the back of the needle. Purl stitches tend to be looser than knit ones, so keep your forefinger closer to the work to help make the stitches even.

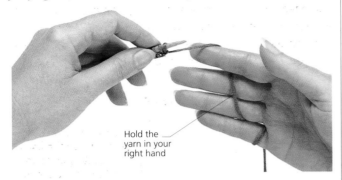

Hold the yarn in your right hand

1 Hold the needle with stitches (cast-on or knit) in your left hand. Wrap yarn around your little finger, under your next two fingers, and over the forefinger of your right hand.

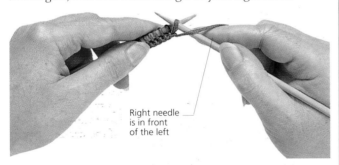

Right needle is in front of the left

2 Keeping the yarn in front of the work, pick up the needle in your right hand and insert the point into the front of the first stitch on the left needle.

3 With your right forefinger, take the yarn over the point of the right needle, and then under it.

4 Draw the loop on the right needle through the stitch and push the new stitch toward the tip of the left needle so you can slip it onto your right needle.

PURL STITCH USING LEFT HAND

With this method, your left forefinger holds the working yarn taut while you scoop up a new loop with your right needle. This action is helped by twisting your left wrist forward to release the yarn and using your middle finger to push the yarn towards the tip of the needle.

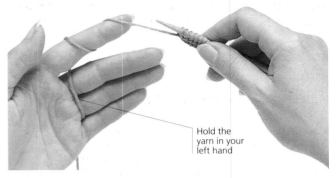

Hold the yarn in your left hand

1 Hold the needle with the stitches in your right hand. Wrap the yarn over your left forefinger, let it fall across your palm, and take up the slack between your last 2 fingers.

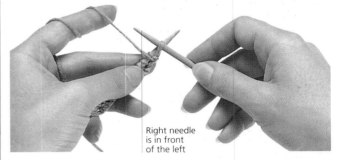

Right needle is in front of the left

2 With the work in your left hand, extend your forefinger slightly, pulling the working yarn in front of the needle. With your thumb and middle finger, push the first stitch toward the tip and insert the right needle into the front of the stitch. Hold stitch with your right forefinger.

3 Twisting your left wrist back slightly, use the forefinger of your left hand to wrap yarn around the right needle.

4 Push down and back with the right needle to draw the loop through the stitch and slip the new stitch onto the right needle. Straighten your left forefinger to tighten new stitch.

CORRECTING MISTAKES

THE SOONER YOU notice an error in your knitting the easier it is to correct. If a stitch has fallen off the needle one row down, you can retrieve it using your knitting needles. If you don't, it will unravel and form a run, and you will need a crochet hook to pick it up. If you knit a stitch incorrectly one or two rows down, you

can unpick it and then correct it in the same way. If a mistake has occurred near the start of your piece, you will have to unravel your work to get close to it. If you are working in stocking stitch or ribbing, always pick up stitches with the knit side toward you, as this is easiest. Be careful not to twist any of the stitches.

Retrieving a dropped knit stitch

1 Insert your right needle into the front of the dropped stitch, picking up the loose yarn behind it.

2 Take your left needle into the back of the stitch and gently lift the stitch up and over the loose yarn and off the right needle.

3 To transfer the new stitch, insert the left needle into the front so that the stitch slips onto it in the correct working position.

Correcting a run of dropped stitches

With knit side of work facing you, insert crochet hook into front of fallen stitch and pick up loose yarn behind. Draw yarn through stitch, forming a new stitch. Continue until you reach top of run. To work on purl side, insert hook into back of stitch and pick up yarn in front.

Retrieving a dropped purl stitch

1 Insert your right needle into the back of the dropped stitch, picking up the loose yarn in front.

2 Take your left needle into the front of the stitch and gently lift the stitch up and over the loose yarn and off the needle.

3 Insert the left needle into the new stitch on the right needle and slip the new stitch onto it in the correct working position.

UNRAVELLING YOUR WORK

*Mark the row in which your error occurred. Take the work off the needles and carefully pull the working thread, until you are **one row** above the error.*

To replace stitches on needle, hold yarn at back, and insert your left needle into front of first stitch below unpicked row. Pull on working yarn to remove top stitch.

INCREASING

IT IS NECESSARY to increase (add stitches), when you are shaping a garment. Increases are also necessary in creating certain stitch patterns, such as bobbles and laces (see pages 48 and 52). Where increases are made in garment shaping, they are often worked in pairs so that the item widens equally on both sides. Where increases are made in stitch patterns, they are combined with decreases (see page 33) so the total number of stitches remains constant.

There are several methods of producing increases. The yarn-over method (see page 32) is visible and is used for lace patterns. The other methods are called invisible. In reality, all increases can be seen but some are more obvious than others and different methods are used at different times.

Bar, raised and lifted increases are all invisible increases, and are typically used in garment shaping. When you are creating a gradual shape, such as a sleeve, it is neater to make the increases two or three stitches in from the sides and to use one of the invisible increases. With a complicated pattern, you will find it easier to add the stitches at the edges.

BAR METHOD

This frequently used technique produces a small bump on the right side of the work, hence its name. It is commonly abbreviated as Inc 1. You knit (or purl) into the front and back of a stitch to make two stitches. This increase can be used near the edge of the work when shaping garments or when making bobbles, where the bump will not matter.

1 Knit a stitch in the usual way but do not remove it from the left-hand needle.

2 Insert right-hand needle into back of the same stitch and knit again.

3 Remove the stitch from the needle. The extra stitch formed by this method produces a small bump on the right side. This will not be noticeable at the edge of the work.

RAISED METHOD

Here, you pick up the horizontal strand between two stitches and knit (or purl) it to make a new stitch. To make it virtually invisible, you have to work into the back of the strand so that it twists. It is effective for shaping darts on mitten or glove thumbs, and is commonly abbreviated make one (M1).

1 Insert your left-hand needle from front to back under the horizontal strand between 2 stitches.

2 Knit (or purl) into the back of the strand on your left-hand needle.

3 Remove stitch from the needle; the twist in the stitch prevents a gap from appearing.

LIFTED METHOD

This increase forms a slant, which needs to be paired with another to balance the work. You have to work both left-side and right-side increases from the centre. This method is particularly suitable for raglan sleeves as the resulting arrows create a fully fashioned appearance. Knit it with a loose tension since this method tends to tighten the work. The increase is made by knitting (or purling) into the horizontal strand below the next stitch to be worked. It is abbreviated as K (or P) up 1.

Paired increases on either edge of a piece of knitting form slanting lines

Right-side increase

1 Insert your right-hand needle from front to back into the top of stitch below the next one to be knitted.

2 Knit the loop you have just picked up in the usual way.

3 Then knit the following stitch normally.

Left-side increase

1 Insert your left-hand needle from back to front into the top of stitch below the last completed stitch.

2 Pull stitch back gently and knit into the front of the loop.

DOUBLE AND MULTIPLE INCREASES

To make two increases in the same stitch (M2), knit, purl, and knit into the front of the stitch. To make more than two stitches, as in bobble and raised patterns (see page 48), continue to knit and purl in the same stitch for the number of stitches that must be made. An increase of, say, five stitches is used to form a large bobble.

YARN OVER VISIBLE INCREASE

This is used for lace and other fancy patterns. This increase method produces a hole, which forms an openwork pattern. The basic technique is to wind the yarn once around the needle to form a loop, which is knitted or purled on the next row. The yarn is wound in different ways depending on where the new stitch falls (see below). This yarn over increase method is abbreviated as yo.

Yarn over in stocking stitch

1 To make a yarn over in stocking stitch, bring the yarn forward to the front of the work, loop it over your right-hand needle (*left*) and knit the next stitch (*right*).

2 The loop and new stitch are on the right-hand needle; knit to the end of the row.

3 On the following row, and with the rest of the stitches, purl the loop in the usual way.

Between purl stitches in reverse stocking stitch

Purl stitch, then take yarn back over right needle then forward under it.

Between two knit stitches in garter stitch

Bring the yarn forward over the right-hand needle, then back under it again.

Between two purl stitches in garter stitch

Take yarn back over right needle, then forward under it.

Between knit and purl stitches in ribbing

After knitting a stitch, bring yarn forward between needles, then back over right-hand needle and forward under it.

Between purl and knit stitches in ribbing

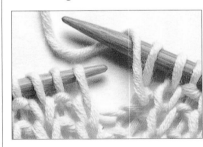

After purling, take the yarn over the right-hand needle from front to back.

DOUBLE AND MULTIPLE INCREASES

Several stitches may be made by the yarn-over method. In stocking stitch, to make a double increase, yo2, on a knit row, bring the yarn forward as for single yarn over but wrap it twice around the right needle before knitting the next stitch. On the next row, purl the first of the new stitches and knit the second.

When making multiple increases, yo3 (4, etc.), bring the yarn forward and then 3, (4, etc.) times around the needle. On the next row, purl and knit the new stitches alternately, always knitting the last new stitch.

DECREASING

CASTING OFF (see page 35) is the preferred method of decreasing when three or more stitches have to be lost, for example, at an underarm. However, if only one or two stitches have to be decreased, as when shaping a garment, any of the three methods described below may be used. Each method is visible and pulls stitches on a diagonal to the right or left. If you are decreasing randomly, or at the edge of the work, the direction of the slant is not important. In symmetrical shaping, however, such as with a raglan sleeve or V-neck, the decreases must be paired, to the right and left of the centre, so that the decreases balance one another. Right and left slants are made by knitting (or purling) two stitches together in their fronts or backs.

Slip-stitch decreases slant in only one direction, so in the same row they are generally used in combination with knitting two stitches together.

KNITTING TWO STITCHES TOGETHER

Decreasing by knitting two stitches together creates a slightly tighter decrease than the slip-stitch method. It is abbreviated K2tog for a right slant; K2tog tbl for a left slant.

Right slant

Knit 2 stitches together through the front of both loops. A slant to the right is used at the left edge of the work.

Left slant

Knit 2 stitches together through the back of both loops. A slant to the left is used at the right edge of the work.

PURLING TWO STITCHES TOGETHER

Decreases to the right are made by purling two stitches together through the front of both loops. This is abbreviated P2tog. For a decrease which slants to the left, purl two stitches together through the back of both loops. This method is abbreviated P2tog tbl.

THE SLIP-STITCH DECREASE

This results in a slightly looser decrease than knitting two stitches together. When made on a knit row, it slants from right to left, and is abbreviated Sl 1, k1, psso. A similar decrease can be made on a purl row, when it slants from left to right. It is abbreviated Sl 1, p1, psso.

On a knit row

1 Slip one stitch knitwise from your left needle onto the right needle then knit the next stitch.

2 Insert your left needle into the front of the slipped stitch and pull it over the knitted one.

3 The right-to-left slant is used on the right side of the centre of the work.

SELVEDGES

THE CAST-ON and cast-off (see page 35) stitches usually form the top and bottom ends of the work, and often have another finish applied to them, such as a fringe or neckband. The sides, known as selvedges, may be sewed into a seam or left exposed. If the sides are to be joined, use one of the simple edges since they are easier to sew. If you are knitting something with exposed edges, such as a scarf, tie, or blanket, use a border. This will be more attractive and help the finished piece lie flat.

Use the slip-stitch edge where there will be an edge-to-edge seam

SIMPLE SELVEDGE

The edge in stocking stitch, is formed by the work's alternate knit and purl rows. Beginning knitters often have trouble keeping this edge tight. Two variations can make this a more stable edge and one more suitable for seams. The slip-stitch edge is suitable when you will be seaming edge-to-edge, the garter-stitch edge is effective for backstitched and oversewn seams.

Slip-stitch selvedge
On all right sides of work (knit rows): slip the first stitch knitwise then knit the last stitch.
   On all wrong sides of work (purl rows): slip the first stitch purlwise then purl the last stitch.

Garter-stitch selvedge
Knit the right-side rows as usual, and knit the first and last stitches of every wrong-side (purl) row.

A garter-stitch edge can be used when there will be a back-stitched seam

The double garter-stitch edge is firm and even

BORDERS

Most pattern instructions do not take special edges into account, so you may have to add two additional stitches on each side. The double garter-stitch edge is firm and even, and will not curl. The double chain edge is decorative as well as firm.

A double chain edge is a more decorative edge

Double garter-stitch edge
On every row: slip the first stitch knitwise and knit the 2nd stitch; knit the last 2 stitches.

Double chain edge
On all right sides of work (knit rows): slip the first stitch knitwise, purl the 2nd stitch. Knit to the last 2 stitches, then purl 1 and slip last stitch knitwise.

CASTING OFF

CASTING OFF PROVIDES a selvedge (finished edge) at the end of your work. This technique is also used in armhole and buttonhole shaping. Plain casting off is the most common and easiest method.

Usually you cast off on the right side of the work and work the stitches in the same way as they were formed, knitting knit stitches and purling purl stitches. It is important that you cast off somewhat loosely, otherwise the edge may pull in and become distorted. If your stitches are too tight, try casting off with a needle one size larger than used for the work, or use the suspended cast off.

PLAIN CAST OFF

This produces a firm, plain edge that is suitable for seaming and armhole and buttonhole shaping.

1 Work your first 2 stitches in pattern. *Keeping the yarn at the back, insert the tip of your left-hand needle through the first stitch.

2 Lift the first stitch over the 2nd stitch and off your needle.

3 Work the next stitch in pattern.* Repeat sequence set out between the asterisks until the desired number of stitches are cast off. Secure yarn at end (see box below).

SUSPENDED CAST OFF

More flexible than the plain cast off, this method produces a looser edge and is preferable if your selvedges tend to be tight.

1 Work first 2 stitches in pattern. *Keeping yarn at the back, insert the tip of your left needle through the first stitch. Lift the first stitch over the 2nd stitch off the right needle, and retain on left needle.

2 Work the next stitch and drop the held stitch when you complete a new stitch.*

3 Repeat the instructions between the asterisks until 2 stitches are left. Knit these 2 together. Secure yarn at end, (see box below).

SECURING THE YARN END

After casting off with either of the two methods above, you will have a single stitch left on your needle. Slip this off your needle, take the yarn end and slip it through the last stitch and pull firmly to tighten the loop. Then, using a tapestry needle, weave the secured yarn end into the seam edge to a depth of 5 cm (2 in) to 8 cm (3 in).

Alternatively, if appropriate, fasten off securely by pulling the yarn through the last loop and leave a length of yarn which can be used for joining seams.

TENSION

AT THE BEGINNING of every knitting pattern you will find the tension – the number of stitches and rows to a given measure that should be obtained using the specified needles and yarn.

This tension is very important to the size and fit of your garment. Before beginning a new project, make a swatch about 10 cm (4 in) square and compare the number of stitches and rows over a given measure to the tension given in the pattern.

CHECKING THE TENSION

Using the given tension as a guide, and the needles and yarn designated, cast on four times the number of stitches that equal 2.5 cm (1 in). Then take your sample and pin it to a flat surface; do not stretch it. Use a ruler, plastic tape measure, or stitch gauge to measure both horizontally and vertically.

Use a tape measure to check the distance between the pins

MAKING ADJUSTMENTS

If your tension does not exactly equal that given, change needle size and knit another sample. One needle size makes a difference of about one stitch over 5 cm (2 in). If you have more stitches to the centimetre, your tension is too tight and you should change to larger needles. If you have fewer stitches, your tension is too loose so use smaller needles.

Measuring horizontally

In stocking stitch, it is easier to measure on the knit side, where each loop represents one stitch. In garter stitch, count the loops in one row only. Place 2 pins 2.5 cm (1 in) apart and count the stitches between them.

Measuring vertically

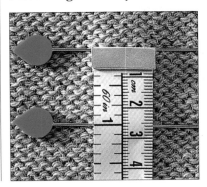

In stocking stitch, it is easier to measure on the purl side (2 ridges equals one row). In garter stitch, a ridge is one row and a valley another. Place 2 pins 2.5 cm (1 in) apart and count the number of rows between them.

THE EFFECT OF YARNS AND PATTERNS

Yarn and pattern also affect tension, so it is especially important to make a sample if you are changing either one from those called for in the instructions. Loosely spun or thick yarns, such as double knitting, will knit up with many fewer stitches and rows than firmly spun yarns, such as silk. Rib and other textured patterns produce much tighter work than do lacy patterns.

4-ply is the finest of the three yarns and produces the smallest square

Double knitting, worked to the same number of stitches, makes a larger piece than 4-ply

Aran yarn is the bulkiest yarn of the three and has fewest stitches to the inch

KNITTING TERMINOLOGY

A SET OF standard abbreviations, terms, and symbols have been devised in order to reduce knitting instructions to their shortest possible length. Otherwise, the row-by-row instructions for even a simple garment could take several pages. Multiples and repeats are commonly found in patterns and a fuller explanation is offered below.

Pattern abbreviations

alt	alternate
beg	beginning
CC	contrasting colour
cn	cable needle
dec(s)	decrease(s), (see page 33)
dp	double pointed
k	knit
k2tog	knit 2 stitches together
k-wise	insert needle as though to knit
inc(s)	increase(s), (see page 30)
lp	loop
M1	make 1 (see page 30)
MC	main colour
p	purl
patt	pattern
psso	pass slipped stitch over the knitted one, (see page 33)
p2tog	purl 2 stitches together
p-wise	insert needle as though to purl
RS	right side
rem	remaining
rep	repeat
rnd(s)	rounds
sk	skip
sl	slip (always slip sts purlwise unless otherwise instructed)
sl st	slip stitch, (see page 33)
ssk	slip, slip, knit decrease (see page 53)
st(s)	stitch(es)
tbl	through back of loop (work into back of stitch)
tog	together
WS	wrong side
yb	yarn behind
yf	yarn forward
yo	yarn over needle, (see page 32)
*	Work instructions immediately following *, then repeat as directed, (see Repeats)
[ ]	Work or repeat all instructions enclosed in brackets as directed immediately after, (see Repeats)
–	The number of sts that should be on your needles or across a row is given after a dash at the end of the row. This serves as a check point, especially after a section of increasing or decreasing.

Repeats

Because a knitting pattern usually consists of sequences of stitches, two devices are used to express this in the shortest possible space. One is the asterisk*, which is placed before the instruction it relates to. For example, *P2, *k2, p2; rep from *, end k2*, means you purl the first two stitches, then for the rest of the row until you are two stitches from the end, you knit two, purl two. The last two stitches are knitted.

Brackets are also used to indicate repeats. For example, *P2 [k2, p2] ten times, k3* means that after purling your first two stitches you repeat the sequence of knitting two and purling two ten times (a total of 40 stitches) before knitting the last three.

Multiples

Preceding each stitch pattern is an instruction about the number of stitches required to complete the pattern across the row. This is expressed as a multiple of a number of stitches, for example, *multiple of 6 sts.* It may also include an additional number to balance the pattern or account for a diagonal, for example, *multiple of 6 sts plus 3*. The number of stitches on the needle must be divisible by the multiple, so for a multiple of 5 sts plus 2, you would need to cast on 5 + 2, 10 + 2, 15 + 2,.... 100 + 2, etc. In the pattern instructions, the multiple is expressed in the following ways:

Multiple of 8 sts plus 2

Row 1: *K4, p4*, k2
Row 2: *P4, k4*, p2

or

Row 1: *K4, p4, rep from *, end k2
Row 2: *P4, k4, rep from *, end p2

TEXTURED PATTERNS

WITH ONLY THE two basic stitches, a wide variety of patterns can be created. Though the techniques are simple, the results are often sophisticated, and lend themselves to use on a wide variety of garments. In combination, knit and purl stitches accentuate each other, creating texture. When they are worked vertically, the knit rows tend to stand out from the purl ones. When they are worked horizontally, in welt or ridge patterns, the purl rows stand away from the knit rows. In textured patterns, the stitches form subtle designs that alter the surface of the fabric.

Vertical rows of knit and purl are known as ribbing, and will stretch in a crosswise direction. This quality is ideal for use on garment edges, and for children's clothes because the garment will expand to accommodate the child. To be sure cuffs and waistbands are snug fitting, use smaller needles than those used for the body of the garment.

KNIT AND PURL CUSHIONS

Use up scrap yarn by working small squares or rectangles in some of your favourite textured stitches; then sew them together for these patchwork cushions. They will serve as records of different knitting stitches.

Combining different yarns with various stitches can make subtle texture changes

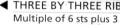
A three by three rib can be knitted in two colour stripes

Ladder stitch panels are interspersed with plain panels of stocking stitch

LADDER ▲
Worked over 11 sts on a background of st st
Row 1 (right side): P2, k7, p2.
Row 2: K2, p7, k2.
Rows 3 and 4: as rows 1 and 2.
Row 5: P.
Row 6: as row 2.
Row 7: as row 1.
Rows 8 and 9: As rows 6 and 7.
Row 10: K.
Rows 1 to 10 form the pattern.

◄ THREE BY THREE RIB
Multiple of 6 sts plus 3
Row 1: *K3, p3; rep from * to last 3 sts, k3.
Row 2: P3, *k3, p3; rep from * to end.
Rows 1 to 2 form the pattern.

MOSS STITCH RIB ▼
Multiple of 11 sts plus 5
Row 1: K5, *[k1, p1] 3 times, k5; rep from * to end.
Row 2: *P5, [p1, k1] 3 times; rep from * to last 5 sts, p5.
Rows 1 to 2 form the pattern.

BROKEN RIB ▲
Multiple of 2 sts plus 1
Row 1 (right side): K.
Row 2: P1, *k1, p1; rep from * to end.
Rows 1 to 2 form the pattern.

MOCK FISHERMAN'S RIB ►
Multiple of 4 sts plus 3.
All rows: *K2, p2; rep from * to last 3 sts, k2, p1.

DIAMOND BROCADE ▲
Multiple of 8 sts plus 1

Row 1 (right side): K4, *p1, k7; rep from * to last 5 sts, p1, k4.
Row 2: P3, *k1, p1, k1, p5; rep from * to last 6 sts, k1, p1, k1, p3.
Row 3: K2, *p1, k3; rep from * to last 3 sts, p1, k2.
Row 4: P1, *k1, p5, k1, p1; rep from * to end.
Row 5: *P1, k7; rep from * to last st, p1.
Row 6: as row 4.
Row 7: as row 3.
Row 8: as row 2.
Rows 1 to 8 form the pattern.

SEEDED TEXTURE ▲
Multiple of 5 sts plus 2

Row 1 (right side): K2, *p3, k2; rep from * to end.
Row 2: P.
Row 3: *P3, k2; rep from * to last 2 sts, p2.
Row 4: P.
Rows 1 to 4 form the pattern.

DOUBLE MOSS STITCH ▶
Multiple of 4 sts plus 2

Row 1: K2, *p2, k2; rep from * to end.
Row 2: P2, *k2, p2; rep from * to end.
Row 3: as row 2.
Row 4: as row 1.
Rows 1 to 4 form the pattern.

SEED STITCH ▲
Multiple of 4 sts

Row 1: *K3, p1; rep from * to end.
Row 2: P.
Row 3: K.
Row 4: P.
Row 5: K1, *p1, k3;* rep from * to last 3 sts, p1, k2.
Row 6: P.
Row 7: K.
Rows 1 to 7 form the pattern.

◀ MOSS STITCH
Multiple of 2 sts plus 1
All rows: K1, * p1, k1, rep from * to end.

CHEVRON RIB ▲
Multiple of 18 sts plus 1

Row 1 (right side): P1, *k1, p2, k2, p2, k1, p1; rep from * to end.
Row 2: *K3, p2, k2, p2, k1, [p2, k2] twice; rep from * to last st, k1.
Row 3: *[P2, k2] twice, p3, k2, p2, k2, p1; rep from * to last st, p1.
Row 4: *K1, p2, k2, p2, k5, p2, k2, p2; rep from * to last st, k1.
Rows 1 to 4 form the pattern.

MARRIAGE LINES ▶

Worked over 17sts on a background of st st

Row 1 (right side): P3, k6, p1, k2, p1, k1, p3.
Row 2: K1, p1, [k1, p2] twice, k1, p5, k1, p1, k1.
Row 3: P3, k4, p1, k2, p1, k3, p3.
Row 4: K1, p1, k1, p4, k1, p2, k1, p3, k1, p1, k1.
Row 5: P3, [k2, p1] twice, k5, p3.
Row 6: K1, p1, k1, p6, k1, p2, [k1, p1] twice, k1.
Row 7: as row 5.

Row 8: as row 4.
Row 9: as row 3.
Row 10: as row 2.
Rows 1 to 10 form the pattern.

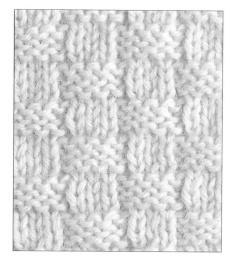

RIPPLE STRIPE ◀

Multiple of 8 sts plus 1

Row 1 (right side): K4, *p1, k7; rep from * to last 5 sts, p1, k4.
Row 2: P3, *k3, p5; rep from * to last 6 sts, k3, p3.
Row 3: K2, *p2, k1, p2, k3; rep from * to last 2 sts, k2.
Row 4: P1, *k2, p3, k2, p1; rep from * to end.
Row 5: K1, *p1, k5, p1, k1; rep from * to end.
Row 6: P.
Rows 1 to 6 form the pattern.

BASKETWEAVE ▲

Multiple of 8 sts plus 3

Row 1 (right side): K.
Row 2: K4, p3, *k5, p3; rep from * to last 4 sts, k4.
Row 3: P4, k3, * p5, k3; rep from * to last 4 sts, p4.
Row 4: as row 2.
Row 5: K.
Row 6: P3, *k5, p3; rep from * to end.
Row 7: K3, *p5, k3; rep from * to end.
Row 8: as row 6.
Rows 1 to 8 form the pattern.

SQUARE LATTICE ◀

Multiple of 14 sts plus 2

Row 1 (right side): K.
Rows 2, 4 and 6: P2, *[k1, p1] twice, k1, p2; rep from * to end.
Rows 3, 5, and 7: K3, *p1, k1, P1, k4; rep from * to last 3 sts, k3.
Row 8: P2, *k12, p2; rep from * to end.
Row 9: K2, *p12; rep from * to end.
Row 10: P.
Rows 11, 13, and 15: K2, *[p1, k1] twice, p1, k2; rep from * to end.
Rows 12, 14, and 16: P3, *k1, p1, k1, p4; rep from * to last 3 sts, p3.
Row 17: P7, *k2, p12; rep from * to last 9 sts, k2, p7.
Row 18: K7, *p2, k12; rep from * to last 9 sts, p2, k7.
Rows 1 to 18 form the pattern.

GARTER STITCH RIDGES ◀

Any number of stitches

Row 1 (right side): K.
Row 2: P.
Rows 3 and 4: as rows 1 and 2.
Rows 5 to 10: P.
Rows 1 to 10 form the pattern.

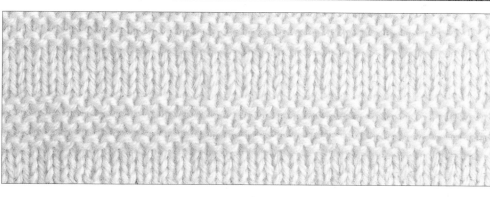

CABLE KNITTING

CABLES CAN TRANSFORM an otherwise simple knitted garment into something really special. They can be used as single panels or combined into an all-over pattern. Originally, fishermen's sweaters were often decorated with cables and patterns that served to identify a man's parish. Heavily textured patterns add to a sweater's warmth and durability. Learning to make cables is within the capabilities of every knitter. If you are adding cable panels to a plain sweater pattern, you must remember that cables tend to decrease the overall width, so plan the pattern and yarn requirements accordingly.

HONEYCOMB ARAN SWEATER

This round-necked cable sweater uses many of the traditional Aran Islands patterns, including a special feature of cable ribbing. The raglan style sleeve makes this ideal for men and women.

The traditional natural undyed wool shows the textured patterns to their full advantage

SPECIAL EQUIPMENT

Cable needles are short double-pointed needles that allow you to hold the stitches to be twisted at the front or back of the work. They can be straight or curved. The curved needle holds the stitches more firmly and keeps them from slipping off.

CABLING BASICS

The basis of all cable patterns is a simple technique whereby stitches are crossed over another group of stitches in the same row. Some of the stitches making up the cable are held at the back (or front) of the work on a special cable needle, while the other stitches are knitted. Then the stitches on the cable needle are knitted, thereby creating a twist.

MAKING CABLES

The cables shown below are 6 stitches wide; these 6 stitches are knitted on the right side and purled on the wrong side.
The stitches on either side are purled on the right side and knitted on the wrong side, i.e. reverse stocking stitch. The length between the twists can be changed as desired; commonly they are crossed every sixth or eighth row. The cables shown here are crossed at the eighth row, having started with a wrong-side row.

Left-hand cable

Right-hand cable

Left-hand cable

Holding the stitches at the back of the work always produces a left-over-right cable.

1 Slip the first 3 stitches onto a cable needle and hold at the back of the work.

2 Then knit the next 3 stitches on the main needle.

3 Finally, knit the 3 stitches held on the cable needle.

Right-hand cable

Holding the stitches at the front of the work always produces a right-over-left cable.

1 Slip the first 3 stitches onto a cable needle and hold at the front of the work.

2 Then knit the next 3 stitches on the main needle.

3 Finally, knit the 3 stitches held on the cable needle.

◀ **LARGE DOUBLE CABLE**
Worked over 20 sts on a background of reverse st st
Row 1 (right side): K.
Row 2: P.
Row 3: C10B, C10F.
Row 4: P.
Rows 5 to 12: Rep rows 1 and 2 four times.
Rows 1 to 12 form the pattern.

MEDALLION MOSS CABLE ▲
Worked over 13 sts on a background of reverse st st
Row 1 (right side): K4, [p1, k1] 3 times, k3.
Row 2: P3, [k1, p1] 4 times, p2.
Rows 3 and 4: as rows 1 and 2.
Row 5: C6F, k1, C6B.
Row 6: P.
Row 7: K.
Rows 8 to 11: rep rows 6 and 7 twice.
Row 12: P.
Row 13: C6B, k1, C6F.
Row 14: as row 2.
Row 15: as row 1.
Row 16: as row 2.
Rows 1 to 16 form the pattern.

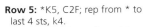

LITTLE WAVE ▲
Multiple of 7 sts plus 4
Row 1 (right side): K.
Row 2: P4, *k2, p5; rep from * to end.
Row 3: K4, *C2F, k5; rep from * to end.
Row 4: P4, *k1, p1, k1, p4; rep from * to end.

Row 5: *K5, C2F; rep from * to last 4 sts, k4.
Row 6: *P5, k2; rep from * to last 4 sts, p4.
Row 7: K.
Row 8: as row 6.
Row 9: *K5, C2B; rep from * to last 4 sts, k4.
Row 10: as row 4.
Row 11: K4, *C2B, k5; rep from * to end.
Row 12: as row 2.
Rows 1 to 12 form the pattern.

◀ **TELESCOPE LATTICE**
Worked over 12 sts on a background of st st
Row 1 and every alt row (wrong side): P.
Row 2: K.
Row 4: *C4B, k4, C4F; rep from * to end.
Row 6: K.
Row 8: *K2, C4F, C4B, k2; rep from * to end.
Rows 1 to 8 form the pattern.

◀ **CROSS RIB CABLE**
Multiple of 11 sts
Row 1 (wrong side): K2, [p1, k1] 4 times, k1.
Row 2: P2, [k1 tbl, p1] 4 times, p1.
Rows 3 to 6: rep rows 1 and 2 twice.
Row 7: as row 1.
Row 8: P2, slip next 4 sts to front on cable needle, [k1tbl, p1] twice from main needle, [k1tbl, p1] twice from cable needle, p1.
Rows 9 to 12: rep rows 1 and 2 twice.
Rows 1 to 12 form the pattern.

SMALL TWIST STITCH CABLE ▲
Multiple of 8 sts plus 3
Row 1 (right side): *K3, p1, k1tbl, p1, k1tbl, p1; rep from * to last 3 sts, k3.
Row 2: P3, *k1, p1tbl, k1, p1tbl, k1, p3; rep from * to end.
Rows 3 to 6: rep rows 1 and 2 twice.

twice.
Row 7: *K3, p1, slip next 2 sts to front on cn, k1tbl, p1, k1tbl from cn, p1; rep from * to last 3 sts, k3.
Row 8: as row 2.
Rows 1 to 8 form the pattern.

OPENWORK AND TWIST ▶

Multiple of 15 sts plus 12

Special abbreviation

T4LR (Twist 4 Left and Right): Slip next 3 sts onto cn and hold at back of work, knit next st from left needle then slip the first st on cn back to left needle, p2 from cn then k1 from left needle.

Row 1 (right side): P1, T4LR, p2, T4LR, p1, *k1, yo, sl 1, k1, psso, p1, T4LR, p2, T4LR, p1; rep from * to end.

Row 2: K1, p1, [k2, p1] 3 times, k1, *p3, k1, p1, [k2, p1] 3 times, k1; rep from * to end.

Row 3: P1, k1, p2, T4LR, p2, k1, p1, *k2tog, yo, k1, p1, k1, p2, T4LR, p2, k1, p1; rep from * to end.

Row 4: as row 2.

Rows 1 to 4 form the pattern.

BRAID CABLE ▲

Multiple of 8 (min. 16 sts) worked on a background of reverse st st. Shown worked over 24 sts

Row 1 (right side): K.

Row 2 and every alt row: P.

Row 3: K.

Row 5: *C8B; rep from * to end of panel.

Row 7: K.

Row 9: K.

Row 11: *C8F; rep from * to end of panel.

Row 12: P.

Rows 1 to 12 form the pattern.

Up   Down

◀ 9 STITCH PLAIT

Worked over 9 sts on a background of reverse st st.

Downward plait

Row 1 (right side): K.

Row 2 and every alt row: P.

Row 3: C6F, k3.

Row 5: K.

Row 7: K3, C6B.

Row 8: P.

Upward plait

Row 1 (right side): K.

Row 2 and every alt row: P.

Row 3: C6B, k3.

Row 5: K.

Row 7: K3, C6F.

Row 8: P.

Rows 1 to 8 form each pattern.

Up   Down

◀ CLAW PATTERN

Worked over 9 sts on a background of reverse st st

Special abbreviations

Cross 4L (Cross 4 Left): Slip next st onto cn and hold at front of work, knit next 3 sts from left needle then knit st from cn.

Cross 4R (Cross 4 Right): Slip next 3 sts onto cn and hold at back of work, knit next st from left needle then knit sts from cn.

Downward claw

Row 1 (right side): K.

Row 2: P.

Row 3: Cross 4L, k1, Cross 4R.

Row 4: P.

Rows 1 to 4 form the pattern.

Upward claw

Row 1 (right side): K.

Row 2: P.

Row 3: Cross 4R, k1, Cross 4L.

Row 4: P.

Rows 1 to 4 form the pattern.

Medallion moss cable

STRIPED MEDALLION CABLE ▶

Worked over 16 sts on a background of reverse st st

Special abbreviations

T8B rib (Twist 8 Back rib): Slip next 4 sts onto cn and hold at back of work, k1, p2, k1 from left-hand needle, then k1, p2, k1 from cn.

T8F rib (Twist 8 Front rib): Slip next 4 sts onto cn and hold at front of work, k1, p2, k1 from left-hand needle, then k1, p2, k1 from cn.

Row 1 (right side): K1, p2, [k2, p2] 3 times, k1.

Row 2: P1, k2, [p2, k2] 3 times, p1.

Row 3: T8B rib, T8F rib.

Row 4: as row 2.

Rows 5 to 14: Rep rows 1 and 2 five times.

Row 15: T8F rib, T8B rib.

Row 16: as row 2.

Rows 17 to 24: Rep rows 1 and 2 four times.

Rows 1 to 24 form the pattern.

▼ ALTERNATING BRAID CABLE

Worked over 6 sts on a background of reverse st st

Row 1 (wrong side): P.

Row 2: K.

Row 3: P.

Row 4: C4B, k2.

Row 5: P.

Row 6: K2, C4F.

Rows 3 to 6 form the pattern.

◀ CELTIC PLAIT

Multiple of 10 sts plus 5 (min. 25 sts) on a background of reverse st st. Shown worked over 25 sts

Special abbreviations

T5B (Twist 5 Back): Slip next 2 sts onto cn and hold at back of work, knit next 3 sts from left needle, then purl sts from cn.

T5F (Twist 5 Front): Slip next 3 sts onto cn and hold at front of work, purl next 2 sts from left needle, then knit sts from cn.

Row 1 (right side): K3, *p4, k6, rep from * to last 2 sts, p2.

Row 2: K2, *p6, k4; rep from * to last 3 sts, p3.

Row 3: K3, *p4, C6F; rep from * to last 2 sts, p2.

Row 4: K2, *p6, k4; rep from * to last 3 sts, p 3.

Row 5: *T5F, T5B; rep from * to last 5 sts, T5F.

Row 6: P3, *k4, p6; rep from * to last 2 sts, k2.

Row 7: P2, *C6B, p4; rep from * to last 3 sts, k3.

Row 8: as row 6.

Row 9: *T5B, T5F; rep from * to last 5 sts, T5B.

Row 10: as row 4.

Rows 3 to 10 form the pattern.

DOUBLE CROSSOVER ▼

Worked over 16 sts on a background of reverse st st

Special abbreviations

T3B (Twist 3 Back): Slip next st onto cn and hold at back, k next 2 sts from left needle, then p st from cn.

T3F (Twist 3 Front): Slip next 2 sts onto cn and hold at front of work, purl next st from left needle, then knit sts from cn.

Row 1 (right side): K2, p4, k4, p4, k2.

Row 2: P2, k4, p4, k4, p2.

Row 3: K2, p4, C4B, p4, k2.

Row 4: as row 2.

Row 5: [T3F, p2, T3B] twice.

Row 6: K1, p2, [k2, p2] 3 times, k1.

Row 7: P1, T3F, T3B, p2, T3F, T3B, p1.

Row 8: K2, p4, k4, p4, k2.

Row 9: P2, C4B, p4, C4B, p2.

Row 10: as row 8.

Row 11: P2, k4, p4, k4, p2.

Rows 12 and 13: as rows 8 and 9.

Row 14: as row 8.

Row 15: P1, T3B, T3F, p2, T3B, T3F, p1.

Row 16: as row 6.

Row 17: [T3B, p2, T3F] twice.

Rows 18 and 19: as rows 2 and 3.

Row 20: as row 2.

Rows 1 to 20 form the pattern.

◀ HONEYCOMB

Multiple of 8 sts

Row 1 (right side): *C4B, C4F; rep from * to end of panel.

Row 2: P.

Row 3: K.

Row 4: P.

Row 5: *C4F, C4B; rep from * to end of panel.

Row 6: P.

Row 7: K.

Row 8: P.

Rows 1 to 8 form the pattern.

ALTERNATED CABLE ▲

Worked over 10 sts on a background of reverse st st

Special abbreviations

T3B (Twist 3 Back): Slip next st onto cn and hold at back of work, knit next 2 sts from left needle, then purl st from cn.

T3F (Twist 3 Front): Slip next 2 sts onto cn and hold at front of work, purl next st from left needle, then knit sts from cn.

Row 1 (right side): P1, k8, p1.
Row 2: K1, p8, k1.
Row 3: P1, C4B, C4F, p1.
Row 4: K1, p2, k4, p2, k1.
Row 5: T3B, p4, T3F.
Row 6: P2, k6, p2.
Row 7: K2, p6, k2.
Rows 8 and 9: as rows 6 and 7.
Row 10: as row 6.
Row 11: T3F, p4, T3B.
Row 12: as row 4.
Row 13: P1, C4F, C4B, p1.
Row 14: K1, p8, k1.
Row 15: P1, C4B, C4F, p1.
Row 16: K1, p8, k1.
Row 17: P1, k8, p1.
Rows 18 and 19: as rows 14 and 15.
Row 20: as row 16.
Rows 1 to 20 form the pattern.

CHAIN CABLE ▶

Worked over 8 sts on a background of reverse st st

Row 1 (right side): K.
Row 2: P.
Row 3: C4B, C4F.
Row 4: P.
Rows 5 and 6: as rows 1 and 2.
Row 7: C4F, C4B.
Row 8: P.
Rows 1 to 8 form the pattern.

SNAKE CABLE ▲

Worked over 8 sts on a background of reverse st st

Row 1 (right side): K8.
Row 2: P8.
Row 3: C8B.
Row 4: P8.
Rows 5 to 10: Rep rows 1 and 2 three times.
Row 11: C8F.
Row 12: P8.
Rows 13 to 16: Rep rows 1 and 2 twice.
Rows 1 to 16 form the pattern.

INTERLACED CABLES ▼

Multiple of 8 sts plus 10

Special abbreviations

T4B (Twist 4 Back): Slip next 2 sts onto cn and hold at back of work, knit next 2 sts from left needle, then purl sts from cn.

T4F (Twist 4 Front): Slip next 2 sts onto cn and hold at front of work, purl next 2 sts from left needle, then knit sts from cn.

Row 1 (right side): P3, k4, *p4, k4; rep from * to last 3 sts, p3.
Row 2: K3, p4, *k4, p4; rep from * to last 3 sts, k3.
Row 3: P3, C4B, *p4, C4B; rep from * to last 3 sts, p3.
Row 4: as row 2.
Rows 5 to 8: as rows 1 to 4.
Row 9: P1, *T4B, T4F; rep from * to last st, p1.
Row 10: K1, p2, k4, *p4, k4; rep from * to last 3 sts, p2, k1.
Row 11: P1, k2, p4, *C4F, p4; rep from * to last 3 sts, k2, p1.
Row 12: as row 10.
Row 13: P1, *T4F, T4B; rep from * to last st, p1.
Rows 14 and 15: as rows 2 and 3.
Row 16: as row 2.
Rows 1 to 16 form the pattern.

WOVEN TRELLIS ▼

Multiple of 12 sts plus 14

Special abbreviations

T4B (Twist 4 Back): Slip next 2 sts onto cn and hold at back of work, knit next 2 sts from left needle, then purl sts from cn.

T4F (Twist 4 Front): Slip next 2 sts onto cn and hold at front of work, purl next 2 sts from left needle, then knit sts from cn.

Row 1 (right side): P3, T4B, T4F, *p4, T4B, T4F; rep from * to last 3 sts, p3.
Row 2: K3, p2, *k4, p2; rep from * to last 3 sts, k3.
Row 3: P1, *T4B, p4, T4F; rep from * to last st, p1.
Row 4: K1, p2, k8, *p4, k8; rep from * to last 3 sts, p2, k1.
Row 5: P1, k2, p8, *C4B, p8; rep from * to last 3 sts, k2, p1.
Row 6: as row 4.
Row 7: P1, *T4F, p4, T4B; rep from * to last st, p1.
Row 8: as row 2.
Row 9: P3, T4F, T4B, *p4, T4F, T4B; rep from * to last 3 sts, p3.
Row 10: K5, p4, *k8, p4; rep from * to last 5 sts, k5.
Row 11: P5, C4F, *p8, C4F; rep from * to last 5 sts, p5.
Row 12: as row 10.
Rows 1 to 12 form the pattern.

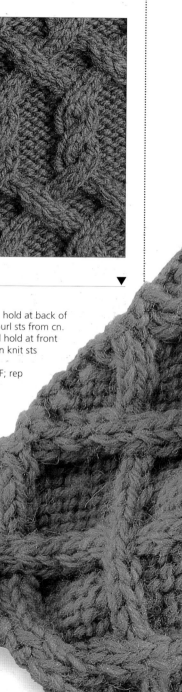

RAISED PATTERNS

A VARIETY OF dramatic effects can be achieved by using stitches to create patterns that stand out from a ground fabric. These stitches are produced by increasing and decreasing techniques, sometimes combined with twist or cable stitches.

Raised stitches come in all sizes, and can be worked in rows or panels, or as all over textures. They can also be combined with lace patterns and cables. Bobbles, popcorns, buds and clusters are some of the most common patterns. A garment that has many motifs will be much thicker and heavier than a plainly knitted one, and will use more yarn. For this reason traditional outdoor wear, such as fishermen's sweaters, is often heavily patterned. To make these stitches, you need only to master the technique of multiple increases in a single stitch. For an easy-to-work pattern that has a strong texture, Popcorn stitch is a popular choice.

BOBBLES

A bobble is a large cluster of stitches that is independent of the knitted ground; it can be worked in stocking stitch or reverse stocking stitch. It is formed by increasing into a single stitch so that three, (four, or five) additional stitches for a small, (medium, or large) bobble are made. Work backwards and forwards on these stitches only. Finally, decrease these extra stitches to the original one. The increases can be made in two ways – using the yarn-over method or working into the front and back of a stitch. The stitches on either side must be worked firmly. Bobbles will make the edge uneven, so start a few stitches in to make the sewing up easier.

Small, medium, and large bobbles

Yarn-over increases
Knit up to your chosen stitch then make a yarn over – insert your right-hand needle into the stitch and knit as usual but do not discard. To make 5 new stitches (a total of 6 stitches), yarn over and knit into the same stitch 3 more times; slip last stitch onto right needle. This may be abbreviated as *yo, k1; rep from * twice (3, 4 times, etc.).*

Working into front and back of stitch
Knit up to your chosen stitch then insert your right-hand needle into it. Leave the stitch on the needle as you knit first into the front and then the back the appropriate number of times. To increase 4 times, making 4 new stitches (a total of 5 stitches), knit into the front and back of the stitch twice and then knit into the front again. Occasionally, an instruction will ask you to increase by alternately knitting and purling into the stitch.

1 For a medium bobble, work up to the chosen stitch. Then increase 3 times into the stitch (4 sts altogether). [We've used the yarn-over method.]

2 Turn work and knit 4 stitches; turn work and purl 4 stitches; turn work and knit 4 stitches; turn work (3 rows of reverse stocking stitch made).

3 Decrease 3 stitches in the row: Sl 2, k2tog, p2sso. Continue in pattern.

4 The completed bobble on a stocking stitch ground.

BUBBLE STITCH AND REVERSE BUBBLE STITCH ▶

Multiple of 8 sts plus 4

Note: Slip all sts p-wise.

Row 1 (right side): K.

Row 2: P.

Row 3: P1, yb, sl 2, yf, *p6, yb, sl 2, yf; rep from
  * to last st, p1.

Row 4: K1, yf, sl 2, yb, *k6, yf, sl 2, yb; rep from
  * to last st, k1.

Rows 5 to 8: rep rows 3 and 4 twice.

Row 9: K.

Row 10: P.

Row 11: P5, yb, sl 2, yf, *p6, yb, sl 2, yf; rep from
  * to last 5 sts, p5.

Row 12: K5, yf, sl 2, yb, *k6, yf, sl 2, yb; rep from * to last 5 sts, k5.

Rows 13 to 16: rep rows 11 and 12 twice.

Rows 1 to 16 form the pattern.

Bubble stitch

Use the reverse
side of the bubble
stitch as the right side

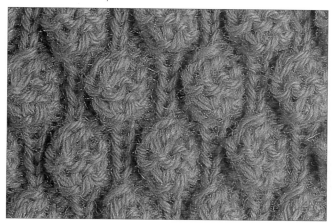

ORCHARD PATTERN ▲

Multiple of 6 sts plus 5

Note: Sts should only be counted
  after rows 6 or 12.

Row 1 (right side): P2, *k into
  front, back, front and back of
  next st, p2, k1, p2; rep from * to
  last 3 sts, k into front, back, front
  and back of next st, p2.

Row 2: *K2, [k1 winding yarn
  round needle twice] 4 times, k2,
  p1; rep from * to last 8 sts, k2,
  [k1 winding yarn round needle
  twice] 4 times, k2.

Row 3: P2, *k4 (dropping extra
  loops), p2, k1, p2; rep from * to
  last 6 sts, k4 (dropping extra
  loops), p2.

Rows 4 and 5: as rows 2 and 3.

Row 6: *K2, p4 tog, k2, p1;
  rep from * to last 8 sts, k2,
  p4tog, k2.

Row 7: P2, *k1, p2, k into front,
  back, front and back of next
  st, p2; rep from * to last 3 sts,
  k1, p2.

Row 8: *K2, p1, k2 [k1 winding
  yarn round needle twice] 4 times;
  rep from * to last 5 sts, k2,
  p1, k2.

Row 9: *P2, k1, p2, k4 (dropping
  extra loops); rep from * to last
  5 sts, p2, k1, p2.

Rows 10 and 11: as rows 8 and 9.

Row 12: *K2, p1, k2, p4tog; rep
  from * to last 5 sts, k2, p1, k2.

Rows 1 to 12 form the pattern.

HONEYCOMB STITCH ▼

Multiple of 4 sts

Special abbreviation

C2B or C2F (Cross 2 Back or Front):
  K into back (or front) of 2nd st on
  needle, then k first st, slipping
  both sts off needle at same time.

Row 1 (right side): *C2F, C2B; rep
  from * to end.

Row 2: P.

Row 3: *C2B, C2F; rep from
  * to end.

Row 4: P.

Rows 1 to 4 form the pattern.

HAZEL NUT ▲

Multiple of 4 sts plus 3

Special abbreviation

HN (Make 1 Hazel Nut): K1 without slipping st off
  left needle, yo, then k1 once more into same st.

Note: Sts should only be counted after rows 4, 5, 6,
  10, 11, or 12.

Row 1 (right side): P3, *HN, p3; rep from * to end.

Row 2: K3, *p3, k3; rep from * to end.

Row 3: P3, *k3, p3; rep from * to end.

Row 4: K3, *p3tog, k3; rep from * to end.

Row 5: P.

Row 6: K.

Row 7: P1, *HN, p3; rep from * to last 2 sts, HN, p1.

Row 8: K1, *p3, k3; rep from * to last 4 sts, p3, k1.

Row 9: P1, *k3, p3; rep from * to last 4 sts, k3, p1.

Row 10: K1, *p3tog, k3; rep from * to last 4 sts,
  p3tog, k1.

Row 11: P.

Row 12: K.

Rows 1 to 12 form the pattern.

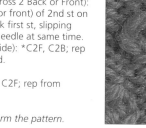

GARTER STITCH CHEVRON ▶
Multiple of 11

Rows 1 to 5: K.
Row 6 (right side): *k2tog, k2, knit into front and back of each of the next 2 sts, k3, ssk; rep from * to end.
Row 7: P.
Rows 8 to 11: rep rows 6 and 7 twice.
Row 12: as row 6.
Rows 1 to 12 rows form the pattern.

BOBBLE FANS   ▲
Worked over 11 sts on a background of reverse st st
Special abbreviations
MB (Make Bobble): [K1, p1] twice all into next st, turn and p4, turn and k4, turn and p4, turn and sl 2, k2tog, p2sso.
T2F (Twist 2 Front): Slip next st onto cn and hold at front of work, purl next st from left needle, then knit st from cn.
T2B (Twist 2 Back): Slip next st onto cn and hold at back of work, knit next st from left needle, then purl st from cn.
T2FW (Twist 2 Front on Wrong side): Slip next st onto cn and hold at front (wrong side) of work, purl next st from left needle, then knit st from cn.
T2BW (Twist 2 Back on Wrong side): Slip next st onto cn and hold at back (right side) of work, knit next st from left needle, then purl st from cn.
Row 1 (right side): P.
Row 2: K.
Row 3: P5, MB, p5.
Row 4: K5, p1tbl, k5.
Row 5: P2, MB, p2, k1tbl, p2, MB, p2.
Row 6: K2, [p1tbl, k2] 3 times.
Row 7: MB, p1, T2F, p1, k1tbl, p1, T2B, p1, MB.
Row 8: p1tbl, k2, p1tbl, [k1, p1tbl] twice, k2, p1tbl.
Row 9: T2F, p1, T2F, k1tbl, T2B, p1, T2B.
Row 10: K1, T2BW, k1, [p1tbl] 3 times, k1, T2FW, k1.
Row 11: P2, T2F, M1 p-wise, sl 1, k2tog, psso, M1 p-wise, T2B, p2.
Row 12: K3, T2BW, p1tbl, T2FW, k3.
Row 13: P4, M1 p-wise, sl 1, k2tog, psso, M1 p-wise, p4.
Row 14: K5, p1tbl, k5.
Row 15: P.
Row 16: K.
Rows 1 to 16 form the pattern.

SCATTERED BOBBLES   ▼
Multiple of 10 sts plus 5 worked on a background of st st
Special abbreviation
MB (Make Bobble): Knit into front, back and front of next st, turn and p3, turn and k3, turn and p3, turn and sl 1, k2tog, psso.
Rows 1 and 3: K.
Rows 2 and 4: P.
Row 5: K7, *MB, k9; rep from * to last 8 sts, MB, k7.
Rows 6, 8 and 10: P.
Rows 7 and 9: K.
Row 11: K2, *MB, k9; rep from * to last 3 sts, MB, k2.
Row 12: P.
Rows 1 to 12 form the pattern.

◀ VERTICAL BOBBLE AND STRIPE
Multiple of 10 sts plus 5
Special abbreviation
MB (Make Bobble): Work [k1, p1, k1, p1, k1] into the next st, turn and k5, turn and k5tog.
Row 1 (right side): P2, k1, *p4, k1; rep from * to last 2 sts, p2.
Row 2: K2, p1, *k4, p1; rep from * to last 2 sts, k2.
Row 3: P2, *MB, p4, k1, p4; rep from * to last 3 sts, MB, p2.
Row 4: as row 2.
Rows 5 to 20: rep rows 1 to 4 four times.
Row 21: as row 1.
Row 22: as row 2.
Row 23: P2, *k1, p4, MB, p4; rep from * to last 3 sts, k1, p2.
Row 24: as row 2.
Rows 25 to 40: rep rows 21 to 24 four times.
Rows 1 to 40 form the pattern.

BUD STITCH   ▲
Multiple of 6 sts plus 5
Note: Sts should only be counted after row 6 or 12.
Row 1 (right side): P5, *k1, yo, p5; rep from * to end.
Row 2: K5, *p2, k5; rep from * to end.
Row 3: P5, *k2, p5; rep from * to end.
Rows 4 and 5: as rows 2 and 3.
Row 6: K5, *p2tog, k5; rep from * to end.
Row 7: P2, *k1, yo, p5; rep from * to last 3 sts, k1, yo, p2.
Row 8: K2, *p2, k5; rep from * to last 4 sts, p2, k2.
Row 9: P2, *k2, p5; rep from * to last 4 sts, k2, p2.
Rows 10 and 11: as rows 8 and 9.
Row 12: K2, *p2tog, k5; rep from * to last 4 sts, p2tog, k2.
Rows 1 to 12 form the pattern.

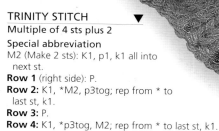

TRINITY STITCH ▼

Multiple of 4 sts plus 2

Special abbreviation

M2 (Make 2 sts): K1, p1, k1 all into next st.

Row 1 (right side): P.

Row 2: K1, *M2, p3tog; rep from * to last st, k1.

Row 3: P.

Row 4: K1, *p3tog, M2; rep from * to last st, k1.

Rows 1 to 4 form the pattern.

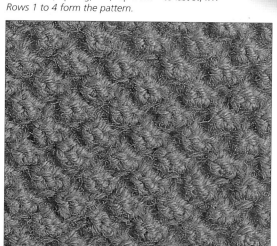

MOCK CABLE ▲

Multiple of 5 sts plus 2

Row 1 (right side): P2, *sl 1, k2, psso, p2; rep from * to end.

Row 2: K2, *p1, yo, p1, k2; rep from * to end.

Row 3: P2, *k3, p2; rep from * to end.

Row 4: K2, *p3, k2; rep from * to end.

Rows 1 to 4 form the pattern.

SINGLE BELL EDGING ▲

Cast on multiple of 12 sts plus 3

Note: Sts should only be counted after rows 1 and 2.

Row 1 (right side): P3, *k9, p3; rep from * to end.

Row 2: K3, *p9, k3; rep from * to end.

Row 3: P3, *yb, ssk, k5, k2tog, p3; rep from * to end.

Row 4: K3, *p7, k3; rep from * to end.

Row 5: P3, *yb, ssk, k3, k2tog, p3; rep from * to end.

Row 6: K3, *p5, k3; rep from * to end.

Row 7: P3, *yb, ssk, k1, k2tog, p3; rep from * to end.

Row 8: K3, *p3, k3; rep from * to end.

Row 9: P3, *yb, sl 1, k2tog, psso, p3; rep from * to end.

Row 10: K3, *p1, k3; rep from * to end.

Row 11: P3, *k1, p3; rep from * to end.

Row 12: as row 10.

Rows 1 to 12 form the edging.

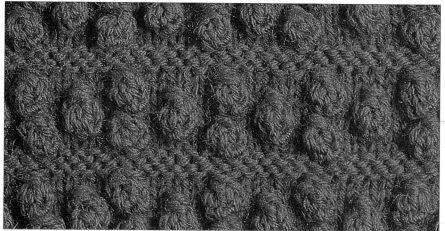

BOBBLE AND RIDGE ▲

Multiple of 6 sts plus 5

Special abbreviation

MB (Make Bobble): Knit into front, back and front of next st, turn and p3, turn and k3, turn and p3, turn and sl 1, k2tog, psso.

Row 1 (right side): K.

Row 2: P.

Row 3: K5, *MB, k5; rep from * to end.

Row 4: P.

Row 5: K2, MB, *k5, MB; rep from * to last 2 sts, k2.

Rows 6, 7 and 8: as rows 2, 3 and 4.

Row 9: P.

Row 10: K.

Rows 1 to 10 form the pattern.

PUFF BALL EDGING ▶

Cast on 13 sts

Row 1 (right side): K2, k2tog, yo2, k2tog, k7.

Row 2: K9, p1, k3.

Rows 3 and 4: K.

Row 5: K2, k2tog, yo2, k2tog, k2, [yo2, k1] 3 times, yo2, k2 – 21 sts.

Row 6: K3, [p1, k2] 3 times, p1, k4, p1, k3.

Rows 7 and 8: K.

Row 9: K2, k2tog, yo2, k2tog, k15.

Row 10: K 12 sts wrapping yarn twice around needle for each st, yo2, k5, p1, k3 – 23 sts (each double wrapped st counts as 1 st).

Row 11: K10, [p1, k1] into next st, slip next 12 sts to right needle, dropping extra loops. Return sts to left needle then k12tog –13 sts.

Row 12: K.

Rows 1 to 12 form the pattern.

OPENWORK PATTERNS

YARN-OVER INCREASES form some of the loveliest and most delicate stitches a knitter can create. Made with fine yarns and needles, openwork patterns are ideal for gossamer shawls, lacy sweaters, or dressy scarves. Where a more robust appearance, or a warmer fabric, is required, use medium-weight yarn to knit patterns with smaller openings.

There are two major categories of openwork pattern – lace and eyelet. Lace is truly openwork, unlike eyelet which is solid work punctuated by small openings. Lace, when combined with other stitches, lends itself to being used as panels. Knit the panels in or near the centre and away from the sides, where they are difficult to shape.

Wool, cottons, silks and cashmere are among the many yarns that knit up beautifully in lace patterns. Cotton lace is often used for trimming curtains, place mats, bed linens, as well as clothes.

OPENWORK BASICS

Openings are formed by yarn-over increases, which are later offset by the same number of decreases so that the number of stitches remains constant. It is important that you work to the correct tension, and with appropriate needles and yarn. Openwork needs stretching before it is fully effective. Therefore, when you are substituting a lace pattern for stocking stitch, cast on less stitches than the width requirement – about three-quarters the number should suffice.

The shawl shown here is worked in a simple openwork pattern with a knitted border worked separately and then sewn onto the main piece.

LACE EDGINGS

Fine crochet cotton edgings make marvellous trims when sewn to bed and table linens. When trimming knitting with a lace edge, first complete the main piece then pick up the required number of stitches for the lace edge (below).

Picking up stitches for an edge

Hold the working yarn behind the completed piece and insert your knitting needle between the rows and the last 2 stitches of each row, from front to back. Take the yarn over the needle as if knitting and draw a loop of the yarn through to form a stitch. Continue until the correct number of stitches have been formed.

This triangular shawl features an attractive leaf pattern and a decorative border

EYELETS

There are two main types of eyelet: the chain and open. Made singly, eyelets can be used as tiny buttonholes or formed into a line for threading ribbon through. Used in combination, with plain rows between, eyelets can be placed vertically, horizontally, or diagonally to form decorative motifs. Do not make eyelets at the beginning or end of a row; work them at least two stitches in from the edge.

A row of open eyelets

Chain eyelet

This is the simplest and most common type of eyelet. It can be combined with the open eyelet in more intricate stitches. It is abbreviated as *yo, k2tog*.

1 Make a yarn-over by bringing your yarn to the front, and then knitting the next 2 stitches together.

2 The yarn-over adds one stitch, but knitting 2 together reduces the stitches to the original number.

3 A chain eyelet has been made in the knitted work.

Open eyelet

To work a slightly larger opening, use this method. This is more suitable for threading ribbon. It is abbreviated as *yo, sl 1 k-wise, k1, psso*.

1 Make a yarn-over by bringing the yarn forward around the front of the needle. Slip the next stitch knitwise, knit the next stitch, and then pass the slipped stitch over.

2 The increase made by the yarn-over has been replaced by the slip-stitch decrease. The number of stitches remains the same.

3 A finished open eyelet.

SLIP, SLIP, KNIT DECREASE

This decrease is especially useful for lace and openwork and leaves a smooth finish, abbreviated as ssk.

1 Slip the first and 2nd stitches knitwise, one at a time, onto the right needle.

2 Insert the left needle into the fronts of these 2 stitches from the left, and knit them together from this position.

3 The completed slip, slip, knit decrease is made.

DIAMOND AND WAVE EDGE ▶

Worked over 13 sts

Note: Sts should only be counted after rows 1 and 20.

Row 1 and every alt row (wrong side): K2, p to last 2 sts, k2.

Row 2: K7, yo, ssk, yo, k4.

Row 4: K6, [yo, ssk] twice, yo, k4.

Row 6: K5, [yo, ssk] 3 times, yo, k4.

Row 8: K4, [yo, ssk] 4 times, yo, k4.

Row 10: K3, [yo, ssk] 5 times, yo, k4.

Row 12: K4, [yo, ssk] 5 times, k2tog, k2.

Row 14: K5, [yo, ssk] 4 times, k2tog, k2.

Row 16: K6, [yo, ssk] 3 times, k2tog, k2.

Row 18: K7, [yo, ssk] twice, k2tog, k2.

Row 20: K8, yo, ssk, k2tog, k2.

Rows 1 to 20 form the pattern.

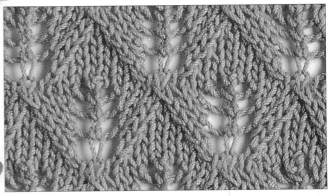

LEAF PATTERN ▲

Multiple of 10 sts plus 1

Row 1 and every alt row (wrong side): P.

Row 2: K3, *k2tog, yo, k1, yo, ssk, k5; rep from *, ending last rep k3.

Row 4: K2, *k2tog, [k1, yo] twice, k1, ssk, k3; rep from *, ending last rep k2.

Row 6: K1, *k2tog, k2, yo, k1, yo, k2, ssk, k1; rep from * to end.

Row 8: K2tog, *k3, yo, k1, yo, k3, sl 1, k2tog, psso; rep from * to last 9 sts, k3, yo, k1, yo, k3, ssk.

Row 10: K1, *yo, ssk, k5, k2tog, yo, k1; rep from * to end.

Row 12: K1, *yo, k1, ssk, k3, k2tog, k1, yo, k1; rep from * to end.

Row 14: K1, *yo, k2, ssk, k1, k2tog, k2, yo, k1; rep from * to end.

Row 16: K1, *yo, k3, sl 1, k2tog, psso, k3, yo, k1; rep from * to end.

Rows 1 to 16 form the pattern.

◀ ENGLISH LACE

Multiple of 6 sts plus 1

Row 1 and every alt row (wrong side): P.

Row 2: K1, *yo, ssk, k1, k2tog, yo, k1; rep from * to end.

Row 4: K1, *yo, k1 sl 1, k2tog, psso, k1, yo, k1; rep from * to end.

Row 6: K1, *k2tog, yo, k1, yo, ssk, k1; rep from * to end.

Row 8: K2tog, *[k1, yo] twice, k1, sl 1, k2tog, psso; rep from * to last 5 sts, [k1, yo] twice, k1, ssk.

Rows 1 to 8 form the pattern.

FEATHER PANEL ▶

Worked over 13 sts on a background of reverse st st

Special abbreviation

S4K (Slip 4 knit): Slip next 4 sts knitwise, one at a time, onto right needle, then insert left needle into fronts of these 4 sts from left, and knit them together from this position.

Row 1 (right side): K.

Row 2: P.

Row 3: K4tog, [yo, k1] 5 times, yo, S4K.

Row 4: P.

Rows 1 to 4 form the pattern.

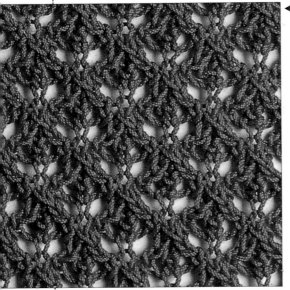

FLEURETTE ▶

Multiple of 6 sts plus 5

Note: Sts should only be counted after rows 1-3, 6-9, and 12.

Row 1 and every alt row (wrong side): P.

Row 2: K2, *k1, yo, ssk, k1, k2tog, yo; rep from *, ending k3.

Row 4: K4, *yo, k3; rep from *, ending k1.

Row 6: K2, k2tog, *yo, ssk, k1, k2tog, yo, sl 2 k-wise, k1, p2sso; rep from *, ending yo, ssk, k1, k2tog, yo, ssk, k2.

Row 8: K2, *k1, k2tog, yo, k1, yo, ssk; rep from *, ending k3.

Row 10: as row 4.

Row 12: K2, *k1, k2tog, yo, sl 2 k-wise, k1, p2sso, yo, ssk; rep from *, ending k3.

Rows 1 to 12 form the pattern.

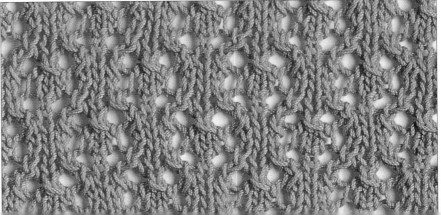

CAT'S PAW ▶

Multiple of 16 sts plus 9

Row 1 and every alt row (wrong side): P.
Row 2: K10, *k2tog, yo, k1, yo, ssk, k11; rep from *, ending last rep k10 instead of k11.
Row 4: K9, *k2tog, yo, k3, yo, ssk, k9; rep from * to end.
Row 6: K10, *yo, ssk, yo, k3tog, yo, k11; rep from *, ending last rep k10 instead of k11.
Row 8: K11, *yo, sl 1, k2tog, psso, yo, k13; rep from *, ending last rep k11 instead of k13.
Row 10: K2, *k2tog, yo, k1, yo, ssk, k11; rep from *, ending last rep k2 instead of k11.
Row 12: K1, *k2tog, yo, k3, yo, ssk, k9; rep from *, ending last rep k1 instead of k9.
Row 14: K2, *yo, ssk, yo, k3tog, yo, k11; rep from *, ending last rep k2 instead of k11.
Row 16: K3, *yo, sl 1, k2tog, psso, yo, k13; rep from *, ending last rep k3 instead of k13.
Rows 1 to 16 form the pattern.

LATTICE STITCH ▼

Multiple of 6 sts plus 1

Row 1 (right side): K1, *yo, p1, p3tog, p1, yo, k1; rep from * to end.
Row 2 and every alt row: P.
Row 3: K2, yo, sl 1, k2tog, psso, yo, *k3, yo, sl 1, k2tog, psso, yo; rep from * to last 2 sts, k2.
Row 5: P2tog, p1, yo, k1, yo, p1, *p3tog, p1, yo, k1, yo, p1; rep from * to last 2 sts, p2tog.
Row 7: K2tog, yo, k3, yo, *sl 1, k2tog, psso, yo, k3, yf; rep from * to last 2 sts, ssk.
Row 8: P.
Rows 1 to 8 form the pattern.

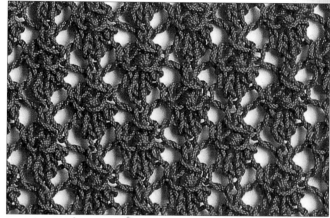

OPENWORK EYELETS ▲

Multiple of 4 sts plus 3

Row 1 (right side): K.
Row 2: P.
Row 3: *K2, k2tog, yo; rep from * to last 3 sts, k3.
Row 4: P.
Row 5: K.
Row 6: P.
Row 7: *K2tog, yo, k2; rep from * to last 3 sts, k2tog, yf, k1.
Row 8: P.
Rows 1 to 8 form the pattern.

WAVE EDGE ▶

Worked over 13 sts

Note: Sts should only be counted after rows 1, 4, 5 or 14.
Row 1 and every alt row (wrong side): K2, p to last 2 sts, k2.
Row 2: Sl 1, k3, yo, k5, yo, k2tog, yo, k2.
Row 4: Sl 1, k4, sl 1, k2tog, psso, k2, [yo, k2tog] twice, k1.
Row 6: Sl 1, k3, ssk, k2, [yo, k2tog] twice, k1.
Row 8: Sl 1, k2, ssk, k2, [yo, k2tog] twice, k1.
Row 10: Sl 1, k1, ssk, k2, [yo, k2tog] twice, k1.
Row 12: K1, ssk, k2, yo, k1, yo, k2tog, yo, k2.
Row 14: Sl 1, [k3, yo] twice, k2tog, yo, k2.
Rows 1 to 14 form the pattern.

◀ FALLING LEAVES

Worked over 16 sts on a background of reverse st st

Row 1 (right side): P1, k3, k2tog, k1, yo, p2, yo, k1, ssk, k3, p1.
Row 2 and every alt row: K1, p6, k2, p6, k1.
Row 3: P1, k2, k2tog, k1, yf, k1, p2, k1, yo, k1, ssk, k2, p1.
Row 5: P1, k1, k2tog, k1, yo, k2, p2, k2, yo, k1, ssk, k1, p1.
Row 7: P1, k2tog, k1, yo, k3, p2, k3, yo, k1, ssk, p1.
Row 8: K1, p6, k2, p6, k1.
Rows 1 to 8 form the pattern.

USING COLOUR

COLOUR IS ANOTHER way of transforming simple shapes. Its use may be subtle or dramatic, providing a mosaic of shades in a complex arrangement.

The simplest way of using colour is to make horizontal stripes. Here, you introduce a new shade at the beginning of a row. To make vertical stripes, use a separate ball of yarn for each colour and, when you get to the end of each block, pick up the new yarn in a way that prevents a hole from appearing. Another effective but easy way of adding colour is to combine two different yarns, working them as one strand. Colour also may be embroidered onto a stocking stitch background using Swiss darning (see page 66).

Simple colour patterns are often shown in chart form. Charts can be coloured or printed in black and white with symbols representing the different colours.

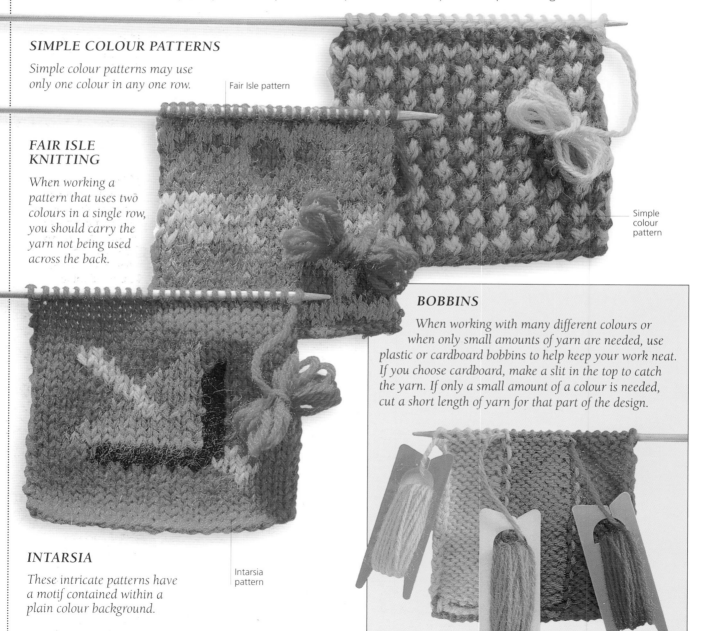

SIMPLE COLOUR PATTERNS

Simple colour patterns may use only one colour in any one row.

Fair Isle pattern

FAIR ISLE KNITTING

When working a pattern that uses two colours in a single row, you should carry the yarn not being used across the back.

Simple colour pattern

INTARSIA

These intricate patterns have a motif contained within a plain colour background.

Intarsia pattern

BOBBINS

When working with many different colours or when only small amounts of yarn are needed, use plastic or cardboard bobbins to help keep your work neat. If you choose cardboard, make a slit in the top to catch the yarn. If only a small amount of a colour is needed, cut a short length of yarn for that part of the design.

ADDING NEW YARN AT START OF ROW

Use this method when knitting horizontal stripes. If you will be using the old colour again, leave it at the side. Make sure any ends are woven neatly into the edge or back of the work.

1 Insert your right needle into the first stitch on the left needle and wrap both the old and new yarns over it. Knit the stitch with both yarns.

2 Drop the old yarn and knit the next 2 stitches with the doubled length of the new yarn.

3 Drop the short end of the new yarn and continue knitting in pattern. On the subsequent row, knit the 3 double stitches in the ordinary way.

ADDING NEW YARN AND WEAVING IN

When joining a colour at the start of a row, use this method to weave in the ends of yarns on the wrong side of the work .

1 Cut the old colour, leaving about 3 inches. With the new yarn, purl the first 2 stitches. Lay the short ends of both the old and new yarns over the top of the needle and purl the next stitch under the short ends.

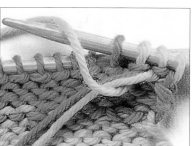

2 Leave the short ends hanging and purl the next stitch over them. Continue until the short ends are woven in.

ADDING NEW YARN WITHIN THE ROW

Use this method when you will be working the original yarn again in the same row. See page 58 for instructions for carrying the yarn along the back.

1 Leaving the old yarn in the back of the work, insert your right-hand needle into the stitch. Wrap the new yarn over the needle and use this to knit the stitch.

2 Knit the next 2 stitches with the doubled length of new yarn.

3 Drop the short end and continue knitting with the new yarn while carrying the old yarn across the back. On subsequent rows, knit the double stitches normally.

MAKING VERTICAL STRIPES OR DESIGNS

This method is known as intarsia and is suitable for knitting motifs. The pattern instructions are always in chart form.

To make vertical stripes or independent blocks of colour, use a separate ball or bobbin of yarn for each colour. Drop the old yarn and pick up the next one from underneath it so the yarns cross. By twisting the yarns in this way, you will prevent a gap appearing in the work. *(Top left.)* Work in the same way for the purl row *(bottom left).*

CARRYING COLOURS ACROSS THE BACK

When working multicolour patterns, you must alternate between two or more balls of yarn. The yarn not in use has to be carried along the back until needed. There are two main methods, stranding and weaving. Stranding is suitable for short distances (5 stitches or less); weaving is better when the yarn is carried 6 stitches or more.

STRANDING

The strands, known as floats, can make knitting more difficult. Floats have to be carried along the back at the correct tension – not too loosely or tightly. With more than two yarns, you will have to drop and pick them up as needed.

If you have only 2 colours in a knit row, hold one in each hand using the methods shown on page 27. (*See above left*). For the purl row (*below left*), follow the instructions for holding the yarn given on page 28.

Do not make your floats longer than 5 stitches, and take care that your strands are the same tension as the knitting.

WEAVING

In this method, the carried yarn is brought alternately above and below each stitch made so that it is woven in. It is best worked using both hands. You can also use it in combination with stranding; for example, weaving in at every third stitch and stranding in between will create a more elastic fabric, which will have a smoother finish.

Yarn above the stitch

Holding one yarn in each hand, knit 1 (*left*) or purl 1 (*right*) with the first colour, and, at the same time, bring the 2nd colour over the tip of the right needle.

Yarn below the stitch

With one yarn in each hand, knit 1 (*left*) or purl 1 (*right*) with the first colour, holding the 2nd colour below the first.

Front of work using stranding method

Back of work

Weaving method showing the front of work

Back of work

COLOUR PATTERNS ARE often charted on graph paper. Each square represents a stitch and each horizontal line of squares is a row of stitches. A coloured-in chart, where the indicated colours fill the graphed squares, is the easiest to follow and has the added advantage of giving you a preview of what the finished work will look like.

Many knitting charts are printed in black and white, and different symbols are used to indicate the different colours. These charts usually come with a colour key, and show only one pattern repeat. In the case of a large multicoloured sweater, the chart may represent the whole garment.

Charts are read from bottom to top; they are usually based on stocking stitch, where the first and all odd-numbered rows are knitted from right to left and all even-numbered rows are purled from left to right. Therefore, the first stitch of a chart is the bottom one on the right. You may find placing a ruler under each row will help you keep track of where you are. When knitting in the round (see page 68), the right side always faces you so that, for every row, you always read every row of the chart from right to left.

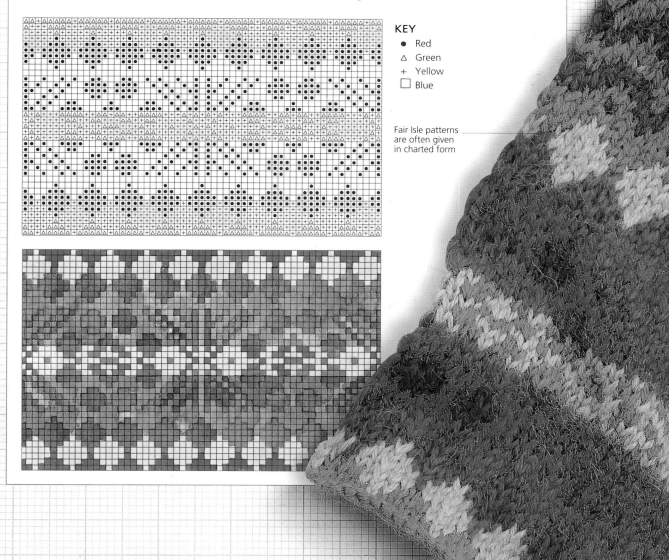

KEY
- ● Red
- △ Green
- + Yellow
- □ Blue

Fair Isle patterns are often given in charted form

FLEUR DE LYS ▶
Multiple of 6 sts plus 3

Rows 1 and 3: K3 MC, *k1 CC, k5 MC; rep from * to end, carrying the threads behind the work.
Row 2: P1 CC, *p3 MC, p3 CC; rep from * to last 2 sts, p2 MC.

Rows 4 and 6: P2 MC, *p1 CC, p5 MC; rep from * to last st, p1 CC.
Row 5: K2 CC, *k3 MC, k3 CC; rep from * to last st, k1 MC.
Rows 1 to 6 form the pattern.

DOT AND SQUARE PATTERN ◀
Multiple of 7 sts plus 4

Row 1 (right side): With MC, k.
Row 2: With MC, p.
Row 3: With CC, k1, sl 2, *k5, sl 2; rep from * to last st, k1.
Row 4: With CC, p1, sl 2, *p5, sl 2; rep from * to last st, p.
Row 5: With MC, k3, *sl 2, k1, sl 2, k2; rep from * to last st, k1.
Row 6: With MC, p3, *sl 2, k1, sl 2, p2; rep from * to last st, p1.
Row 7 and 8: as rows 3 and 4.
Rows 1 to 8 form the pattern.

TWO-COLOUR RIBS ▼
Multiple of 4 sts

Row 1: *K2 MC, p2 CC; rep from * to end, carrying the threads behind the work.
Row 2: *P2 MC, k2 CC; rep from * to end.
Rows 1 to 2 form the pattern.

GREEK KEY PATTERN ▲
Multiple of 10 sts plus 2

Row 1 (right side): With MC, k.
Row 2: With MC, p.
Row 3: With CC, k1, *k8, sl 2; rep from * to last st, k1.
Row 4 and every alt row: Using the same colour as previous row, purl, slipping all sts slipped on previous row.
Row 5: With MC, k1, *sl 2, k4, sl 2, k2; rep from * to last st, k1.
Row 7: With CC, k1, *k2, sl 2, k4, sl 2; rep from * to last st, k1.
Row 9: With MC, k1, *sl 2, k8; rep from * to last sk, k1.
Row 11: With CC, k.
Row 13: With MC, *k4, sl 2, k4; rep from * to last 2 sts, k2.
Row 15: With CC, k2, *sl 2, k2, sl 2, k4; rep from * to end.
Row 17: With MC, *k4, sl 2, k2, sl 2; rep from * to last 2 sts, k2.
Row 19: With CC, *k6, sl 2, k2; rep from * to last 2 sts, k2.
Row 20: as row 4.
Rows 1 to 20 form the pattern.

ZIGZAG ▼
Multiple of 12 sts plus 3

Cast on with MC and knit one row.

Row 1 (right side): With CC, k1, sl 1, k1, psso, *k9, sl 2, k1, p2sso; rep from * to last 12 sts, k9, k2tog, k1.
Row 2: With CC, k1, *p1, k4 (k1, yo, k1) in next st, k4; rep from * to last 2 sts, p1, k1.
Rows 3 and 4: With MC, rep rows 1 and 2.
Rows 1 to 4 form the pattern.

COLOUR MOTIFS

COLOUR KNITTING CAN be as simple or as intricate as you wish. In theory, any pattern that can be drawn out on graph paper can be transferred to knitting, but the more colours you have in any one row, the more practice you will need to master the techniques of picking up and joining the new colour, and carrying the unused colour behind the work. In more complicated colour patterns, stranding and weaving can be combined with intarsia. An example of this is found in the Old Rose motif shown on page 63.

You can use most of these patterns to stand as single motifs, or arrange them in repeats in rows or diagonals. Plot them out on graph paper to fit the shape of the garment pieces you are knitting.

Big Bow
You can use a large single motif to work on a pocket, or a border round the hem of a sweater. Space the motifs as close or as far apart as you like. The colours you choose will affect the look of the pattern; avoid using too strong a background.

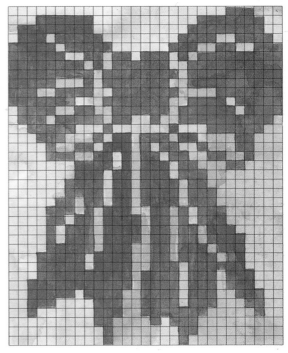

Little Bows
A row of small bows can be knitted in the same colour, alternating colours, or a string of different colours, according to your mood. Use a small border like this around the sleeves and hem of a cardigan.

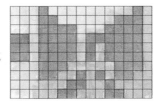

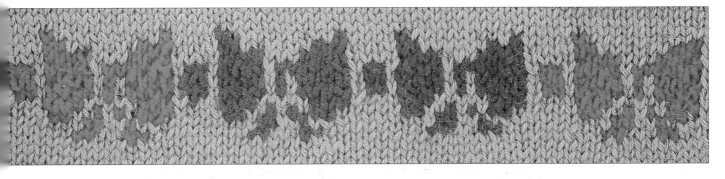

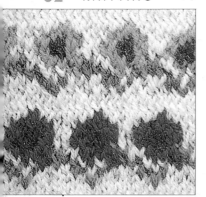

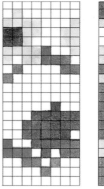

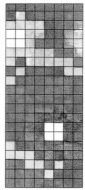

Bavarian Flowers

Small, neat rows of this flower repeat (*left*) would make an all-over pattern. Notice that the dark and light colourways create a completely different effect.

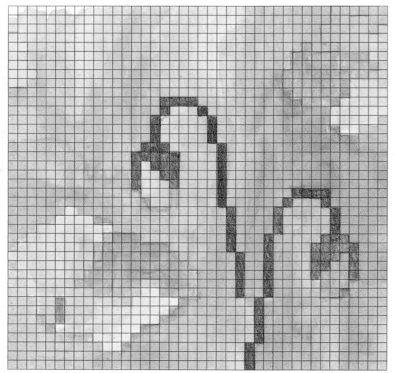

Welsh Poppies

For a hotter colour variation, knit the flowers in bright reds. This motif (*below, left*) could be spaced wide apart on jackets or cardigans.

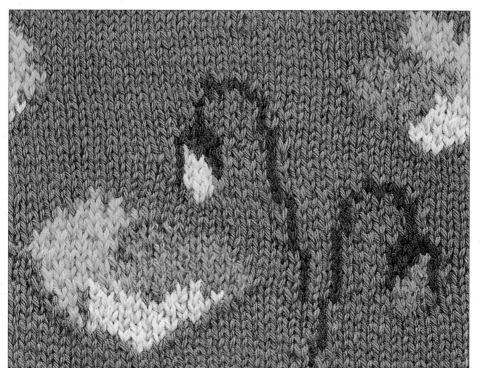

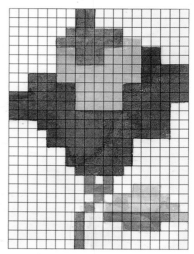

Purple Flower

The simple shape of this pretty flower (*above*) takes on a richness by the use of six colours.

Old Rose

A classic old rose pattern (*right*) reminiscent of upholstery chintzes, with carefully shaded petals and leaves. Use this as a single motif on a dressy cardigan.

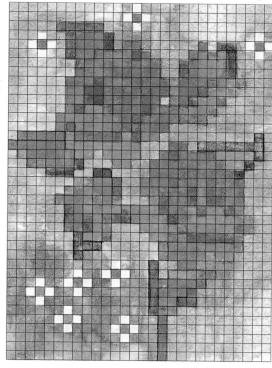

Single Anemone

This flower and leaf motif (*below*) could be spaced over the background and set into diagonal lines. The edge of the motif must be carefully knitted.

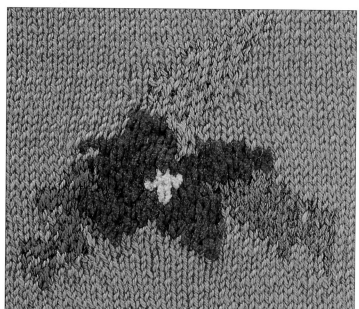

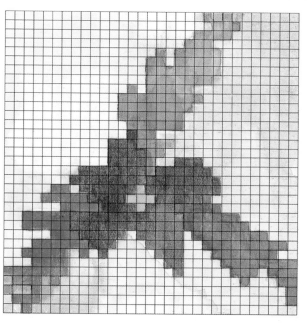

Anemone border

A flower border (*right*) with overlapping petals can be adapted into many different colorways; use it to set off the Single Anemone pattern as a border trim on a cardigan.

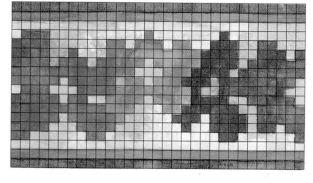

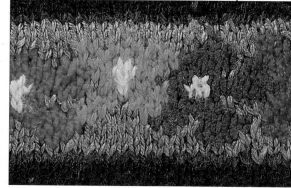

Sitting Cat
Slightly spooky cat would make a good repeating pattern particularly worked in black.

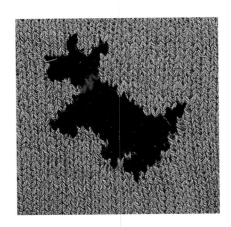

Jumping Scottie
A simple but effective pattern that could work well at almost any scale. Could be combined with its mirror image.

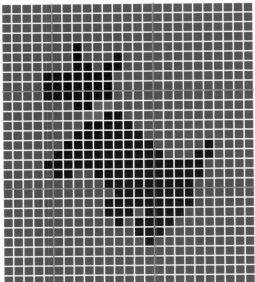

Falling Leaf
Worked here in a tweed wool for more interest.

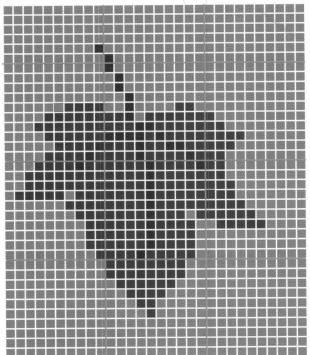

BUTTONHOLES

THERE ARE FOUR basic types of buttonholes – horizontal, vertical, round and loop. The horizontal is hardwearing and is the most commonly used. It is suitable for light and medium weight garments. The vertical type is better when the knitting will have a vertical pull, such as on pocket flaps. Round buttonholes are worked for small buttons on baby clothes (see eyelets page 53). Loops are suitable for thick jackets, and are sewn to the edge of the knitting.

It is essential that the size and position of the buttonhole matches the button to be used. In general, a horizontal buttonhole extends one stitch beyond the button, a vertical hole extends one row above it, and a round hole or loop aligns exactly with the button.

Horizontal buttonhole

Knit up to buttonhole position. On a right-side row, cast off number of stitches required for size of button and then knit to end of row. On next row, work up to stitch before buttonhole and knit into front and back of this stitch. Cast on one stitch less than number cast off. Knit to end of row.

Vertical buttonhole

Turn work at base of buttonhole, holding unused stitches on spare needle. Work on first set of stitches to the depth needed, ending on a right-side row. Join new yarn, and work one less than this number of rows on 2nd set of stitches. Slip these back onto original needle and knit across.

Loop

Mark 2 fixing points on wrong side. With a blunt-ended needle, secure yarn firmly to one point, then loop it over to the 2nd fixing point and take a small stitch. Continue looping and securing yarn until the required thickness has been achieved. Then buttonhole stitch over the loops.

Buttonhole stitch

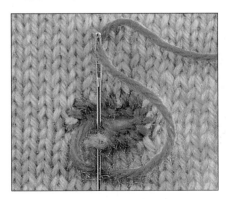

This stitch is used to cover loops (*above*) and to neaten other buttonholes. Work from right, using a blunt-ended needle. Bring yarn out on right side just below edge. Take a straight downwards stitch with thread under needle, pull up stitch to form a loop knot at buttonhole edge and repeat. Work stitches close together.

Buttonstand

With some patterns you may need to knit a buttonstand – an extra area of fabric onto which buttons are sewn. To knit a buttonstand, simply cast on the extra number of stitches required at the end of a row, then work across these and the rest of the stitches until you reach the required depth. Cast off the extra stitches.

Knitted buttons

With scrap yarn, cast on 14 stitches. With yarn for button, knit 5 rows; leaving about 8 inches, cut yarn. With this yarn, sew through stitches in last row. Unpick scrap yarn; with another length of yarn, sew through loops. Draw both ends tight and fasten. Stuff button with yarn, and sew up. Use threads to sew on.

EMBROIDERING KNITTING

SIMPLE EMBROIDERY STITCHES enrich any knitted garment by adding extra colour and texture. Four of the most popular stitches are shown here – Swiss darning, cross stitch, long and short, and bullion knot. Swiss darning follows the same stitch pattern as the knitting, and can be used instead of colour knitting (see page 56) to work motifs, or in combination with colour knitting to add areas of colour. Cross stitch is a quick and easy pattern stitch; bullion knots provide interesting texture. Long and short stitch is useful for filling solid shapes in free-form embroidery. You can also experiment with other common stitches – including chain stitch, daisy stitch and running stitch.

EMBROIDERY BASICS

It is often easier to embroider on knitting before the garment has been assembled, but after it has been blocked (see page 71). The golden rule is to work with the knitted fabric and not against it. Do not pull the embroidery stitches too tight or the knitting will pucker, and always work with a blunt-ended tapestry needle or yarn needle to avoid splitting the knitted stitches. Embroider with a yarn of the same type and thickness as the knitting – if the embroidery yarn is too thin it will sink into the knitted stitches, and if it is too thick it will stretch the knitting and look lumpy. You can also use embroidery floss or tapestry wool instead of knitting yarn. These products are sold in small, economical amounts and come in a wide range of beautiful colours. Bear in mind that you may need to work with several strands to match the thickness of the knitting yarn.

Swiss darning worked on a knitted pocket can form a striking initial or monogram

Swiss darning in vertical rows on stocking stitch

1 Bring needle out on right side of knitting under strand at the bottom of a knit stitch (base of V-shape). Insert needle from right to left behind knit stitch directly above and pull the yarn snug.

2 Insert needle under same strand where the thread emerged for first half-stitch. Bring needle out under the connecting strand of the knit stitch directly above it.

Swiss darning in horizontal rows on stocking stitch

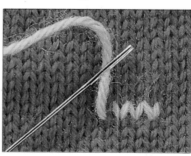

1 Bring the needle up on the right side under the connecting thread at the bottom of a knit stitch. Insert needle from right to left behind the knit stitch above, and pull the yarn snug.

2 Insert needle under the same strand where thread emerged for the first half stitch. Bring needle up again under the connecting strand of the stitch to the left of it.

Cross stitch

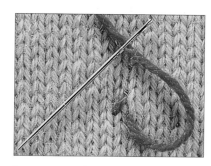

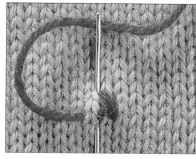

1 Bring yarn out at the front of the work at the bottom of a knit stitch, and take a diagonal stitch up to right. Bring the needle out directly below, and pull the yarn snug.

2 To complete the cross, insert the needle directly above where it first emerged. If making a 2nd cross stitch, bring it out at bottom to left and continue as in step 1.

Stem stitch

Work from left to right, taking regular, slanted backstitches. The thread should always emerge on the left of the previous stitch.

Long and short stitch

1 Baste the outline shape with contrasting thread (this is removed afterwards). Count down the knitted rows vertically, and bring needle out at front of work about 2 knit stitches inside outline.

2 Insert needle at outline, and bring it out at left of previous stitch and one knit stitch down. Repeat using long and short stitches alternately, closely following the outline. Work stitches in following rows to fill shape.

Bullion knot

1 Similar to a French knot (see page 132), this stitch may be worked singly or in clusters. Bring yarn out at front of work at the position for the knot. Make a backstitch the size of the knot(s) required, bringing needle out at front next to first stitch. Twist yarn around needle point as many times as required to equal the backstitch length.

2 Hold your left thumb on the coiled yarn and pull needle through the coils. Then turn needle back to where it was first inserted, and pull yarn through to the back of the work so that the bullion knot lies flat.

A combination of different embroidery stitches can be used very effectively

Knots form the centres of the flowers, which are worked in long and short stitch

KNITTING IN THE ROUND

KNITTING IN THE round is a more ancient art than flat knitting, and many of the antique pieces and traditional garments you will see in museums have been knitted in this way. Since the knitting is worked as a continuous spiral there are no seams to sew up, and a stronger garment is produced. Another advantage is that the right side of the knitting is always facing you, so if you are working a colour pattern you can see it clearly at all times. Knitting stocking stitch is simplified because you knit every row or round. Purling every row produces reverse stocking stitch.

There are two main ways of working in the round: with a flexible circular needle or with four or more double-pointed straight needles. A circular needle can hold three times as many stitches as a straight needle so it is the best way of knitting large items such as skirts. Small items, such as socks, collars and mittens are usually produced with four or more straight needles rather than a circular needle.

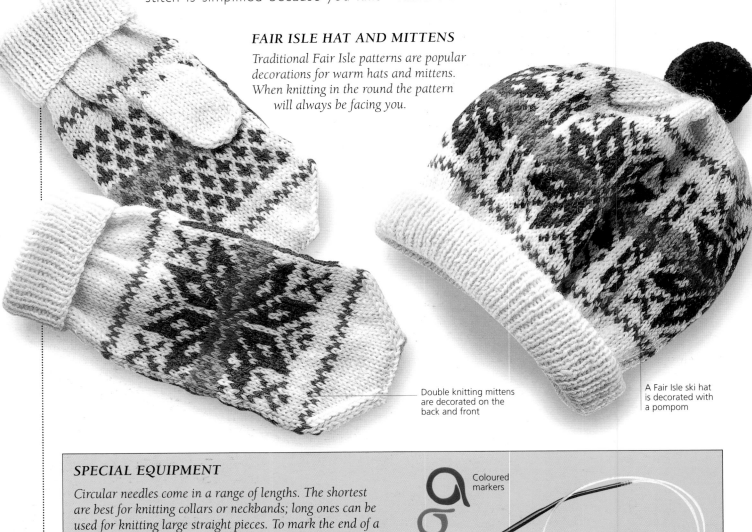

FAIR ISLE HAT AND MITTENS

Traditional Fair Isle patterns are popular decorations for warm hats and mittens. When knitting in the round the pattern will always be facing you.

Double knitting mittens are decorated on the back and front

A Fair Isle ski hat is decorated with a pompom

SPECIAL EQUIPMENT

Circular needles come in a range of lengths. The shortest are best for knitting collars or neckbands; long ones can be used for knitting large straight pieces. To mark the end of a round, coloured markers are useful. Double-pointed needles come in sets of four or more, and in different lengths.

Coloured markers

Circular needle

Set of double-pointed needles

KNITTING WITH A CIRCULAR NEEDLE

Choose a circular needle about 5 cm (2 in) smaller than the circumference of the knitting to avoid stretching the stitches. If you haven't used this type of needle before, just work as if each pointed end is a separate needle.

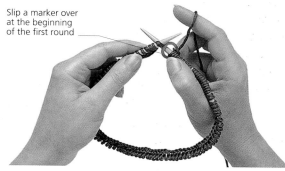

Slip a marker over at the beginning of the first round

1 Cast on the number of stitches needed, then slip a marker between the first and last stitches so that you can see where the first round starts. Hold the needle tip with the last cast-on stitch in your right hand, and the tip with the first cast-on stitch in your left hand. At this point it is crucial to check for any twisted stitches by making sure the cast-on edge is facing in toward the centre of the needle. When knitting the first stitch of the round, pull the yarn firmly to avoid a gap.

2 Knit until you reach the marker, then slip the marker over. You are now ready to start the second round. Check again to see if any stitches are twisted. If so, unravel the first row – twisted stitches cannot be corrected in any other way.

To knit flat work on a circular needle

The last cast-on stitch is on left-hand point

A circular needle is ideal for knitting large flat pieces. Hold the needle tip with the last cast-on stitch in your left hand and the needle tip with the first cast-on stitch in your right hand. Knit as with ordinary needles across the row, ending with the last stitch, then turn your work around so that the wrong side is facing you. Purl across the row. Continue to work back and forth, knitting and purling.

KNITTING WITH DOUBLE-POINTED NEEDLES

Double-pointed needles usually come in sets of four, but sometimes as many as six needles can be used. The working method is always the same: one needle is used to knit off the stitches that are equally divided between the other needles.

1 To knit with 4 needles, cast on one third of the stitches onto each of 3 needles. When you complete the stitches on one needle, hold the next one parallel and above it with the point a little bit further forward than the lower one. (Alternatively, cast on all the stitches on one needle and then divide them between the other needles.)

2 Place the 3 needles in a triangle and make sure the bottom edges of all the stitches are facing the centre. Place a marker after the last stitch.

3 Use the 4th needle to knit into the first cast-on stitch. Pull the yarn extra firmly on this stitch to avoid a gap in the work. When you have knitted all the stitches off the first needle, use it as the working needle to knit the stitches off the 2nd needle, then use this needle to work the stitches off the 3rd needle.

The marker will show you where each new round starts

4 Continue knitting in this way, holding the 2 working needles as you would normally, and dropping the needles not in use to the back of the work. When you reach the marker, slip it and start the next round.

TRIMMINGS

THE RIGHT TRIMMING can add that special finishing touch to your knitted garment. Pompoms are fun on children's hats, a fringe is the perfect edging for a scarf, and tassels make a jacket look smart or home furnishings more professionally finished. All can be made in the same or contrasting yarn.

Pompoms

1 Cut 2 cardboard circles to desired size. In centres, cut a hole about one third of total diameter. Place circles together and wrap yarn as shown.

2 Continue wrapping yarn until the centre holes are completely filled. If you run out of yarn, wrap a new length in and leave the ends dangling at the outer edge.

Tie a length of yarn between cardboard circles

3 Cut through yarn around edges. Ease circles slightly apart and wrap a length of yarn tightly around strands a few times, and secure with a firm knot. Pull off cardboard. Fluff out pompom, and trim with sharp scissors.

Trimmed and finished pompom

Fringe

1 Wrap yarn around a cardboard rectangle slightly deeper than desired length of fringe. Cut along one edge to make the strands. Take several strands and fold.

2 With a crochet hook, draw loop of strands through edge stitch, then pull cut ends through loop to form a loose knot. Adjust and trim.

Tassels

1 Wrap yarn around cardboard cut to desired length. Thread length of yarn under top loops, and tie tightly; leave one end long. Cut through yarn at lower edge.

2 Hide knot and short end of yarn under tassel strands. Wind long end tightly around strands to form a neat top. Thread needle with long end of yarn and push under binding and out through top of tassel. Trim ends if necessary.

BLOCKING & PRESSING

BEFORE A KNITTED garment is sewn together it must be blocked. This means that each knitted piece is shaped to the measurements given in the pattern. The process also helps smooth out any stitch irregularities and flattens curling edges. Before blocking, weave in all the loose ends. The beauty of the garment is in its hand knitted appearance – be careful not to over-press and obliterate this look.

BLOCKING

You will need a large, flat, padded surface. A table covered with a folded blanket and topped with a clean white sheet works well. Place each knitted piece wrong side up on the padding, smooth it out, and pin the corners to the padding with straight steel pins. Take care not to stretch or distort the basic shape, and make sure the knit rows run in straight lines. Then take a tape measure and check the length and width of each piece against those given in the pattern. Stretch or shrink the piece as necessary, and continue pinning at fairly close intervals all around the edges. The edges should be quite smooth: if each pin draws out a point of the knitting, you are either stretching it too much or are not using enough pins.

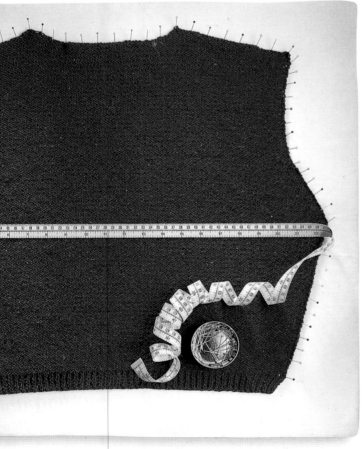

Block the piece to the measure given in the pattern instructions

PRESSING

After pinning cotton and wool, press very lightly under a damp cloth with a warm iron. Alternatively, hold a steaming iron very close to, but not touching, the knitting. Leave until completely dry. For synthetic yarn, check label instructions.

Stocking and garter stitch

Press or steam each part of the knitting. If pressing, lift up and re-apply the iron since moving it over the surface of the cloth will distort the stitches.

Embossed patterns

Hold a steaming iron or steamer just above the knitting. If you press, use a damp cloth and unpin the piece immediately and lightly pat it into shape so that the texture doesn't become flattened.

Ribbing

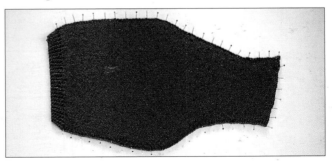

If the garment is all ribbing, use minimum pinning so that the ribbing isn't under any tension. If the ribbing is attached to stocking stitch, omit the pins on the ribbing section altogether. After pressing or steaming, immediately unpin the piece and ease the ribbing into its correct shape.

SEAMS

ONCE YOU'VE FINISHED knitting all the pieces of a garment, you have to sew them together. Don't be tempted to rush this process because clumsy seaming can completely ruin beautiful knitting. Seams should be sewn with a blunt-ended tapestry needle and matching yarn. If the garment yarn is not smooth, use plain yarn in a matching or slightly darker colour, making sure the washing instructions are compatible. A ladder-stitch seam is best for straight edges, and can be almost invisible. Backstitch seams make a small ridge inside the garment. If you are joining two pieces of horizontal knitting, use the grafting method.

ORDER OF SEAMING

If given, always follow the assembling instructions included with the pattern. Due to special design features, your pattern instructions may vary slightly from the basic steps listed below:

1 Shoulder seams
2 Set in sleeves (*see below*)
3 Side and sleeve seams: seam in one continuous line of stitching
4 Collar: sew right side of collar to wrong side of neckline, matching centre back of both pieces
5 Buttonbands
6 Pockets
7 Hems

Backstitch seam

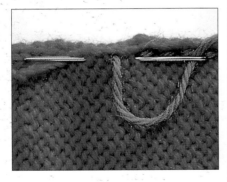

Place the pieces to be joined, right side to right side, carefully matching up the rows of knitting stitch for stitch. Baste together with contrasting yarn. Work backstitch along the seam about 5 mm (¼ in) in from edges, sewing into the centre of each stitch and checking that the stitches correspond on both pieces. To work backstitch: bring needle one stitch ahead at starting edge, insert it one stitch back and bring it out one stitch ahead of emerging thread. Repeat to end and remove basting thread.

Ladder-stitch seam

Place the 2 pieces in your left hand, edge to edge, and with the 2 right sides facing you. Match the knitting row by row. Pick up the strand between the first and 2nd stitches on one edge, and then the strand between first and 2nd stitches on the other edge. Take care to match the tension of the knitting.

To set in sleeves

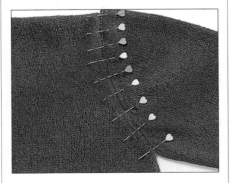

The sleeve cap is often slightly larger than the armhole. The following steps will ensure a good fit. Fold the sleeve in half lengthways and mark the centre cap. Match it to the shoulder seam on the garment and pin in position. Then pin the 2 pieces together at intervals, easing in the sleeve fullness. Sew the sleeve into the armhole.

Grafting

Slip the stitches off the needles; in order to prevent your work from unravelling, press lightly with a steam iron or thread a piece of yarn through the stitches. Place the 2 pieces face up on a padded surface, with the 2 edges to be joined abutting. Thread a tapestry needle with matching yarn; you will need about 3 times the length of the seam to be joined.

Insert needle from back to front through first loop on lower piece. *Insert needle from front to back through first loop on upper piece; then from back to front on 2nd upper loop.

Insert needle from front to back in first lower loop, then from back to front in 2nd lower loop. Repeat from *, always going from front to back through a loop you have already gone through from back to front.

CARING FOR YOUR KNITS

KNITTED GARMENTS CAN be pulled out of shape all too easily during washing and drying. Handle garments gently, particularly when they are wet. Some specially treated wool yarns and many acrylic yarns are machine washable, and most yarns will benefit from a short, fast spin before being laid out flat to dry. Check the instructions on the yarn label first, and, if you are in any doubt, use the method given below.

TROUBLE-SHOOTING

Here are some tips for keeping your knitted garments in great condition:

- Snags should never be cut. Ease the yarn back in position with a blunt tapestry needle, and, if necessary, catch with a few small stitches on the wrong side.
- Some yarns are prone to pilling (tiny balls of fluff caused by rubbing). Lay the garment flat and pick off the balls gently by hand. They may also be removed by brushing lengthways with the edge of a stiff, dry synthetic sponge. A small shaver can also be bought from stores for this purpose.
- The texture of mohair can be improved by brushing very gently with a metal 'teazel'.
- Stains require immediate action. Most will respond to cold water. Dab or soak the area – don't rub. Oil-based stains should be treated with an appropriate solvent on the wrong side, following the manufacturer's instructions. Rinse afterward.

MACHINE WASHING

Use only when indicated on the yarn label. Turn the garment inside out and wash on the appropriate cycle. To avoid stretching, place garment in a loosely tied pillowcase before washing. Then, wash it on the woollen programme. Remove the garment when damp, lay it on a flat surface away from direct heat or sunlight, and pat it into its original shape. Leave until completely dry.

The pillowcase prevents the garment stretching in the machine's drum

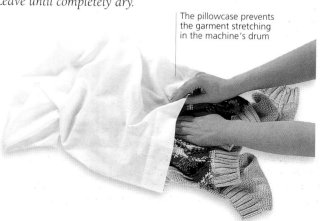

HAND WASHING

Large items should be washed separately in lukewarm water, using a mild detergent made especially for knitwear. If you think strong colours will run, wet a corner of the garment and press it on a white cloth. If it makes a stain, use cold water for a few washes.

1 Work in lather by gently squeezing and pressing the knitting up and down. Never rub or twist. Rinse thoroughly with several changes of lukewarm water.

2 Do not wring; squeeze out excess moisture. Then roll in a clean towel to soak up as much moisture as possible; repeat with a second towel if necessary.

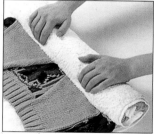

3 Spread the article out on a flat surface, away from direct heat, and ease it into its original shape. Leave until completely dry.

STORAGE

Dust can damage knitted garments. To prevent this, store knitwear flat in a cupboard, drawer, or in a container under the bed, not on an open shelf. Always wash your knits before storage. Never hang up knitted garments as their weight will cause them to stretch out of shape.

CROCHET

CROCHET IS AN ANCIENT CRAFT practised all around the world, and every year another generation of designers rediscovers its appeal. New stitch patterns are regularly created and with the wealth of attractive patterns and yarns available it is not surprising that crochet remains an extremely popular pastime.

Big and bold or light and lacy, crochet is versatile and lends itself to a variety of uses. Tools and materials are minimal – all you need are a single hook and a ball of yarn – making crochet extremely portable. Like knitting, it is formed from a continuous length of yarn but only one stitch at a time is made. By using a large hook and thick yarn, you can create chunky hats and sweaters. If you choose a thin hook and fine yarn, a combination of stitches will make patterns that rival lace in their delicacy.

Easy to work in rows or rings, all the well-loved stitches – and some interesting variations – are included, enabling you to create a fabulous range of items for the home.

CONTENTS

HOOKS & YARNS

CROCHET HOOKS COME in different sizes and materials. There are fine steel hooks and larger ones of aluminium, plastic or wood. Avoid the cheaper plastic versions that may have rough edges. Yarns are sold by weight and/or length. Beginners will find it helpful to choose a smooth yarn in a heavy weight that is not likely to untwist while you work. Generally, the coarser the yarn, the larger the hook needed. Sometimes a hook size is given on the label: use this as a starting point, but it is essential to obtain the tension stated in a pattern (see page 89). Fancy yarns can be worked with a larger hook than a smooth yarn of similar weight. If you are mixing more than one yarn in a garment, check that they share the same care instructions.

YARNS

There are basic standard terms which describe the most popular weights of yarns and some of their suitable uses. These yarns may be made of different numbers of strands spun together, 2-, 3- and 4-ply are all common. There is often an overlap within these terms so the following is a guide:

Fine weight or 2-ply is usually used for lace work and edgings. It is approximately half the thickness of 3-ply, or finer. 3-ply is used for delicate garments and baby wear. Four-ply is middle of the weight range, for sweaters, cardigans, or shawls, and is the standard on which other yarn weights are based.

Double knitting suits chunkier jackets and sweaters, and is equivalent to two strands of 4-ply. Aran weight is equivalent to three strands of 4-ply, and is used for heavy afghans or jackets. Chunky, for warm outdoor garments, is equivalent to four strands of 4-ply or two strands of double knitting.

Fine weight

3-ply

4-ply

Double knitting

Aran

Chunky

HOOKS

Steel and aluminium hooks come in a large range of sizes, but wooden hooks are also popular. Tunisian crochet needs the very long hook shown on the right.

CROCHET HOOK SIZES

Aluminium and plastic hooks

Size	mm
2	7.00
3	6.50
4	6.00
5	5.50
6	5.00
7	4.50
8	4.00
9	3.50
10	3.25
11	3.00
12	2.50
13	2.25
14	2.00

Steel hooks

Size	mm
000	3.00
00	2.50
0	–
1	2.00
1 1/2	1.75
2 1/2	1.50
3	1.25
4	1.00
5	1.00
5 1/2	0.75
6	0.75
6 1/2	0.60
7	0.60

BEGINNING TO CROCHET

CROCHET WORK, like knitting, is created from a continuous length of yarn. However, in crochet a single hook is used to work one stitch at a time. To begin crocheting, you start with a slip knot then continue to make loops (called chains) to form your foundation chain, from which you make your first row. You can hold the hook and yarn as you like, but we show the two most common ways or you can devise a method to suit yourself. The tension of the yarn is controlled with either your middle or forefinger. With practice, you will learn to control the yarn evenly and develop uniform chains.

LEFT-HANDED CROCHETERS

Illustrations show hook and yarn positions of a right-handed person. If you are left-handed, hold the working yarn in your right hand and hold the hook exactly as shown, but in the left hand. If it helps, hold this book in front of a mirror to follow the correct working positions.

Making a slip knot

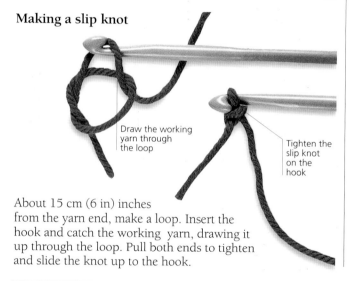

Draw the working yarn through the loop

Tighten the slip knot on the hook

About 15 cm (6 in) inches from the yarn end, make a loop. Insert the hook and catch the working yarn, drawing it up through the loop. Pull both ends to tighten and slide the knot up to the hook.

HOLDING THE HOOK

Both methods are equally good, so use whichever feels most comfortable.

Pencil position
Grasp the flat part of the hook between thumb and forefinger as if it were a pencil with the stem above your hand.

Hold the hook as if it were a pencil

Knife position
With the stem against your palm and your thumb on the flat part, grasp the hook between thumb and fingers.

Hold the hook in the knife position

CONTROLLING THE YARN

The way you hold the yarn allows it to flow easily with the right tension. You can wrap the yarn around your little finger, over the next two fingers, and catch it with your forefinger – when your middle finger will control the yarn. Or you can wrap the yarn around your little finger, then under your next two fingers and over your forefinger – when your forefinger will control the yarn. With thick yarn, you can catch it between your fourth and fifth fingers. Use the method that you feel comfortable with.

Forefinger method
Pass working yarn around little finger, under next 2 fingers and over forefinger. With hook through slip loop, and holding slip knot between thumb and middle finger, prepare to make first chain by raising your forefinger.

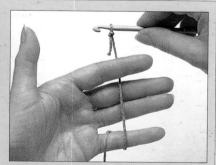

Middle finger method
Pass working yarn around little finger, and over other fingers. With hook through slip loop, and holding slip knot between thumb and forefinger of your left hand, prepare to make first chain by raising your middle finger.

CHAIN STITCH (CH)

Chain stitch is usually used to form the foundation for the first row in crochet. It is also used as part of a pattern stitch, to make spaces between stitches, for bars in openwork (see page 109), and for the turning chains at the beginnings of rows/rounds (see page 82).

Foundation chain

The foundation chain should be worked loosely and evenly to ensure that the hook can enter each loop easily on the first row. The hook and your tension will determine the size of the chains. Do not try to make them loose by pulling them as you make them, since this tightens up previously made chains. If the chains are too tight, ensure that the yarn is flowing through your fingers easily, or use a larger hook than you will use for the rest of your work. The length of the foundation chain will be specified in the pattern instruction.

Making a chain stitch

1 Hold hook in your right hand. Keeping working yarn taut, grasp slip knot with thumb and middle finger of your left hand. Push hook forward and take hook under (anti-clockwise), behind and then over yarn, so that yarn passes round hook and is caught in it. This is called yarn round hook – or *yrh*.

2 Draw hook and yarn back through the slip loop to form the first chain stitch.

3 Repeat steps 1 and 2. After making a few chains in this way, move your left hand up so that you are holding the work directly under the hook for maximum control, and continue.

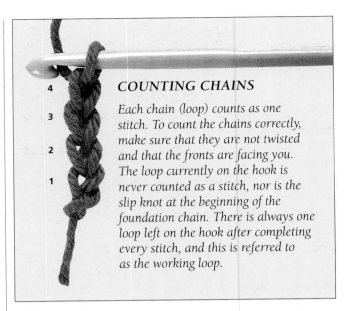

COUNTING CHAINS

Each chain (loop) counts as one stitch. To count the chains correctly, make sure that they are not twisted and that the fronts are facing you. The loop currently on the hook is never counted as a stitch, nor is the slip knot at the beginning of the foundation chain. There is always one loop left on the hook after completing every stitch, and this is referred to as the working loop.

SLIP STITCH (SL ST)

Some of the earliest crochet work found was done in continuous slip stitch or single crochet. However, this stitch is now only used to join a row into a round (see page 102), to decrease (see page 91), and for joining seams (see page 116).

1 Make a length of evenly worked foundation chain.

2 Insert the hook from front to back under the top of the 2nd chain (*ch*) from the hook. Wrap the yarn around the hook (*yrh*).

3 Draw yarn through the 2 loops now on the hook, making a slip stitch. To continue working slip stitch, insert the hook into the next and each chain, and repeat step 2 as required.

BASIC CROCHET STITCHES

IT IS EASY to learn crochet stitches because they are all made in the same way. Apart from the chain and the slip stitch, there are five basic crochet stitches, which vary in height (there are others, but these are used infrequently). The difference in the height or length of these stitches is determined by the number of times the yarn is wrapped around the hook. As each stitch has a flatter appearance on the front than

on the back, the crocheted piece has more texture when worked in rows and turned because you see both the fronts and the backs of the stitches. The surface has a smoother, flatter look when worked in rows/rounds without turning, as it always shows the front of the stitches.

DOUBLE CROCHET

This is a simple compact stitch. It is found in many pattern designs and forms a firm, smooth surface.

HALF TREBLE CROCHET

Between double and treble crochet in size, this stitch produces a slightly looser surface with an attractive ridge.

DOUBLE TREBLE CROCHET

Three times as high as double crochet, this stitch forms a looser texture.

Double treble crochet

Half treble crochet

Double crochet

Treble crochet

TREBLE CROCHET

Twice as high as double crochet, this stitch works up quickly. It is the most commonly used stitch.

Triple treble crochet

TRIPLE TREBLE CROCHET

This extremely long stitch is commonly used in fancy stitch patterns, but is not generally used continuously to make a whole piece, except where it is linked (see page 84).

MAKING THE BASIC STITCHES

WHEN YOU ARE working the basic stitches onto the foundation chains, insert the hook from front to back under the top loop of each chain. On subsequent rows, unless instructed otherwise, insert your hook from front to back under the top two loops of each stitch. Turn the work at the end of each row, then make extra chains, called turning chains, to bring the hook level with the height of the stitches in the new row (see page 82). The turning chains may or may not count as stitches at the beginning of a row, according to the pattern. They do count as a stitch in the basic stitch patterns below.

Double crochet (dc)

1 Make a foundation chain. Skip 2 ch and insert hook under top loop of 3rd ch *(right)*. Yrh and draw yarn through chain loop only *(far right)*.

2 There are 2 loops on the hook. Yrh and draw through both loops.

3 Double crochet made. Continue working dc into the next and all following chains to the end of the row.

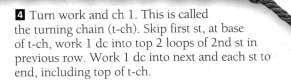

4 Turn work and ch 1. This is called the turning chain (t-ch). Skip first st, at base of t-ch, work 1 dc into top 2 loops of 2nd st in previous row. Work 1 dc into next and each st to end, including top of t-ch.

Half treble crochet (htr)

1 Make a length of foundation chain. Skip 2 ch, yrh and insert the hook under top loop of 3rd ch. Yrh.

2 Draw the yarn through the chain loop only; (there are now 3 loops on hook). Yrh.

3 Draw yarn through all 3 loops. Half treble crochet made. Continue working htr into next and all following chs to end of row.

4 To make the next and following rows of htr, turn work and ch 2. This turning chain counts as first htr in new row. Skip first st, which is at base of t-ch. Work 1 htr, inserting hook under top 2 loops of 2nd st in previous row. Work 1 htr into next and each st to end, including into top of t-ch.

Treble crochet (tr)

1 Make a length of foundation chain. Skip 3 ch, yrh and insert the hook under the top loop of the 4th ch. Yrh.

2 Draw yarn through ch loop only (there are now 3 loops on hook). Yrh.

3 Draw yarn through 2 loops only (2 loops on hook). Yrh.

4 Draw yarn through these 2 loops. Treble crochet made. Continue working tr into the next and all following chains to the end of the row.

5 To make next and following rows of tr, turn work and ch 3. This t-ch counts as first tr in new row. Skip first st which is at base of t-ch. Work 1 tr inserting hook under top 2 loops of 2nd st in previous row. Work 1 tr into next and each st to end, including into top of t-ch.

Double treble crochet (dtr)

1 Make a length of foundation chain. Skip 4 ch, yrh twice and insert hook under the top loop of the 5th ch. Yrh.

2 Draw yarn through ch loop only; (there are now 4 loops on hook). Yrh.

3 Draw yarn through 2 loops only; (3 loops on the hook). Yrh.

4 Draw yarn through 2 loops only, yrh again. Draw yarn through remaining 2 loops. Double treble made. Continue working dtr into the next and all following chains to the end of the row.

5 To make next row of dtr, turn work and ch 4. This t-ch counts as first dtr in new row. Skip first st which is at base of t-ch. Work 1 dtr, inserting hook under top 2 loops of 2nd st in previous row. Work 1 dtr into next and each st to end of row, including into t-ch.

Triple treble (ttr)

1 Make a length of foundation chain. Skip 5 ch, yrh 3 times and insert hook under top of the 6th ch, yrh and draw it through the ch loop only; (there are now 5 loops on the hook). *Yrh.

2 Draw yarn through 2 loops only.

3 Repeat from * three times more.

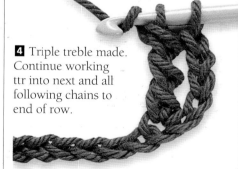

4 Triple treble made. Continue working ttr into next and all following chains to end of row.

5 To make the next and following rows of ttr, turn the work and ch 5. This t-ch counts as the first ttr in the new row. Skip the first st, which is at the base of the t-ch. Work 1 ttr, inserting the hook under the top 2 loops of the 2nd st in the previous row. Work 1 ttr into next and each st to the end of row, including into top of t-ch.

TURNING CHAINS (T-CH)

*To bring the hook up to the height of the stitches, you must add turning chains at the beginning of each row. Each stitch has its own number of chains: the table gives the numbers when the t-ch counts as the first stitch. Sometimes the t-ch may **not** be counted as a stitch (see Straight Edges). Some instructions say ch 2 and turn.*

Stitch	Add to foundation chain	Skip at beginning of foundation row (counts as first st)	For turning chain counts as first st
Double crochet	1	2	1
Half treble	1	2	2
Treble	2	3	3
Double treble	3	4	4
Triple treble	4	5	5
Quad treble	5	6	6

STRAIGHT EDGES

To obtain straight edges and keep the number of stitches constant, you need to make the turning chains in one of two ways. The first is most common, but the second is used with very short stitches, or to avoid the gap created by using the turning chain as a stitch. However, the second method creates slightly uneven edges. The instruction to work "even" in a pattern means to work without any increasing or decreasing.

Turning chain counts as first stitch

Skip the first stitch of the previous row at the base of the turning chain. When you reach the end of the row, work a stitch into the top of the turning chain of the previous row.

Turning chain does not count as stitch

Work into the first stitch at the base of the turning chain. When you reach the end of the row, do not work into the top of the previous turning chain.

WORKING IN ROWS

Crochet is normally worked in rows to produce the desired width, and the work is turned between each row: the right side of the work will not always be facing you.

The first row is made by working across the foundation chain from right to left (if you are left-handed, work from left to right).

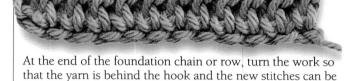

At the end of the foundation chain or row, turn the work so that the yarn is behind the hook and the new stitches can be worked into the tops of those in the previous row.

FASTENING OFF

To prevent the work from unravelling when you have finished, it is necessary to fasten the end.

Complete the final stitch, then cut the working yarn and pull it through the last loop on the hook. Pull the yarn tight to close the loop. Thread the working end of the yarn into a tapestry or yarn needle and weave it into the back of the work.

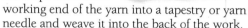

COUNTING STITCHES

To count short stitches, such as double crochet (as shown), it is easier to look at the tops. For longer stitches, count the upright stems – each is counted as a single stitch.

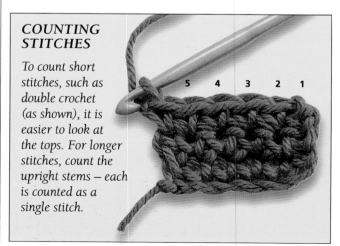

BASIC STITCH VARIATIONS

YOU CAN ACHIEVE interesting textural effects by working the basic stitches, but then inserting the hook into a different part of the work instead of into the top two loops of each stitch. For example, you can work under one top loop at a time, between the stitches, or around the stem of the stitch. All crochet stitches can be worked with these variations, but some produce more interesting effects than others. As well as adding surface texture, these stitches will make a garment thicker and warmer. To begin any of these stitch variations, first make a length of foundation chain and work one row in your chosen stitch.

WORKING UNDER ONE LOOP

By continually working into only the back loop (abbreviated as bl as in bldc), you can create a pattern with a ridged effect. Working into only the front loop (fl) makes a less pronounced ridge with a horizontal line. This technique works well with the shorter stitches, for example double crochet and half treble crochet.

To work into the back loop

From the 2nd row onwards work your chosen crochet stitch normally (for example, htr as shown here), but insert the hook into the back loop of each stitch.

To work into the front loop

From the 2nd row onwards work your chosen crochet stitch normally (for example, dc as shown here), but insert the hook into the front loop only of each stitch.

Stitch worked into back loop

Stitch worked into front loop

WORKING BETWEEN TWO STITCHES

This technique of working between the stitches of the previous row is quick and easy, and produces a slightly thicker fabric with a more open look.

To work between two stitches

From the 2nd row onwards work your chosen crochet stitch normally (for example, tr as shown here), but insert hook between stems and below all horizontal threads connecting stitches.

WORKING SPIKES

Spikes are arrow-shaped loops of yarn on the surface of the work. They are made by inserting the hook lower down than usual, for example, into one or more rows below the previous one (pattern instructions will always specify where).

To make a simple dc spike

Insert hook into base of next stitch (*left*), yrh and draw it through up to height of a dc in this row, (2 loops on hook) (*right*). Yrh and draw it through both loops. Dc spike made.

WORKING AROUND THE STEM (RAISED STITCHES)

A raised effect can be achieved by working around the stems of the stitches in the previous row, either in the front (raised front, abbreviated rf), or in the back (raised back, abbreviated rb). Rows can be worked all in front or all in back, or alternatively one or more stitches around the back then one or more stitches around the front, to produce a large variety of stitch patterns.

To work raised stitches around the front

First work a row of your basic stitch, such as the tr shown here. From 2nd row onwards, make each stitch normally, but insert hook in front and from right to left around stem of stitch below *(right).*

A raised stitch worked around the front

To work raised stitches around the back

Work exactly the same as for raised stitches to the front, except insert the hook in back and from right to left around stem of stitch below *(right).*

The finished stitch worked around the back

WORKING LINKED STITCHES

Longer stitches can be linked to each other down their sides to eliminate the space between the stems of the stitches. This creates an effect as if several rows of shorter stitches had been worked in the same direction at the same time.

To work a linked double treble

1 Insert the hook down through the upper of the 2 horizontal loops around the stem of the last stitch made; yarn round hook.

2 Draw a loop through, insert the hook down through the lower horizontal loop of the same stitch, yrh, draw a loop through. (There are now 3 loops on hook.)

3 Insert hook for next stitch, yrh, draw it through stitch only, [yrh and draw it through 2 loops only] 3 times. Linked dtr made.

To start a row with a linked double treble, treat 2nd *(left)* and 4th chains from the hook as the upper and lower horizontal loops of last stitch made.

CROCHET TERMINOLOGY

CROCHET PATTERN INSTRUCTIONS indicate, in abbreviated form, how many and what kind of stitches to work and where to insert the hook. They assume you are familiar with the basic stitches and other procedures and that you understand these abbreviations.

Pattern abbreviations

across	to the end of the row
alt	alternate
approx	approximate(ly)
beg	beginning
bet	between
bl	insert hook under back loop only. Eg. bldc – back loop double crochet
ch(s)	chain or chain stitch(es)
ch sp(s)	chain space(s)
cl	cluster
cont	continue
dc	double crochet
dc2tog	work 2 dc together
dec	decrease
dtr	double treble crochet
dtr2tog	work 2 dtr together
fl	insert hook under front loop only. Eg. fldc – front loop double crochet
foll	following
gr	group
htr	half treble crochet
htr2tog	work 2 htr together
in	inches
in next	sts to be worked into same stitch
inc	increase
lp(s)	loop(s)
nc	not closed (see Clusters, page 106)
patt	pattern
p or pc	picot
rf	raised front. Eg. rfdc – raised front double crochet
rb	raised back. Eg. rbdc – raised back double crochet
rem	remaining
rep	repeat
rnd	round
sk	skip
sl st	slip stitch
sp(s)	space(s)
st(s)	stitch(es)
t-ch(s)	turning chain(s)
tog	together
tr	treble crochet
tr2tog	work 2 tr together
ttr	triple treble crochet
ttr2tog	work 2 ttr together
yrh	yarn round hook
*	Work instructions immediately following *, then repeat as directed, (see Repeats)
[ ]	Work or repeat all instructions enclosed in brackets as directed immediately after, (see Repeats)

Unless otherwise specified:
• Do not turn the work at the end of a row/round.
• Always count the turning chain as a stitch (see page 82).
• Work into the next available stitch in the previous row.
• Always insert the hook under both top loops of a stitch, unless it is a chain space or loop.
• The instruction, *1 dc*, means work one double crochet into next sitch, and *5 tr*, work 1 tr into each of next 5 sts.
• For a cluster, the instruction *tr3tog*, or *dtr5tog*, means that each stitch is worked into a separate stitch, before joining.
• If all parts of the cluster are to be worked into the next stitch, the instruction would say *tr5tog in next*.

Multiples
In the stitch glossaries the pattern gives the number of stitches required in the row and the number of chains to work for the foundation chain in this way: *Multiple of 5 sts plus 2, plus 2 for foundation ch*. This means make 9, 14, 19, etc, chains in order to work with 7, 12, 17, etc. stitches.

Brackets [ ] or parentheses ( )
These are used in three distinct ways:
• To simplify repetition – see Repeats.
• To indicate at the end of a row/round the total number of stitches that have been worked in that row/round. For example, *(24 dc)* means that the row/round counts as 24 double crochet stitches.
• To give information about different sizes.

Right side/wrong side (RS/WS)
Even if a crochet pattern is reversible it is usual to define a right side. When working in the round, the right side is normally facing you. Where the work is turned between rows, instructions specify the first right side row. If you are directed to keep the right side facing you when working rows, fasten off at the end of each row and rejoin the yarn.

Repeats
Instructions within brackets are worked the number of times stated, for example *[ch 1, skip 1 ch, 1 tr] 5 times*. A single asterisk marks the beginning of a pattern repeat sequence. For example **ch 1, skip 1 ch, 1 dc; rep from * across*. A double asterisk indicates a smaller repeat in the main repeat sequence. The instruction: *rep from * to last st* means work complete repeats until only one stitch remains.

Working into the back and front loops alternately makes a broken texture

◀ **BACK AND FRONT LOOP HALF TREBLE CROCHET**

Multiple of 2 sts, plus 1 for foundation ch

Row 1: Skip 2 ch, htr across, turn.
Row 2: Ch 2, *1 blhtr, 1 flhtr; rep from * to last st, 1 htr, turn.
Row 2 forms the pattern.

BACK LOOP HALF TREBLE CROCHET ▼

Any number of sts, plus 1 for foundation ch

Row 1: Skip 2 ch, htr across, turn.
Row 2: Ch 2, blhtr across, turn.
Row 2 forms the pattern.

Working into the back loops only produces a ridged effect

HALF TREBLE CROCHET BETWEEN STITCHES ▼

Any number of sts, plus 1 for foundation ch

Row 1: Skip 2 ch, htr across, turn.
Row 2: Ch 2, *1 htr inserting hook between stems of next 2 sts and below all horizontal connecting threads; rep from * across, turn.
Row 2 forms the pattern.

BACK AND FRONT LOOP DOUBLE CROCHET ▲

Multiple of 2 sts, plus 1 for foundation ch

Row 1: Skip 2 ch, dc across, turn.
Row 2: Ch 1, *1 bldc , 1 fldc; rep from * to last st, 1 dc, turn.
Row 2 forms the pattern.

ALTERNATE ROWS BACK AND FRONT LOOP TREBLE CROCHET ▲

Any number of sts, plus 2 for foundation ch

Row 1: Skip 3 ch, tr across, turn.
Row 2: Ch 3, bltr across, turn.
Row 3: Ch 3, fltr across, turn.
Rows 2 and 3 form the pattern.

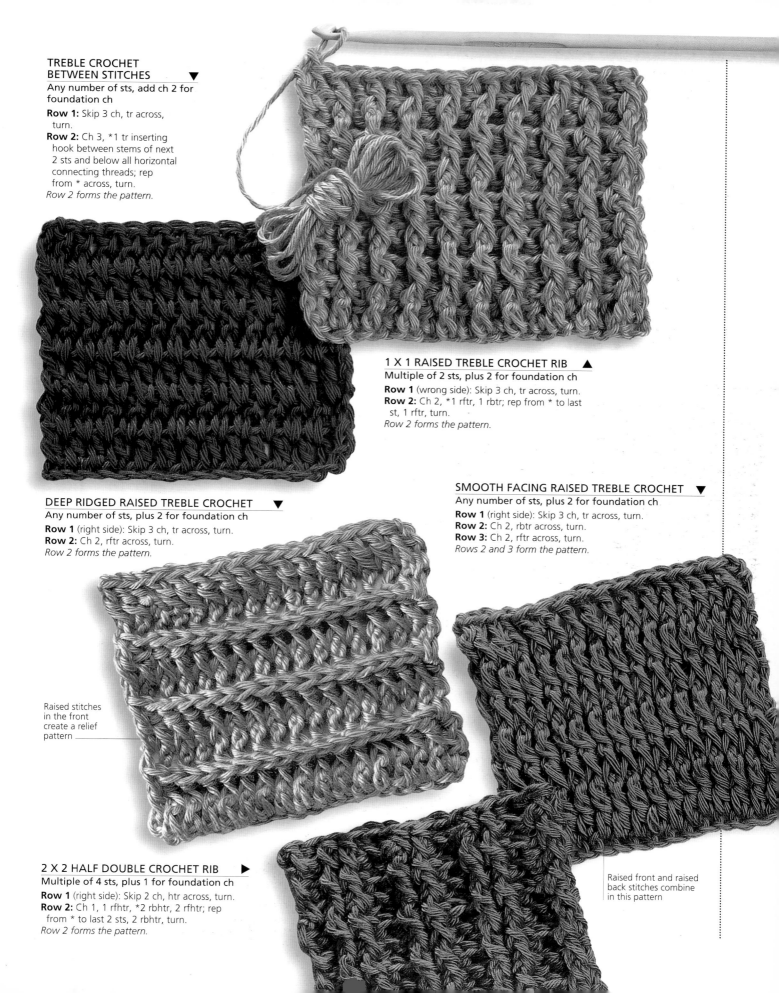

TREBLE CROCHET BETWEEN STITCHES ▼

Any number of sts, add ch 2 for foundation ch

Row 1: Skip 3 ch, tr across, turn.

Row 2: Ch 3, *1 tr inserting hook between stems of next 2 sts and below all horizontal connecting threads; rep from * across, turn.

Row 2 forms the pattern.

1 X 1 RAISED TREBLE CROCHET RIB ▲

Multiple of 2 sts, plus 2 for foundation ch

Row 1 (wrong side): Skip 3 ch, tr across, turn.

Row 2: Ch 2, *1 rftr, 1 rbtr; rep from * to last st, 1 rftr, turn.

Row 2 forms the pattern.

DEEP RIDGED RAISED TREBLE CROCHET ▼

Any number of sts, plus 2 for foundation ch

Row 1 (right side): Skip 3 ch, tr across, turn.

Row 2: Ch 2, rftr across, turn.

Row 2 forms the pattern.

Raised stitches in the front create a relief pattern

SMOOTH FACING RAISED TREBLE CROCHET ▼

Any number of sts, plus 2 for foundation ch

Row 1 (right side): Skip 3 ch, tr across, turn.

Row 2: Ch 2, rbtr across, turn.

Row 3: Ch 2, rftr across, turn.

Rows 2 and 3 form the pattern.

Raised front and raised back stitches combine in this pattern

2 X 2 HALF DOUBLE CROCHET RIB ▶

Multiple of 4 sts, plus 1 for foundation ch

Row 1 (right side): Skip 2 ch, htr across, turn.

Row 2: Ch 1, 1 rfhtr, *2 rbhtr, 2 rfhtr; rep from * to last 2 sts, 2 rbhtr, turn.

Row 2 forms the pattern.

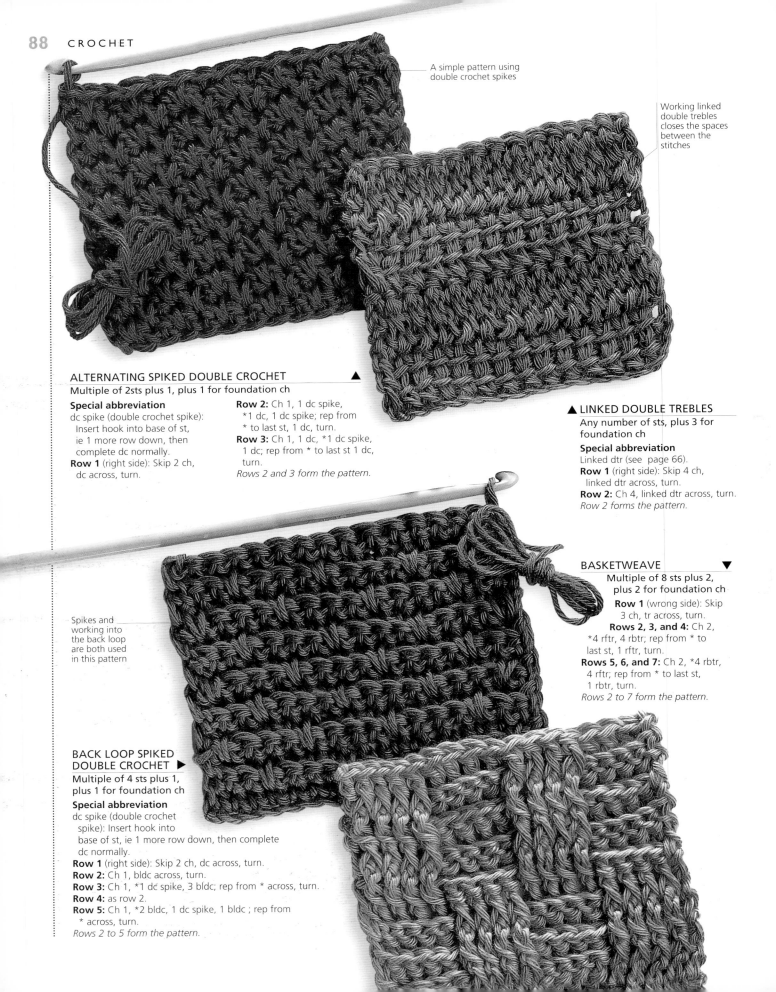

A simple pattern using double crochet spikes

Working linked double trebles closes the spaces between the stitches

ALTERNATING SPIKED DOUBLE CROCHET ▲
Multiple of 2sts plus 1, plus 1 for foundation ch

Special abbreviation
dc spike (double crochet spike): Insert hook into base of st, ie 1 more row down, then complete dc normally.
Row 1 (right side): Skip 2 ch, dc across, turn.

Row 2: Ch 1, 1 dc spike, *1 dc, 1 dc spike; rep from * to last st, 1 dc, turn.
Row 3: Ch 1, 1 dc, *1 dc spike, 1 dc; rep from * to last st 1 dc, turn.
Rows 2 and 3 form the pattern.

▲ LINKED DOUBLE TREBLES
Any number of sts, plus 3 for foundation ch
Special abbreviation
Linked dtr (see page 66).
Row 1 (right side): Skip 4 ch, linked dtr across, turn.
Row 2: Ch 4, linked dtr across, turn.
Row 2 forms the pattern.

BASKETWEAVE ▼
Multiple of 8 sts plus 2, plus 2 for foundation ch
Row 1 (wrong side): Skip 3 ch, tr across, turn.
Rows 2, 3, and 4: Ch 2, *4 rftr, 4 rbtr; rep from * to last st, 1 rftr, turn.
Rows 5, 6, and 7: Ch 2, *4 rbtr, 4 rftr; rep from * to last st, 1 rbtr, turn.
Rows 2 to 7 form the pattern.

Spikes and working into the back loop are both used in this pattern

BACK LOOP SPIKED DOUBLE CROCHET ▶
Multiple of 4 sts plus 1, plus 1 for foundation ch

Special abbreviation
dc spike (double crochet spike): Insert hook into base of st, ie 1 more row down, then complete dc normally.
Row 1 (right side): Skip 2 ch, dc across, turn.
Row 2: Ch 1, bldc across, turn.
Row 3: Ch 1, *1 dc spike, 3 bldc; rep from * across, turn.
Row 4: as row 2.
Row 5: Ch 1, *2 bldc, 1 dc spike, 1 bldc ; rep from * across, turn.
Rows 2 to 5 form the pattern.

TENSION

THE NUMBER OF stitches and rows required to make a piece of crochet of a specific size depends upon four things: the yarn, the hook size, the stitch pattern and the individual crocheter. The tension is given at the beginning of every crochet pattern. This indicates the number of stitches and rows in a particular measure, and the entire design is based around this. To achieve the best results, you **must** follow the tension. But since crochet is a true hand craft, each person's work will be slightly different. Before beginning a project, make a swatch to ensure that your tension matches that given. If you want to change the yarn or the stitch pattern, you can usually do so as long as you make sure you can still match the tension.

CHECKING THE TENSION

Using the weight of yarn, hook size, and stitch pattern given with the instructions, crochet a sample at least 10 cm (4 in) square. Place the finished sample right side up on a flat surface, taking care not to stretch it out of shape.

Measuring stitches

Lay your ruler across the sample at the bottom of a row of stitches. Insert 2 pins vertically 2.5 cm (1 in) apart. Count the number of stitches between the pins. If a pin falls in the middle of a stitch, measure 5 cm (2 in).

Measuring rows
Now turn your ruler vertically and lay it along one side of a column of stitches. Avoiding the edges, place pins horizontally 10 cm (4 in) apart. Count the rows between the pins. If a pin falls in the middle of a row, measure 5 cm (2 in).

MAKING ADJUSTMENTS

If your tension does not correspond with that given in the instructions, change to a bigger or smaller hook and crochet another sample. Fewer stitches and rows than indicated means your work is too loose and you should try a smaller hook. More stitches and rows than shown means it is too tight and you should try a larger hook. Occasionally you may find it impossible to match the tension of both stitches and rows at the same time, in which case you should match the tension and compensate by working more or fewer rows.

THE EFFECT OF YARNS AND PATTERNS

Weight of yarn and stitch pattern affect tension, so always work a sample before altering written instructions. Fine yarn will work with more stitches to the inch than heavier yarn, as will yarn worked with a smaller hook.

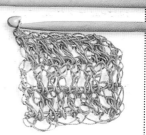

A thick yarn and a finer yarn worked on the same hook size will result in different numbers of stitches per cm

The same yarn and stitch worked on different size hooks will work up to a different tension

Different stitch patterns worked with the same hook and yarn will also produce different numbers of stitches per cm

INCREASING

MANY CROCHET ITEMS are made of rectangles worked evenly throughout (see page 82). There are times, however, when it is necessary to shape your work. To widen the fabric, you increase or add stitches. This may be done at the beginning and/or the end of a row, or at one or more places within a row.

WORKING SINGLE INCREASES

When it is necessary to increase by a single stitch, the simplest way is to work twice into the same stitch.

At the beginning of a row

When the turning chain counts as a stitch (*see page 82*), use one of these methods. Skip the first st as usual and work 2 sts into the 2nd st, or work 1 st into the first st that you usually skip.

At the end of a row

Work 2 sts into the last st (this will be the turning chain, if it counts as a st).

REPEATED SINGLE INCREASES

When you are making single increases one above another, work each subsequent pair into either the first or second of the previous pair consistently, so as to maintain vertical lines of increase. To slant them to the right on a right side row, work each increase pair into the first of the previous pair; to slant them to the left, work them into the second.

Across a row

Mark the position for each increase. Pattern instructions usually tell you exactly where to place these, but if not, spread them evenly. Work 2 stitches into each marked stitch.

MULTIPLE INCREASES

To increase by more than two stitches at the edge, make additional chain sts. The method is the same for all the basic stitches. Here the turning-chain counts as a st. When several stitches at once are made at an edge, a sharp angle is created.

At the beginning of a row

Add the the number of increases needed to the number of turning-chains being used. For example, if you are working trebles (tr), which need 2 t-ch, and want to add 5 sts, you will need to work 7 ch. Skip 3 ch (counts as 1 tr) and work 1 tr into each of the remaining 4 new ch sts, making 5 new sts, including turning-chain.

At the end of a row

To make the first additional stitch, insert the hook through the lower part of the last stitch made, picking up the single, vertical thread on its left-hand side. Continue inserting the hook into the base of the stitch just completed to work the required number of additional stitches.

DECREASING

IT MAY BE necessary to shape your crochet work by subtracting stitches; these decreases may be made at the beginning and/or the end of a row, or at set at various places within the row. You can also narrow your work by skipping one or more stitches, but this method may leave holes. Unless you want to create holes as a decorative effect, it is preferable to decrease by crocheting two or more stitches together.

REPEATED SINGLE DECREASES

When working single decreases one above another in mid row, work consistently either the first or the second part of the decrease cluster into the top of the previous cluster so as to maintain vertical lines of decrease. (See Repeated Single Increases, page 90.)

MULTIPLE DECREASES

To decrease more than two or three stitches, work multiple decreases at the ends of rows. The t-ch counts as a stitch. This method creates a sharp angle. Treble crochet (tr) is shown here, but the method is the same for all basic stitches

At the beginning of a row

Work slip st over each st to be subtracted. Then, make the required number of turning chains to form a new edge st and continue the row in pattern from there.

At the end of a row

Work in pattern until you reach the stitches to be decreased. Leave these sts unworked, turn and make the t-ch for the first st of the next row.

WORKING STITCHES TOGETHER AS ONE (STITCH CLUSTER)

To decrease 1, 2, 3, sts, etc. work 2, 3, 4, sts, etc. together. At the beginning of a row, when the t-ch counts as first st, work the 2nd and 3rd sts together to make a single decrease and the 2nd, 3rd, and 4th together to make a double decrease.

At the end of a row

Work the last 2, 3, or 4 sts together. In mid row work 1, 2, or 3 consecutive sts together in the appropriate positions *(see also Increasing and Repeated Single Decreases).*

At the beginning of a row
Double crochet

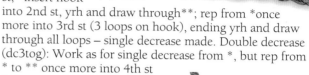

Single decrease (dc2tog): Make 1 ch (counts as 1 dc), skip first st, *insert hook into 2nd st, yrh and draw through**; rep from *once more into 3rd st (3 loops on hook), ending yrh and draw through all loops – single decrease made. Double decrease (dc3tog): Work as for single decrease from *, but rep from * to ** once more into 4th st (4 loops on hook) before ending.

Half treble crochet

Single decrease (htr2tog): Make 2 ch (counts as 1 htr), skip first st, *yrh, insert hook into next (2nd) st, yrh and draw through**; rep from * once more into next (3rd) st (5 loops on hook), ending yrh and draw through all loops – single decrease made. Double decrease (htr3tog): Work as for single decrease from *, but rep from * to ** once more into next (4th) st (7 loops on hook) before ending.

Treble crochet

Single decrease (tr2tog): Make 3 ch (counts as 1 tr), skip first st, *yrh, insert hook into next (2nd) st, yrh and draw through, yrh and draw through 2 loops only**; rep from * once more into next (3rd) st (3 loops on hook), ending yrh and draw through all loops – single decrease made. Double decrease (tr3tog): Work as for single decrease from *, but rep from * to ** once more into next (4th) st (4 loops on hook) before ending.

Double treble crochet

The method is the same for longer crochet stitches, such as double treble crochet.

Making a single decrease in double treble crochet

WORKING WITH COLOUR

COLOURED YARNS ARE used to create stripes, geometric patterns, and simple pictures in sharp contrasts or subtle gradations. Crochet stitches are generally larger and more varied than knitted ones and are perfect for overlapped and relief effects as well as variegated row structures. These stitches are best used for their own unique character, boldly and with imagination. Single yarns may be used, or strands of more than one giving both variegated colour and additional warmth. Yarns may be plain colour, two-tone, or patterned in different ways – heather mixtures, mottled or multicoloured yarns.

HORIZONTAL STRIPES

Use single colours for one or more whole rows to create horizontal stripes. Carry the yarns not in use up the side of the work or cut them off and rejoin as required.

VERTICAL STRIPES AND INTARSIA

For blocks of colour, join a separate ball for each colour area or stripe, which avoids floats entirely. There is no need (as there is in knitting) to twist the yarns around each other at the changeovers to prevent holes appearing.

Working stripes is the simplest way of introducing a new colour

Work with separate coloured balls for intarsia

Jacquard includes all-over multicoloured, geometric, and picture patterns

TEXTURED EFFECTS

Richly textured effects can be achieved using different types of yarn along with changes of colour. Multicoloured yarns create a new effect when combined with plain colours or textured yarns. Bouclé and mohair multicoloured yarns are shown worked together in this basketweave pattern sample.

Textured stitches and yarns combined make a rich fabric

JACQUARD

When yarn is joined in the middle of a row, the yarn not in use is carried along the back of work. This will form loops, or floats, which may catch in wear and must be worked over every few stitches, or encased during right side rows.

YARN ENDS

Provided you can do so without interfering with the visual effect, it is advisable to work over yarn ends whenever possible. Remember that all stray ends must finally be woven into the wrong side.

CHARTS

Most multicolour patterns are presented in the form of graphs, in which each square corresponds to one stitch – normally double crochet, since it is the smallest, squarest stitch. There are two main rules for following colour chart grids: always change to next colour required just before you complete the previous stitch and follow odd-numbered rows from right to left and even-numbered from left to right (chart always represents right side of the work).

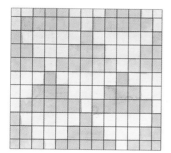 

JOINING NEW YARN

When working horizontal stripes, change to the new yarn at the end of the row just before completing the last stitch. This way, the new colour is ready to work the turning chain. When working in the round, work the last stitch with the old colour and use the new colour to make the joining slip stitch.

1 Just before you pick up for the last time to make the last stitch with the old colour, drop the old yarn and pick up the new yarn.

2 Draw new yarn through to complete the old stitch – the working loop is now ready in the new colour. This sample is in tr, but the same principle applies to all other stitches.

Before working the next stitch, make sure old yarn is kept to the wrong side of the work, or carried along the tops of the next few stitches so that it will become encased.

CHANGING YARN

Change the yarns as for joining, just before you complete the last stitch with the old colour. Draw up the float in the new colour evenly, making sure the old yarn is appropriately positioned. Double crochet is illustrated here, but the same principle applies to all other basic stitches.

RE-JOINING YARN

Occasionally you will need to join yarn into a piece of crochet that has been fastened off, in order to make a fresh start.

Insert the hook into the appropriate place. Start with a slip knot (or a simple loop, if you prefer) and draw this through. Make the appropriate turning chain for the first new stitch (ch 3 for 1 tr shown here).

FLOATS

To help the tension of floats be more even, catch them into the work every few stitches. When finished, cut in half any unacceptably long float threads and weave them in.

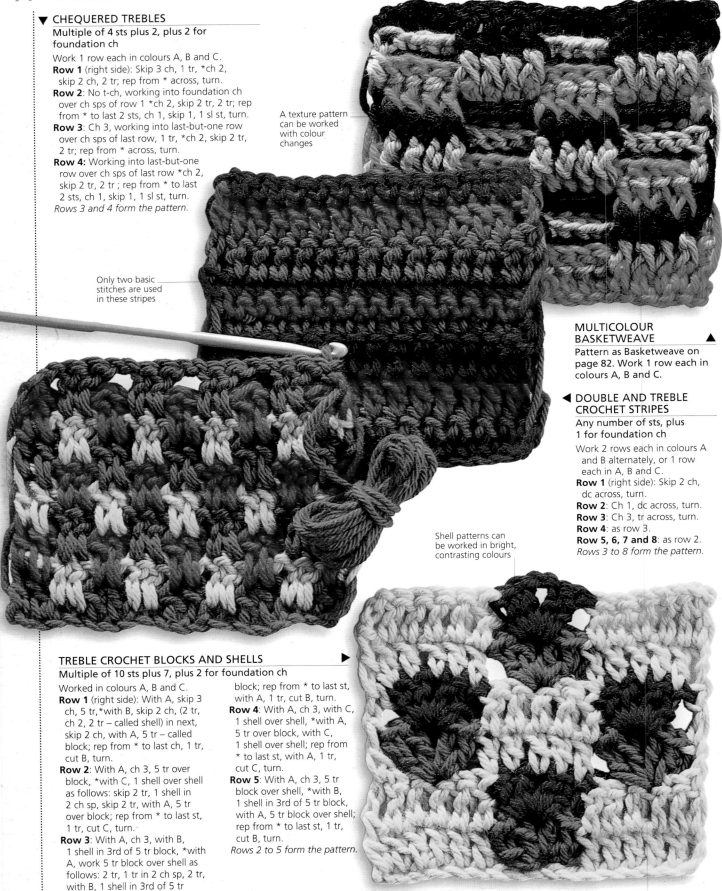

▼ CHEQUERED TREBLES

Multiple of 4 sts plus 2, plus 2 for foundation ch

Work 1 row each in colours A, B and C.

Row 1 (right side): Skip 3 ch, 1 tr, *ch 2, skip 2 ch, 2 tr; rep from * across, turn.

Row 2: No t-ch, working into foundation ch over ch sps of row 1 *ch 2, skip 2 tr, 2 tr; rep from * to last 2 sts, ch 1, skip 1, 1 sl st, turn.

Row 3: Ch 3, working into last-but-one row over ch sps of last row, 1 tr, *ch 2, skip 2 tr, 2 tr; rep from * across, turn.

Row 4: Working into last-but-one row over ch sps of last row *ch 2, skip 2 tr, 2 tr ; rep from * to last 2 sts, ch 1, skip 1, 1 sl st, turn.

Rows 3 and 4 form the pattern.

A texture pattern can be worked with colour changes

Only two basic stitches are used in these stripes

MULTICOLOUR BASKETWEAVE ▲

Pattern as Basketweave on page 82. Work 1 row each in colours A, B and C.

◄ DOUBLE AND TREBLE CROCHET STRIPES

Any number of sts, plus 1 for foundation ch

Work 2 rows each in colours A and B alternately, or 1 row each in A, B and C.

Row 1 (right side): Skip 2 ch, dc across, turn.

Row 2: Ch 1, dc across, turn.

Row 3: Ch 3, tr across, turn.

Row 4: as row 3.

Row 5, 6, 7 and 8: as row 2.

Rows 3 to 8 form the pattern.

Shell patterns can be worked in bright, contrasting colours

TREBLE CROCHET BLOCKS AND SHELLS ▶

Multiple of 10 sts plus 7, plus 2 for foundation ch

Worked in colours A, B and C.

Row 1 (right side): With A, skip 3 ch, 5 tr,*with B, skip 2 ch, (2 tr, ch 2, 2 tr – called shell) in next, skip 2 ch, with A, 5 tr – called block; rep from * to last ch, 1 tr, cut B, turn.

Row 2: With A, ch 3, 5 tr over block, *with C, 1 shell over shell as follows: skip 2 tr, 1 shell in 2 ch sp, skip 2 tr, with A, 5 tr over block; rep from * to last st, 1 tr, cut C, turn.

Row 3: With A, ch 3, with B, 1 shell in 3rd of 5 tr block, *with A, work 5 tr block over shell as follows: 2 tr, 1 tr in 2 ch sp, 2 tr, with B, 1 shell in 3rd of 5 tr block; rep from * to last st, with A, 1 tr, cut B, turn.

Row 4: With A, ch 3, with C, 1 shell over shell, *with A, 5 tr over block, with C, 1 shell over shell; rep from * to last st, with A, 1 tr, cut C, turn.

Row 5: With A, ch 3, 5 tr block over shell, *with B, 1 shell in 3rd of 5 tr block, with A, 5 tr block over shell; rep from * to last st, with A, 1 tr, cut B, turn.

Rows 2 to 5 form the pattern.

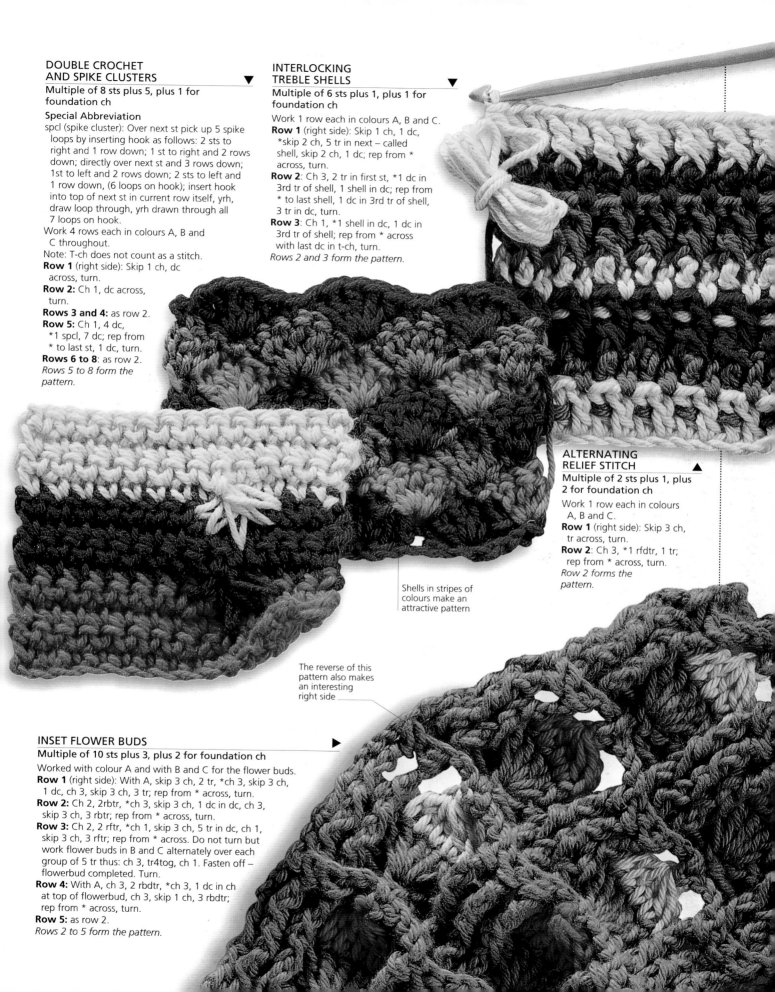

DOUBLE CROCHET AND SPIKE CLUSTERS ▼

Multiple of 8 sts plus 5, plus 1 for foundation ch

Special Abbreviation

spcl (spike cluster): Over next st pick up 5 spike loops by inserting hook as follows: 2 sts to right and 1 row down; 1st to right and 2 rows down; directly over next st and 3 rows down; 1st to left and 2 rows down; 2 sts to left and 1 row down, (6 loops on hook); insert hook into top of next st in current row itself, yrh, draw loop through, yrh drawn through all 7 loops on hook.

Work 4 rows each in colours A, B and C throughout.

Note: T-ch does not count as a stitch.

Row 1 (right side): Skip 1 ch, dc across, turn.

Row 2: Ch 1, dc across, turn.

Rows 3 and 4: as row 2.

Row 5: Ch 1, 4 dc, *1 spcl, 7 dc; rep from * to last st, 1 dc, turn.

Rows 6 to 8: as row 2.

Rows 5 to 8 form the pattern.

INTERLOCKING TREBLE SHELLS ▼

Multiple of 6 sts plus 1, plus 1 for foundation ch

Work 1 row each in colours A, B and C.

Row 1 (right side): Skip 1 ch, 1 dc, *skip 2 ch, 5 tr in next – called shell, skip 2 ch, 1 dc; rep from * across, turn.

Row 2: Ch 3, 2 tr in first st, *1 dc in 3rd tr of shell, 1 shell in dc; rep from * to last shell, 1 dc in 3rd tr of shell, 3 tr in dc, turn.

Row 3: Ch 1, *1 shell in dc, 1 dc in 3rd tr of shell; rep from * across with last dc in t-ch, turn.

Rows 2 and 3 form the pattern.

Shells in stripes of colours make an attractive pattern

ALTERNATING RELIEF STITCH ▲

Multiple of 2 sts plus 1, plus 2 for foundation ch

Work 1 row each in colours A, B and C.

Row 1 (right side): Skip 3 ch, tr across, turn.

Row 2: Ch 3, *1 rfdtr, 1 tr; rep from * across, turn.

Row 2 forms the pattern.

The reverse of this pattern also makes an interesting right side

INSET FLOWER BUDS ►

Multiple of 10 sts plus 3, plus 2 for foundation ch

Worked with colour A and with B and C for the flower buds.

Row 1 (right side): With A, skip 3 ch, 2 tr, *ch 3, skip 3 ch, 1 dc, ch 3, skip 3 ch, 3 tr; rep from * across, turn.

Row 2: Ch 2, 2rbtr, *ch 3, skip 3 ch, 1 dc in dc, ch 3, skip 3 ch, 3 rbtr; rep from * across, turn.

Row 3: Ch 2, 2 rftr, *ch 1, skip 3 ch, 5 tr in dc, ch 1, skip 3 ch, 3 rftr; rep from * across. Do not turn but work flower buds in B and C alternately over each group of 5 tr thus: ch 3, tr4tog, ch 1. Fasten off – flowerbud completed. Turn.

Row 4: With A, ch 3, 2 rbdtr, *ch 3, 1 dc in ch at top of flowerbud, ch 3, skip 1 ch, 3 rbdtr; rep from * across, turn.

Row 5: as row 2.

Rows 2 to 5 form the pattern.

MORE STITCH VARIATIONS

ONE OF THE great strengths of crochet is the versatility of the stitches. Change the height of your stitches from row to row, and you will see many different textures and stripe widths. Within a row, stitches of different heights will produce wave shapes and surface texture. Additional texture can be achieved by crossing stitches to produce a cable effect, or working them into different places. Making long stitches – reaching down below the level of the previous row and picking up around the stem – results in raised surface stitches, which are particularly striking when made in contrasting colours.

Simple crossed stitch

1 To make a pair of simple crossed stitches (tr shown here), first skip 1 and work 1 tr into next stitch (*left*). Then work 1 tr, inserting hook into previous skipped stitch (*right*).

2 The crossed tr wraps up and encases previous tr. (*See page 97, Crossed Trebles.*)

Cable crossed stitch (back)

1 To begin cable, first skip 3 sts and then work 3 ttr normally (shown here worked on tr).

2 With hook behind sts, insert it from front. Work 1 ttr into each of 3 skipped sts.

Cable crossed stitch (front)

Work entirely in front of the previous stitches (holding them aside at back if necessary) after inserting hook so as not to encase the stitches, as in Simple Crossed Stitch (*left*).

RAISED SURFACE STITCHES

*There are many variations of raised surface stitches, but they are all made in a similar way. The method shown left involves skipping stitches in the background fabric and working around the stem. The surface stitches must be longer than the background stitches. When skipping a stitch would result in a hole, work the raised surface stitch **together with** the background stitch, like a decrease cluster (see page 91). In this typical example the background is made with alternate rows of dc and tr.*

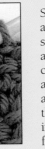

Skip sts in dc row and work raised surface sts in dtr around stem of chosen stitch. Work at front, alternately a few sts to left and then to right, inserting hook from right to left.

Leaving last loop of each stitch on hook, work raised surface stitch, then background dc (there are now 3 loops on hook). Yrh and draw through all loops to complete cluster.

◀ **DOUBLE AND TREBLE CROCHET**

Any number of sts, plus 1 for foundation ch

Row 1 (wrong side): Skip 2 ch, dc across, turn.
Row 2: Ch 3, tr across, turn.
Row 3: Ch 1, dc across, turn.
Rows 2 and 3 form the pattern.a

TREBLE CROCHET V STITCH ▶

Multiple of 2 sts, plus 2 for foundation ch

Row 1 (right side): Skip 3 ch, 2 tr in next, * skip 1 ch, 2 tr in next; rep from * to last 2 ch, skip 1 ch, 1 tr, turn.
Row 2: Ch 3, *skip 2 sts, 2 tr in between 2nd skipped st and next; rep from * to last 2 sts, skip 1 st, 1tr, turn.
Row 2 forms the pattern.

STACKING DOUBLE AND TREBLE CROCHET ▲

Multiple of 2 sts plus 1, plus 1 for foundation ch

Note: T-ch does not count as a stitch.

Row 1 (right side): Skip 1 ch, 1 dc, *1 tr, 1 dc; rep from * across, turn.
Row 2: Ch 1, 1 dc, *1 tr, 1 dc; rep from * across, turn.
Row 2 forms the pattern.

MULTI STITCH WAVE ▲

Multiple of 14 sts plus 1, plus 1 for foundation ch

Special Abbreviation
wave (worked over 14 sts): 1 dc, 2 htr, 2 tr, 3 dtr, 2 tr, 2 htr, 2 dc.
reverse wave (worked over 14 sts): 1 dtr, 2 tr, 2 htr, 3 dc, 2 htr, 2 tr, 2 dtr.
Work 2 rows each in colours A and B alternately throughout.
Row 1 (right side): Skip 2 ch, *wave; rep from * across, turn.
Row 2: Ch 1, dc across, turn.
Row 3: Ch 4, *reverse wave; rep from * across, turn.
Row 4: as row 2.
Row 5: Ch 1, *wave; rep from * across, turn.
Row 6: as row 2.
Rows 3 to 6 form the pattern.

This stitch can also be worked in brightly coloured shapes

TREBLE CROCHET DIAGONAL BLOCKS ▼

Multiple of 7 sts plus 4, plus 3 for foundation ch

Row 1 (right side): Skip 2 ch, 2 tr in next, *skip 3 ch, 1 dc, ch 3, 3 tr; rep from * to last 4 ch, skip 3 ch, 1 dc turn.
Row 2: Ch 3, 2 tr in first dc, *skip 3 ch, (1 dc, ch 3, 2 tr) in 3 ch loop, 1 tr in dc; rep from * ending skip 2 tr, 1 dc, turn.
Row 2 forms the pattern.

▲ CROSSED TREBLES

Multiple of 2 sts, plus 2 for foundation ch

Special Abbreviation
2 ctr (2 crossed treble crochet): Skip next st, 1 tr, 1 tr in skipped st, working so that the crossed tr wraps and encases the previous tr (see Simple crossed stitch, page 96).
Row 1 (right side): Skip 3 ch, *2 ctr; rep from * to last st, 1 tr, turn.
Row 2: Ch 1, dc across, turn.
Row 3: Ch 3, *2 ctr; rep from * to last st, 1 tr, turn.
Rows 2 and 3 form the pattern.

CHEVRONS & MOTIFS

THE BASIC STITCHES can be combined with increasing and decreasing to create zigzags, chevrons and curves. The same plain stitch, increased and decreased alternately at frequent intervals at the same place in each row, will create a zigzag shape. Using increasing and decreasing in several different ways, you can make a variety of other geometric shapes for motifs to be made up into patchwork items.

SIMPLE CHEVRONS

In these patterns the same row shape is maintained and all rows are parallel throughout. If given the instruction to work even when working chevrons, you must continue increasing and decreasing as established to create the chevrons, but keeping the same number of stitches in each row and the edges of your fabric straight.

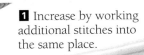

1 Increase by working additional stitches into the same place.

2 Decrease by joining stitches together into clusters (*see page 91*).

If the row shapes are to change, for instance so that zigzags alternate with straight rows or angles reverse, then you must use stitches of graduated heights at the same time as increasing and decreasing.

Zigzags and straight rows are combined in this piece

TRIANGLE MOTIFS

There are numerous ways of combining simple triangles to make patchwork covers or bedspreads. These bedcovers have long formed a large and popular part of traditional crochet.

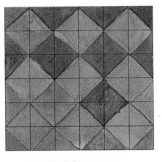

Increase triangle
Start with a single stitch and increase at both edges simultaneously. Make a foundation chain of 3 ch. Skip 2 ch, 2 dc in next, turn (3 sts – right side). Work 11 more rows in dc, making single inc at end of every row and also at beginning of 4th, 7th, and 10th rows (17 sts at end of Row 12).

Decrease triangle
Start with a foundation row the desired length of a triangle side and then decrease at both edges simultaneously to a single stitch. Work a foundation chain of 18 ch. Skip 2 ch, dc across to last 2 ch, dc2tog, turn (16 sts – right side). Work 11 more rows in dc, making single dec at end of every row and also at beginning of 3rd, 6th, and

Make a diamond by crocheting an increase triangle followed by a decrease triangle

BOBBLES

CROCHET WAS DEVELOPED mainly to meet the nineteenth century demand for lace. But it can also be used to create a lovely array of textured effects. The easily-made bobbles shown here involve the same skills already learned for increasing and decreasing.

A relief effect is created whenever you work a stitch taller than the stitches on either side, for example, a double treble crochet in a row of double crochet; the taller stitch cannot lie flat, but sticks out from the surface. Similarly, if you work more than one stitch into

the same place and then join the group into one at the top, the excess will stand out from the surface. The taller and greater the number of stitches in the cluster, the more pronounced the bobble.

Variations can be made using different numbers of stitches and inserting the hook in different positions.

Completed bobbles on double crochet

Popcorn stitch

Work 5 stitches into same place (*left*). Remove hook from working loop. Insert it from front to back under top 2 loops of first stitch in group. Pick up working loop and draw it through. To make popcorn stand out towards back of work, insert hook from back through to front (*right*).

Puff stitch

The puff stitch is about to be completed

Work a cluster of htr (*above*). Yrh, insert hook into st, yrh, draw loop through loosely. Without tightening other loops on hook, repeat 4 times. Yrh and draw through all loops on hook (*right*). To secure, leave last of 11 loops on hook, yrh and draw through the remaining 2 loops.

Bobble

Work a decrease cluster of 5 tr (or whatever amount you like) all into same place, in a row made otherwise of dc (*left*). *Yrh, insert hook into st, yrh, draw a loop through, yrh, draw through 2 loops; repeat from * 4 more times always inserting hook into same stitch (6 loops on hook). Yrh and draw yarn through all loops to complete (*right*). The bobble is more pronounced when worked during wrong side rows.

Bullion stitch

1 Yrh, say 7 times, as if making a long stitch. Insert hook, yrh, and draw through st. Yrh, draw through all loops.

2 Allow enough yarn to be drawn through loops to give them enough room to stand up as far as you wish. Yrh once more and, taking care not to allow stem of bullion to tighten, draw through to complete (*right*).

VERTICAL POPCORNS WITH RAISED DOUBLE TREBLES ▼
Multiple of 11 sts plus 3, plus 2 for foundation ch
Special Abbreviation
pop: Popcorn made with 5 dtr
 (see page 99).
Row 1 (right side): Skip 3 ch, 2 tr,
 *ch 2, skip 3 ch, 1 pop, ch 1,
 1 pop, ch 1, skip 3 ch, 3 tr; rep
 from * across, turn.
Row 2: Ch 3, 1 rbdtr, 1 tr, *ch 3,
 skip (1 ch, 1 pop), 2 dc in ch sp,
 ch 3, skip (1 pop, 2 ch), 1 tr,
 1 rbdtr, 1 tr; rep

from * across, turn.
Row 3: Ch 3, 1 rfdtr, 1 tr, *ch 2,
 skip 3 ch, 1 pop, ch 1, 1 pop,
 ch 1, skip 3 ch, 1 tr, 1 rfdtr,
 1 tr; rep from * across, turn.
Rows 2 and 3 form the pattern.

DIAGONAL SPIKE PUFF ▲
Multiple of 3 sts plus 2, plus 2 for foundation ch
Special Abbreviation
spfcl (spike puff cluster): Yrh, insert hook in next st, yrh, draw
 through, yrh, draw through 2 loops, (yrh, insert hook from front
 in 3rd previous st, yrh, draw through loosely) twice (6 loops on
 hook), yrh, draw through all loops.
Row 1 (right side): Skip 3 ch, *2 tr, 1 spfcl; rep from * to
 last st, 1 tr, turn.
Row 2: Ch 3, *2 tr, 1 spfcl; rep from * to last st,
 1 tr, turn.
Row 2 forms the pattern.

PUFFS AND RAISED CROSSES PANEL ▶
Worked over 11 sts on a background of tr
Special Abbreviation
Puff: Made as htr5tog in same place
 (see page 99).
nc (not closed): see Clusters page 106.
Row 1 (right side): 11 tr.
Row 2 (wrong side): *1 rbdtr, 1 puff,
 1 rbdtr**, 1 tr; rep from * once more
 and from * to ** again.
Row 3: *1 trnc in first, skip puff, 1 rfdtrnc
 around next (3 loops on hook), yrh, draw
through all loops, 1 tr in puff, 1 trnc in next,
1 rfdtrnc around st before previous puff crossing
in front of previous rfdtr, yrh, and draw through
3 loops as before**, 1 tr; rep from * once more
and from * to ** again.
Rows 2 and 3 form the pattern.

POPCORNS AND TREBLE CROCHET ▲
Multiple of 6 sts plus 1, plus
2 for foundation ch
Special Abbreviation
pop: Popcorn made with 5 tr
 (see page 99).
Work 1 row each in colours
 A, B and C throughout.
Row 1 (right side): Skip 3 ch,
 tr across, turn.
Row 2: Ch 1 (does not count as
 st), *1 dc, ch 1, skip 1; rep from
 * to last st, 1 dc, turn.
Row 3: Ch 3, *skip (1 ch, 1 dc),
 (1 pop, ch 1, 1 tr, ch 1, 1 pop)
 in next ch sp, skip (1 dc, 1 ch),
 1 tr; rep from * across, turn.
Row 4: as row 2.
Row 5: Ch 3, tr across, turn.
Rows 2 to 5 form the pattern.

◀ BOBBLE PANEL
Worked over 13 sts on
a background of alt tr
(right side) and dc rows.

Special Abbreviation
bob (bobble): tr5tog in same
 place (see page 99).
Note: Work each rfdtr around
 tr st 2 rows below.
Row 1 (right side): 13 tr.
Row 2 (wrong side): 4 dc,
 1 bob, 3 dc, 1 bob, 4 dc.
Row 3: 1 rfdtr, 1 tr, 1 rfdtr,
 7 tr, 1 rfdtr, 1 tr, 1 rfdtr.
Row 4: 6 dc, 1 bob, 6 dc.
Row 5: as row 3.
Rows 2 to 5 form the pattern.

DOUBLE BULLIONS

Multiple of 6 sts plus 2, plus 1 for foundation ch

Special Abbreviation
bst: Bullion stitch made with (yrh) 7 times (see page 99).
Note: t-ch counts as stitch only on right side (bullion stitch) rows.
Row 1 (wrong side): Skip 1 ch, 1 dc, ch 1, skip 1 ch, 1 dc, * ch 2, skip 2 ch, 1 dc; rep from * to last 2 ch, ch 1, skip 1 ch, 1 dc, turn.
Row 2: Ch 3, 1 tr in ch sp, *1 tr, 2 bsts in 2 ch sp, 1 tr, 2 tr in 2 ch sp; rep from * across, working last tr in last dc, turn.
Row 3: Ch 1, 1 dc, ch 1, skip 1, 1 dc, *ch 2, skip 2, 1 dc; rep from * to last 2 sts, ch 1, skip 1, 1 dc, turn.
Row 4: Ch 3, 1 bst in next ch sp, *1 tr, 2 tr in next ch sp, 1 tr **, 2 bsts in 2 ch sp; rep from * to last 6 sts and from * to ** again, 1 bst in next ch sp, 1 tr, turn.
Row 5: as row 3.
Rows 2 to 5 form the pattern.

PUFFS AND DOUBLE CROCHET ▲

Multiple of 4 sts plus 1, plus 1 for foundation ch

Special Abbreviation
puff: Made as htr4tog in same place (see page 99).
Row 1 (right side): Skip 2 ch, dc across, turn.
Row 2: Ch 1, 1 dc, *1 puff, 3 dc; rep from * across, omitting 1 dc at end of last rep, turn.
Row 3: Ch 1, dc across, turn.
Row 4: Ch 1, *3 dc, 1 puff; rep from *to last 4 sts, 4 dc, turn.
Row 5: as row 3.
Rows 2 to 5 form the pattern.

BULLION WAVES ▶

Multiple of 10 sts plus 2, plus 1 for foundation ch

Special Abbreviation
bst: Bullion stitch made with (yrh) 10 times (see page 99).
Note: t-ch counts as stitch only on right side (bullion stitch) rows.
Row 1 (wrong side): Skip 1 ch, dc across, turn.
Row 2: Ch 3, *5 tr, 5 bsts; rep from * to last st, 1 tr, turn.
Row 3: Ch 1, dc across, turn.
Row 4: Ch 3, *5 bsts, 5 tr; rep from * to last st, 1 tr, turn.
Row 5: as row 3.
Rows 2 to 5 form the pattern.

CROSSED TRIPLE ▼ TREBLE CABLE PANEL

Worked over 19 sts on a background of dc

Note: See page 96 for crossed stitches.
Row 1 (wrong side): 19 tr.
Row 2 (right side): 1 rfdtr, 1 tr, skip 3, 3 ttr, going in back of last 3 ttr work 3 ttr in 3 skipped sts, 1 tr, 1 rfdtr, 1tr, skip 3, 3 ttr, going in front of last 3 ttr but not encasing them, work 3 ttr in 3 skipped sts, 1 tr, 1 rfdtr.
Row 3 (wrong side): as row 1, except work rbdtr instead of rfdtr over 1st, 10th and 19th sts to keep raised ridges on right side of fabric.
Rows 2 and 3 form the pattern.

TREBLE CROCHET BOBBLES ▼

Multiple of 4 sts plus 1, plus 2 for foundation ch

Row 1 (right side): Skip 3 ch, tr across, turn.
Row 2: Ch 1, 1 dc, *tr5tog in next, 3 dc; rep from * to last 3 sts, tr5tog in next, 2 dc, turn.
Row 3: Ch 3, tr across, turn.
Row 4: Ch 1, *3 dc, tr5tog in next; rep from * to last 4 sts, 4 dc, turn.
Row 5: as row 3.
Rows 2 to 5 form the pattern.

WORKING IN THE ROUND

THIS TECHNIQUE IS used to make motifs, and larger fabrics such as tablecloths. Unlike normal crochet, you work around a central ring and increase regularly every round to keep the work flat. If you increase too much or too little the fabric will curl. The shape of the fabric made in the round may be any shape depending upon the position of the increases.

An enormous number of patchwork-style fabrics can be made from motifs. Lace stitches can be incorporated as in the pretty lace doilies shown here.

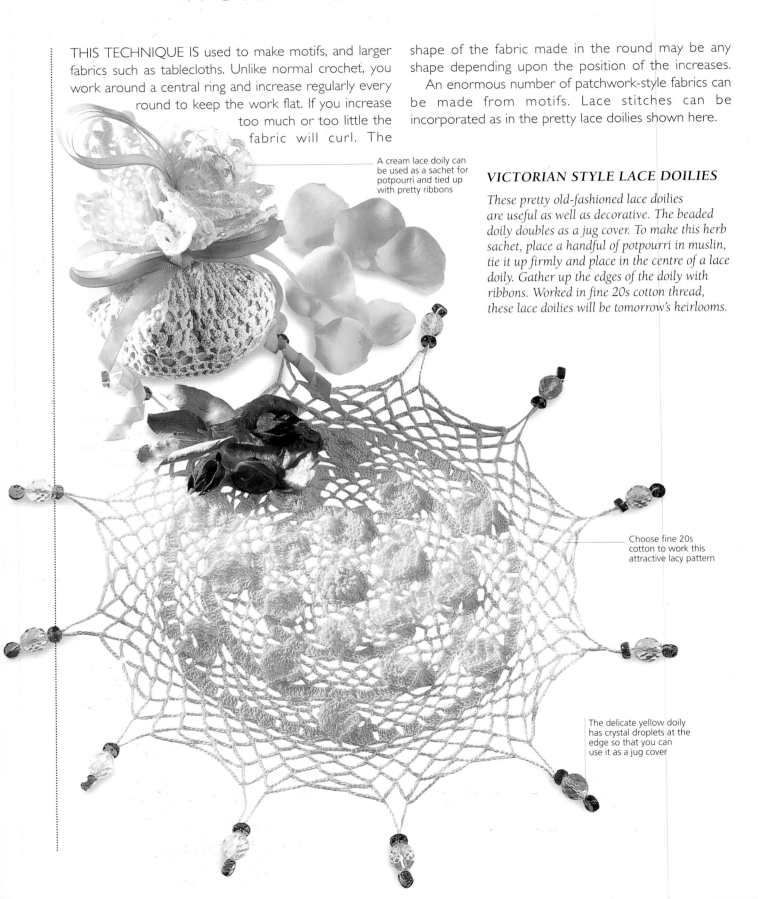

A cream lace doily can be used as a sachet for potpourri and tied up with pretty ribbons

VICTORIAN STYLE LACE DOILIES

These pretty old-fashioned lace doilies are useful as well as decorative. The beaded doily doubles as a jug cover. To make this herb sachet, place a handful of potpourri in muslin, tie it up firmly and place in the centre of a lace doily. Gather up the edges of the doily with ribbons. Worked in fine 20s cotton thread, these lace doilies will be tomorrow's heirlooms.

Choose fine 20s cotton to work this attractive lacy pattern

The delicate yellow doily has crystal droplets at the edge so that you can use it as a jug cover

FOUNDATION RING

Working in the round starts with a foundation ring; the one most often used is closed by working a slip stitch into the first chain (first method below). When it is important to be able to close any central hole in the fabric, use the second method.

Chain foundation ring

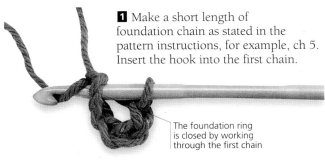

1 Make a short length of foundation chain as stated in the pattern instructions, for example, ch 5. Insert the hook into the first chain.

The foundation ring is closed by working through the first chain

2 Close the ring with a slip stitch, (yrh and draw through).

Yarn loop foundation ring

1 Make a loop in yarn. Hold bottom of loop with fingers which normally hold work. Insert hook through loop, yrh and draw through. Make correct turning chain (chain 1 for double crochet) and work first round into loop ring, making sure you encase short end of yarn.

2 Close the round with a slip stitch. Close up the centre of the ring by drawing the short end of the yarn tight. Secure it by weaving it into the wrong side of the work.

MOTIFS

On the stich glossary overleaf, unless otherwise specified:
1 Close the foundation chain ring by working a slip stitch into the first chain.
2 At the beginning of each round work a turning chain to stand as the first stitch of the first pattern repeat (see table page 64).
3 At the end of each round close with a slip stitch into the top of this first stitch.
4 Do not turn between rounds – right side is always facing.

WORKING IN THE ROUND

There are two main methods of working in the round: making one continuous spiral or a series of joined rounds. In the latter case, each round is completed and joined with a slip stitch, but before starting the next round, make a turning chain to match the height of the following stitches (even if the work is not actually turned between rounds). For turning chain table see page 82.

1 Make the correct number of chains for the turning chain, for example, ch 4 for dtr.

Work turning chains after the foundation ring

Working into the centre of the foundation ring

2 Insert hook into centre of foundation ring; work stitches as required for first round.

3 To close the round, work a slip stitch into the top of the turning chain.

All the stitches are worked into the foundation ring

4 Before working another round, make the required turning chain.

A turning chain is worked at the beginning of each round

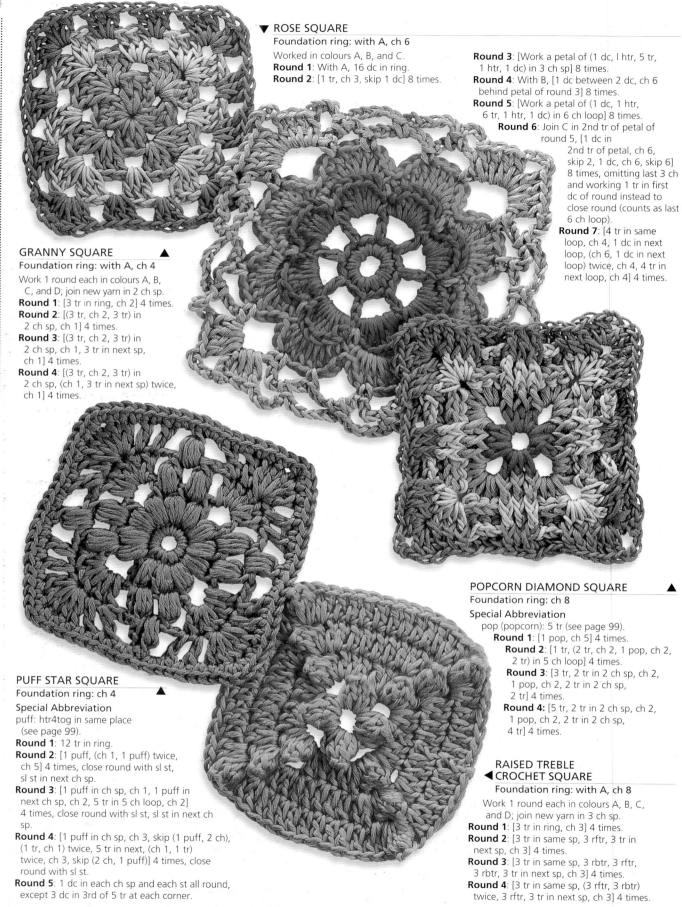

ROSE SQUARE ▼

Foundation ring: with A, ch 6

Worked in colours A, B, and C.
Round 1: With A, 16 dc in ring.
Round 2: [1 tr, ch 3, skip 1 dc] 8 times.

Round 3: [Work a petal of (1 dc, l htr, 5 tr, 1 htr, 1 dc) in 3 ch sp] 8 times.
Round 4: With B, [1 dc between 2 dc, ch 6 behind petal of round 3] 8 times.
Round 5: [Work a petal of (1 dc, 1 htr, 6 tr, 1 htr, 1 dc) in 6 ch loop] 8 times.
Round 6: Join C in 2nd tr of petal of round 5, [1 dc in 2nd tr of petal, ch 6, skip 2, 1 dc, ch 6, skip 6] 8 times, omitting last 3 ch and working 1 tr in first dc of round instead to close round (counts as last 6 ch loop).
Round 7: [4 tr in same loop, ch 4, 1 dc in next loop, (ch 6, 1 dc in next loop) twice, ch 4, 4 tr in next loop, ch 4] 4 times.

GRANNY SQUARE ▲

Foundation ring: with A, ch 4

Work 1 round each in colours A, B, C, and D; join new yarn in 2 ch sp.
Round 1: [3 tr in ring, ch 2] 4 times.
Round 2: [(3 tr, ch 2, 3 tr) in 2 ch sp, ch 1] 4 times.
Round 3: [(3 tr, ch 2, 3 tr) in 2 ch sp, ch 1, 3 tr in next sp, ch 1] 4 times.
Round 4: [(3 tr, ch 2, 3 tr) in 2 ch sp, (ch 1, 3 tr in next sp) twice, ch 1] 4 times.

POPCORN DIAMOND SQUARE ▲

Foundation ring: ch 8

Special Abbreviation
pop (popcorn): 5 tr (see page 99).
Round 1: [1 pop, ch 5] 4 times.
Round 2: [1 tr, (2 tr, ch 2, 1 pop, ch 2, 2 tr) in 5 ch loop] 4 times.
Round 3: [3 tr, 2 tr in 2 ch sp, ch 2, 1 pop, ch 2, 2 tr in 2 ch sp, 2 tr] 4 times.
Round 4: [5 tr, 2 tr in 2 ch sp, ch 2, 1 pop, ch 2, 2 tr in 2 ch sp, 4 tr] 4 times.

PUFF STAR SQUARE ▲

Foundation ring: ch 4

Special Abbreviation
puff: htr4tog in same place (see page 99).
Round 1: 12 tr in ring.
Round 2: [1 puff, (ch 1, 1 puff) twice, ch 5] 4 times, close round with sl st, sl st in next ch sp.
Round 3: [1 puff in ch sp, ch 1, 1 puff in next ch sp, ch 2, 5 tr in 5 ch loop, ch 2] 4 times, close round with sl st, sl st in next ch sp.
Round 4: [1 puff in ch sp, ch 3, skip (1 puff, 2 ch), (1 tr, ch 1) twice, 5 tr in next, (ch 1, 1 tr) twice, ch 3, skip (2 ch, 1 puff)] 4 times, close round with sl st.
Round 5: 1 dc in each ch sp and each st all round, except 3 dc in 3rd of 5 tr at each corner.

RAISED TREBLE CROCHET SQUARE ◄

Foundation ring: with A, ch 8

Work 1 round each in colours A, B, C, and D; join new yarn in 3 ch sp.
Round 1: [3 tr in ring, ch 3] 4 times.
Round 2: [3 tr in same sp, 3 rftr, 3 tr in next sp, ch 3] 4 times.
Round 3: [3 tr in same sp, 3 rbtr, 3 rftr, 3 rbtr, 3 tr in next sp, ch 3] 4 times.
Round 4: [3 tr in same sp, (3 rftr, 3 rbtr) twice, 3 rftr, 3 tr in next sp, ch 3] 4 times.

SPIRAL HEXAGON
Foundation ring: ch 5

Note: This motif is worked as a continuous spiral without joining between rounds. Hint: mark last dc of each round with contrasting thread.

Round 1: [Ch 6, 1 dc in ring] 6 times.
Round 2: [Ch 4, 1 dc in next sp] 6 times.
Round 3: [Ch 4, 1 dc in next sp, 1 dc in next dc] 6 times.
Round 4: [Ch 4, 1 dc in next sp, 2 dc] 6 times.
Round 5: [Ch 4, 1 dc in next sp, 3 dc] 6 times.
Rep for as many rounds as desired, increasing number of dc in each of 6 sections of each round as established. From round 10 work 5 instead of 4 ch in each sp. End with ch sp then 1 sl st in next dc.

FLOWER WHEEL
Foundation ring: ch 5

Round 1: 12 dc in ring.
Round 2: [2 tr, ch 3] 6 times.
Round 3: Sl st in tr and in next ch, [(tr3tog, ch 4, tr3tog) in ch sp, ch 4] 6 times.
Round 4: [(2dc, ch 3, 2 dc) in ch sp] 12 times.

▲ FLOWER POWER
Foundation ring: ch 6

Round 1: 12 dc in ring.
Round 2: [1 dc, ch 7, skip 1] 5 times, 1 dc, ch 3, skip 1, 1 dtr in top of first dc (counts as 6th 7 ch loop).
Round 3: [5 tr in ch loop, ch 3] 6 times.
Round 4: [5 tr, ch 3, 1 dc in ch loop, ch 3] 6 times.
Round 5: [tr5tog, (ch 5, 1 dc in next loop) twice, ch 5] 6 times.
Round 6: Sl st in each of next 3 ch, [1 dc in ch loop, ch 5] 18 times.
Round 7: Sl st in each of next 3 ch, [1 dc in ch loop, ch 5, 1 dc in ch loop, ch 3, (5 tr, ch 3, 5 tr) in ch loop, ch 3] 6 times.

SPIKE MEDALLION
Foundation ring: with A, ch 6 ▼

Worked in colors A and B.
Special Abbreviations
dcsp2 (spike double crochet 2 rounds below): insert hook 2 rounds below st indicated, i.e. into top of round 1, yrh, draw loop through and up to height of current round, yrh, draw through both loops on hook (see Spikes, page 83).
pc (picot): Ch 3, sl st in dc first worked.

Round 1: With A, 16 dc in ring.
Round 2: With B, [2 dc, (1 dc, ch 9, 1 dc) in next, 1 dc] 4 times.
Round 3: [1 dc, skip 2 dc, (2 htr, 17 tr, 2 htr) in 9 ch arch, skip 2 dc] 4 times.
Round 4: Rejoin A in dc, [1 dcsp2, ch 5, skip 5, 1 dc, 1 pc, (ch 5, skip 4, 1 dc, 1 pc) twice, ch 5, skip 5] 4 times.

TREBLE CROCHET CLUSTER HEXAGON
Foundation ring: with A, ch 6. Work 1 round each in colours A, B, C, D, and E; join new yarn in ch sp ▲

Round 1: [tr3tog in ring, ch 3] 6 times.
Round 2: [(tr3tog, ch 3, tr3tog) in 3 ch sp, ch 3] 6 times.
Round 3: Join C in 3 ch sp, linking 2 pairs of cls, [(tr3tog, ch 3, tr3tog) in 3 ch sp, ch 3, tr3tog in next sp, ch 3] 6 times.
Round 4: Join D in 3 ch sp between 1st pair of cls, [(3 tr, ch 2, 3tr) in 3 ch sp, (3 tr in next 3 ch sp) twice] 6 times.
Round 5: Join E in 3 ch sp, [2 dc in 3 ch sp, 12 dc] 6 times.

SHELLS, CLUSTERS & LACE

ATTRACTIVE PATTERNS can be made by grouping stitches together in shells or clusters. Shells are formed by working a group of stitches into the same place, whereas a cluster is made of several adjacent stitches joined together at the top. Work these closely together, or for a delicate look, increase the spacing.

SHELLS

These may be all of the same stitch, or of varying stitch heights to create an asymmetric shape. Shells may also contain chains to create spaces. If no stitches are skipped, working more than one stitch into the same place will make an increase (see page 90). If groups of stitches are worked at intervals with other shells between them, no increase is created. See Interlocking Treble Shells, page 95.

CLUSTERS

A cluster is a group of stitches worked into one stitch or space then drawn together at the top with a loop. A shell and a cluster in combination can make a starburst.

1 Work the required number of stitches, leaving last loop of each on hook *(see right).* These are sometimes called not closed (nc).

2 Yrh; draw the yarn through all loops as in Treble Crochet Whorls *(see page 107).*

LACE

Lacework consists of shells and clusters as well as meshes (see page 108), single chains, and arches or loops, including picots. There are two ways of working over chains. Working into a space underneath a chain is quicker and easier, so use the second method unless otherwise instructed.

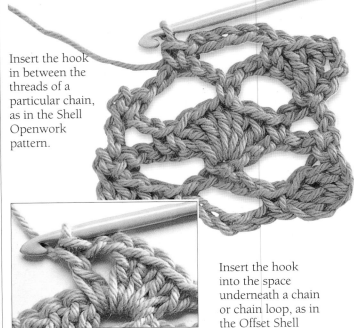

Insert the hook in between the threads of a particular chain, as in the Shell Openwork pattern.

Insert the hook into the space underneath a chain or chain loop, as in the Offset Shell pattern.

PICOTS

These single or multiple chain loops are anchored together for decoration. They are often featured in Irish crochet lace networks (see page 108), and are frequently used as edgings (see page 112).

To make this simple picot the instructions would state, *1 dc in ch sp, (ch 3, sl st in 3rd ch from hook – called picot),* as in the Shells with Picot pattern.

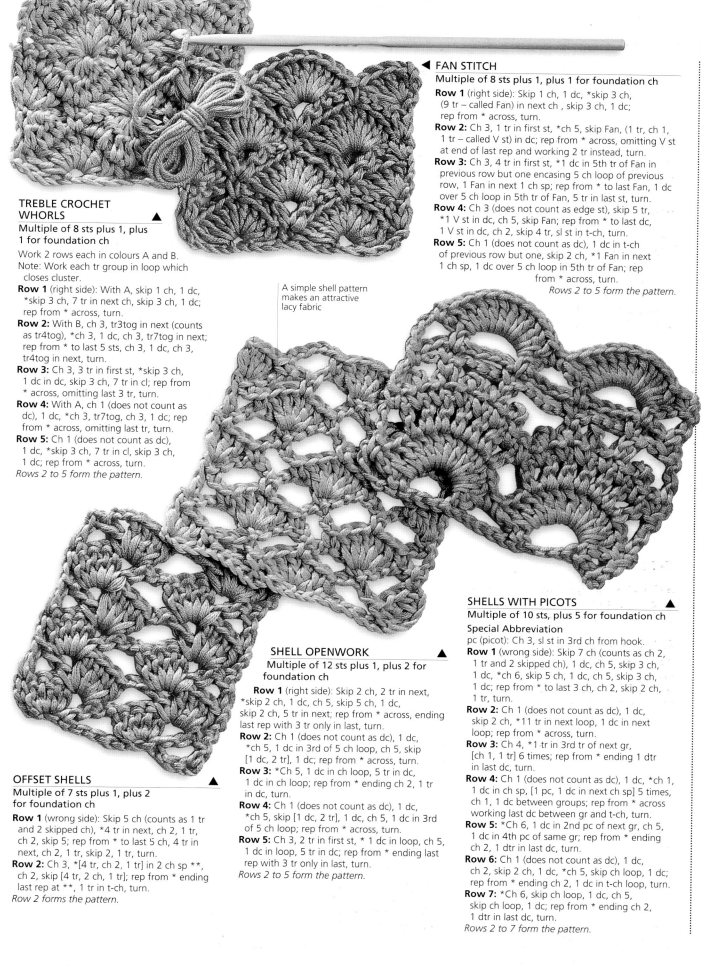

TREBLE CROCHET WHORLS ▲

Multiple of 8 sts plus 1, plus 1 for foundation ch

Work 2 rows each in colours A and B.
Note: Work each tr group in loop which closes cluster.

Row 1 (right side): With A, skip 1 ch, 1 dc, *skip 3 ch, 7 tr in next ch, skip 3 ch, 1 dc; rep from * across, turn.

Row 2: With B, ch 3, tr3tog in next (counts as tr4tog), *ch 3, 1 dc, ch 3, tr7tog in next; rep from * to last 5 sts, ch 3, 1 dc, ch 3, tr4tog in next, turn.

Row 3: Ch 3, 3 tr in first st, *skip 3 ch, 1 dc in dc, skip 3 ch, 7 tr in cl; rep from * across, omitting last 3 tr, turn.

Row 4: With A, ch 1 (does not count as dc), 1 dc, *ch 3, tr7tog, ch 3, 1 dc; rep from * across, omitting last tr, turn.

Row 5: Ch 1 (does not count as dc), 1 dc, *skip 3 ch, 7 tr in cl, skip 3 ch, 1 dc; rep from * across, turn.

Rows 2 to 5 form the pattern.

◄ FAN STITCH

Multiple of 8 sts plus 1, plus 1 for foundation ch

Row 1 (right side): Skip 1 ch, 1 dc, *skip 3 ch, (9 tr – called Fan) in next ch , skip 3 ch, 1 dc; rep from * across, turn.

Row 2: Ch 3, 1 tr in first st, *ch 5, skip Fan, (1 tr, ch 1, 1 tr – called V st) in dc; rep from * across, omitting V st at end of last rep and working 2 tr instead, turn.

Row 3: Ch 3, 4 tr in first st, *1 dc in 5th tr of Fan in previous row but one encasing 5 ch loop of previous row, 1 Fan in next 1 ch sp; rep from * to last Fan, 1 dc over 5 ch loop in 5th tr of Fan, 5 tr in last st, turn.

Row 4: Ch 3 (does not count as edge st), skip 5 tr, *1 V st in dc, ch 5, skip Fan; rep from * to last dc, 1 V st in dc, ch 2, skip 4 tr, sl st in t-ch, turn.

Row 5: Ch 1 (does not count as dc), 1 dc in t-ch of previous row but one, skip 2 ch, *1 Fan in next 1 ch sp, 1 dc over 5 ch loop in 5th tr of Fan; rep from * across, turn.

Rows 2 to 5 form the pattern.

A simple shell pattern makes an attractive lacy fabric

OFFSET SHELLS ▲

Multiple of 7 sts plus 1, plus 2 for foundation ch

Row 1 (wrong side): Skip 5 ch (counts as 1 tr and 2 skipped ch), *4 tr in next, ch 2, 1 tr, ch 2, skip 5; rep from * to last 5 ch, 4 tr in next, ch 2, 1 tr, skip 2, 1 tr, turn.

Row 2: Ch 3, *[4 tr, ch 2, 1 tr] in 2 ch sp **, ch 2, skip [4 tr, 2 ch, 1 tr]; rep from * ending last rep at **, 1 tr in t-ch, turn.

Row 2 forms the pattern.

SHELL OPENWORK ▲

Multiple of 12 sts plus 1, plus 2 for foundation ch

Row 1 (right side): Skip 2 ch, 2 tr in next, *skip 2 ch, 1 dc, ch 5, skip 5 ch, 1 dc, skip 2 ch, 5 tr in next; rep from * across, ending last rep with 3 tr only in last, turn.

Row 2: Ch 1 (does not count as dc), 1 dc, *ch 5, 1 dc in 3rd of 5 ch loop, ch 5, skip [1 dc, 2 tr], 1 dc; rep from * across, turn.

Row 3: *Ch 5, 1 dc in ch loop, 5 tr in dc, 1 dc in ch loop; rep from * ending ch 2, 1 tr in dc, turn.

Row 4: Ch 1 (does not count as dc), 1 dc, *ch 5, skip [1 dc, 2 tr], 1 dc, ch 5, 1 dc in 3rd of 5 ch loop; rep from * across, turn.

Row 5: Ch 3, 2 tr in first st, * 1 dc in loop, ch 5, 1 dc in loop, 5 tr in dc; rep from * ending last rep with 3 tr only in last, turn.

Rows 2 to 5 form the pattern.

SHELLS WITH PICOTS ▲

Multiple of 10 sts, plus 5 for foundation ch

Special Abbreviation
pc (picot): Ch 3, sl st in 3rd ch from hook.

Row 1 (wrong side): Skip 7 ch (counts as ch 2, 1 tr and 2 skipped ch), 1 dc, ch 5, skip 3 ch, 1 dc, *ch 6, skip 5 ch, 1 dc, ch 5, skip 3 ch, 1 dc; rep from * to last 3 ch, ch 2, skip 2 ch, 1 tr, turn.

Row 2: Ch 1 (does not count as dc), 1 dc, skip 2 ch, *11 tr in next loop, 1 dc in next loop; rep from * across, turn.

Row 3: Ch 4, *1 tr in 3rd tr of next gr, [ch 1, 1 tr] 6 times; rep from * ending 1 dtr in last dc, turn.

Row 4: Ch 1 (does not count as dc), 1 dc, *ch 1, 1 dc in ch sp, [1 pc, 1 dc in next ch sp] 5 times, ch 1, 1 dc between groups; rep from * across working last dc between gr and t-ch, turn.

Row 5: *Ch 6, 1 dc in 2nd pc of next gr, ch 5, 1 dc in 4th pc of same gr; rep from * ending ch 2, 1 dtr in last dc, turn.

Row 6: Ch 1 (does not count as dc), 1 dc, ch 2, skip 2 ch, 1 dc, *ch 5, skip ch loop, 1 dc; rep from * ending ch 2, 1 dc in t-ch loop, turn.

Row 7: *Ch 6, skip ch loop, 1 dc, ch 5, skip ch loop, 1 dc; rep from * ending ch 2, 1 dtr in last dc, turn.

Rows 2 to 7 form the pattern.

MESHES & FILETS

GRIDS OF SQUARES or diamonds characterise most crochet patterns. These can be in the form of closed or openwork fabric. Crochet meshes are often embellished, not only with shells (see page 106) and picots (see page 112), but with Clones knots and with the filled spaces of filet lace.

CLONES KNOTS

These are named after an Irish town that was an early centre for lace making.

1 To make the knot: Ch 3, *yrh, take hook under ch loop just made, yrh, bring hook back again over ch loop; repeat from * 4 more times (there are now 9 loops on the hook).

2 Yrh and draw through all loops, sl st in 1st of 3 ch.

FILET CROCHET

This is a smooth background of regular squares. Patterns are created by leaving some squares open (spaces) and filling others (blocks). Characteristic images range from simple geometrics to detailed representations of birds and flowers. Filet work is used for edgings as well as for tablecloths, curtains, and clothes.

Filet mesh can be filled with blocks or bars and lacets

CHARTS

Pattern instructions usually come on graph paper. Remember, unless otherwise stated, to read odd rows of a chart from right to left, even rows from left to right. You can usually adapt and use any squared chart as a pattern for filet work.

On filet charts, the spaces are represented by blank squares and the blocks by filled-in squares. The filet ground's vertical stitches are usually treble crochet and the horizontal bars ch 2 spaces. Occasional special features called bars and lacets are drawn as they look.

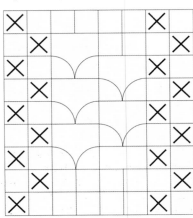

MAKING FILET MESH

For the foundation chain, make a multiple of 3 ch for each square required (which in turn will be a multiple of the number of squares in the pattern repeat), plus 1. Add 4 if the first square is a space, but only 2 if it is a block.

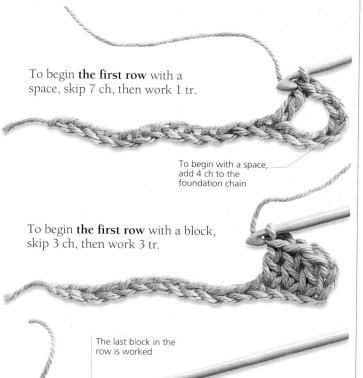

To begin **the first row** with a space, skip 7 ch, then work 1 tr.

To begin with a space, add 4 ch to the foundation chain

To begin **the first row** with a block, skip 3 ch, then work 3 tr.

The last block in the row is worked

Thereafter, work each space as: ch 2, skip 2, 1 tr. Work each block as: 3 tr.

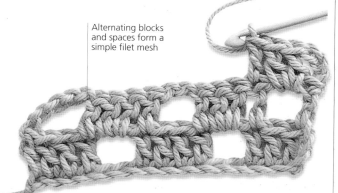

Alternating blocks and spaces form a simple filet mesh

    From row 2, at the beginning of each row, ch 3 to count as the edge stitch (tr), skip the first tr, and then, for each space, ch 2, skip 2 ch (or next 2 tr of a block), 1 tr in next tr; and for each block, work 2 tr in 2 ch sp (or in next 2 tr of a block), 1 tr in next tr.

BARS AND LACETS

Each structure occupies 2 squares and is usually worked alternately.

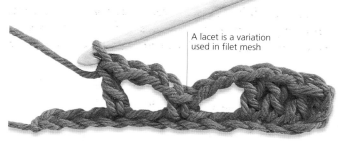

A lacet is a variation used in filet mesh

lacet – ch 3, skip 2, 1 dc, ch 3, skip 2, 1 tr.

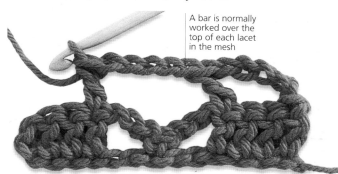

A bar is normally worked over the top of each lacet in the mesh

bar – ch 5, skip lacet (or 2 squares), 1 tr.

Filet Variation 1

Sometimes filet charts are interpreted with 1 ch for the spaces. Each square is then narrower.

Filet Variation 2

A mesh with 1-ch spaces and offset squares, that is, with the vertical stitches (tr) worked into the chain spaces of the previous row,

Variation 1

Variation 2

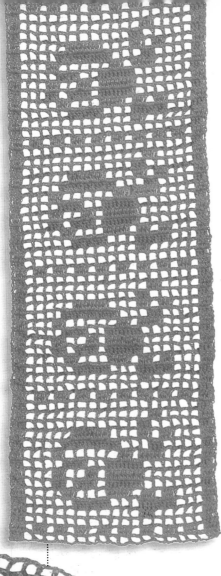

PUFF TRELLIS ▶

Multiple of 3 sts plus 1, plus 1 for foundation ch

Special Abbreviation

Puff V st: [htr3tog, ch 3, htr3tog] in same place (see page 73).

Row 1 (right side): Skip 1 ch, 1 dc, *ch 3, skip 2 ch, 1 dc; rep from * across, turn.

Row 2: Ch 4, 1 dc in ch loop, *ch 3, 1 dc ch loop; rep from * across, ending ch 1, 1 tr in last st, turn.

Row 3: Ch 3,*1 puff V st in dc; rep from * across, ending 1 tr in t-ch loop, turn.

Rows 2 and 3 form the pattern.

◀ FILET ROSE INSERTION

Foundation: Ch 60

Row 1 (right side): Skip 3 ch, 3 tr, [ch 2, skip 2, 1 tr] 17 times, 3 tr, turn (19 squares).

Follow chart from row 2 for pattern, repeating rows 3 to 16 as required.

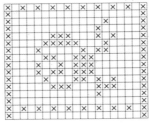

BASIC TRELLIS ▶

Multiple of 4 sts plus 2, plus 4 for foundation ch

Row 1 (right side): Skip 5 ch, 1 dc, *ch 5, skip 3 ch, 1 dc; rep from * across, turn.

Row 2: *Ch 5, 1 dc in 5 ch loop; rep from * across, turn.

Row 2 forms the pattern.

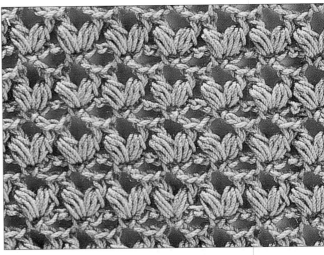

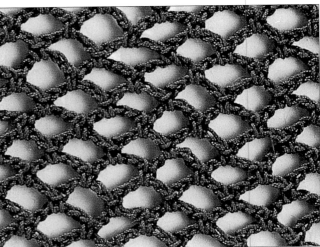

FILET BUTTERFLIES ▼

Multiple of 54 sts (18 squares) plus 7 (2 squares plus 1 st), plus 4 for foundation ch

Row 1 (right side): Skip 7 ch, 1 tr, *ch 2, skip 2, 1 tr; rep from * across, turn.

Follow chart from row 2 for pattern, repeating rows 2 to 33 as required.

Delicate filet mesh butterflies are worked in simple blocks and spaces

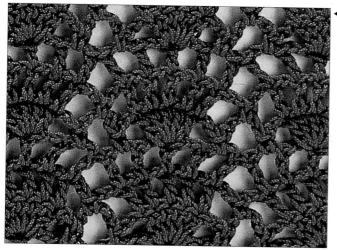

FOUNTAIN NETWORK ◄

Multiple of 12 sts plus 5, plus 1 for foundation ch

Row 1 (right side): Skip 1 ch, 1 dc, *ch 5, skip 3 ch, 1 dc, ch 2, skip 3 ch, 5 tr in next, ch 2, skip 3 ch, 1 dc; rep from * to last 4 ch, ch 5, skip 3 ch, 1 dc, turn.

Row 2: Ch 5 (counts as 1 tr and ch 2), *1 dc in 5 ch loop, ch 2, skip 2 ch, 1 tr in tr, [ch 1, 1 tr] 4 times, ch 2, skip 2 ch; rep from * to last 5 ch loop, 1 dc in 5 ch loop, ch 2, 1 tr in dc, turn.

Row 3: Ch 4 (counts as 1 tr and ch 1), 1 tr in first st, *skip [2 ch, 1 dc, 2 ch], 1 tr in tr, [ch 2, skip 1 ch, 1 tr] 4 times; rep from * ending skip [2 ch, 1 dc, 2 ch], [1 tr, ch 1, 1 tr] in t-ch loop, turn.

Row 4: Ch 1 (does not count as dc), 1 dc, skip [1 ch, 2 tr], *ch 5, 1 dc in 2 ch sp, ch 2, skip [1 tr, 2 ch], 5 tr in tr, ch 2, skip [2 ch, 1 tr], 1 dc in 2 ch sp; rep from * ending ch 5, 1 dc in t-ch loop, turn.

Rows 2, 3 and 4 form the pattern.

FILET DIAMOND BORDER ►

Foundation: ch 36

Note: For multiple increases and decreases see pages 72 to 73.

Row 1 (right side): Skip 3 ch, 3 tr, [ch 2, skip 2, 1 tr] twice, 3 tr, [ch 2, skip 2, 1 tr] 5 times, [3 tr] twice, turn.

Follow chart from row 2 for pattern, repeating rows 2 to 12 as required.

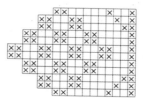

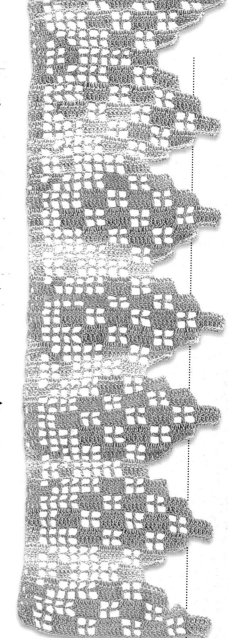

BLOCK, BAR AND LACET ▲

Multiple of 6 sts plus 1, plus 2 for foundation ch

Row 1 (right side): Skip 3 ch, tr across, turn.

Row 2: Ch 3, skip first tr, *ch 5, skip 5, 1 tr; rep from * across, turn.

Row 3: Ch 3, skip first tr, *ch 3, 1 dc in ch loop, ch 3, – called lacet, 1 tr in tr; rep from * across, turn.

Row 4: Ch 3, skip first tr, *ch 5, skip lacet, 1 tr; rep from * across, turn.

Row 5: Ch 3, *5 tr in ch loop, 1 tr in tr; rep from * across, turn.

Rows 2 to 5 form the pattern.

DOUBLE CROCHET NETWORK ►

Multiple of 8 sts plus 1, plus 1 for foundation ch

Note: t-ch does not count as st, except on row 4, 10, etc.

Row 1 (right side): Skip 1 ch, 3 dc, *ch 5, skip 3 ch, 5 dc; rep from * across, omitting 2 of 5 dc at end of last rep, turn.

Row 2: Ch 1, 1 dc, *1 dc, ch 3, 1 dc in 5 ch loop, ch 3, skip 1 dc, 2 dc; rep from * across, turn.

Row 3: Ch 1, 1 dc, *ch 3, 1 dc in 3 ch sp, 1 dc, 1 dc in 3 ch sp, ch 3, skip 1 dc, 1 dc; rep from * across, turn.

Row 4: Ch 5 (counts as 1 tr and 2 ch), * 1 dc in 3 ch sp, 3 dc, 1 dc in 3 ch sp **, ch 5; rep from * to 2nd last 3 ch sp and from * to ** again, ch 2, 1 tr in last dc, turn.

Row 5: Ch 1, 1 dc, *ch 3, skip 1 dc, 3 dc, ch 3, skip 1 dc, 1 dc in 5 ch loop; rep from * across, turn.

Row 6: Ch 1, 1 dc, *1 dc in 3 ch sp, ch 3, skip 1 dc, 1 dc, ch 3, skip 1 dc, 1 dc in 3 ch sp, 1 dc; rep from * across, turn.

Row 7: Ch 1, 1 dc, *1 dc, 1 dc in 3 ch sp, ch 5, 1 dc in 3 ch sp, 2 dc; rep from * across, turn.

Rows 2 to 7 form the pattern.

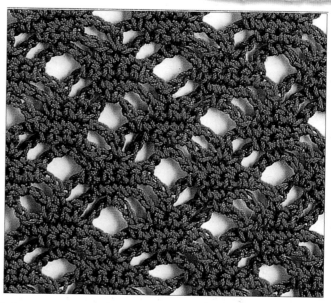

EDGINGS

CROCHET WORK WILL usually lie flatter and have a better finish if an edging is added. Crochet edges and borders can also be used to trim a finished article. If edges or borders are a foundation for your main piece, make them first. If you are to attach them afterwards, make them separately. When working edgings, use a smaller size hook than you used for the main piece. This will give the edging a firmer finish.

DOUBLE CROCHET EDGING

This basic edging, worked with the right side facing, neatens and strengthens the fabric, and can cover any float threads or stray short ends. (The two rows shown here were worked in a contrasting colour for clarity.) It is also a good foundation for a more decorative edging.

BUTTONHOLE LOOPS

Loops for buttons may be made in an edging row by skipping the required number of stitches and working chains instead. If you need extra edging rows, work dc into the loops.

CORDED EDGE

This is a very effective edging, usually worked after one round of dc and with the right side facing. Work it in dc, but from left to right.

PICOT EDGING

Picots of varying size and complexity are a regular feature of crochet edgings. To make this triple picot work [ch 3, sl st in 3rd ch from hook] 3 times, then sl st into the top of the last dc made (see Triple Picot below).

WORKING CORNERS AND EDGES

Normally you work one stitch into each stitch across the top of a row and into the underside of a foundation chain. Work 3 stitches into a corner and along the side of the fabric at the rate of 1 stitch per dc row. As a guide, you will need to use 1 and 2 stitches alternately per htr row, 2 stitches per tr row, 3 stitches per dtr row, etc.

Making the corded edge

*Working from left to right, insert the hook into the next stitch to the right, yrh. Draw the loop through the work, below the loop which remains on the hook, and up to the left, into the normal working position (*left*). Yrh and draw the loop through to complete 1 corded dc (*right*). Repeat from *.

PUFF STITCH
Multiple of 2 sts

Note: All rows worked right side facing.
Row 1: With yarn matching main fabric, dc.
Row 2: With contrasting colour, working from left to right and inserting hook from front to back work * ch1, skip 1, htr3tog; rep from * ending with a sl st.
Main fabric represented here by a row of tr.

TRIPLE PICOT　　　▲
Multiple of 5 sts

Note: All rows worked right side facing.
Row 1: With yarn matching main fabric, dc.
Row 2: With contrasting colour, *5 dc, [ch 3, sl st in 3rd ch from hook] 3 times, sl st in top of last dc made; rep from *.
Main fabric represented here by a row of tr.

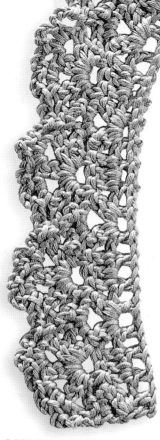

◀ PICOT SCALLOPS

Multiple of 8 sts plus 1, plus 2 for foundation ch

Row 1 (right side): Skip 3 ch, 1 tr, *ch 1, skip 1, 1 tr; rep from * to last ch, 1 tr, turn.

Row 2: Ch 5 (counts as 1 tr, ch 2), tr2tog in first, *skip [1 tr, 1 ch], 3 tr, skip [1 ch, 1 tr], [tr2tog, ch 4, tr2tog – called 2cl] in ch sp; rep from * across, omitting last 2 ch and tr2tog from last 2cl and working 1 tr in same loop, turn.

Row 3: Ch 3 (counts as 1 htr, ch 1), 1 dc in 2 ch sp, *skip cl, [ch 3, 1 dc – called picot], skip 1, 1 pc, 2 pc in 4 ch loop; rep from * across, omiting 2nd pc at end of last rep and working ch 1, 1 htr in same loop, turn.

Row 4: Ch 1 (does not count as dc), 1 dc, *ch 1, skip 1 pc, [tr2tog, (ch 3, tr2tog) twice] in next pc, ch 1, skip 1 pc, 1 dc in next pc; rep from * across, turn.

Row 5: Ch 1 (does not count as dc), 1 dc, skip 1 ch, *[2 pc in next 3 ch loop] twice, skip 1 ch, 1 pc in dc; rep from * across.

SHAMROCK STRIPES ▲

Foundation: with A, ch 19

Work 2 rows each in colours A, B, C and D, throughout.

Row 1 (wrong side): With A, skip 5 ch, 1 tr, ch 1, skip 1, 2 tr, ch 8, skip 9, [1 tr, (ch 3, 1 tr) 3 times] in last ch, turn.

Row 2: [In 3 ch sp work (1 dc, 1 htr, 3 tr, 1 htr, 1 dc – called petal)] 3 times, ch 6, skip 6 ch, 1 tr in each of last 2 ch of loop, (2 tr – called blk), [ch 1, skip 1, 1 tr] twice, turn.

Row 3: With B, ch 4 (counts as 1 tr, ch 1), skip 1, 1 tr, ch 1, skip 1, (4 tr – called blk), 1 tr in each of next 2 ch, ch 8, in centre tr of 2nd petal work [1 tr, (ch 3, 1 tr) 3 times], turn.

Row 4: as row 2, except work blk of 6 tr.

Row 5: With C, as row 3, except work blk of 8 tr.

Row 6: as row 2, except work blk of 10 tr.

Row 7: With D, ch 4 (counts as 1 tr, ch 1), skip 1 ch, 1 tr, ch 1, skip 1, 2 tr, ch 8, skip 9, (1 tr, [ch 3, 1 tr] 3 times) in last tr, turn.

Rows 2 to 7 form the pattern.

DEEP SEA SHELLS ▼

Foundation: ch 11

Row 1 (right side): Skip 3 ch, 2 tr, ch 2, skip 2, 1 tr, ch 2, skip 2, [1 tr, ch 3, 1 tr] in last ch, turn.

Row 2: Ch 5, [3 tr, ch 1, 3 tr] in 3 ch sp, ch 2, skip 2 ch, 1 tr, ch 2, skip 2 ch, 3 tr, turn.

Row 3: Ch 3, 2 tr, ch 2, skip 2 ch, 1 tr, ch 2, skip 2 ch, [1 tr, ch 3, 1 tr] in 1 ch sp *, ch 2, (1 tr, [ch 1, 1 tr] 7 times) in 5 ch loop **, 1 dtr in 1st ch made of foundation, turn.

Row 4: Ch 2, skip 2, 1 dc in ch sp, [ch 3, 1 dc in ch sp] 6 times, ch 2, skip 2 ch, [3 tr, ch 1, 3 tr] in 3 ch sp, ch 2, skip 2 ch, 1 tr, ch 2, skip 2 ch, 3 tr, turn.

Row 5: as row 3 to *, turn.

Row 6: as row 2.

Row 7: as row 3 to **, 1 dc in 2 ch sp of last-but-two row.

Row 8: as row 4.

Rows 5 to 8 form the pattern.

BULLION SPIRALS ▶

Foundation: ch 12

Special Abbreviation

Bst (Bullion stitch): See page 99, made with yrh 10 times.

Row 1 (right side): Skip 3 ch, 1 tr, skip 3 ch, (1 tr, [1 Bst, 1 tr] 3 times – called shell) in next, skip 3 ch, (3 tr, ch 2, 3 tr – called V st) in next, turn.

Row 2: Ch 7, skip 3 ch, [3 tr in next] 4 times, V st in 2 ch sp, ch 3, 1 dc in centre Bst of shell, ch 3, 1 tr in each of last 2 sts, turn.

Row 3: Ch 3, 1 tr, skip 3 ch, shell in dc, skip 3 ch, V st in 2 ch sp, turn.

Rows 2 and 3 form the pattern.

PICOT ARCHWAY

Multiple of 8 sts plus 1, plus 1 for foundation ch

Row 1 (right side): Skip 2 ch, dc across, turn.

Row 2: Ch 1, dc across, turn.

Row 3: Ch 1 (does not count as dc), 1 dc, *ch 3, 2 tr in next, skip 2, 1 dc; rep from * across, turn.

Row 4: Ch 4 (counts as 1 tr, ch 1), 1 tr in first, * 1 dc in 3 ch loop, ch 6, 1 dc in 3 ch loop, (1 tr, ch 3, 1 tr – called V st) in dc; rep from * omitting 2 of 3 ch in last V st, turn.

Row 5: Ch 1, 1 dc in 1 ch sp, *[5 tr, ch 5, sl st in 5th ch from hook, 5 tr] in 6 ch loop, 1 dc in next ch loop; rep from * across.

BUTTONS, CORDS & FINISHES

YOU CAN ADD finishing touches to garments by using matching or contrasting crochet trims. Buttons and cords will liven up children's garments, or women's accessories such as purses. The addition of slip stitches to the surface of a finished crochet piece creates an effect somewhat like weaving.

BUTTONS

Easy to make, chunky crochet buttons offer a colourful, lively way of enhancing handmade garments and accessories. For a crochet loop buttonhole, see page 112.

Bobble Button

Foundation: Ch 2. Note: close each round with sl st in first dc.
Round 1 (right side): 6 dc in 2nd ch from hook.
Round 2: Ch 1, 2 dc in each tr (12 sts).
Round 3: Ch 1, 1 dc in each dc *(top right)*.
Round 4: Ch 1, (1 dc, skip 1) 6 times (6 sts). Pack button with small amount of yarn *(bottom right)*.
Round 5: Ch 1, (1 dc, skip 1) 3 times. Cut length of yarn to close opening and sew button in place.

CORDS

Ties and drawstrings can be worked quickly and easily in contrasting colours to add bright and decorative touches to crochet or knitted children's clothes and accessories.

Round Cord

Foundation ring: Ch 5 (or as required for thickness of cord). Work in spiral around ring as follows: 1 sl st in top loop of each ch and then of each sl st, until cord reaches required length. For a faster-growing cord, work in dc or tr.

Flat Cord

Ch 2, 1 dc in 2nd ch from hook, turn and work 1 dc in ch at back of dc just made; *turn and work 1 dc, inserting hook down through 2 loops at back of dc just made; rep from * until cord is required length.

SURFACE CHAINS

Plaids require careful planning, but any crocheted design, particularly one with a network of chain spaces, may be decorated in this way with vertical or horizontal lines.

Making surface chains

1 Make a slip knot in new yarn. With right or wrong side facing as required, insert hook down through chosen chain space. Yrh underneath work, draw through work and loop on hook.

2 *Insert hook down through next chain space or selected position, yrh underneath fabric, draw through fabric and loop on hook; rep from * as required.

Make one chain beyond edge of work and fasten off. It is important to work loosely so as not to distort the background stitches. It may help to use a larger hook than you used for the main work. Short ends of yarn should be worked over and encased during any subsequent edging rounds or darned into the wrong side of the piece.

Right side

Wrong side

TUNISIAN CROCHET

TUNISIAN CROCHET (sometimes referred to as afghan stitch) is traditionally worked with a special hook, which is longer than usual, has a uniform diameter, and a knob (or sometimes another hook) at the other end. The technique is a cross between knitting and crochet. The finished work resembles knitting, but the stitches are thicker and firmer. For Tunisian crochet, you should expect to use a hook at least two sizes larger than you would ordinarily use with the same yarn in regular crochet.

The odd-numbered rows are worked from right to left, as loops are picked up and retained on the hook. In the even-numbered rows, the loops are worked off again from left to right.

FOUNDATION ROW

An enormous range of plain, textured, multicoloured, and openwork stitch patterns are all possible in Tunisian crochet. Most patterns are worked with the same two rows given below. Unless a double-ended hook is involved, the work is never turned and so the right side is always facing.

Make a length of foundation chain with the same number of chains as the number of stitches required in the finished row, plus 1 chain for turning.

Row one (forward)

Skip 1 ch, *insert the hook in the next ch, yrh, draw the loop through the ch only and keep on the hook; rep from * across. Do not turn the work.

Row two (return)

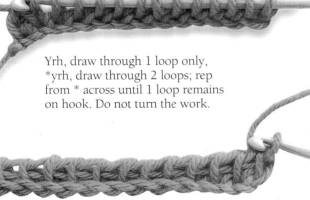

Yrh, draw through 1 loop only, *yrh, draw through 2 loops; rep from * across until 1 loop remains on hook. Do not turn the work.

The finished foundation row forms the basis of most Tunisian crochet patterns.

TUNISIAN SIMPLE STITCH

Work basic forward and return foundation row as at left.

Forward (row 3 and all odd rows): Count loop on hook as first st and start in 2nd st. *Insert hook at front and from right to left around single front vertical thread, yrh, draw through and keep on hook; rep from * across. Do not turn.
Return (even rows): Same as row two.

TUNISIAN KNIT STITCH

Work basic forward and return foundation row as at left.

Forward: Count loop on hook as first st and start in 2nd st. *Insert hook from front through fabric and below chs formed by previous return row to right of front vertical thread and left of back thread of same loop, yrh, draw loop through and keep on hook; rep from * across. Do not turn.
Return: Same as row two.

FINISHING & JOINING

FOR A POLISHED, professional look, take special care when finishing and joining your work – its whole appearance and durability depend on it. Make sure all stray ends of yarn are woven neatly and securely into the wrong side. Seams can be sewn, or joined with a crochet hook as below.

JOINING WITH A HOOK

Crochet seams are strong, and quick to work. Slip stitch is the most invisible, and double crochet makes a ridge that can be a feature on the right side. The number of stitches to work per row end is the same as for edgings (see page 112).

Slip stitch seam

Place the pieces right sides together. *Insert hook through both edge stitches, yrh and draw through to complete 1 sl st; rep from *, working loosely.

Double crochet seam

Place the pieces right sides together (or wrong sides together for a visible seam) and work as for slip stitch seam, using double crochet instead of slip stitch.

Double crochet and chain

A useful variation of the double crochet seam, this is used when less bulk and/or greater flexibility is called for. Work 1 dc and 1 ch alternately.

Flat slip stitch seam

Place the pieces edge to edge and wrong sides up. Work 1 sl st into each edge alternately. (*See also alternative right.*)

JOINING MOTIFS

Straight edges may be joined in the normal way. However, when there are many pieces, particularly squares and triangles, it is worthwhile connecting pairs of motifs in a continuous seam to avoid repeated fastening off.

Alternative flat slip stitch seam

A neat, flat seam may be made using the tops of stitches, as for example, with motifs made in the round. Lay the pieces edge to edge and right sides up. Insert the hook down through the top loop only of each corresponding pair of stitches and join with slip stitch.

Filler motifs join as well as decorate

Many motifs have a final round of picots or loops, and these may be used to join motifs to each other as that round is being worked. Typically the centre chain of a loop is replaced by a sl st or dc worked into a loop of the adjacent motif.

After joining, small motifs, which add decoration and strength, can be worked in the spaces between. The main motifs shown here are Flower Wheel, (*see page 105*). For the filler motifs work: Foundation ring: Ch 5. Round 1: [1 dc in ring, ch 2, sl st in motif, ch 2, 1 dc in ring] 4 times.

BLOCKING AND PRESSING

Cotton lace work usually needs careful pinning and pressing. Other crochet, particularly a textured piece, hardly ever requires this treatment. Pinning the article, misting with a fine spray, and leaving it to dry naturally may be just as effective. Be sure to use rust-proof pins.

HAND DYED YARNS

ALTHOUGH STORE-BOUGHT yarns come in a wide range of colours, you might want to try something a little different. Experiment with dyeing yarns and you can guarantee your finished crochet will be unique.

MAKING HANKS

Start with white 100 per cent cotton yarn. Some yarns are available in hanks. If, however, you are starting with a ball or cone of yarn, you will need to unwind it and then rewind it into a loose hank. The easiest way to create hanks is to use the back of a straight chair. Simply wind the yarn around the back in a clockwise direction. When finished, tie the hank loosely with short lengths of yarn in two or three places.

The hank below is an example of a variegated yarn where there are 3 colours plus additional shades where 2 dyes overlap. Beginners may find it easier to start with single colour, in which case, only one immersion is needed.

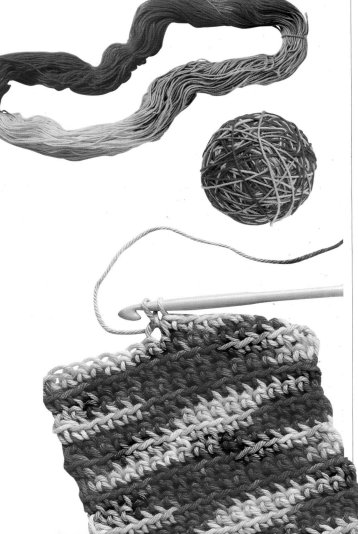

DYEING YARN

Use cold water dyes and be careful to follow the manufacturer's instructions to ensure the dyed yarn remains colourfast. Wear rubber gloves when handling the dyes.

1 Wash the hank of yarn in soapy water then rinse thoroughly in several changes of clean water. Wring out excess water and leave damp.

2 Dissolve the dye powder and mix with water, soda and salt, according to the manufacturer's instructions. Pour each colour into a separate bucket or deep bowl. For this yarn, three different colours have been used.

3 Immerse a portion of the hank into one of the buckets of dye. Here, about half the yarn is immersed in yellow dye. Place a wooden spoon or stick across the top of the bucket, to support the yarn and keep the undyed part out of the dye. You will need to leave the yarn immersed in the dye for about 1 hour.

4 Remove the yarn from the dye and squeeze out excess. Then immerse another portion of the hank in another colour – here, a quarter of the yarn is dipped in blue dye. Then repeat with a third colour until the desired result has been achieved.

5 Wash the dyed yarn in soapy water and rinse thoroughly, then leave to dry before winding into a ball. The dyed yarn is then ready to use.

EMBROIDERY

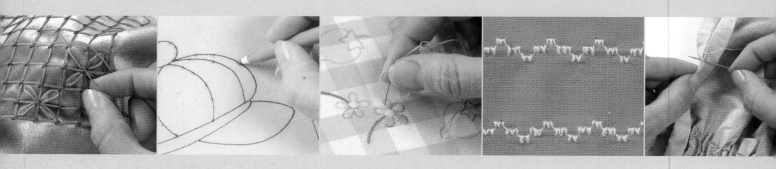

MUSEUMS AROUND THE WORLD are filled with examples of beautiful embroidery. A good collection will contain embroidered garments such as waistcoats and christening gowns, as well as samplers, pictures, covered boxes and altar pieces. Not content with using silk, wool or cotton threads, skilled embroiderers used metal threads and added beads and sequins. Special effects continue to be highly prized and sought after on both garments and furnishings.

In the following pages you will discover the vast range of options open to you as you explore this exciting craft. The variety of individual stitches is enormous and the myriad ways stitches can be combined and applied – to plain or patterned fabric – means that highly original work is within everyone's reach. Many people enjoy working cross stitch projects, but there is always the possibility of decorating garments with more ambitious stitches. Working with colour and texture is another avenue of inspiration that will enable you to create unique pieces of work of which to be proud.

More recently, sewing machines have brought a new dimension to decorative stitching – speed. Even with the simplest of machines, you can embellish items with colourful borders and motifs as well as creating free-hand designs.

CONTENTS

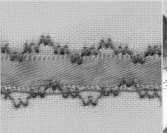

TOOLS & MATERIALS

THERE IS AN enormous range of background fabrics and threads for any embroidery project. The ones you choose will affect the results of your work. When making your selections, keep in mind that the fabric should be suitable for the finished item – for example, hardwearing and washable for a cushion cover. Also, be certain that the needle and thread will pass through the fabric easily without splitting the woven threads. Your only other essential piece of equipment is a small, sharp pair of scissors.

FABRICS

Plain or patterned fabric are suitable for embroidery. Woven or geometric patterns are especially useful for stitches that need guidelines to keep them a regular size. A wide range of even-weave fabrics for counted-thread techniques (such as cross stitch) is available. An even-weave fabric has the same number of warp and weft threads per square inch. For example 18-count means that there are 18 threads to the inch. One of the most popular fabrics for embroidered pictures is 14-count Aida cloth. This is also available with a woven coloured grid to make stitch counting from charts easier. The coloured threads are removed when the stitching is finished.

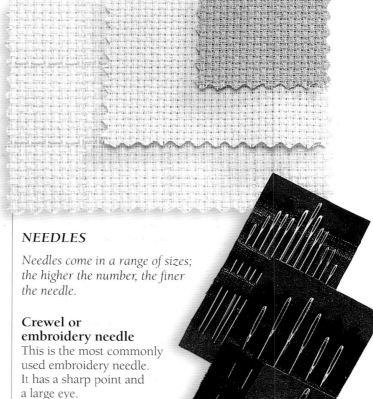

EMBROIDERY THREADS

These come in a wide range of colours. Some popular thread types are shown below, but don't be afraid to experiment with other yarns supplied for knitting, crochet, and canvas work.

Embroidery floss
A loosely twisted 6-strand thread that is easily divided into single threads.

Pearl cotton
A strong, twisted non-divisible thread with a high sheen.

Flower thread
A fine non-divisible thread with a matte finish.

Matte embroidery cotton
A thick, soft, tightly twisted thread.

Crewel yarn
Fine 2-ply wool or acrylic yarn. Also used in tapestry work.

Persian yarn
Loosely twisted 3-strand wool or acrylic yarn; this is easily divisible.

NEEDLES

Needles come in a range of sizes; the higher the number, the finer the needle.

Crewel or embroidery needle
This is the most commonly used embroidery needle. It has a sharp point and a large eye.

Chenille needle
Similar to a crewel needle, but this has a thicker stem. It is suitable for working with heavier threads on a coarse background fabric.

Tapestry or yarn needle
A thick-stemmed, large-eyed needle with a round-pointed end. Used for lacing embroidery stitches and for pulled threadwork.

Beading needle
A fine, long needle for sewing on tiny beads.

Stretcher frames
These stretch the work very evenly. A frame usually consists of four pieces of wood, with a roller at the top and bottom to which strips of webbing are nailed. Two flat sides fit into the rollers and are secured by pegs or screws.

Stretcher frame

Hoops (round frames)
These are made of wood, metal, or plastic, and come in a variety of sizes, ranging from 12.5 cm to 25 cm (5 to 10 in) in diameter. The frame has two hoops that are placed one inside the other, stretching the fabric between them. The outer hoop opens, and has a screw to adjust the tension.

Hoop

EMBROIDERY FRAMES

These hold the fabric taut while you work. A frame isn't essential for small pieces of embroidery, but it does make the work easier to handle and quicker to stitch. Since the fabric is held at an even tension, the stitches themselves will be more even. Also, holding the frame instead of the fabric keeps the work cleaner than working without one.

There are two basic types of frames, the round frame (called a hoop) and the straight-sided frame. The hoop is the most commonly used because it is lightweight and portable,

and it only takes a few seconds to mount the fabric in it correctly. Straight-sided frames, known as stretcher frames, have a roller at the top and bottom and are generally used for large pieces of embroidery such as wall hangings; it takes longer to mount the work, but the fabric is quickly moved into a new position. Both types of frames are available on floor or lap stands, which allow you to keep both hands free.

OTHER USEFUL EQUIPMENT

Pairs of large and small sharp scissors for cutting your fabric and thread are absolutely essential. You'll also want dressmaker's carbon paper and special pencils for transferring your embroidery designs to fabric. Other useful items include a thimble, needle threader, and masking tape to prevent fabric edges from fraying.

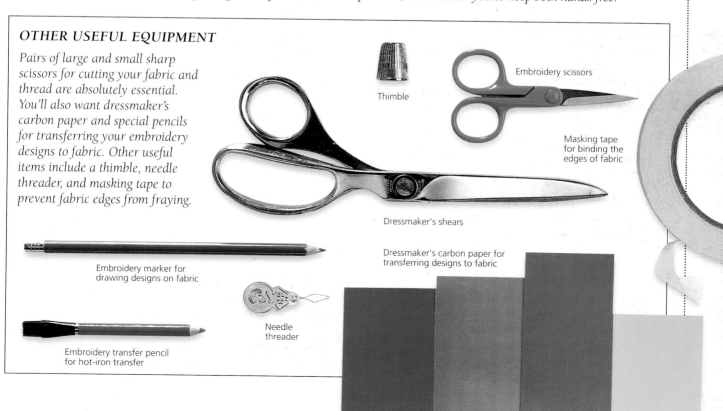

Thimble

Embroidery scissors

Masking tape for binding the edges of fabric

Dressmaker's shears

Dressmaker's carbon paper for transferring designs to fabric

Embroidery marker for drawing designs on fabric

Needle threader

Embroidery transfer pencil for hot-iron transfer

PREPARING A FRAME

LIGHTWEIGHT ROUND FRAMES, called hoops, are ideal for small pieces of fabric, while straight-sided frames, or stretcher frames, are better for larger pieces.

These latter take longer to set up as the fabric has to be stitched to the roller webbing at the top and bottom, and then laced to the sides of the frame.

HOOPS

Before placing the fabric, loosen the tension screw on the outer hoop. The hoop can be repositioned on the fabric as you complete each small area of stitching.

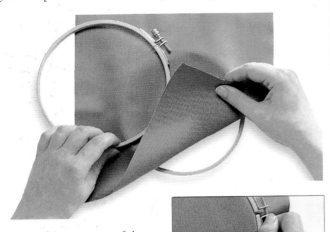

Lay the fabric on top of the inner hoop, with the section to be embroidered facing you (*above*). Make sure that the fabric is smooth. Push the outer hoop down on top of the fabric on the inner hoop. Gently pull the fabric taut. Tighten the upper hoop by turning the screw, so that the fabric is stretched like a drum and held firmly in position (*right*).

Irregular shapes

1 Baste the irregular shape onto a larger piece of fabric, with the woven threads of each aligned.

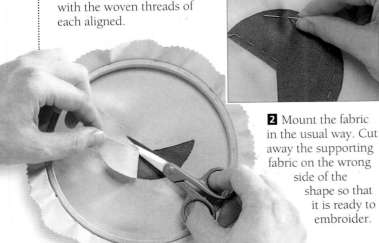

2 Mount the fabric in the usual way. Cut away the supporting fabric on the wrong side of the shape so that it is ready to embroider.

PROTECTING YOUR WORK

You can bind your hoop to prevent fine fabrics from sagging and losing their shape while you work. For a large piece of embroidery, change hoop position every time a section is completed. When you reposition your work be sure to protect finished stitches with a layer of tissue paper.

Wrap woven tape around the inner hoop as shown, and secure the end with a few stitches (*left*). Place the fabric on the lower hoop and lay white tissue paper on top. Mount the fabric and paper, then tear away the paper (*right*).

STRAIGHT-SIDED FRAMES

Before you mount the fabric, hem all the edges, or bind them with 2 cm (³⁄4 in) wide cotton tape. Mark the centre point of the fabric on the top and bottom edges.

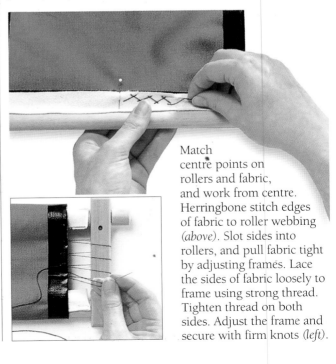

Match centre points on rollers and fabric, and work from centre. Herringbone stitch edges of fabric to roller webbing (*above*). Slot sides into rollers, and pull fabric tight by adjusting frames. Lace the sides of fabric loosely to frame using strong thread. Tighten thread on both sides. Adjust the frame and secure with firm knots (*left*).

EMBROIDERY TECHNIQUES

ONCE YOU HAVE transferred your design to the fabric, you are ready to start the embroidery. If the fabric weave is very open and loose, you will need to bind the edges so that they don't fray – use one of the simple methods given below. When working, try to keep the back of the work as neat as possible by weaving the thread ends behind existing stitches and avoiding large gaps between stitches.

CUTTING AND BINDING FABRIC

The fabric should be cut 5 cm (2 in) larger all around than the overall design. But if you want to mount or frame the completed embroidery, add twice this amount 10 cm (4 in). Take care to cut the fabric straight, following the warp and weft threads of the weave of the fabric.

Binding fabric prevents edges from fraying while you work and is essential on loosely woven fabric. Either tape the edges with masking tape or neaten raw edges with machine zigzag stitch. Alternatively, turn the edges under and sew in place.

PREPARING THE THREADS

The working thread should be 45 cm (18 in) or less. Longer threads will get tangled, lose their sheen, and fray.

When stitching a large area in one colour, cut skeins into 45 cm (18 in) lengths before you start. Fold bundles in half width-wise, and tie a thread around loop end. Use as needed.

Embroidery floss, matte embroidery cotton and Persian yarn are all loosely twisted threads that can be separated into finer strands. It is best to separate them when you need them.

STARTING AND FINISHING WORK

Don't make a knot when you are starting or finishing a length of thread. Knots show through the work, creating an uneven appearance. Instead, use a small backstitch (page 129), or weave the end into existing stitches on the back of the work.

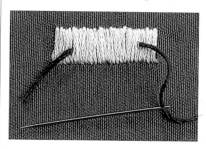

Start a new thread by sliding needle under wrong side of some stitches, keeping thread end about 4 cm (1¹/₂ in) long. Bring needle up on right side of fabric and continue.

To secure thread at the end of stitching, slide the needle under 4 cm (1¹/₂ in) of the worked stitches on wrong side of work, and then cut thread.

EMBROIDERING THE DESIGN

Always work in a good light and in a comfortable position. Follow the guidelines carefully, inserting the needle on the outside of each line, so that none of the lines will show when the work is finished.

Choose the right needle for the fabric and thread, and try to keep the stitch tension even. Where possible, use a stabbing motion with the needle, and always pull the thread through carefully. Stitching will make the thread twist, particularly if you are working knotted stitches. If this starts happening, just let the needle drop and hang freely for a few seconds until the thread untwists.

Don't make the stitches too long, especially if you are working an article that will receive a lot of wear or be handled frequently. When your embroidery is finished you may find that the long stitches tend to snag and break if they get caught on other objects. For the same reason, on the back of the work, if there is a gap of more than 2 cm (³/₄ in) between stitches, secure the first stitch and start the next one with a new piece of thread.

ENLARGING & REDUCING

INSPIRATION FOR EMBROIDERY designs can be found almost anywhere. Start by looking at old embroidery, art postcards, photographs, book illustrations or wallpaper. Since the original design is unlikely to be the right size, you will need to enlarge or reduce it. The easiest way to do this is with a photocopier, or you may use the grid method shown below. This involves transposing the outline shapes of the basic design from one grid to another of a different size. You will need some good quality tracing paper, a ruler and a set square.

INSPIRATION FOR DESIGN

You can find ideas for designs from all kinds of things such as plates, tiles, leaves, shells or flowers. Old objects, such as this trinket box or book, often have attractive decorations that could easily be copied for embroidery designs. If the design has a lot of detail, try to simplify the outlines to suit the scale of your work.

To enlarge a design

1 Trace shapes on tracing paper, and go over all lines with a black felt-tip pen. Enclose the design in a rectangle. Draw a diagonal line from bottom left-hand corner to top right-hand corner.

2 Place traced rectangle on a sheet of paper large enough for the final design. Align left-hand and bottom edges. Tape down tracing; extend the diagonal line on the tracing across paper.

3 Remove paper and complete diagonal line. At height of new design, using a set square, draw a horizontal line to cross the diagonal. From this point draw a vertical line down to bottom edge.

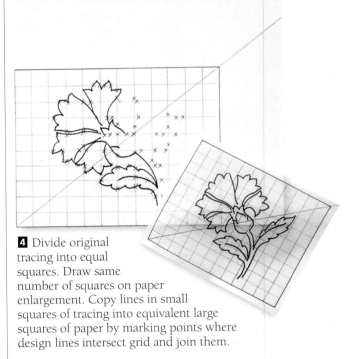

4 Divide original tracing into equal squares. Draw same number of squares on paper enlargement. Copy lines in small squares of tracing into equivalent large squares of paper by marking points where design lines intersect grid and join them.

To reduce a design

Start with step 1 of enlargement instructions; then tape a small piece of paper in the bottom left-hand corner of the tracing. Draw a diagonal line on the paper to correspond to the diagonal line on the tracing. Draw the required width and height of the embroidery on the paper as in step 3. Divide the tracing into squares, and then divide the paper into the same number of squares. Transfer the design as in step 4.

TRANSFERRING A DESIGN

THERE ARE FIVE methods of transferring an original design to fabric. The method you choose as the most suitable will depend on the type of design and texture of the fabric. First iron the fabric, then cut it to size (see page 123). Carefully position the design on the fabric before you transfer it by your chosen method.

Drawing freehand

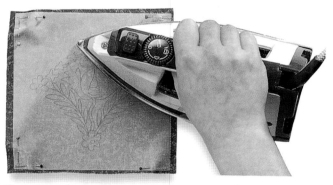

Designs can be drawn directly onto the right side of fabric with a pencil or embroidery marker – a fine-tipped water-soluble pen. Any lines that show afterward can be removed by damping the fabric. In the case of sheer fabrics such as organdy, muslin, or voile, draw the design on paper and go over the lines with a medium black felt-tip pen. When the ink is dry, place the fabric over the paper, and trace the design onto the fabric.

Hot-iron transfer

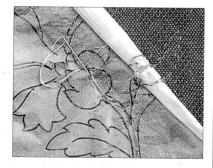

Copy your design onto tracing paper. Turn the paper over and trace the lines with an embroidery-transfer pencil. Position the paper, transfer side down, on the fabric, and pin together. With an iron on low heat, press down for a few seconds; do not move the iron because this may cause smudges. Before unpinning, pull back a corner of the tracing paper to check that the transfer is visible on the fabric.

Basting through tissue paper

This method is suitable for coarse fabric. Trace the design onto white tissue paper and pin in position on the fabric. Baste over the traced lines, through the paper and fabric, using small uniform stitches. Gently tear off tissue paper. If it doesn't come away easily, gently score the basting lines with a needle. When you have completed the embroidery, remove the basting stitches with tweezers.

Tracing with dressmaker's carbon paper

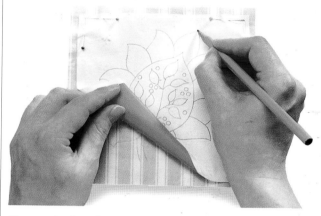

Dressmaker's carbon paper is made especially for use on fabrics, and is nothing like stationery carbon paper. It works best on smooth fabrics. Use a light colour on a dark fabric, and a dark colour on a light fabric. Draw the design on thin paper. Place the carbon paper, ink side down, between the fabric and the design. Pin together at the corners, or hold down firmly with one hand. Trace over all the lines of the design with a tracing wheel, or a hard-pointed object, pressing down firmly. Check that you haven't missed any lines before you remove the design and the carbon paper.

Tracing-paper templates

This is a way of transferring simple shapes. It works well on any type of fabric, and is particularly useful for repeating motifs. Draw the design onto thick tracing paper and cut out each separate piece. Pin all the shapes in position on the fabric. Draw around them if the fabric is smooth or baste around them if the fabric is coarse. Use the templates again for a repeating motif. Use clear plastic for a more durable, re-useable template.

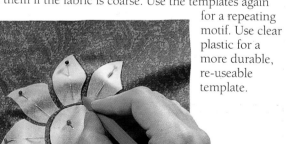

HEIRLOOM STITCHES

THROUGHOUT THE AGES, and in every culture, people have made use of needle and thread to create a wide range of decorative textiles – to be worn, used or displayed. These varied examples from Europe, North America and the Far East – demonstrating the effects of different stitches – can be used as inspiration for your own imaginative efforts.

Victorian beaded purses were a popular accessory

These late 19th century North American Indian cuffs have two strips of beads twisted together and couched to the edge

The flowers on this Chinese boy's hat are embroidered in satin stitches

Insects have seeding and single straight stitch details worked over the satin stitch

The scalloped edge is worked in buttonhole stitch

Motifs of couched beadwork with small clusters of beads stitched in individually

The flowers on this English 1820s hem are worked in padded satin stitch.

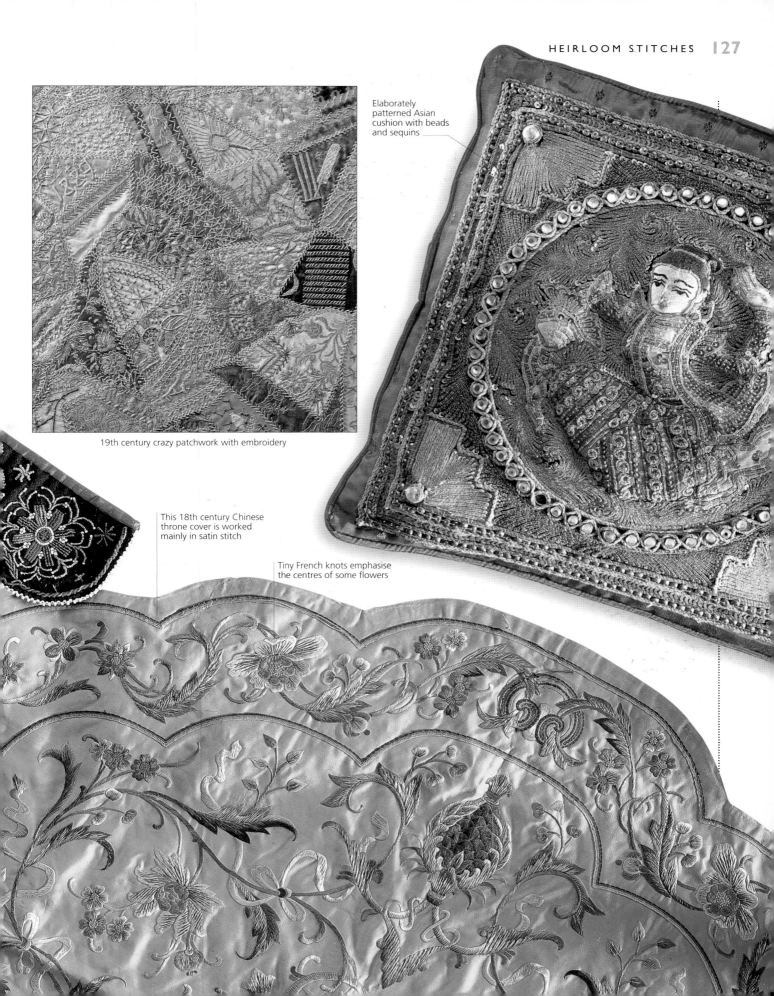

Elaborately
patterned Asian
cushion with beads
and sequins

19th century crazy patchwork with embroidery

This 18th century Chinese
throne cover is worked
mainly in satin stitch

Tiny French knots emphasise
the centres of some flowers

FLAT STITCHES

IT MAY SEEM there is an infinite variety of embroidery stitches. In fact, they are all variations on a few basic stitches, categorised into four groups: flat stitches, crossed stitches, looped stitches, and knot stitches.

The flat stitches are perhaps the simplest and easiest to learn; those shown on page 129 are based on two of the oldest known stitches: running stitch and backstitch. They are all formed with flat, straight stitches. The stitches can be worked in varying sizes, grouped with other stitches in different combinations, or worked in different directions to form borders, outlines, and blocks of colour in your designs.

CROSSED STITCHES

BASIC CROSS STITCH is probably the most popular of all the embroidery stitches; it is quick and easy to master, and can be worked singly or in rows. One stitch fills a small square. This means that designs can be worked out in grid form; it is simple to work out your own design on graph paper, shading the squares with coloured pencils. There is a wide variety of crossed stitches, and all are formed by stitches crossing each other at differing angles (see page 130). To work a neat row of crossed stitches, the head and base of each stitch should be the same number of rows apart. If the threads in the fabric are too fine to count, work the stitches between two lines of basting stitches and remove them afterward.

LOOPED STITCHES

CHAIN STITCH IS the most important of the looped stitches. It is an extremely versatile stitch, which can be worked in thick yarns or fine silk threads. All the stitches in this group are formed from loops that are held in place with small stitches (see page 131). They can be used both for outlining and for filling shapes. When used as filling stitches, they are generally worked in rows, and stitched in the same direction, to create an all over texture.

KNOTTED STITCHES

KNOTTED STITCHES PRODUCE various exciting surface textures and look particularly attractive when worked with thick thread. They are formed by looping the thread around the needle, and then pulling the needle through the loops to form a knot or twist on the surface of the fabric (see page 132). If you haven't tried a particular knotted stitch before, work several samples on a piece of scrap fabric first because it takes a little practice to get the tension of the knots even. To avoid your thread getting into tangles, always hold the loops of thread down with your left thumb when you pull the needle through.

Running stitch

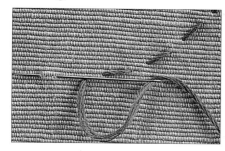

Take several small, even stitches at one time. The stitches on the wrong side of the fabric are usually half the size or less of the stitches on the right side.

Laced running stitch

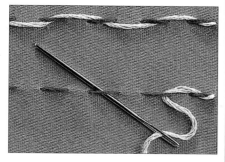

Lace the running stitches with a round-pointed needle by sliding it between the stitches and the fabric. Take the needle alternately through the bottom of one stitch and then the top of the next stitch. Do not pick up any fabric.

Whipped running stitch

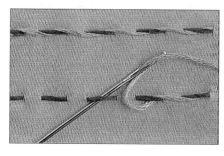

Work a row of running stitches. With a round-pointed needle, weave contrasting thread through each stitch from top to bottom, sliding the needle between the stitches and the fabric. Do not pick up any fabric.

Double running stitch

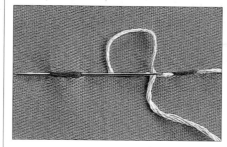

Work a row of running stitches. In same direction, work a second row, in same or a contrasting colour, to fill spaces between stitches in first row.

Backstitch

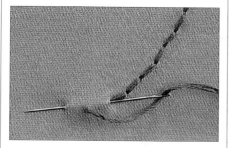

Take a small backward stitch, and bring the needle through to the right side again in front of the stitch you just made. Take another backward stitch, inserting the needle at the point where the first stitch stops. Keep the length of the stitches even.

Stem stitch

Work from left to right, taking regular, slanted backstitches. The thread should always emerge slightly above the previous stitch.

Encroaching satin stitch

Work the first row as for satin stitch. Work subsequent rows so that the head of the new stitch is between the bases of the stitches above.

Split stitch

Work in the same way as stem stitch, but the thread of the new stitch should split the thread of the previous stitch.

Straight stitch

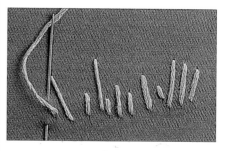

These single, spaced stitches may vary in size. Do not make them too long or too loose.

Satin stitch
Work the straight stitches against each other to completely fill area. Make sure stitches are fairly short and uniform.

Seed stitch
Work very small uniform stitches to cover area to be filled, changing stitch direction as desired. For a stronger effect, work two stitches close together instead.

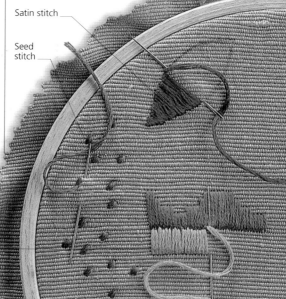

Satin stitch

Seed stitch

Encroaching satin stitch

Basic cross stitch

1 Work one or more evenly spaced diagonal stitches in one direction.

2 Cover with one or more diagonal stitches worked in opposite direction.

Long-armed cross stitch

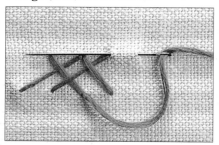

1 Bring the needle through at the stitch base line and take a long diagonal stitch to the right, at desired height of stitches. Measure the diagonal stitch, and bring out needle half this distance to the left, on the top line.

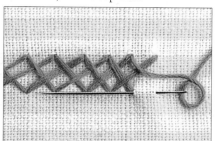

2 Take a diagonal stitch to base line, insert needle directly below the point where needle was inserted on top line. Bring needle out directly below the point where it emerged on the top line.

A wide variety of star shapes can be created using crossed stitches

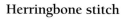

Herringbone stitch

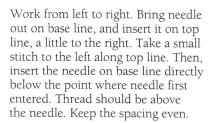

Work from left to right. Bring needle out on base line, and insert it on top line, a little to the right. Take a small stitch to the left along top line. Then, insert the needle on base line directly below the point where needle first entered. Thread should be above the needle. Keep the spacing even.

Tacked herringbone stitch

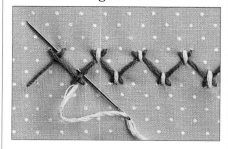

Work a row of herringbone stitch. In a contrasting coloured thread, working from right to left, sew each cross together with a small vertical stitch.

Closed herringbone stitch

Work in the same way as herringbone stitch but with no spaces left between the stitches. The diagonals should touch at the top and bottom.

Basket stitch (Step 1)

Basket stitch (Step 2)

Basket stitch

1 Work from left to right. Take a diagonal stitch from the base line to the top line, with the needle inserted vertically downward through the design lines.

2 Take a vertical downward stitch to the left and into the same holes as the two previous crossed stitches.

Zigzag stitch

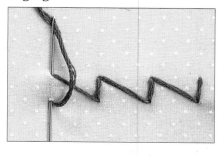

1 Work from right to left. Take alternate upright and long diagonal stitches to the end of the row.

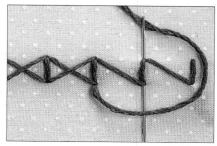

2 Work from left to right. Take upright stitches into the same holes as the previous upright stitches, and reverse the direction of the diagonal stitches so they cross each other.

Chain stitch

Bring the needle out at the position for the first stitch. Loop thread and hold it down with your left thumb. Insert the needle where it first emerged, and bring the tip out a short distance below this point. Keep the thread under the tip of the needle, and pull the needle through. To make the next stitch, insert the needle into the hole from which it has just emerged.

Lazy daisy stitch (detached chain stitch)

Work a single chain stitch, as described above. To secure the stitch, insert the needle just below the base of the loop and bring it out at the position for the next chain stitch.

Blanket stitch

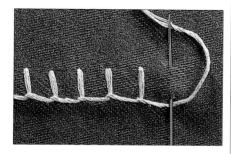

Work from left to right. Bring the thread out at the position for the looped edging. Insert the needle above and a little to the left of this point as shown, and take a straight downward stitch, with the thread under the tip of the needle. Pull up the stitch to form the loop, and repeat.

Chequered chain stitch

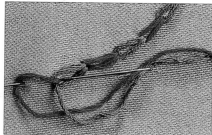

Thread the needle with two contrasting coloured threads. Work as for chain stitch, keeping the thread not in use above the point of the needle.

Open chain stitch (ladder stitch)

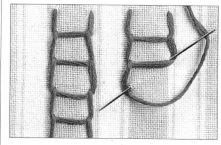

Bring needle out at left guideline. Hold thread down with left thumb, and insert needle at right guideline, opposite point where thread emerged. Bring needle out again at left guideline, with thread under needle. Continue anchoring right side as for left.

Feather stitch

Work vertically from top to bottom. Bring needle out at top centre. Hold thread down with your left thumb, and insert needle to right and slightly below. Take a small slanting stitch toward the centre, with thread under needle. Insert needle again on left side, and take a slanting stitch down toward the centre, with thread under needle. Work looped stitches to left and right alternately.

Double feather stitch (fancy)

This is worked in the same way as feather stitch, but two stitches are taken instead of one.

Closed Cretan stitch

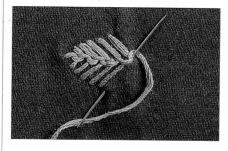

1 Bring the needle through centrally at left side of shape. Take a small stitch on the lower guideline, with the needle pointing inwards and the thread under the tip of the needle.

2 Take a small stitch on upper guideline, with needle pointing inwards and thread under needle. Repeat steps 1 and 2 until shape is filled.

Open Cretan stitch

Work by making short vertical stitches downwards and upwards alternately, with the thread always held down to the right under the tip of the needle.

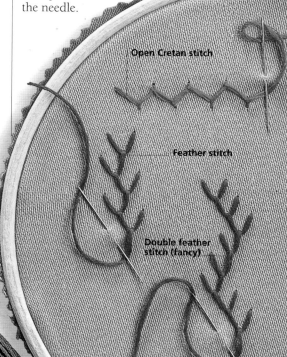

Open Cretan stitch

Feather stitch

Double feather stitch (fancy)

French knot

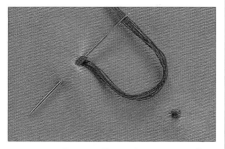

Bring out the needle at the position for the knot. Twist the needle 2 or 3 times around the thread. Turn the needle and insert it just above where the thread first emerged. Holding the working thread taut with the left hand, pull the thread through to the back of the work. For a larger knot, use 2 or more strands of thread.

Bullion knot

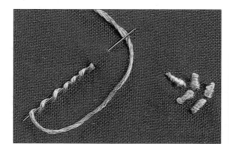

Make a backstitch, the size of the knot required, bringing the needle half way out at the point where it first emerged. Twist the thread around needle as many times as required to equal the size of backstitch. Holding your left thumb on the coiled thread, pull the needle through. Then turn the needle back to where it was inserted, and pull the thread through to the back of the work, so that the bullion knot lies flat.

Scroll stitch

Bring the needle out on the guideline. Loop thread to right. Insert needle in loop, and over working thread as shown. Pull through to form a knot.

Coral stitch

Work from right to left. Bring the thread out, and hold it with your left thumb along the line to be worked. Take a small stitch under and over the looped working thread. Pull thread through to form knot. The spacing of the knots can be varied as required. *(See top right.)*

Zigzag coral stitch

Bring the needle out at top left. Lay thread across fabric to right margin to form first diagonal. Loop the thread; insert the needle and take a small diagonal stitch, bringing the needle tip out at the centre of the loop. Pull the needle through the loop to form the knot. Lay the thread across the fabric to left margin for second diagonal, and repeat knot stitch. Continue knotting at right and left margins alternately for form zigzag.

Four-legged knot stitch

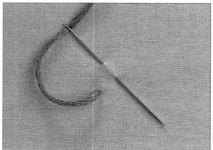

1 Take a vertical stitch and bring the needle out at centre right, ready to form horizontal leg of cross.

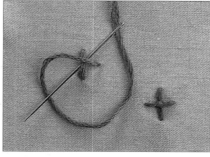

2 Slide the needle between the vertical stitch and the fabric, without picking up any fabric. Loop the thread around the needle, and pull the needle through to form the knot. Take a small horizontal stitch to left, to form last leg of cross *(see above right)*.

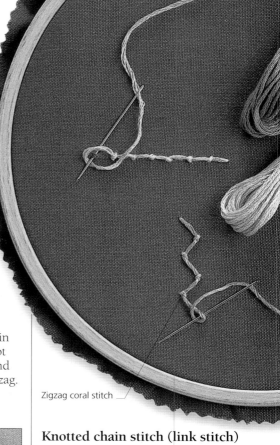

Zigzag coral stitch

Knotted chain stitch (link stitch)

1 Take an upward diagonal stitch, and bring out the needle directly below the point where it has just been inserted. Slide the needle between the stitch and the fabric, keeping the looped thread on the left.

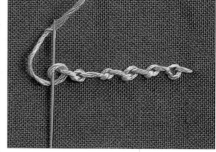

2 Loop the working thread under the tip of the needle and pull through to form the knot.

SAMPLERS

The word sampler comes from the Latin "exemplum", meaning an example to be followed. In the 16th and 17th century, samplers were worked by the high born ladies of the European courts as a method of recording stitches and designs. In the 18th to 19th century they became the province of the school room, to teach the alphabet, a skill necessary for marking bed linen. The designs became more stylised, with decorative borders, religious scripts, and pictures of the home or school. The name of the young embroiderer and the date were usually incorporated.

Detail from a modern cross-stitch sampler

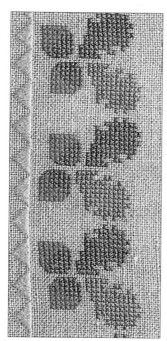

A house motif from a modern cross-stitch sampler with straight-stitch detail

The strawberry (above) is still a favourite motif. It was first used as a Christian symbol denoting perfect righteousness. Flowers and fruit (right) are worked in cross stitch, stem stitch, and satin stitch

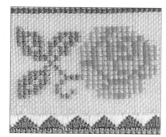

Alphabet detail from a modern sampler, based on an 1822 design

COUCHING & LAIDWORK

COUCHING IS A quick and easy method of laying one strand of thread on the fabric, and catching it down at intervals with a separate strand of thread. More than one strand can be laid down at a time to create bold outlines. Textured and metallic threads, which won't pass through the fabric easily, can be laid down with finer thread. It is also useful for filling large shapes rapidly to produce solid areas of colour.

Laidwork is really a continuation of couching. Long threads (grid threads) are laid on the fabric in a grid pattern, and then secured at the intersections with a separate thread. The method produces quite complicated looking lattice filling stitches.

For the best results, use an embroidery frame in order to keep the fabric taut, and make sure that the grid threads are evenly spaced.

Basic method

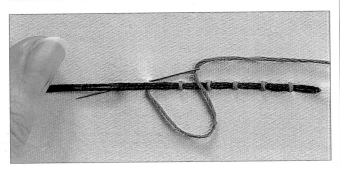

Work from right to left. Bring out the strand to be laid and use your left thumb to hold it in place. Bring out the working (couching) thread just below the laid strand. Take a vertical stitch over the laid strand, bringing the needle out to the left, below the laid strand, ready for the next stitch. At the end of the line, take both the couching thread and laid thread through to back of work, and secure.

To fill an area

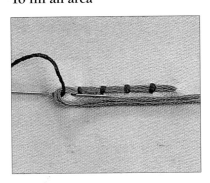

1 Work a line of basic couching. At the end of the line, turn the loose laid thread to the right and take a horizontal stitch across the turning point.

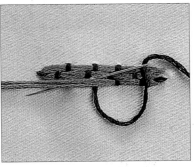

2 Turn the work upside-down and couch 2nd row of threads next to first, placing stitches between those on the previous row. Continue until the area is filled.

To couch a circle

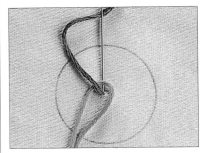

1 Bring out the needle with the laid thread at the centre of the circle, and pass the needle through the looped couching thread.

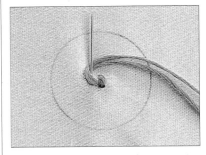

2 Insert the needle at the centre to secure the laid thread. With your left thumb, guide the laid thread into a spiral, and couch over it.

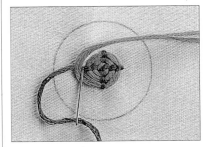

3 Make sure all the couching stitches line up as shown, as if on the spokes of a wheel. Bring threads to the back and secure.

Variations

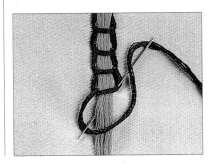

Couching can be worked with 2 contrasting coloured threads, and with open chain stitch as shown here (see page 131).

Squared laidwork (open lattice)

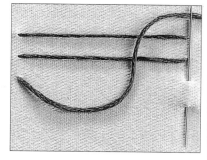

1 To lay horizontal threads, bring needle out at top left-hand guideline, lay thread across to opposite point on right guideline. Insert needle, and bring it out below this stitch, ready to form next horizontal thread. Continue back and forth until all horizontal threads are laid, keeping tension fairly loose so that stitches do not pucker. At end of last stitch, take thread to back of work and secure.

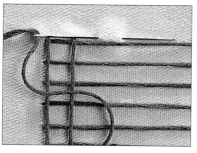

2 To create the lattice effect, lay the vertical stitches across the horizontal threads in the same manner.

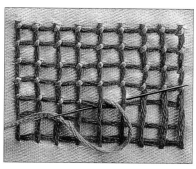

3 Bring out the couching thread at the top left corner of the grid. Secure each intersection of the vertical and horizontal threads with a small, slanting stitch.

Variations

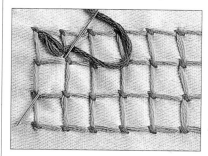

1 Make the squared laidwork, and make a series of 4 detached chain stitches (*see page 131*) within 4 lattice squares. Make the anchoring stitch at the centre of the 4 squares.

2 Work any further chain-stitch groups with a lattice space between them.

EMBROIDERED PARTY SHOES

Plain black velvet children's shoes can be dressed up with embroidery and circles couched in metallic thread – and transformed into sophisticated party slippers for that first grown-up evening out. The same techniques in cotton thread could be applied to canvas shoes for the beach.

Spirals of metallic gold thread make little coin-like motifs

Lazy daisy stitch decorates an open lattice of laidwork

LETTERING

EMBROIDERED INITIALS, MONOGRAMS, and messages are used to personalize clothes and gifts. Cross stitch is the traditional way to work the name and date on samplers, and is still the most popular lettering stitch for embroidered pictures.

The smooth, even look of satin stitch is perfect for scrolled initials on, for example, table linen, pillowcases, towels and handkerchiefs. You can use techniques such as padded satin stitch, braidwork, and openwork to add variety to your lettering designs.

Any design incorporating lettering should be easy to read. You can trace examples of alphabets from books and magazines. Transfer the outlines of the letters on to your background fabric. If possible, work on a frame or hoop so that you can keep the stitches even and prevent the fabric from puckering.

The letters and words in a full name or message must be spaced out carefully. Trace all the words onto paper. Then hold the paper away from you and study the effect. If necessary, adjust the spacing before transferring the lettering to the fabric.

SATIN STITCHES

Two variations on satin stitch (see page 129) are ideal for working initials. Before you embark on a monogram, practice working the shapes to obtain a smooth outline.

Satin stitch initials personalise a blue handkerchief

Padded satin stitch

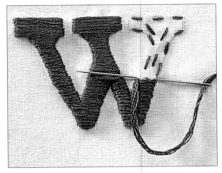

Raising the satin stitch above the surface of the fabric gives it more definition. Fill in outlined area with satin stitch. Then, working in a different direction, add a 2nd layer of satin stitch.

Negative satin stitch

This is an effective technique for monograms and crests. Choose a simple, well defined letter shape. Work the background in satin stitch, leaving the letters in unstitched fabric. Outline the design in stem stitch *(see page 129)* or chain stitch *(see page 131)*.

BRAID AND RIBBON LETTERING

For joined lettering, try to plan out the design so that only one piece of ribbon or braid is required for the complete design. If you must add a separate piece, place it underneath the ribbon or braid previously laid down. Raised braids can be couched in a matching or contrasting colour.

Fine ribbon and braid can be used for lettering. Hem the short ends by pressing the narrow raw edges to the wrong side. Stitch in place down the centre with small running stitches or backstitches.

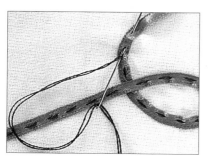

When you reach an intersection, leave a gap in the running stitches. On the return, thread the ribbon or braid through this gap, and continue stitching.

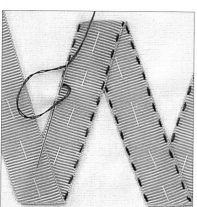

A wide braid or double-sided ribbon may be twisted over to form angles and corners for straight-sided lettering. Baste in position and press. Then stitch along both edges so that they lie flat and even.

OPENWORK

Satin stitch lettering looks very attractive against a fine openwork background. Work the lettering first, then the background, and outline the letters in stem stitch. Two useful openwork filling stitches are shown below.

Cloud filling stitch

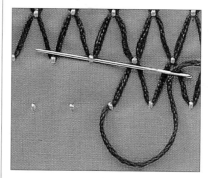

Work rows of small, vertical, evenly spaced stitches across the background area. Use a tapestry needle to lace a second thread through these stitches to form a trellis pattern.

Wave stitch

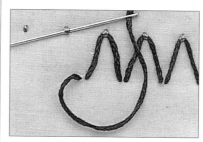

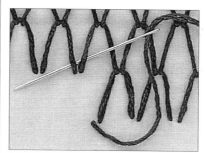

1 Work a row of small, evenly spaced vertical stitches. Bring out needle below and to the right of last stitch, and work a row of arched loops by passing the needle under the vertical stitches.

2 On following rows, continue to make arched loops by passing the needle under the pairs of stitch bases in the row directly above.

A background of openwork stitches emphasises the satin stitch letter

PULLED THREADWORK

THIS TECHNIQUE HAS been used for centuries to decorate clothing and household items. Stitches are looped around the fabric threads and pulled tightly, to make holes. This combination of stitches and holes creates lacy patterns. Threadwork was traditionally done on cream or white linen with matching thread. Today, we have a wider choice of fabrics, and many of the patterns look lovely when worked in colours.

TOOLS AND MATERIALS

Work on an even-weave fabric, using a thread that is similar in weight to a single thread of the fabric you are using. The working thread must be fairly strong. Pearl cotton, soft embroidery cotton and crochet cotton are all suitable. Use a round-pointed needle to exaggerate the holes, but make sure it will still slip between the threads easily. Working in a frame isn't essential, but it helps to have both hands free to count the threads and pull the stitches tight.

BASIC WORKING METHOD

If necessary, finish raw edges to prevent fraying (see page 123). Run a line of tacking stitches in a contrasting colour across the length and width of the fabric to help you count the stitches, and remove them when the work is finished.

Work the stitch patterns in rows, starting at the centre and moving outward. Count the fabric threads carefully, and always pull the embroidery thread tight.

Secure the first thread with a few backstitches on the wrong side of the work. Then, when you have finished a row of the pattern, unpick the backstitches, and weave the loose thread under some of the embroidery stitches. Secure all other threads by weaving the ends under worked stitches.

The size of stitches can be varied by stitching over more or fewer threads than the numbers stated in the instructions.

Pin stitch hem

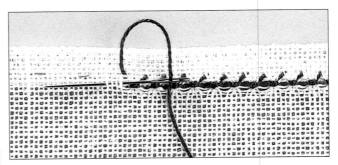

1 Bring needle out on right side, 2 threads above folded hem. Insert needle 2 threads down (through single thickness) just under hem, and bring it out 4 threads to left. Backstitch over same 4 threads and pull tight.

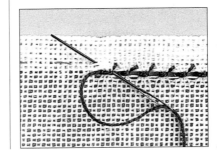

2 Take a 2nd backstitch over the 4 threads, and bring out needle 2 stitches above hemline to start next stitch sequence.

TO MITRE THE CORNERS ON A HEM

If you want to make place mats or napkins with pulled-threadwork borders, you must mitre the corners of the hems so that they lie flat.

1 Press raw edges to wrong side of fabric. Turn under folded edge again by the same amount to form a double hem, and press. Open fabric.

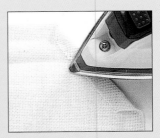

2 Crease marks will form 4 squares at each corner. Taking one corner at a time, cut off corner by cutting inner square in half diagonally. Fold in sides so that edges just meet at inner corner of inner square. Turn under raw edges.

3 Refold and tack hems. Slip stitch mitred corner edges. Machine or hand stitch hem.

Coil filling stitch

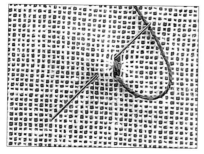

1 Bring out needle on right side. Take 2 vertical satin stitches across 4 threads, into same holes. Take a 3rd satin stitch into top hole, bringing out needle 4 threads to left, on base line of stitches just worked.

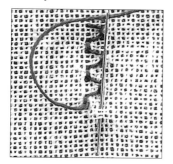

2 To begin next row, bring needle out 4 threads below and 2 threads to right of stitches just worked. Continue working rows from right to left, and left to right, alternately.

Honeycomb stitch

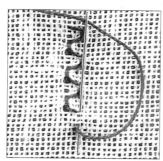

1 Bring the needle out on right side of work. Insert needle 3 threads to right, and bring it out 3 threads down. Take a backstitch into base of stitch just made, and bring it out 3 threads down. Insert needle 3 threads to the left, and bring it out 3 threads down. Take a backstitch into the base of stitch just made, and bring it out 3 threads down. Repeat sequence to end of row.

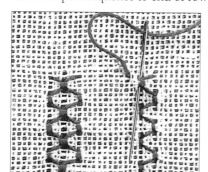

2 Turn the work at end of row, and embroider the next row in the same way.

Honeycomb stitch forms a regular lattice filling, and is worked from top to bottom

Faggot stitch

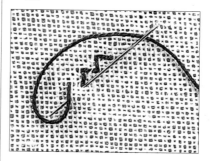

1 Bring out needle on right side of fabric. Work diagonally, and take horizontal and then vertical stitches over an equal number of threads alternately.

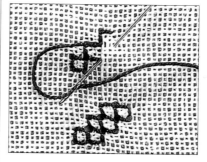

2 On the next row, make squares by working into the holes of the previous row.

Coil filling stitch is made from groups of satin stitches worked in horizontal rows

Faggot stitch is a useful basic stitch for patterning and background filling

Chessboard filling stitch

1 Work 3 rows of satin stitch from left to right, and right to left, alternately. Each satin stitch is worked over 3 threads, and each block is made up of 3 rows of 8 stitches.

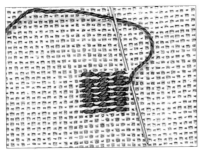

2 At end of 3rd row, turn the work as shown, and bring out needle 3 vertical threads down and one horizontal thread to the left, ready to start next block.

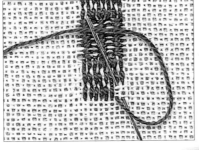

3 Repeat step 1. Work all other blocks in the same way, turning the work after each to change the stitch direction.

Diagonal raised band

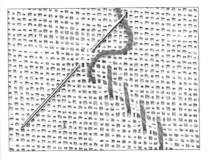

1 Bring needle out on right side at bottom right-hand corner. Insert it 6 threads up to form first vertical stitch, and bring it out 3 threads down and 3 to left. Pull thread very tight to make a ridged effect. Repeat.

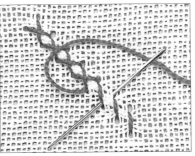

2 Insert needle 6 threads to right to form first horizontal stitch, and bring it out 3 threads down and 3 to left, ready to start next stitch. Pull tight. Repeat.

Wave stitch

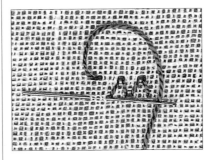

1 Working from right to left, bring needle out on right side of work, and insert it 4 threads down and 2 to the right, to form the first diagonal stitch. Bring it out 4 threads to the left and insert it at the point where the thread emerged.

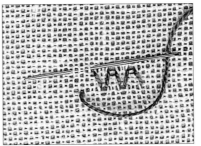

2 Bring out the needle, 4 threads to the left in line with top of V-shape formed, to start the next diagonal stitch. Repeat to end of row.

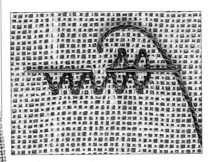

3 To start second row, insert needle 8 threads down from top of V-shape formed. Turn the work upside-down and work second row of zigzags as in step 1.

Chessboard filling stitch is shown in blue, diagonal raised band in red, and wave stitch in green

DRAWN THREADWORK BORDERS

IN DRAWN THREADWORK, some of the warp and weft threads of the fabric are removed, and the remaining threads in the drawn area can then be pulled together in clusters with the embroidery thread to form open patterns. The technique is used mainly for border decorations on tablecloths and place mats.

TOOLS AND MATERIALS

If you are a beginner, you will find it easier to remove the threads from a coarse open-weave fabric rather than a closely woven one. To hem stitch the border, use stranded cotton or pearl cotton similar in thickness to a single thread of the ground fabric you have chosen, and work with a round-pointed tapestry needle.

How to remove the fabric threads

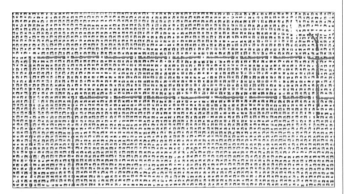

1 Cut your chosen fabric to size, allowing for a mitred hem around all 4 sides (*see page 138*). Mark out the hem allowance with a row of basting stitches or an embroidery marker. Decide on the number of threads that will make up the depth of the border and mark the inner border line, then mark the centre point on each side.

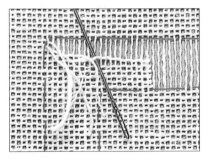

2 Using a pair of sharp embroidery scissors, carefully cut horizontal fabric threads at the centre mark on each side of border. Gently ease out threads with a tapestry needle until you reach corners.

3 Trim loose thread ends. Then fold them back, and backstitch over ends. Remove basting stitches. Turn up hem allowance, and baste in position, ready for hem stitching.

Hem stitch

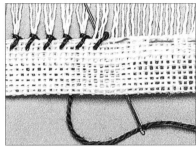

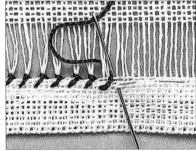

1 Work from left to right on the wrong side of the fabric. Bring needle out 2 threads below hem, and opposite first loose thread in border. Take a diagonal stitch to right, and insert needle under first 3 or more loose threads in border; pull together.

2 Take vertical stitch, bringing needle out on wrong side, to right of bundle and 2 threads below hem. Repeat.

Ladder stitch variation

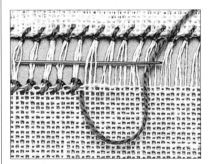

Complete a row of hem stitch. Turn the work upside-down and work hem stitch along opposite edge of border, catching the same loose threads into bundles, forming a ladder-like pattern.

To finish corners

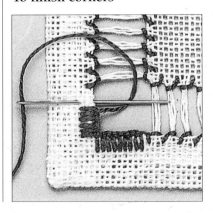

If the open squares at the corners are small, they can be left as they are, or they can be reinforced with blanket stitch (*see page 131*).

SMOCKING

AN ATTRACTIVE WAY of reducing the fullness in fabric is to gather material into tiny pleats, and work over them with embroidery stitches. The patterns can be worked in one stitch only or several stitches can be combined into elaborate patterns, according to the effect desired. When the embroidery is finished, the gathering stitches are removed and the fabric relaxes slightly. Extensively used in the eighteenth and nineteenth centuries to fashion comfortable garments for rural working men, it remains a popular and interesting way to shape and decorate clothes for children and adults. It also can be used for accessories, and all sorts of items for the home such as cushions, lampshades, and curtains.

MATERIALS AND TOOLS

Any type of fabric can be smocked if it is supple enough to be gathered. Regular repeating patterns, such as checks and dots, are popular because the pattern can be used as a guideline for the gathering stitches. Work with a crewel needle and strong cotton thread for the gathering stitches. The embroidery can be worked in either embroidery floss, pearl cotton, or matte embroidery cotton.

CUTTING THE FABRIC

Smocking is always worked before a garment is made up. The amount of fabric needed is usually three times the finished width of the smocked area. Less fabric is required when working on a thick material.

GATHERING THE FABRIC

Work the rows of gathering stitches from right to left, on the wrong side of the fabric, using a strongly contrasting thread. The contrast colour will help you remove the gathering thread easily when the smocking is finished.

To gather fabric

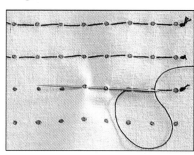

1 Cut a length of thread, longer than row of dots to be gathered, and tie a knot. Make running stitches along each row, picking up a piece of the fabric at each dot. Leave thread ends loose.

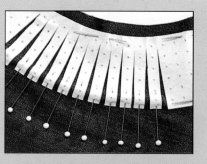

2 Pull up each gathering thread to the required width and tie together in pairs at the end of the rows. Make sure all pleats are even and that gathers are not pulled too tightly.

MARKING THE FABRIC FOR GATHERING

The rows for the gathering stitches are marked on the wrong side (in America, on the right). The easiest way to do this is with a smocking-dot transfer. This is an iron-on transfer with rows of equally spaced dots printed across it. The space between dots is usually 5 to 8 mm (¹/₄ to ³/₈ in), and between rows usually 8 mm to 1cm (³/₈ to ¹/₂ in). In general, the finer the fabric, the closer the dots and rows. Make sure the dots are in line with the threads of the fabric, then iron in position, following the hot-iron transfer method on page 125.

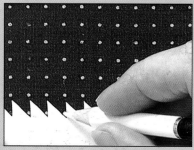

To mark a curved area, such as a yoke, slash the transfer and pin in place before ironing.

You can make your own guide from thin cardboard and mark out dots in pencil. Position the points on a row of dots, and mark the next row at the base of each V.

SMOCKING STITCHES

These stitches are worked on the right side of the gathered fabric. All the stitches shown here are worked from left to right, beginning at the top left-hand corner. Make sure the embroidery thread is attached and fastened off very securely. Hold the needle parallel to the gathering threads, and take the stitches through about one-third of the depth of each pleat, to keep them elastic, and to ensure that the embroidery thread doesn't become entangled with the gathering thread. Leave the first row of gathers free of embroidery so that the smocked panel can be joined to another piece. Smocking stitches vary considerably in tension, so work a sample first to see how tight or loose a stitch will be. Intricate patterns can be made with a combination of smocking stitches, although equally impressive results can be achieved by working only one or two. Other embroidery stitches such as lazy daisy (see page 131), cross stitch (see page 130) and chain stitch (see page 131) may be worked over two or more pleats between the rows of smocking for extra decoration. The gaps between rows should not be too wide or the pleats will puff out.

Stem stitch

Working it like a basic stem stitch, use this stitch for the top row of smocking. Bring needle out to left of first fold. Take a stitch through top of each fold, keeping thread below needle.

Cable stitch

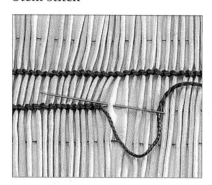

1 Bring needle out to left of first fold. With the thread below the needle, take a stitch over the 2nd fold, and bring the needle out between the first and 2nd folds.

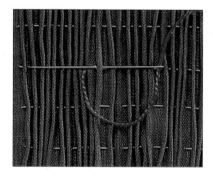

2 With thread above needle, take a stitch over 3rd fold, and bring needle out between 2nd and 3rd folds. Continue to the end of the row, keeping the thread alternately above, then below, needle.

Wheat stitch

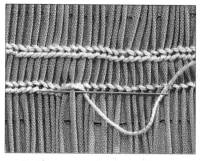

This variation of stem stitch produces a tight stitch. Work a row of stem stitch, then work a second row just below, keeping the thread above the needle to alter stitch direction.

Double cable stitch

Work one row of cable stitch, starting with the thread below the needle. Work a 2nd row underneath it, starting with the thread above the needle.

Honeycomb stitch

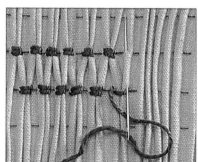

1 This stitch is worked across 2 lines of gathering stitches. Bring needle out at left of first fold on top of line of gathering stitches, and take a backstitch over first 2 folds to draw them together. Take a 2nd stitch over 2 folds, bringing needle out at lower line of gathering stitches, between first and 2nd fold.

2 Take a backstitch over 2nd and 3rd folds to draw them together. Take a 2nd stitch over these folds, bringing needle out at top line of gathering stitches, between 2nd and 3rd fold.

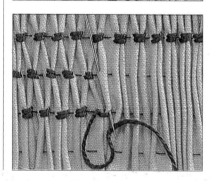

3 Continue working stitches on top and bottom lines of gathering stitches alternately.

Wave stitch

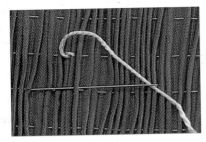

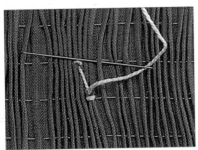

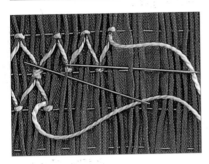

1 Work across 2 lines of gathering. Bring needle out left of first fold on top line. With thread above needle, take a stitch over 2nd fold. Bring it out between first and 2nd folds. With thread at lower line, and above needle, take stitch over 3rd fold. Bring needle out between 2nd and 3rd folds.

2 With thread below needle, take stitch over 4th fold. Bring it out between 3rd and 4th folds. With thread at top line and below needle, take a stitch over 5th fold. Bring it out between 4th and 5th folds.

3 Next row, work between 3rd line of gathering and bases of stitches above.

Trellis diamond

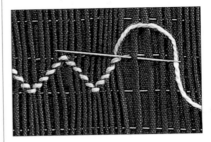

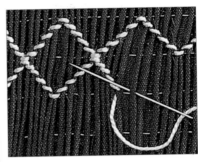

1 Work one row of stem stitch in a chevron pattern between 2 lines of gathering stitches, keeping thread below needle when working up, and above needle on the way down.

2 Start at 2nd line of gathering stitches, and work another row of stem stitch chevron pattern between lines 2 and 3, inverting chevrons to form a diamond trellis.

Surface honeycomb stitch

1 Work across 2 lines of gathering. Bring the needle out to left of first fold, on the top line. With the thread above the needle, take a stitch over and to the left of the 2nd fold. With the thread at the

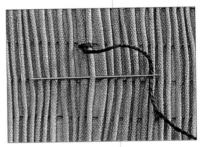

lower line and above the needle, insert the needle between the 2nd and 3rd folds; bring it out to the left of the 2nd fold.

2 With the thread below the needle, take a stitch over 2nd and 3rd folds: Bring it out to left of 3rd. With the thread at the top line and below the needle, insert the needle

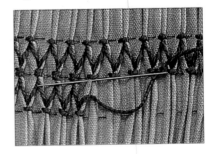

between 3rd and 4th folds. Work next row between the 2nd and 3rd rows of gathering stitches.

This drawstring bag is worked in trellis diamond and surface honeycomb stitches

TO FINISH

When a smocked piece is finished, steam press on the wrong side, or lay a damp cloth on top and lightly pass a hot iron over the work, taking care not to flatten it. Then remove the gathering threads.

If you find that the smocking is too tight, take out the gathering stitches, lay the work wrong side on the ironing board, and pin it out to size. Steam press as above.

BEADS & SEQUINS

THROUGHOUT THE AGES, in every culture, and in every part of the world beads and sequins have been used to add extra sparkle and richness to textiles and to denote the wearer's wealth and standing. Fashions change, and today we see beading on everything from glittering evening clothes to T-shirts. However, beads and sequins can also be used creatively to highlight areas on embroidered pictures and hangings – for example, a single pearl bead looks wonderful in the centre of a flower, or two flashing green sequins can suggest a cat's eyes.

BEADING

Use an ordinary sewing needle for beads with large holes. If, however, the beads have very small holes, you will need a fine beading needle, see page 120.

Sewing on beads individually

Bring out the needle and thread the bead. If the bead is round, insert needle back through same hole. With a long shaped bead, hold down with the thumb and insert needle close to edge of bead. Repeat.

Couching rows of beads

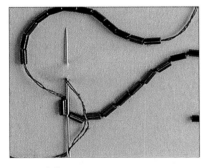

Use two needles. Bring out first needle, and thread beads. Bring out 2nd needle close to left of first bead and take a small stitch over thread. Slide next bead up, and repeat.

Strand fringe

Tie first bead onto thread, and knot securely. (If beads are large, start with a small bead.) Thread beads for one fringe strand; secure to hem with a small backstitch. Repeat for each strand.

APPLYING SEQUINS

With matching sewing thread, sequins may be stitched on almost invisibly. An embroidery thread in a contrasting colour can add to the decorative effect.

Two-stitch method

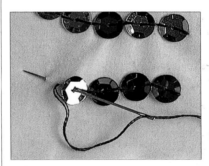

Use to secure one or more sequins. Bring out needle and thread sequin. Take a backstitch over right edge of sequin and bring out needle at left edge. Stitch through sequin again and repeat.

Invisible stitching

Bring out needle and thread on sequin. Take a stitch over its left edge; place a 2nd sequin so that right edge covers eye of first. Bring out needle at left edge of 2nd sequin and insert needle in its eye.

Securing sequins with beads

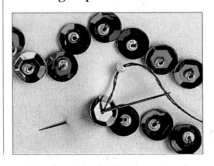

Bring out needle; thread on a sequin and a bead. Insert needle through sequin eye and pull thread so that bead holds sequin in its place. Bring out needle at position for next sequin.

SPECIAL EFFECTS

ONCE YOU HAVE mastered the basic embroidery stitches, you might like to experiment with some of the traditional forms of embroidery that depend upon a combination of stitches to achieve a particular effect. Four of the the most popular are shown here – blackwork, whitework, stumpwork, and crewel work.

CREWEL WORK

This type of embroidery gets its name from the very fine wool yarn with which it is worked. Since it is difficult to create small, intricate stitches in wool, the designs are generally bold and free-flowing. Crewel work has always been popular for home furnishings, and also looks very decorative on clothing and accessories. Traditional themes include exotic animals, birds, flowers and trees. The basic shapes are usually worked in a simple outline stitch and then filled in with a variety of broader stitches. Choose a firm, medium-weight fabric on which to stitch your designs.

Crewel-work design

This landscape shows how outline shapes can be enhanced with textured filling stitches. Branches are worked in stem stitch, berries are French knots, and the foreground is satin stitch. Useful stitches include split and herringbone.

STUMPWORK

This is an interesting way of making embroidery more three-dimensional. It is done by combining padded appliqué and embroidery stitches. Stumpwork was very popular in the last century for decorating boxes and screens. It is also very effective on pictures and wall hangings. Choose lightweight fabrics for the best results.

Appliqué shapes are stitched to a background fabric and one end is left open for stuffing. Once the appliqué is stitched closed, you can embroider the surrounding area and the padded shapes.

Raised stitches with a clearly defined surface texture – such as padded satin stitch, couching – and any of the knotted stitches combine well with padded appliqué.

Padded appliqué

1 Cut out your appliqué shape, slightly larger than finished size, and hand stitch to right side of fabric (*see appliqué, page 182*). Leave a small section open to insert the stuffing. Push in some wadding and distribute it evenly.

The petals are embroidered with seeding and couching

2 Sew up the opening neatly by hand. The padded appliqué motif may then be left as it is or decorated with embroidery stitches or even beadwork.

French knots decorate this appliquéd heart

WHITEWORK

*The general name given to any type of
white embroidery on white fabric, whitework
is a beautiful way of decorating fine bed linen,
tablecloths, and blouses.*

   *When only one colour is used for both the back-
ground and the embroidery, subtle contrasts, such
as the look of the thread against the fabric and the
texture of the stitch, become important. Most surface
stitches will be enhanced by working them in a thread
with a high sheen on a matte background fabric. Bands
of pulled and drawn threadwork (see pages 138 to 141)
will add texture to the design. For a stronger contrast, hem
sections of fabric with a close buttonhole stitch to prevent
fraying, then cut away sections within the stitching. This
is called cutwork, and the basic method is given below.*

   *The pillow-case shown right is worked with high-sheen
pearl cotton thread on crisp linen. It has a cutwork border,
and strongly defined surface embroidery done with whip
stitch and French knot. The narrow satin ribbon is threaded
through a band of open chain stitch.*

Cutwork border
is edged with
buttonhole stitch

Cutwork

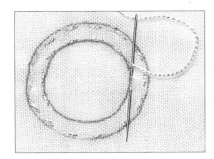

1 This is easier
to work in a frame.
Outline the section
of the background
fabric that is to be
cut away with a
small running
stitch in embroidery
floss or cotton
pearl thread.

2 Work a close
buttonhole stitch
in matching thread
around this outline.
The ridged edge of
the buttonhole stitch
should just cover the
running stitch, as
shown above.

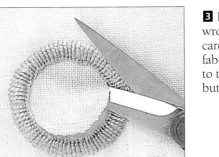

3 From the
wrong side of fabric,
carefully cut out the
fabric shape close
to the base of the
buttonhole stitching.

BLACKWORK

*A form of counted-thread embroidery, blackwork depends on
simple stitches worked in one colour over a precise number of
fabric threads; it forms repetitive geometric patterns, and the
spacing of the stitches creates dark, medium, and light areas
within the design. Traditionally, the embroidery is worked in
black thread on linen. It was very popular in Tudor times,
and was used to decorate clothing and bed linen.*

   *Work the design using backstitch, running stitch, double
running stitch, and cross stitches for stars. Outline different
patterned shapes in chain stitch, stem stitch, or couching.
Work small parts of the design in satin stitch to create solid
black areas to contrast with lighter, open-stitch patterns.
A combination of straight and crossed stitches can be used
to form elaborate borders and large motifs, as shown below.*

BLOCKING & MOUNTING

ONCE FINISHED, MOST pieces of embroidery only require a light pressing on the wrong side of the background fabric. However, if the work has become badly distorted, it will need to be soaked and blocked to remove any creases and to ease it back into shape. There are as many ways to display finished work as there are different types of embroidery. If you plan on framing your work, it must first be mounted.

PRESSING

Never put an iron on the right side of a piece of embroidery as it will flatten the stitches, and may scorch the piece. Place

the embroidery, right side down, on a padded surface. Cover it with a damp or dry cloth (depending on the type of fabric used). With the iron at the correct setting for the fabric, press very gently all over.

MOUNTING

To frame embroidery, the piece first must be mounted on hardboard. The board should be cut to the same size as the work, or slightly larger to accommodate a cardboard mat or

a frame with an edge that might hide some of the stitching. Press the finished embroidery, and lay it right side down on a table. Centre the hardboard on top, and turn the edges of the fabric to the back of the board. Lace the edges together with strong thread, taking evenly spaced stitches. Carefully pull the stitches tight, and secure with a few backstitches. Fold and lace the side edges in the same way, pulling evenly so that the work is stretched smoothly across the board.

BLOCKING

Check that the background fabric and the yarns will not run when wet, otherwise the piece will have to be blocked dry. With modern fabrics this isn't usually a problem, but

care should be taken with old or ethnic fabrics. Soak the embroidery in cold water, and roll it in a clean towel to remove the excess moisture. Cover a soft board with plastic or cotton, and pin it in position. Lay the embroidery on top of the covered board, right side up. Using steel pins, pin the piece at each corner, keeping the pins outside the area of work. Stretch the embroidery, and pin at 2.5 cm (1 in) intervals, starting at the centre. Leave pinned until completely dry.

CLEANING

Dust, dirt and moths are the main enemies of embroidery. Regular inspection, a gentle hand wash and careful storage will guard against all three. If the embroidery is delicate,

play it safe: take it to a specialist rather than attempting to clean it yourself. Most modern embroidery threads are colourfast, but you should still test them before washing. You can either test scraps of the threads in hot water or press a wet cotton ball against the wrong side of the work and check for staining. Dark colours and shades of red are the most likely to run; if this happens, take the piece to a reliable dry cleaner. If the embroidery is lined, the lining should be removed and washed separately. It is a good idea to measure your upholstery covers before washing so that they can be blocked to the correct size afterwards.

ALPHABETS

MANY EMBROIDERED ITEMS are personalised with the addition of monograms, names or words. On the following pages you wlll find a selection of alphabets. These can be enlarged (or reduced) as necessary and then traced onto transfer paper. To get the best effect with the cross-stitch alphabet, choose the size of cloth with the threads per square inch (see page 120) that best shows letters that are fifteen squares high.

Aa Bb Cc Dd Ee
Ff Gg Hh Ii Jj
Kk Ll Mm Nn Oo
Pp Qq Rr Ss Tt
Uu Vv Ww Xx
Yy Zz
1 2 3 4 5 6 7 8 9 0

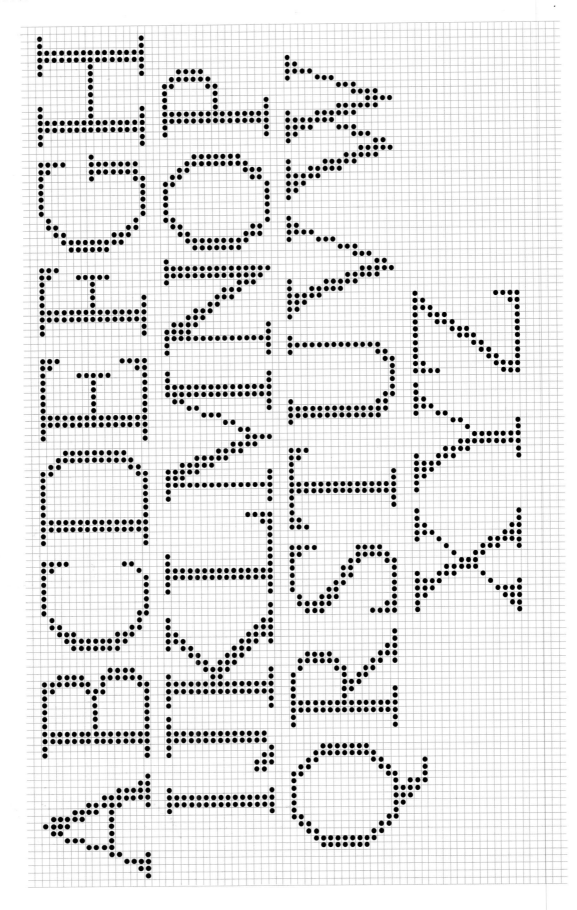

Aa Bb Cc Dd
Ee Ff Gg Hh Ii
Jj Kk Ll Mm
Nn Oo Pp 2q
Rr Ss Tt Uu Vv
Ww Xx Yy Zz
1 2 3 4 5 6 7 8 9 0

MACHINE EQUIPMENT

FOR MACHINE EMBROIDERY it is essential to have an electric sewing machine with a foot pedal, which leaves both hands free to manipulate the fabric. The machine does not have to be complicated; the most basic swing needle (zigzag stitch) machine is all you need to complete any of the projects in this book. Make sure you are familiar with the way your own machine works, how to operate its various controls, alter tension and so on.

TEETH OR FEED

In normal stitching mode, the teeth, which are alongside the needle plate, automatically feed the fabric under the needle. When darning or free stitching, you need to move the fabric in various directions so these teeth must be disconnected or lowered.

MACHINE NEEDLES

Standard needles are labelled with US, British, and continental sizes. For most sewing purposes, using medium-weight fabrics, a 12-80 or 14-90 is suitable but for embroidery, a thicker needle, such as a 16-100, is preferable. If you are not sure which needle to use, practice on a spare scrap of fabric.

Ballpoint needles
These are used when stitching synthetics and jersey fabrics.

Jeans needles
A tapered shape and very sharp point can penetrate tough denim fabrics; also useful for embroidering heavy fabrics or multiple layers.

MACHINE FEET

Open-toe presser foot (A)
Used for most straight and zigzag stitching. this has a "window" of transparent plastic – or may be made entirely of transparent plastic – which allows a good view of stitches in progress.

Darning or quilting foot (B)
This has a spring that enables it to move smoothly over uneven surfaces and allows flexible movement for stitching in different directions.

Cording foot (C)
Used for couching threads or cords, with a groove ensuring that the cord is fed through into the correct position for the needle to stitch over it.

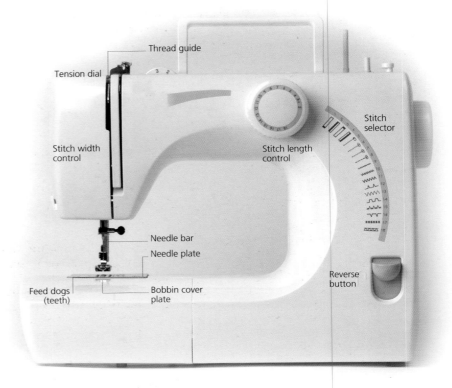

Thread guide
Tension dial
Stitch selector
Stitch width control
Stitch length control
Needle bar
Needle plate
Reverse button
Feed dogs (teeth)
Bobbin cover plate

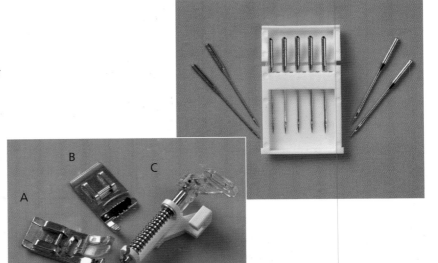

MACHINE THREADS

Ordinary sewing thread is good to experiment with when you are embarking on machine embroidery for the first time. But you will soon want to use some of the more unusual threads specially designed and manufactured for machine embroidery. Also, embroidery threads are often finer and more loosely twisted than mercerised sewing thread, and the fibres have better covering properties.

Cotton and polyester

These embroidery threads behave well with most machine techniques, both with set stitches and freehand embroidery. Look out for matt threads, shiny threads, variegated shades, and even fluorescent colours. Threads made from blended fibres tend to be stronger and less likely to break.

Rayon threads

These offer a subtle, silky sheen. Look for variegated colours and threads that are so shiny they look almost pearlescent. These speciality threads tend to be slightly more expensive that ordinary sewing thread so you may wish to economize by using a less expensive thread of a similar weight and thickness in the bobbin.

Metallic threads

Include types that appear almost to be made of pure spun gold or silver to those which are blended with other threads to produce a more subtle sparkle or glitter. Some metallic threads are easier to work with than others and you will need to experiment to find the ones you like best.

LINING, INTERFACING AND OTHER SUPPORTS

When it comes to embroidery there are easy fabrics and there are "difficult" ones such as very lightweight and sheer fabrics, velvet, lace, and silks, which will require some kind of support or reinforcement before you start to stitch.

You can use a firm, closely woven fabric such as calico or linen as a backing, or one of the special materials designed for the purpose.

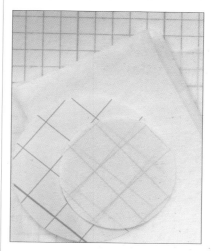

Interfacing

This is available in various weights and in fusible (iron-on) and non-fusible versions. One that is printed with a grid is useful when measuring and cutting.

Bonding web

A double-sided fusible interfacing, this is invaluable in machine appliqué as it will fix one fabric to another. Medium and heavyweight bonding webs attach fabrics without the need for stitching while lightweight webs, which are softer and more flexible, are usually used in association with stitching and are more suitable for delicate fabrics.

Stabilizers

Non-woven materials which look and feel similar to interfacing, these are used as supports under areas of hand or machine embroidery or appliqué. Some have an adhesive backing, protected by a layer of paper, while others are usually tacked in place and the excess torn away after the stitching is completed.

Vanishing fabrics

These are usually used alone to create machine lace but have their uses as a backing for delicate, sheer, or fragile fabrics, too.

MACHINE STITCHES

MANY PROJECTS including those in this book can be completed using the most basic sewing machine provided that it has a swing needle – meaning that it can produce a zigzag stitch. There is no need for a sophisticated machine though, if you have one, you may enjoy substituting other stitches for the ones shown on a project.

MAKING STITCH SAMPLERS

Achieving decorative effects using set stitches is easy. In most instances, your sewing machine can be set up as for normal sewing. Before embarking on any new project, however, it is a good idea to practice the stitches on a spare piece of fabric, in case minor adjustments need to be made to stitch tension. Sewing a sample of each stitch will also help you to decide upon the appropriate width and length to which you should set the dials on your machine.

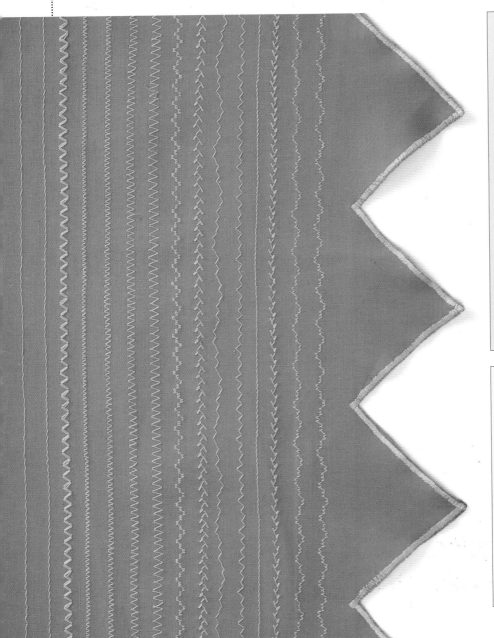

QUILTING FOOT

Using this attachment – sometimes also referred to as a darning foot – will allow you move flexibility when stitching, making it easier to stitch in wavy lines and round shapes, not just in straight lines.

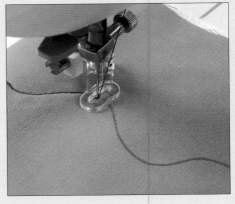

TENSION

Thread tension will affect the quality and appearance of your stitches. As a general rule, if the upper tension is too tight, 'locks' (loops of thread) will appear on the surface of the fabric so you will need to decrease the tension. If the tension is too loose, locks will appear on the reverse, so increase the tension. Check your machine's instruction manual for tips on adjusting tension.

BASIC MACHINE STITCHES

Straight stitch

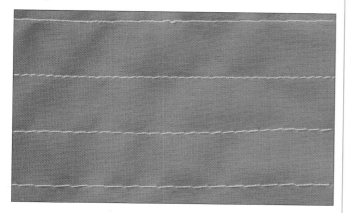

This is the basic sewing machine stitch and, while it is most often used for seams, it also can create decorative lines. When used for freestyle embroidery (see page 160), straight stitch can be made to produce a very different effect.

Straight stitch variation

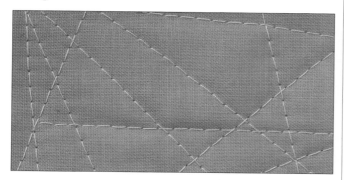

Simply by crossing lines of straight stitch, you can create interesting patterns, either random or more formally arranged. This is also a useful device for quilting two or more layers of fabric.

Herringbone

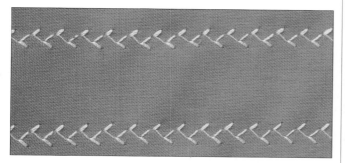

If your machine has this stitch, use it directly on the fabric as surface decoration or to hold down the edges of ribbons and braids. It's also good around the edges of appliqué shapes. You may be able to vary the width and length of the stitch, which will produce different effects.

Zigzag stitch

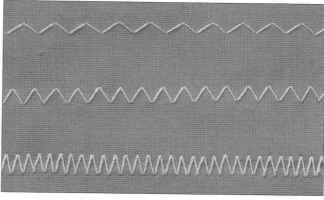

By altering the stitch length and width dials, you can produce lots of variations on the basic zigzag, from an open pattern (top) to a closed "satin stitch" (bottom).

Zigzag stitch variation

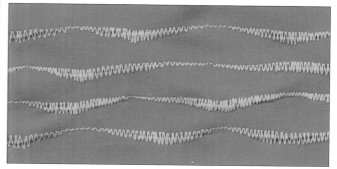

By altering the width of a close zigzag as you stitch, you can create some interesting effects. (Some machines produce this stitch pattern automatically.)

Lightning stitch

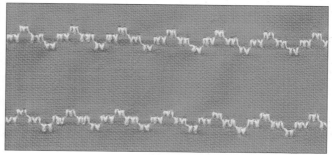

A widely available stitch choice (check your manual). Your machine may produce a similar stitch, or the same stitch with a different name. This is useful for decorative borders and to hold down the edges of ribbons and braids.

DESIGNING FOR A MACHINE

MOST DESIGNS – apart from the simplest lines of decorative stitching or couching – will require some planning and will involve transferring the outlines of a design onto the fabric before you start to stitch. It's also important to consider the suitability of your design: frequently washed items, for example, need firm and flat stitches while little-worn or purely decorative items can take looser stitches and beads.

PLANNING A DESIGN

Machine embroidery, when thickly applied, tends to distort the fabric, so you may also need to use stabilising or interlining materials (see page 153).

Some fancy threads, especially metallics, are more difficult to work with than others, so start with blended threads and progress to the more unusual types when you have gained confidence. Experiment on scraps of fabric and use these experiments to help you come up with your final design.

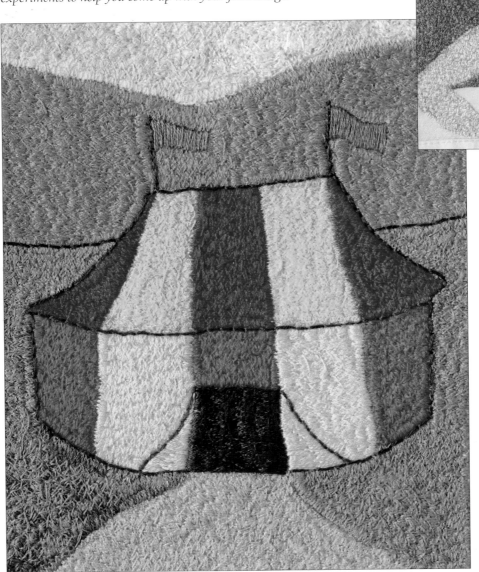

For the big top (left), the stitching covers every part of the fabric for a richly embroidered effect. For the strongman (top), areas of the design have been filled in with freestyle zigzag stitches, leaving a background of unworked fabric.

TRANSFERRING DESIGNS

Several different methods are described on page 125 and these are suitable also for machine embroidery. When using a stabilising fabric, bonding web or interlining, the design often can be drawn on this instead of on the actual fabric.

MEASURING

Each of the projects in this book includes a list of the materials needed to complete the project. When customising a project, however, or embarking on your own designs, you will need to work out how much fabric, thread or other materials you will need. When measuring, always remember to add generous seam allowances; this also applies if the fabric is to be stretched in a hoop or frame.

STITCH CHOICE

Before embarking upon a project, work some sample stitching on a spare piece of the fabric you will be using. This will help to determine whether the stitch is suitable for the fabric, and whether or not the tension, or the width or length of the stitch needs to be adjusted. It is also an opportunity to practise the stitch, to give you more confidence, especially when tackling a new technique for the first time.

SAMPLES

Keep any stitch samples or other experiments. They are a useful reference. You may also be able to incorporate some of them into future projects, or turn them into greetings cards.

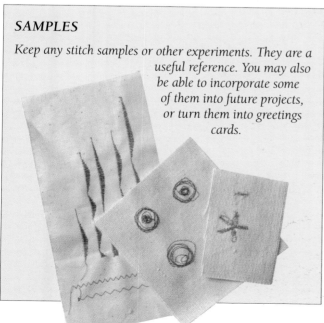

THREAD CHOICE

If you are new to machine embroidery, start by using the same type of thread – preferably a standard sewing thread or a plain machine embroidery thread – in both the needle and the bobbin. As you gain confidence, you can experiment with different thread combinations and you will discover which threads are easiest and most difficult to use.

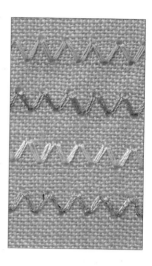

FABRIC CHOICE

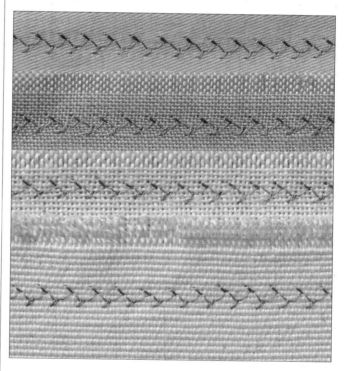

For set stitches, almost any fabric can be used, though evenly woven cottons and linens are the easiest to work with, especially for a beginner.

For freestyle embroidery, you must have a firm, stable base. Medium to heavy fabrics made from natural fibres such as cotton, linen and silk are the best. Really firm fabrics can sometimes be used without any kind of support but, as a general rule, the fabric should be stretched in a hoop. With fine fabrics, you may need to use more than one layer or back the fabric with a stabiliser or support.

Shiny or synthetic fabrics are the most difficult to work with. Synthetics are liable to tear, shiny fabrics to slip and stretchy fabrics to distort.

BORDER MOTIFS

A MACHINE-EMBROIDERED border can be as simple as a line of topstitching along a hem or a zigzag stitch holding a length of cord in place. Utilise the stitches your machine can produce in a creative way — and incorporate other materials such as lace, ribbons, braids, cords and fabric strips — and you can create a range of border designs quickly and easily with the minimum of effort but the maximum impact.

HOW TO CREATE SIMPLE BORDERS

By using the most basic set stitches to hold down ribbons and cords of various widths and materials, you can create richly textured borders.

SCALLOPED EDGE

If your machine offers this scalloped satin stitch effect as an option, you can use it to produce a fancy edging. Thread the top and bottom with the same thread and make sure the stitch is set to form a close zigzag. The fabric should be trimmed close to the stitching — but take care not to cut any of the threads.

Using straight stitch

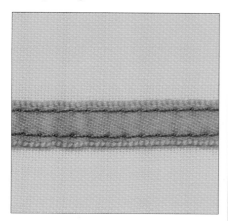

Straight stitch is not just for sewing seams: it can be decorative in its own right. Stitch lines of straight stitch directly on to your fabric, or pin and tack a length of ribbon and use straight stitch to hold it in place.

Using zigzag stitch

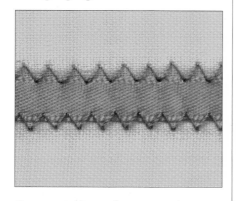

Once again, lines of zigzag can be very decorative but they also have a practical application in holding down the edges of a length of ribbon or braid. Use a thread colour to match the ribbon for a subtle effect, or a contrast colour for greater impact.

Using fancy stitches

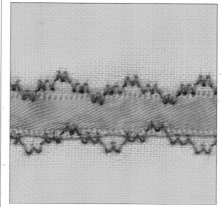

The variety of stitches at your disposal will depend on the type and sophistication of the sewing machine you are using – but even the most basic machine nowadays offers some fancy stitches which can produce highly decorative borders used alone or with lengths of pretty ribbon.

Couching lines of cord

Use a basic zigzag stitch and standard presser foot to hold down a length of cord. Set the stitch width so that the needle goes into the fabric at either side of the cord. This method can be used to place a cord along the edge of a piece of fabric, or for creating straight lines of couching.

Couching with a special foot

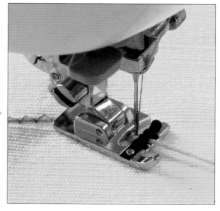

Using a special cording foot allows more flexibility, as the cord – or sometimes two or more cords at a time – are fed through the grooves and trapped by stitches as you go along. The diameter of the groove will limit the thickness of the cord that can be fed through, but it still allows you the freedom to use a variety of cords, including thick metallic threads, and six-stranded embroidery threads (as shown here). With a cording foot, you can move the fabric quite freely as you stitch, so this method can be adapted to create wavy, looped or zigzag borders. To hold down the cord, use a matching or contrasting thread to create various different effects.

FREESTYLE MACHINE EMBROIDERY

USING YOUR SEWING machine to create freestyle patterns opens up a world of new possibilities. Once you have got to grips with the small adjustments you need to make to your machine, and you have practised the techniques on a few spare scraps of fabric, you will be able to move on to more ambitious projects.

FREESTYLE BASICS

The main difference between set stitching and freestyle is that the feed dogs, which usually move the fabric as you stitch, are lowered or covered so that you are free to move the fabric as you wish, in any direction.

Another difference is that you may choose to remove the foot altogether, or to replace the standard presser foot with one suitable for embroidery. Check the accessories that are supplied with your machine: there may be a darning foot, quilting foot or embroidery foot. You will recognise it by the spring mechanism on the needle bar, which allows the foot to move smoothly over uneven fabrics but it has a small ring through which the needle enters the fabric and which exerts a little pressure on that small area of fabric immediately under the needle. For novices, the foot also offers some protection to your fingers.

Before you start to stitch, set the stitch type to straight stitch or zigzag and the stitch length to zero. The zigzag width can be altered according to the effect you wish to achieve: you can decide this by stitching on a small sample of fabric before you embark on a bigger project.

In this example, freestyle zigzag is used to cover the background fabric completely, resulting in a richly embroidered effect that is quick and easy to achieve, even for a relative beginner.

CREATING FREESTYLE EMBROIDERY

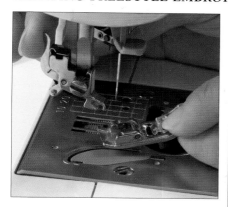

1 Remove the presser foot. You can replace it with a quilting or darning foot, if you wish, or simply leave it off..

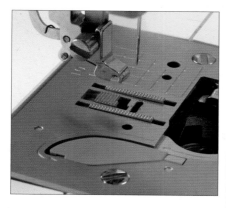

2 Lower the feed dogs. Check your manual to see how to do this.

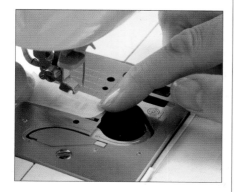

3 If your machine does not allow you to lower the feed dogs, cover them with self-adhesive tape.

4 Draw your design on the fabric. You can draw shapes freehand, use a template (as shown), or any of the methods described on page 125.

5 Stretch the fabric in an embroidery hoop. If the fabric is very thin or unstable, you may need to back it with one of the materials described on page 153.

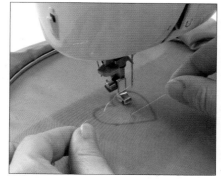

6 Place the fabric flat on the bed of the machine, and lower the drop feed lever. Insert the needle, then lift it and draw the lower thread through to the surface.

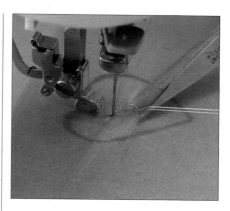

7 Hold both threads as you begin to stitch. After you have made a few stitches, snip off the thread.

8 Move the fabric back and forth and from side to side as you stitch, holding the edges of the hoop. In this case, the stitch used is straight stitch.

9 This method can also be used with zigzag stitch. Once again, make a few initial stitches before snipping off the thread ends.

MACHINE EMBROIDERED FABRICS

AS WELL AS BEING used to decorate fabrics, machine embroidery can be used to create new fabrics. You simply need to use a special material to support the stitching that is afterwards removed completely from the finished work. Start with a small, manageable project such as the corsage on page 274. As you become more accomplished, you will be able to create fabrics ranging from wispy, gossamer-like lace to more robust pieces – and have great fun in the process.

Using one of a number of special fabrics that are removed after stitching (see page 153, you can build up a network of interlocking stitches that produce a lacy effect. It is essential that the stitching should overlap.

The special fabrics used for this method are available from most shops that sell embroidery materials and fall into three basic types.

COLD WATER-SOLUBLE MATERIALS

Available in a variety of types, resembling fine netting, film, fabric or paper, they are ideal for very fine work and are the most commonly available. Being transparent, it is easy to see the stitches being created as you work. Cold water soluble film has been used for the projects in this book.

HOT WATER-SOLUBLE FILM

Stronger and stiffer than cold water-soluables, this can be worked without using a frame. It has the texture and appearance of fine silk and tends to be more expensive than the cold water type but is only suitable for use with threads that are colourfast and that can stand up to very hot water.

VANISHING MUSLIN

This is a loose-weave fabric which, when heated, disintegrates. It is quite stiff, allowing it to be worked without the use of a hoop, but it is also quite brittle and produces a dust when heated that can be an irritant.

CREATING MACHINE LACE FABRICS

1 Draw your design on a piece of vanishing fabric. Stretch the fabric in a hoop.

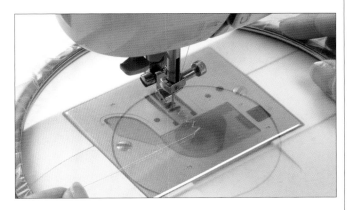

2 Lower the drop feed lever, insert the needle, lift it and draw the lower thread through to the surface. Hold both threads as you begin to stitch.

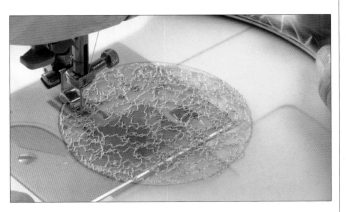

3 After you have made a few stitches, snip off the thread ends close to the fabric, then carry on stitching, moving the hoop in circular motions and making sure that you create a network of overlapping stitches.

4 When you are satisfied that the piece is finished, and that the lines of stitching are all interlinked, remove the vanishing fabric according to the manufacturer's instructions (for example, by dissolving it in cold water).

VANISHING FABRICS

When using vanishing fabrics for the first time, you are advised to use cold water soluble fabric which is the least expensive and most readily available. Most types resemble a sheet of plastic, and must be stretched in a hoop. Begin stitching with a fine-gauge needle and thin thread and move the fabric smoothly as you sew, as jerky movements will invariably cause the material to tear. Any tears, small or large, can, however, be repaired by laying another piece of the materials under the hole and proceeding to stitch. Once you are confident about using the fabric, you can experiment with different threads.

OVERLAPPING STITCHES

It is important to remember that, when stitching on any vanishing fabric, the lines of stitching must overlap and connect or, when the support is removed, the stitching will unravel.

5 Once you have finished stitching, excess vanishing fabric can be trimmed away. Keep these small pieces as they can be used again for other projects, to mend tears or to reinforce small areas of stitching.

PATCHWORK & QUILTING

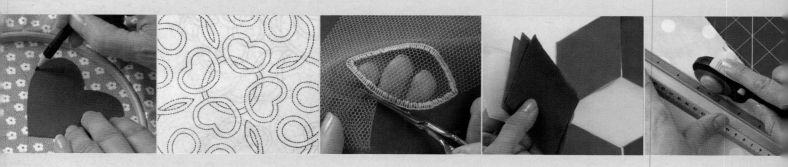

ALWAYS HIGHLY POPULAR, PATCHWORK AND QUILTING can be used to reproduce treasured designs, as well as create the heirlooms of tomorrow. For generations, these crafts were the hub of social gatherings, where quilters contributed their talents towards the completion of a single quilt. While both patchwork and quilting techniques can be used alone, they are most often combined into intricate patterns.

The designs used in patchwork and quilting originate from many different cultures but are generally inspired by everyday objects — let your imagination guide you, as the opportunities for experimentation are endless. The techniques are easy to master, and machine stitching and different cutting techniques make them even more accessible.

Whether you create your own design or use one of the hundreds of established pattern blocks, your choice of colours, textures and fabrics — and their position — will make your project truly unique.

CONTENTS

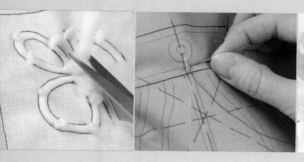   

EQUIPMENT

PATCHWORK AND QUILTING require little in the way of speciality equipment. The correct needle and thread are important and, depending on the complexity of your design, you may need a template, a rotary cutter and board (see page 170), and a quilting hoop. One other vital piece of equipment is a steam iron, which is used in every step of creating patchwork. Steam helps set seams and removes wrinkles from the fabric.

PATCHWORK AND QUILTING TOOLS

The correct needle will make your patchwork or quilting much easier. Most fabric shops sell packs of needles specifically for quilting. Apart from the equipment described below, most of the other tools needed are likely to be found in your sewing box.

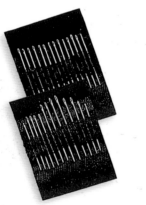

Thimble
Absolutely necessary for quilting – if you have never used a thimble before, you should learn to use one now.

Thread
Use No. 50 cotton thread for hand sewing and a No. 40 cotton thread or a polyester/cotton thread for machine sewing. Always use a 100% cotton thread for quilting.

Needles
Sharps are used for hand sewing; betweens for quilting. A size 8 between needle is recommended for beginners.

Pins
Smooth, fine dressmaker's pins with glass or plastic heads are recommended.

Beeswax
Run your thread over a cake of beeswax to strengthen the thread and prevent it from kinking when hand sewing or quilting.

Embroidery scissors
Use these to clip into seam allowances or to cut thread.

Seam ripper
To remove machine-sewn stitches.

Dressmaker's shears
Use these for cutting fabric only. They should be extremely sharp.

Templates
Used for cutting pattern pieces, these are plastic or metal, or can be made from cardboard or clear acetate (*see page 168*).

Quilting hoop
Wooden hoops, around 35 cm (14 in) diameter, help to keep an even tension on your work as you are quilting.

FABRICS & PATTERNS

MOST TRADITIONAL-STYLE patchwork quilts are constructed of printed fabrics. However, this should not keep you from experimenting with a variety of textures, colours, and designs and exploring the different effects created. Let your imagination and taste guide you. Beginners should use only 100% cotton fabrics, which are easy to work with, keep a crease, and wear well. Choose those with a medium weave, since loosely woven fabrics have little strength and tightly woven fabrics will be difficult to quilt. Wash fabrics in hot water to test for shrinkage and colourfastness, and iron carefully before using.

COLOUR VALUE

In art, value is the relative lightness or darkness of a colour. In patchwork, this quality can be more important than the colour itself. A design can differ substantially depending upon the placement of fabrics of different values. For the best results, combine a mix of light, medium, and dark values.

In addition, colour values are affected by surrounding fabrics. This can be a useful point to exploit if you are working with a limited number of colours and wish to make the best possible use of their difference in value.

PRINT SCALE

Medium-scale prints, which can be compact or widely-spaced are generally the best for patchwork. Small-scale prints can add a subtle texture to a design, while large-scale prints can give the impression of more than one fabric. Stripes and plaids can also be used.

Small-scale prints

Medium-scale prints

Large-scale prints

Stripes and plaids

WADDING

A soft, fibrous material, this is used as a filling between a quilt top and back. Wadding can be bought in a roll of different widths, fibres, and weights. Different weights will suit various quilting purposes.

TEMPLATES

TEMPLATES ARE DURABLE patterns used for cutting out the pieces of a patchwork design. They can be purchased from speciality shops, and are available in metal and plastic in a variety of shapes. Plastic and window templates can be positioned on the fabric to create special effects. Window templates provide for the seam allowance other types do not.

It is also easy to make your own templates. Accuracy is extremely important, so be sure to measure carefully and use sharpened dressmaker's pencils when making the templates and marking the lines on fabric. Always mark patchwork pieces on the wrong side of the fabric. Sharp cutting tools are also necessary for making templates from cardboard or plastic.

TEMPLATE-MAKING SUPPLIES

If you are making a quilt with many pieces, make several templates for each piece and discard when they are worn out.

Marking tools
Use a dressmaker's pencil for all types of fabric.

Template material
Medium-weight cardboard and plastic can be used. Graph paper can be glued to the template to aid cutting.

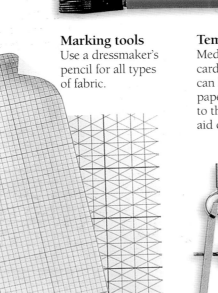

Cutting tools
A utility knife and a metal-edge ruler or scissors will cut through cardboard or plastic.

Temporary adhesive
Use this for sticking paper templates to cardboard and for securing appliqué pieces temporarily to base fabric.

Measuring equipment
A transparent plastic ruler is useful for marking out seam allowances and templates. A compass is extremely useful for drafting curved templates.

MAKING TEMPLATES

Trace pattern pieces from a book, magazine or other source. Alternatively, draw your own design on graph paper. For machine sewing templates or window templates you will need to add a 5 mm (¼ in) seam allowance all around each pattern piece. Label the pieces with letters and the pattern name, then draw a grainline (see below).

1 Cut out your paper pieces and spray the wrong side with temporary adhesive. Leaving 1 cm (½ in) between pieces, press onto a sheet of medium-weight cardboard or clear acetate.

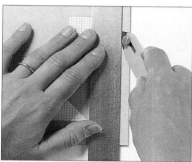

2 Place the cardboard or acetate on a cutting mat or stack of newspaper and use a utility knife and a metal-edge ruler to cut out the templates – either along the edge of the paper or along the marked seamline.

3 For complicated or curved designs, mark notches in the edges of templates to aid in matching the pieces when you sew them together. Cut out notches using a utility knife.

CUTTING OUT FABRIC PIECES

Mark the seamline and cutting lines on the wrong side of the fabric if you are hand sewing. Mark just the outer cutting line if you are machine sewing. As a general rule, mark the longest edge of a patchwork piece along the fabric grain.

For hand sewing

1 Position the pieces at least 1 cm (½ in) apart when marking them on fabric.

2 Either mark the cutting lines, or judge by eye, and cut the pieces apart.

For machine sewing

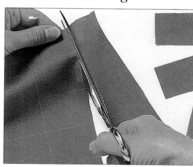

When marking the shapes on fabric, position pieces with edges touching.

GRAIN OF FABRIC

Selvedges are the finished edges of fabric. The lengthwise grain or warp runs parallel to the selvedges and has little give. The crosswise grain or weft runs perpendicular to selvedges and has a slight give. A fabric has its maximum give when it is cut on the bias, which runs at a 45° angle to the selvedges. This information is essential when it comes to positioning and cutting out patchwork pieces. For example, the borders of a quilt should be strong, therefore cut them with the longest edges on the length-wise grain of the fabric. Curved patchwork should be cut with the curves on the bias of the fabric so that the pieces are easier to manipulate.

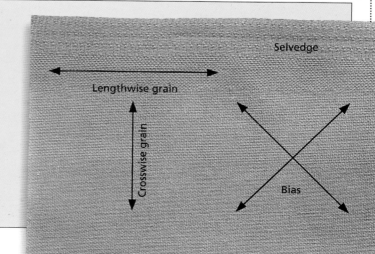

ROTARY CUTTING

ROTARY CUTTING is a fast and accurate method of cutting patchwork pieces without using templates. It is particularly effective when cutting long strips for sashing, borders, bindings, and for Seminole patchwork (see page 178).

ROTARY CUTTING EQUIPMENT

A few simple tools will enable you to cut your pieces without templates.

Roll the blade of the cutter against the ruler. The lines aid in measuring fabric

Cutting mat
This self-healing surface will grip the fabric to prevent slipping, and will keep the rotary cutter's blade sharp.

Rotary ruler
Made in clear plastic and marked with straight and angled lines. Roll the blade against the ruler's edge.

Rotary cutter
This accurately cuts through several fabric layers. Buy one with a large blade, and change the blade often.

Cutting material

1 Align the selvedges evenly, and iron fabric. If the grain of the fabric is not straight, align it before cutting pattern pieces.

2 Place fabric on cutting board with raw edges at right and selvedges at top. Place a set square along straight fold of fabric. Place rotary ruler against left edge of set square. Remove set square.

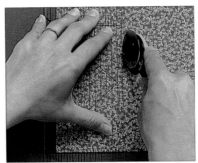

3 Press down firmly on the rotary ruler to prevent shifting. Run the blade of rotary cutter along edge of the ruler, keeping the blade upright. Move your hand carefully up the ruler as you cut. Always push the blade away from you.

4 Fold fabric in half again, aligning fold with selvedges and matching cut edges. Using rotary ruler, measure desired width of strip. With line of ruler along cut edge, cut a strip as you did in Step 3.

5 To make squares, cut a strip 1 cm (¹⁄₂ in) wider than the finished size of the square. Cut off selvedges, then place the ruler over the strip and cut a piece to the same width as the strip to create 4 squares.

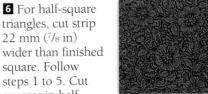

6 For half-square triangles, cut strip 22 mm (⁷⁄₈ in) wider than finished square. Follow steps 1 to 5. Cut squares in half.

7 For quarter-square triangles, use strip 32 mm (1¹⁄₄ in) larger than finished long edge. Repeat to step 6 and cut triangles in half.

PATTERNS

A QUICK WAY to determine the difficulty of a patchwork design is to count the number of pieces in the design – the more pieces there are, the more difficult the design will be, and the more time it will take you to complete it. It is also helpful to study a design to see how many seams need matching, whether several seams must match at one point, and whether there are set-in patches or curved seams. Beginning quilters should select designs with few pieces and seams that are easy to match, such as the Shoo Fly design. The designs shown on here are graded in order of difficulty. Work your way up gradually to the more challenging designs and have the satisfaction of seeing your skills improve.

EASY

Shoo Fly is one of the easiest patchwork patterns to construct. It is composed of nine squares, four of which are pieced from right-angle triangles. Both blocks are made using fabrics in the same colour family. The same design can look very different depending upon the scale of the overall pattern; experiment to see the various effects.

MEDIUM

Grape Basket is a block of medium difficulty. There are many more seams than in Shoo Fly. The illustrations show a variety of fabrics, creating an old-fashioned block, and the graphic look achieved by using solid colours.

Shoo Fly

DIFFICULT

Diamond Star is a challenging block because there is an eight-seam join in the middle and the pieces at the edges must be inset (see page 177). The large illustration shows plaids and stripes, which have to be carefully matched. The inset illustration shows how contrasting values create a feeling of depth.

Diamond Star

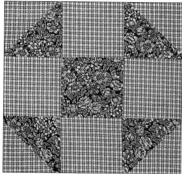

Shoo Fly variation

Grape Basket

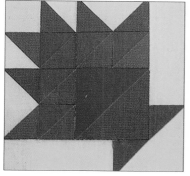

Grape Basket variation

Diamond Star variation

PIECING

ACCURACY IS CRUCIAL when joining many little patchwork seams together. Always sew pieces with the right sides of the fabric together and the raw edges exactly even with each other.

Seam allowances in patchwork are 5 millimetres (quarter of an inch) wide whether you are sewing by hand or machine, and must be marked on the patches when sewing by hand. Hand sewing takes more time but produces a unique look. Stitches made by hand must be evenly spaced, and not too crowded. Today, quilters often machine-piece the quilt top, to save time, and do the quilting by hand.

If machine sewing, use a standard straight stitch at 10 to 12 stitches per 2.5 cm (one inch). The edge of the presser foot or a line on the throat plate of the sewing machine should be used as a stitching guide.

HAND PIECING

Work with 45 cm (18 in) lengths of matching thread knotted at the end. It helps to run the thread over a cake of beeswax to strengthen it and prevent it tangling as you work. Sewing lines are marked on the wrong side of the fabric; seams are sewn from corner to corner along the marked lines.

Holding the needle correctly is essential for good sewing

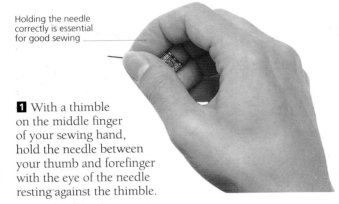

1 With a thimble on the middle finger of your sewing hand, hold the needle between your thumb and forefinger with the eye of the needle resting against the thimble.

2 Hold the fabric so that you can see the sewing lines on each side. Make 2 backstitches at the beginning of the seam and work evenly spaced running stitches along the marked seam lines.

3 Check your stitching to ensure that they are exactly on the marked lines, front and back. Make 2 backstitches at the opposite corner.

Tacking

Use a temporary stitch to secure the pieces before sewing them together. For easy removal, use light coloured thread that will contrast with the fabric. Make spaced running stitches about 5 mm (¹/₄ in) long.

Joining rows

1 Hold the sewn pieces together with the right sides facing, matching the seams carefully, and inserting pins where necessary to secure the pieces.

2 At each seam, knot or backstitch the thread, then insert needle through seam allowance to other side so that you are leaving seam allowances free. Knot or backstitch again before sewing the rest of the seam.

Hand sewing over papers

1 Using outer edge of a window template, cut out fabric pieces. Use inner edge to cut out papers. Centre a paper on wrong side of a fabric piece, then pin. Fold one seam allowance over paper without creasing it; tack one stitch through fabric and paper, leaving tail of thread free and unknotted.

2 Fold adjacent seam allowance over paper, forming a sharp corner. Tack over corner to secure, bringing needle up in middle of next seam allowance. Repeat for remaining edges. Cut thread, leaving end free. Remove pin. Press gently and repeat for other patches.

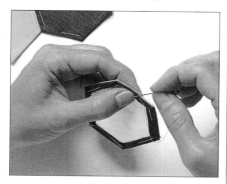

3 To join, place pieces with right sides facing, matching corners. Whip stitch edges together from corner to corner, backstitching at each end. Do not sew in papers. Remove tacking stitches and papers. Gently press finished work.

MACHINE SEWING

Before joining the patchwork pieces, test the sewing machine's tension by stitching on a fabric scrap.

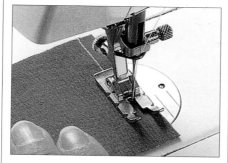

1 Hold the patches together; pin if necessary. Place the edge of the patches beneath the presser foot. Lower it and needle into the edge of the fabric. Stitch forward slowly, guiding the fabric with your hand. At end of the seam, pull out a length of thread and break it.

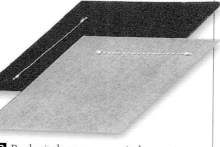

2 Backstitch to secure stitches, using reverse lever on sewing machine, or make stitches tiny. It isn't necessary to backstitch at each edge of each patch – only where you know that a seam or edge will be under stress, or when setting in *(see page 177)*.

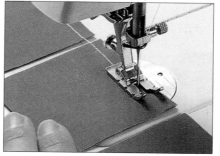

3 Patches can be sewed together in a chain to save time and thread. Feed each new set of patches beneath presser foot. Feed dogs will draw them beneath needle. Cut chain apart with scissors after sewing, and press seam allowances.

CORRECTING MISTAKES

If stitches cause the fabric to pucker, remove them carefully.

Use a seam ripper to remove unwanted stitches. Cut through every 3rd or 4th stitch on one side. On the opposite side, pull the thread – it should lift away easily.

Joining rows

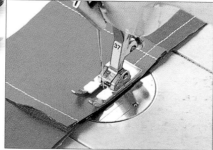

Make sure that the matching seam allowances are pressed in opposite directions to reduce bulk and to make matching the seam easier. Pin the pieces together directly through the stitching, and to the right and left of the seam to prevent the pieces from shifting as you sew.

To save time, several sections of patches can be sewn up at one sitting and then snipped apart

BASIC PATCHWORK

FOR YOUR FIRST patchwork pattern, choose one of the simpler ones – we show some patterns here in order of increasing difficulty. The assembly diagrams will help you construct the patchwork blocks. Draw these patterns on graph paper to the desired size, and make templates (see page 168) to mark and cut out the patches you need. When pieces are asymmetrical, such as in the Box design, you will need to reverse some of the pieces when cutting out. Simply flip the template over and mark the outline on the fabric as usual. Blocks are assembled in sections, starting with the smallest pieces and building up from these.

Turnstyle
This four-patch design is relatively simple, and a good starting point for beginners. It is made up of identical quarters which are rotated through a circle in order to make the pattern. It is also known as Oh Susannah. Cut 4 dark and 4 light of A, and 4 medium of B. (Total of 12 pieces.)

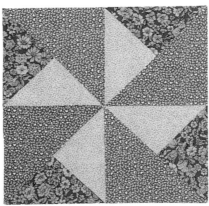

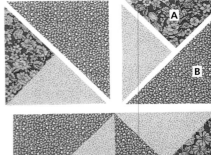

Prairie Queen
This is a nine-patch block where all the patches are pieced except the centre one. The corner patches are half-square triangles, and the others simple quarters. Cut 8 medium and 8 dark of shape A, 4 light and 4 bright of B; and 1 bright of C, making 25 pieces in all.

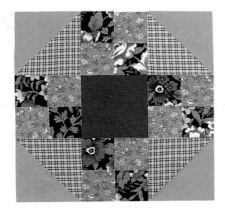

Old Tippecanoe
Irregular sized patches make up this block. If shape A is the basic square, shape B is its quarter-square triangle, and shape C is its half-square triangle. You will need 1 dark of shape A; 8 light, 4 medium, and 8 bright of shape B; and 4 dark of shape C. There are 25 pieces in all.

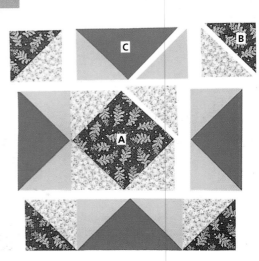

Cross & Crown

A more complex nine-patch block where the 4 corner patches are pieced. Cut 8 bright and 8 dark of shape A; 4 bright of shape B; 4 light of shape C; 4 bright of shape D; and 1 light of shape E; a total of 29 pieces.

A cushion with a Cross & Crown pattern – a variation on a nine-patch block

Basket of Scraps

This is an irregular block that is made with straight seams. It is fairly complex as it is composed of 7 different shaped pieces. You need 2 light and 2 bright of shape A, 1 medium of B, 2 medium of C, 1 dark of D, 2 medium of E, 2 dark of F, and 1 medium of G; a total of 13 pieces.

Box

A complex pattern where shape A has to be reversed in order to cut the pieces. Cut 4 pieces of shape A (1 check, 1 bright, 1 medium, and 1 dark), and 8 pieces of A reverse (1 check, 1 bright, 3 medium, and 3 dark). You will also need 4 light of shape B; 2 stripe and 2 bright of shape C; and 4 light of shape D; a total of 20 pieces.

SPECIAL TECHNIQUES

PATCHWORK CHALLENGES a sewer's ingenuity. There are times when you will need to execute some intricate manoeuvres to create certain types of designs involving complex seams and joins. These techniques may seem daunting to the beginner patchworker, but are easily mastered with a bit of experience. Practise some of these techniques with scrap fabrics so that you'll be confident when you begin a project.

CURVED SEAMS

Curved seams have to be eased to fit so the pieces join smoothly and the seam does not pull or pucker.

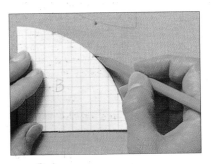

1 Cut out pieces with curves on bias of fabric. When joining curved edges, curves bend in opposite directions. Mark evenly spaced notches on seamline for matching.

2 Match central notches on both pieces and pin together, then align side edges and pin. Match and pin any other notches, then continue pinning, easing and smoothing pieces to fit.

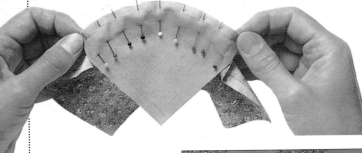

3 Sew pieces together by hand or machine, securing beginning and end of seam with backstitches. Carefully press seam allowance toward darker fabrics, clipping where necessary so seam allowance lies flat and the front of the work lies flat.

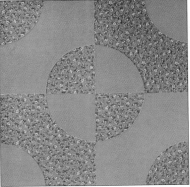

EIGHT-SEAM JOIN

Sew the diamonds together, beginning and ending the seam with backstitches 5 mm (¹/₄ in) from the edges. Sew two pairs of diamonds together to form each half of the design.

1 To hand sew halves together, insert a pin through point of centre diamond on wrong side of one piece, 5 mm (¹/₄ in) away from edge to be joined. The same pin should be inserted through right side of other piece at same point.

2 Pin the remainder of the seam, then stitch carefully. Press from the wrong side, opening up the seam allowance around the centre point to reduce the bulk.

The points of the pieces should all meet accurately at one centre point in the finished point.

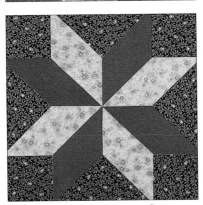

A machine-sewn eight-seam join should look like this on the back.

The stitching passes directly over the point of the uppermost diamond

SETTING IN

This is done when you have to sew a piece into an angle formed by joined pieces. When sewing the initial pieces, end your stitching 5 mm (¹/₄ in) from the edge. Backstitch or knot the end. Mark a dot on the corner of the piece to be inset to show the position of the corner.

Hand sewing

1 If sewing by hand, pin the patch to be inset into the angle with right sides together, matching the dots exactly. Stitch seam from the outer edge toward the centre. Make a backstitch at the central dot.

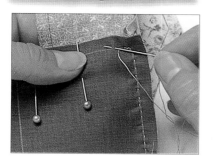

2 Swing the adjacent edge of the patch to align it with the other edge of the angled piece, then continue stitching the adjacent seam backstitching at the end.

Machine sewing

1 To sew by machine, pin the patch to be inset into the angle with right sides together, matching the dots exactly. Stitch the seam from the centre toward the outer edge. Break the thread.

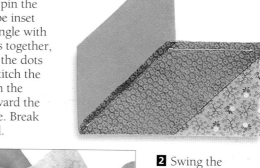

2 Swing the adjacent angled piece to the other edge of the patch and pin. Stitch from centre to outer edge. There should be no puckers on the right side of the work. Clip off any threads. Press carefully.

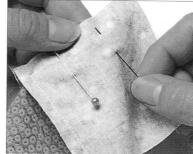

The seams are carefully matched at the corners

PRESSING

Always press seam allowances to one side to make the seams stronger, not open as in dressmaking. If possible, press seam allowances toward the darker fabric. If this is not possible, trim the seam allowance so that the dark fabric does not show through to the right side. If you are pressing small patchwork pieces, it may be easier to press from the right side: place the light piece of the patchwork wrong side down on the ironing board, then with the tip of the iron, smooth the dark fabric upward and open.

Finger pressing

To save time or when sewing over wadding, use this method to crease fabrics in position without an iron. Run your index finger or a thumbnail several times over the area until the crease holds.

Hand sewing

Because the seam allowances are left free, you must open them up before pressing, in order to reduce the bulk at the join.

Machine sewing

Press every piece before it is crossed by another. Always press intersecting seam allowances in opposite directions. After joining, press the new seam allowance toward darker fabric.

SEMINOLE PATCHWORK

CREATED BY THE Seminole Indians of Florida around the turn of the century, this form of patchwork is a variation on strip piecing. Seminole patchwork has become increasingly popular and is often used for long borders and insertions. You will need a rotary cutter, and it is essential that you are accurate when matching and sewing seams. Although the finished result looks intricate, the method is not difficult.

Cutting and sewing the strips

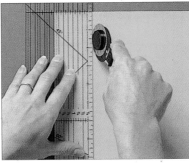

1 Choose a pattern from below and, using a rotary cutter, cut the required number of strips. Coat the strips lightly with spray starch to make them easier to handle, and press. Sew the strips together in the combinations given with the design. Press the seam allowances toward the darker fabrics.

2 Cut the strips into pieces of the required width, and arrange on your cutting mat to follow the design shown.

3 Sew the pieces together in a chain (*see page 173*) either alternating the pieces or offsetting them as directed. Press the strip carefully.

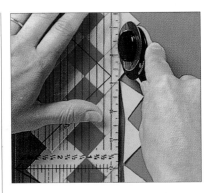

4 Use a rotary cutter to trim the top and bottom edges evenly if necessary. Remember to leave a 5 mm (¼ in) seam allowance all round.

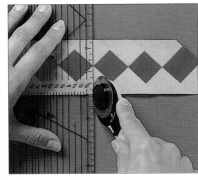

5 You can straighten the angled ends of Seminole patchwork by making a straight cut through the patchwork. If you have seams that do not quite match, make your cut through this area.

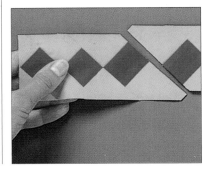

6 Re-arrange the pieces, aligning the diagonal edges. Sew these edges together, matching the seams carefully.

NOTE:
The instructions on these pages assume you are working with 112 cm (45 in) wide fabrics. Cut all the strips across the full width of the fabric, then trim off 1 cm (½ in) from selvedge ends, to leave you with a 110 cm (44 in) long strip.

The colourful strips of Seminole patchwork are easy to master

Pattern 1

Cut 1 light 2 cm (³/₄ in) strip, 1 dark 2 cm (³/₄ in) strip, and 2 medium 3.5 cm (1½ in) strips. Sew together to make a pieced strip 7.5 cm (3 in) wide. Cut the strip into 3.5 cm (1½ in) pieces. Invert 1 piece and sew the pieces together, matching the seams.

Pattern 2

For the A pieces, cut 2 dark 4.5 cm (1³/₄ in) strips, 2 medium 3.5 cm (1½ in) strips and 1 bright 3.5 cm (1½ in) strip. Sew together to make a pieced strip 15 cm (6 in) wide. For the B pieces, make a pieced strip as follows: cut 1 dark 9.5 cm (3³/₄ in) strip, 1 medium 3.5 cm (1½ in) strip, and 1 dark 4.5 cm (1³/₄ in) strip. Sew together to make a pieced strip, 15 cm (6 in) wide. Cut the pieced A and B strips into 3.5 cm (1½ in) pieces. Arrange one B piece on each side of an A piece, with one of the B pieces in an inverted position, as shown. Arrange the pieces so that the medium squares line up on each side of the bright square. Sew together, matching the seams.

Invert every alternate B piece in order to complete the pattern sequence

The basic pieced strip made up of five strips in graded widths

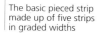

Pattern 3

For A, cut 2 dark 3.5 cm (1½ in) strips, 2 medium 5 cm (2 in) strips and 1 bright 2.5 cm (1 in) strip. Sew together to make a pieced strip 15 cm (6 in) wide. Cut strip into 3.5 cm (1½ in) pieces. For B, cut 5 bright 3.5 cm (1½ in) strips. Cut these into 15 cm (6 in) lengths – a total of 28 pieces. Arrange an A piece on each side of a B. Offset the pieces by 1 cm (½ in); sew together, alternating A and B.

LOG CABIN PATCHWORK

THIS PATCHWORK TECHNIQUE involves sewing strips of fabric around a central shape to produce a variety of effects. It is essential that you work with strongly contrasting fabrics so that one half of the block is light and the other half is dark. Identical Log Cabin blocks can be arranged to make numerous different pattern combinations.

There are two main ways to sew a Log Cabin block. One is to sew all the pieces onto a muslin base. This is a good method for combining fabrics of different weights and textures as the base provides a firm foundation. However, the finished product will be difficult to quilt since there is an extra layer of fabric that must be sewn through. You can get around this by using wadding for the base, or placing the wadding on the base and sewing and quilting at the same time.

The second method, shown here, does not require any templates, unless you are using an unusual shape for the centre of the block. Rotary cutting will simplify the cutting process and save time.

TRADITIONAL LOG CABIN BLOCK

The red square in the middle represents the hearth of the log cabin, while the strips symbolise the logs of the cabin walls. The dark and light portions of the block show the effect of sunshine and shadow on the cabin in day and night. To construct the block, begin in the middle and work around in a anticlockwise direction.

Working without templates

1 Make sure the light and dark fabric you choose contrast sharply. Cut strips to desired width plus 1 cm (¹/₂ in) seam allowance – making sure to cut across entire width of fabric.

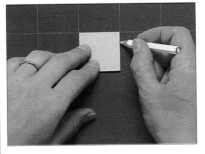

2 The centre can be any shape, although it is usually a square. If you choose another shape, you must make a template and cut the shape with a rotary cutter. Red is traditionally used for the centre.

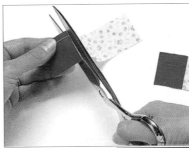

3 With right sides facing, place the centre square against a light strip, matching the edges. Stitch, then cut the strip even with the square. Press the seam allowance towards the centre.

4 Alternatively, if you wish to use the same fabric for all the first strips in your quilt, sew the centre pieces to the first strip one after another, leaving only a small space between each. Cut the pieces apart, trimming them to the same size as the centre square.

5 Choose a different light fabric for the 2nd strip and sew to the pieced centre, trimming away the excess fabric so it is even with the centre. Press lightly.

6 Again, to make all the blocks exactly the same, sew these pieces to the 2nd strip leaving only a small space between each. Cut the pieces apart, trimming them to the same size as the pieced centre. Continue adding around centre if you want every block to have the same fabric arrangement.

7 Pick a dark fabric for the 3rd strip. Continuing anticlockwise, sew the pieced centre to the 3rd strip, trimming away the excess strip so it is even with the centre. Press lightly.

8 Select a different dark fabric for the 4th strip. Sew to the pieced centre, trimming away the excess fabric as before. Press lightly.

9 Continue working anticlockwise, adding 2 light strips, then 2 dark strips in turn around the centre. Avoid placing the same fabrics next to each other. Trim the strips and press lightly after each addition.

10 Once you have made the required number of blocks for your quilt or wall hanging, arrange the blocks in a variety of positions to see the different effects you can achieve by transposing the dark and light portions of the blocks. Examples are shown here.

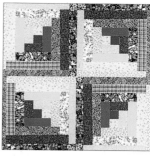

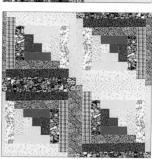

An arrangement of Log Cabin blocks makes a strong pattern

APPLIQUÉ

IF YOU HAVE EVER patched a pair of jeans or sewn a badge onto a child's school uniform then you have appliquéd. The word means applied, and the technique is simply to stitch one fabric on top of another. Functional or purely decorative, appliqués can be hand or machine made, and the stitches used to secure the appliqués to the background fabric can be invisible, such as a slip stitch, or visible and part of the decorative effect, such as satin stitch.

APPLIQUÉ QUILT

Huge stylized strawberry motifs are appliquéd down the centre and sides. The motif is quilted in the resulting spaces while its shape is echoed in the quilting on the background.

In appliqué work, you can use many different fabrics in one project, provided that the finished item will not be subjected to heavy wear and frequent washing. The combination of diverse fabrics, such as tweeds, corduroys, silks, and satins, and the use of buttons, beads, and sequins, can create marvellous effects. Beginners may wish to appliqué using felt because it is easy to work with and doesn't fray. Or, choose tightly woven 100% cotton fabrics that are not likely to fray.

APPLIQUÉ DESIGNS

If you are a beginner, select an appliqué design with straight lines or gradual curves and a relatively small number of large or medium-sized pieces. As you become adept at turning the edges under smoothly and sewing them invisibly to a fabric background, you can graduate to more complex shapes and designs. Templates for hand and machine appliqué have no seam allowances so that you can mark the exact outline of the piece on the fabric. Basting lines on your base fabric will help you place the appliqué pieces.

Cutting appliqués

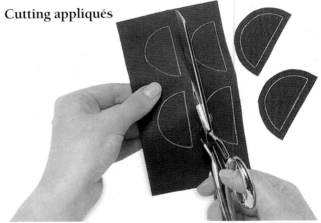

Make templates to finished size (*see page 168*. Mark outline on right side of fabric, leaving 1 cm (¹/₂ in) in between each. Cut out pieces, adding a 5 mm (¹/₄ in) seam allowance.

Preparing the base fabric

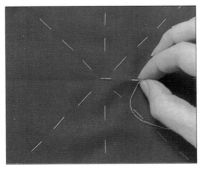

Cut fabric for base 2.5 cm (1 in) larger than desired size. Fold base in half horizontally, vertically, and then diagonally, and press folds. Open fabric and baste along each fold with contrasting thread. Press flat.

HAND APPLIQUÉ

Floral, geometric, or pictorial themes all work well in appliqué. If necessary, enlarge or reduce your design and transfer it to paper.

1 Draw design and label each piece by letter. Trace design and make a template for each appliqué. Label each template with the correct letter. Mark outline of appliqués on right side of fabric and cut, adding a 5 mm (¹/₄ in) seam allowance.

2 Use tip of a sharp pair of scissors to clip into curved edges perpendicular to marked outline of piece; do not clip beyond the outline. Make extra clips along deep curves for ease in turning.

3 Using a design tracing, pencil outlines of pieces on right side of base about 5 mm (¹/₄ in) within outline, to avoid marks showing around edges.

4 Following placement lines, arrange appliqués on the base. Position the background pieces first, with foreground pieces overlapping if necessary. Pin or baste pieces to base.

5 Turn raw edges of the appliqués 5 mm (¹/₄ in) to the wrong side, using the tip of your needle as a tool for turning.

6 Using matching thread and making tiny invisible slip stitches, sew the appliqués to the base fabric, starting with the background pieces and finishing with the appliqués that are topmost.

7 Turn completed design to wrong side and very carefully cut away base fabric within all the larger appliqué pieces, leaving a 5 mm (¹/₄ in) seam allowance. This prevents any puckers, and makes quilting easier.

8 Remove the pins or tacking threads after the appliqué is finished. Press the appliqués lightly on a thick towel so that the seam allowances do not show through to the right side.

SPECIAL APPLIQUÉ TECHNIQUES

Complex shapes will require you to use special techniques in order to achieve a smooth edge to your appliqué pieces, and prevent the seam allowance from distorting the shape.

Points

Trimming your seam allowance will help you make neat points

1 First clip into seam allowance 5 mm (¹/₄ in) from tip on each side and trim seam to 3 mm (¹/₈ in). Trim off point 3 mm (¹/₈ in) from turning line. Fold point to wrong side along turning line.

2 Fold one edge of appliqué 5 mm (¹/₄ in) to wrong side. Press, then tack in place. Fold 2nd edge to wrong side, overlapping first edge at top and bottom. Steam and tack.

Valleys

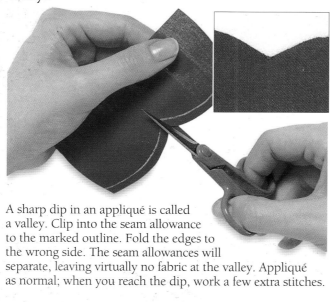

A sharp dip in an appliqué is called a valley. Clip into the seam allowance to the marked outline. Fold the edges to the wrong side. The seam allowances will separate, leaving virtually no fabric at the valley. Appliqué as normal; when you reach the dip, work a few extra stitches.

Circles

1 Make a thin cardboard template to the exact size of the circle required. Cut out a circle of fabric for the appliqué piece 1 cm (¹/₂ in) larger in diameter than the template just prepared.

2 Work a row of tacking stitches close to the edge of the fabric circle.

3 Place the cardboard template in the middle of the wrong side of the fabric circle. Gently pull the tacking stitches to gather the edge of the fabric circle around the cardboard template. Make a few backstitches to secure the end of the thread.

4 Press the circle gently so that there are no puckers on right side. Then, remove the cardboard from the circle without distorting shape.

MACHINE APPLIQUÉ

Before starting, change to a new needle and a zigzag foot; use 100% cotton thread to match the appliqué. Because the seam allowances are not turned under, technically you do not need to add an allowance when cutting out your pieces. However, it is not easy to keep the pieces from puckering when stitching very close to the edges. Therefore, the steps shown here show a seam allowance, which is trimmed away after stitching. Test your stitch on a scrap of fabric. Use a standard width of 3 mm (1/8 in) for medium-weight fabrics. Fine fabrics will require a narrow stitch width, and heavy fabrics need a wider one. The tension should be even and should not pucker the fabric. If the bobbin thread shows through to the right side, loosen the top tension of the sewing machine .

1 Cut out the appliqués and prepare the base as directed on page 182. Follow steps 1, 2, and 4 for Hand Appliqué. Arrange the pieces in their correct position on the base fabric and attach, using a fabric glue stick and basting stitches.

2 Machine stitch along the marked outline of each appliqué, using matching thread to make short straight stitches.

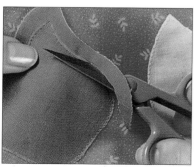

3 Using sharp embroidery scissors, carefully trim away the excess seam allowance beyond the stitching line, cutting as close to your machine stitches as possible.

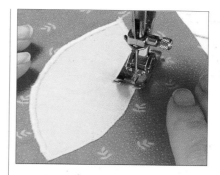

4 Zigzag stitch over line of stitches, covering raw edges of fabric. Gently guide fabric around curves so that machine sews smoothly. Work slowly so that you have complete control over your stitching.

STITCH EFFECTS

Use zigzag satin stitch to add details that are too small to make in fabric, such as veining on leaves, or to delineate flower petals. You can also use machine embroidery stitches to create a variety of other embellishments. A highly contrasting thread will also create special effects in machine appliqué, with black or dark grey creating a stained glass appearance.

Perfect points on leaf shapes can be achieved with a little care

Embroidery details such as the spots and antennae on this ladybird, are made with tiny satin stitches

LACE & INSERTION APPLIQU

FINE FABRICS CAN be decorated with solid, lace or net motifs. These are applied to the surface of ground fabric and outlined with hand embroidery to secure them. The ground fabric is then cut away from beneath them, in order to create light behind the motifs and a more interesting effect. As well as commercially available motifs from notions departments, vintage slips are another good source.

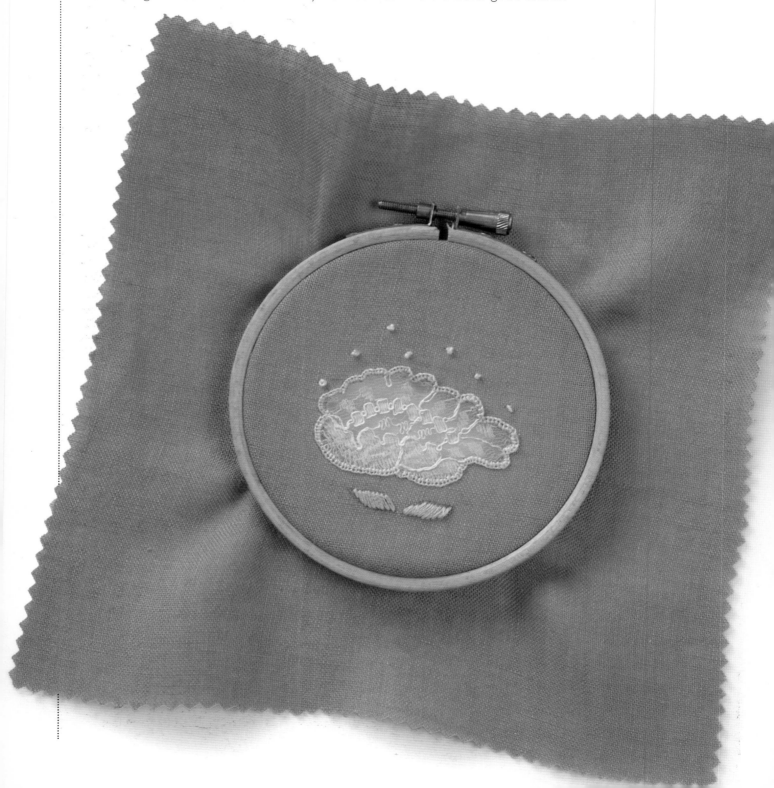

WORKING APPLIQUÉS
Lace Applique

1 Firmly stretch your ground fabric in a hoop and then pin and baste the lace motif(s) on top.

2 Work around the edges of the motif with close blanket stitch (see page 131) or satin stitch (see page 129 (to cover the edges.

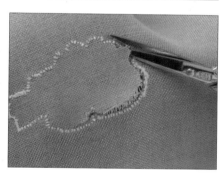

3 When the motif is completely outlined, remove the fabric from the frame and cut away the ground fabric from beneath, using blunt ended scissors.

EMBROIDERED DECORATION

To augment a motif, stitching can be used to reinforce a theme. Here, some French knots (see page 132) and satin stitch leaves have been added to suggest a flower.

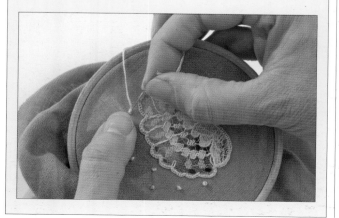

Solid motif on net ground

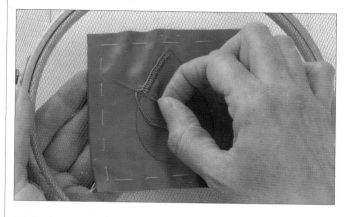

1 Mark the design on your ground fabric and then baste this on top of the net. Stitch over the outlines through both layers, using close blanket stitch (see page 131).

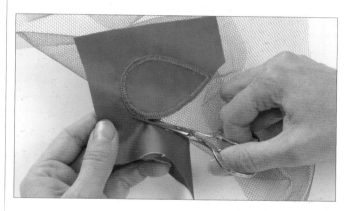

2 When you have finished stitching, remove the basting threads and cut away the surplus material outside the motif close to the design lines, using blunt-ended scissors.

Net motif on a solid ground

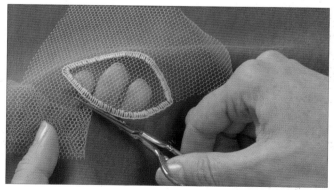

Mark the design on the ground fabric and then baste the net on top of it. Stitch over the outlines through both layers of fabric using close blanket stitch (see page 131) and then remove basting threads. Using blunt-ended scissors, cut away the ground from inside the motif and excess net around it.

CRAZY PATCHWORK

PROBABLY THE EARLIEST type of patchwork, this technique was born out of the necessity to mend tattered clothing or blankets. During the Victorian era crazy patchwork evolved into an art form in its own right when women used it as a medium for displaying their fine needlework skills.

Crazy patchwork can be as simple or as elaborate as you wish to make it. It is an enjoyable technique that can make use of all the bits of fabric that you hate to part with, but that you can't use in a larger project. To make a Victorian-style crazy quilt, collect all the rich silks, brocades, and velvet fabrics you can find. Sew them in a random fashion to a base fabric, then embroider over the seams with silk embroidery floss in a variety of fancy patterns. You can also stitch small motifs in the middle of some of the patches.

This flower has a chain stitch stem. Metallic thread is used for the couched surface decoration

Padded appliqué emphasises the cat's shape. The face is worked in small, straight stitches

Here, the details are worked in straight stitch, buttonhole, and double feather stitch. Sequins add an exotic touch

FOLDED STAR

THIS TYPE OF patchwork is composed of folded rectangles, arranged in overlapping layers to form a star design on a base of lightweight foundation fabric. 5.5 by 10 cm (2½ by 4 in) rectangles are positioned on the base in rounds so that their centres are aligned with lines on the base. Folded star pattern is ideal for wallhangings and cushions or could be framed as a sampler. Highly contrasting fabrics make the most of this technique and one colour of fabric should be arranged in each round. To achieve a perfect star, the points of each round must be the same distance away from the centre. The folds conceal unfinished edges that could fray from wear and frequent washing and the folding also means that the amount of fabric used makes the finished work thick and heavy, so this pattern is not suitable for a quilt top.

MARKING QUILTING PATTERNS

THERE ARE A NUMBER of ways to transfer a quilt design to the fabric; the important thing to bear in mind is that many methods leave discernible lines that will have to be covered by your stitching.

VISIBLE AND INVISIBLE METHODS

All designs are marked on the top layer of the item to be quilted. Using chalk, silverpoint pencil, pins, or water-soluble or fading ink will produce lines that are easily removed or practically invisible while dressmaker's carbon paper, and tracing with a regular or coloured pencil will leave more permanent marks.

Design know-how

It's important to bear in mind that when you create your own patterns using a transfer pencil on paper, or use printed iron-on transfers, the pattern will be reversed on the fabric. You can correct this on your own designs by drawing them in mirror image.

PRICK AND POUNCE

This is a traditional technique that is ideal to use with intricate designs. You can buy perforated patterns or draw your own design on paper. Then prick holes down all the lines of the design with a hand or unthreaded sewing machine needle. Pounce, a type of powder, is no longer available but you can use talcum powder or dust chalk. Position your design over your material and using powder or chalk on a cotton ball, rub this gently over the holes. Alternatively, you also can use a washable colour marker to dot through the holes.

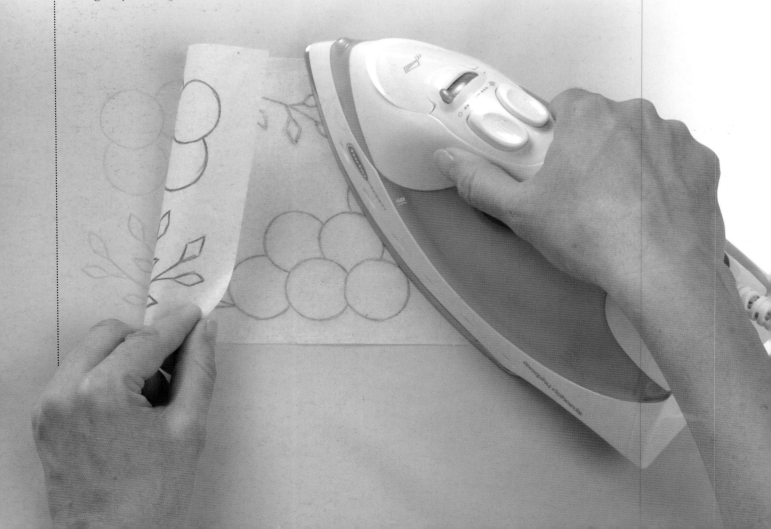

METHODS FOR MARKING PATTERNS

Using Templates

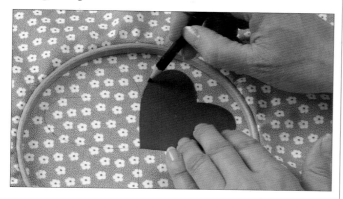

Place your template on the fabric's right side. With a pencil, trace around the outside of the shape. If your fabric is very pale, you may be able to trace through it; in this case place your template or stencil (see below) underneath.

Using stencils

Place your stencil on the fabric's right side. With a pencil, trace around the inside for a stencil.

For Repeating Patterns

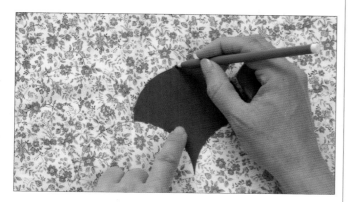

If you are using a template to draw a repeating shape, work from the centre outward. If you like, mark the template with a notch where the shapes overlap. Make sure you first tack horizontal and vertical centring lines so you have a guide as to placing the templates evenly across your fabric.

Using dressmaker's carbon paper

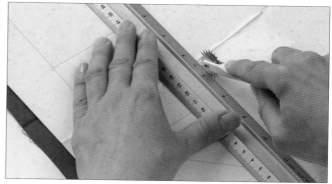

Choose a colour close to that of your top fabric. Lay it face down on the fabric's right side and place your pattern on top. Run a dressmaker's tracing wheel over all the lines. A dotted line will emerge. For small or intricate patterns, use a pencil or ballpoint pen instead of a wheel.

Using iron-on transfers

Transfer pencils can be used to draw a design onto paper, which can be transferred to your fabric by pressing with a warm iron.

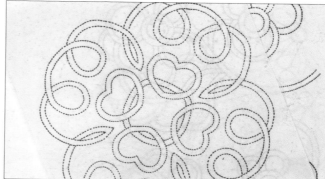

Iron-on printed transfer papers are also available; these will leave dark lines that will not wash out, so your stitching must be thick enough to cover the lines. Some quilting patterns are available with less noticeable silver-grey transfer lines.

QUILT PATTERNS

PATTERNS CAN COVER the entire top or be used just for borders. The important thing is that they have evenly-spaced lines – and plenty of them – to secure the wadding. Because of their generally smaller scale, border patterns work best on baby quilts or to trim garment sleeves and hems.

WORKING WITH PATTERNS

The earliest quilts were often stitched in straight and diagonal lines, creating simple squares and diamond shapes. More elaborate motifs can be created using templates, stencils or perforated patterns. The patterns shown here can be enlarged to suit your own project and transferred using the techniques on pages 190-91. If you want to create your own designs for a simple outline shape, bear in mind that the filling lines are there to secure the wadding. Always try to create an evenly spaced design.

Leaf

WHOLECLOTH MOTIFS

The Leaf (opposite) and Medallion and Clam shell designs (below) are all examples of patterns that are suitable for the entire quilt top.

BORDER PATTERNS

The Connecting hearts and Grape vine patterns (below)can be used to make a suitable border to work continuously around a quilt.

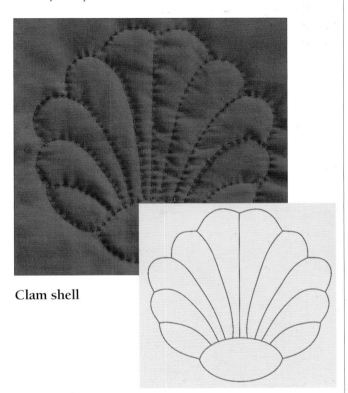

Clam shell

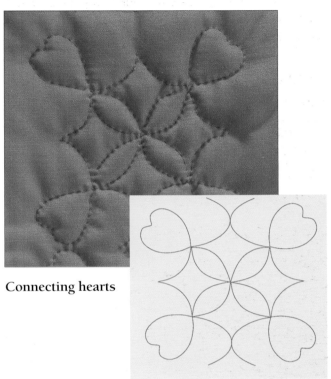

Connecting hearts

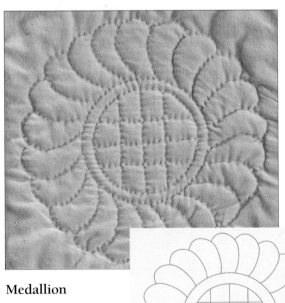

Medallion

Grape vine

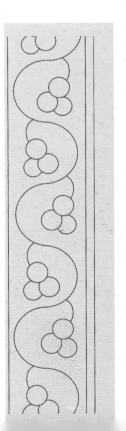

CONSTRUCTING A QUILT

THERE ARE MANY ways to join patchwork blocks together to make a quilt. Each method produces very different results, even when the same patchwork blocks are used. Shown here are some of the traditional ways of joining patchwork blocks. Sashing refers to fabric strips that surround each block of a quilt. In edge-to-edge, the blocks are sewn directly together. Connector squares, or posts, join the short sashing strips that frame individual blocks. Appliqué is used to hide seams and decorate the blocks.

SCRAP QUILT

This Evening Star scrap quilt features blocks set together with grey sashing strips and navy posts (connector squares).

EDGE-TO-EDGE SETTING

This variation on the Card Trick design has a pieced ribbon border. The blocks form a secondary pattern.

SASHING

The medallion style blocks of this Lone Star quilt are framed with green sashing.

BALTIMORE QUILT

The seams between the blocks of this Baltimore Album style quilt are decorated with red appliqué made to resemble lace.

ASSEMBLING A QUILT

A QUILT IS a sandwich composed of three layers – the quilt top, the wadding, and the quilt back. The layers are held together with quilting stitches (see pages 196 and 197) or by tying (see page 204). Tack the layers carefully before you quilt to prevent creases and puckers forming on the back of the finished quilt.

Putting quilt layers together

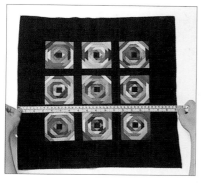

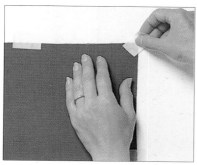

1 Measure your quilt top to find the size of quilt back. Add a 5 cm (2 in) margin all round. This will be trimmed off later. You may have to join pieces for quilt back, but usually only one central seam is required. If the quilt is large, you may need to join 3 pieces.

2 Press the quilt back carefully and lay it on a large flat surface, wrong side up. If you can, tape edges of quilt back in place to prevent fabric from shifting as you work.

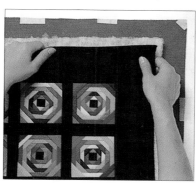

3 Cut a piece of wadding the same size as the quilt top. Place in the centre of the quilt back. Carefully iron the quilt top and remove any loose threads or bits of fabric. Then, place it right side up on the wadding.

4 Pin the layers together with long straight pins so that they don't shift while tacking.

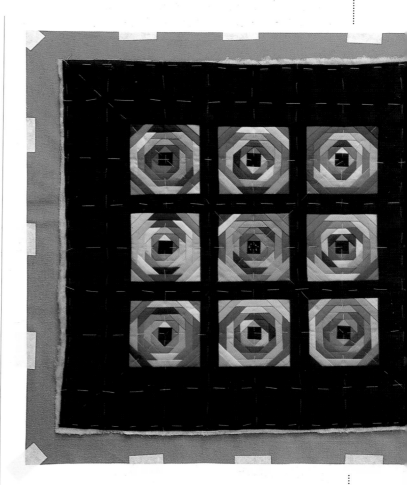

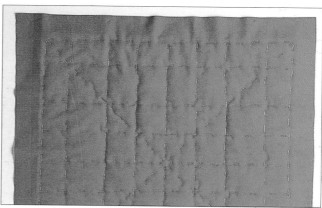

5 Tack the quilt together from the centre out to the edges, first horizontally and vertically, then diagonally in each direction. Secure any open areas of quilt with additional tacking, working out from the centre.

HAND QUILTING

THE MAIN PURPOSE of quilting is to hold the top, wadding, and backing layers together to prevent them from shifting when the quilt is being used or washed. Quilting stitches are simply running stitches that pass through all three layers, anchoring the layers together firmly. The stitches can be worked on plain fabric or pieced work, according to the design. Quilting stitches also help bring your quilt to life by providing another design that adds dimension to your work, and serves to highlight or offset the piecing.

1 Cut a 45 cm (18 in) length of quilting thread and knot the end. Pass thread through top of quilt, pulling it so that knot becomes buried in wadding. The knot will make a popping sound as it passes through quilt top.

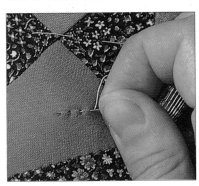

2 You may want to use a thimble. With one hand below the quilt to guide the needle upward, begin working a series of running stitches through all 3 layers of quilt. The stitches should be the same length on the front and back.

3 Try to make 3 or 4 stitches at a time, rocking needle from surface to quilt back and up to surface again, then pull stitches through. If quilt is in a frame, you can pull quite firmly, which will give your stitches greater definition.

4 If you have trouble pulling the needle through, use a balloon to grip the needle.

5 When you reach the end of your length of thread, make a knot close to the surface of the quilt. Then make a backstitch through the quilt top and wadding, pulling the knot beneath the surface and burying it in the wadding.

USING A HOOP

Quilting frames can be quite bulky, and few of us have the room for one. Luckily, any size project can be quilted using a large (50 cm/20 in) hoop specifically designed for this purpose. (You will still need to baste the quilt.) The tautness, or surface tension, of the quilt in the hoop can vary from very firm to slightly pliant – experiment to find the tension you prefer.

1 Unscrew wing nut on your hoop and separate inner and outer rings. Place inner ring on a flat surface, then position centre of your project over it. Place outer ring over inner, and tighten screw after adjusting tension.

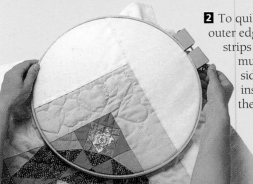

2 To quilt the outer edges, baste strips of muslin to sides, then insert in the hoop.

MACHINE QUILTING

QUICKER THAN HAND quilting, machine quilting is sometimes an effective way of finishing those quilts that are too thick to stitch by hand. Use a medium colour printed fabric for the quilt back. The secret to successful machine quilting is to maintain an even tension between the top thread and the bobbin, so test your tension on a scrap quilt "sandwich", and adjust before sewing the quilt itself.

SETTING UP THE MACHINE

Use a size 80/12 needle, and use a 50 three-ply mercerized cotton thread. Wind the bobbin with thread to match the quilt back so that any uneven stitches will not show. If the quilt is well basted and not too thick, you can use a regular presser foot. Work at a table large enough to support the entire quilt – if it hangs off, it will hinder the operation. If the top is being pushed ahead of the wadding, use a walking foot (see below).

Quilting by machine

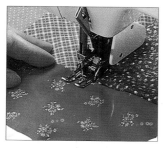 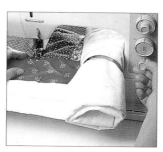

1 To secure the thread ends at the beginning or end of a line of stitching, stitch forward and reverse several times, then cut off the surplus threads close to the surface of the quilt.

2 You can use a spacer guide, which attaches to the walking foot, to sew parallel lines without marking them.

3 Place your hands on each side of the needle and smooth the quilt as you sew. Pulling or pushing the fabric may cause skipped stitches or puckers on the back. Check the back often to catch problems as they occur.

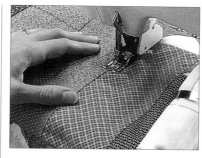

4 First stabilise the quilt by basting as straight a line as possible down the horizontal and vertical centres of piece. Then quilt each quarter in turn, from centre outward to edges.

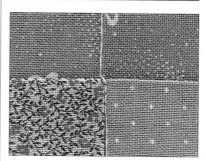

5 Beginners should try a small project first. The simplest technique is to stitch-in-the-ditch, which means to stitch as close to the seam as possible, opposite the pressed seam allowances.

6 If you are sewing along a seam where the position of the seam allowances alternate, just make a small stitch across the intersection and alternate your quilting line too.

7 Roll large quilts in a scroll-like fashion and only uncover the area you wish to quilt. Secure the roll with bicycle clips.

WALKING FOOT

You can use a walking foot (or even feed foot) with most sewing machines. This contains a set of feed dogs similar to those in the throat plate. With both sets working in unison, the fabric layers move evenly beneath the needle.

CONTOUR QUILTING

CONTOUR QUILTING IS really very simple. Instead of quilting a design onto your fabric, you use a printed fabric for the top of your item and stitch along some of its lines either by hand or by machine. Contour quilting can be used to great effect on garments, accessories and wall hangings.

FABRIC CHOICE

Contour quilting works well not only on pictorial printed fabrics, such as florals, but also on stripes and abstract designs – as long as the designs are relatively big and bold. It's also effective with pre-printed patchwork fabric. It is not necessary to quilt every line on a pattern; not only is this tedious but the effect of the quilting may be lost. Choose a few bold lines to work along and, if necessary, to hold the fabrics together; use straight quilting lines on the remainder of the fabric. Experiment with the same or contrasting thread to see which gives the best result.

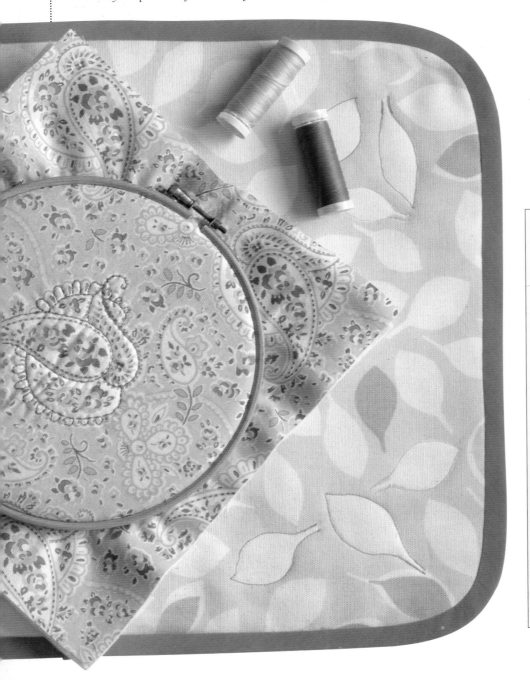

METALLIC THREADS

Extra sparkle can be added to printed fabrics if metallic thread is used for the quilting stitches. Use small lengths of thread (metallic threads fray easily) and running stitches made by hand along some of the dominant lines.

CONTOUR QUILTING TECHNIQUES

Basic contour quilting

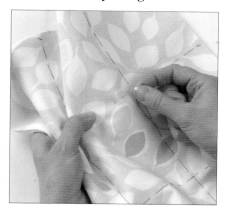

1 Place your backing fabric face down and top with the wadding. Cover with your printed fabric. Tack all three layers together with several lines of tacking stitches in all directions.

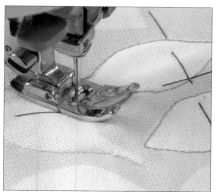

2 Using a machine set to a medium-length straight stitch, start sewing the shapes nearest the centre of your piece and work outwards.

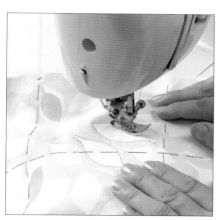

3 Continue sewing along the major lines, carefully changing direction and working around any irregular shapes to prevent the fabric bunching.

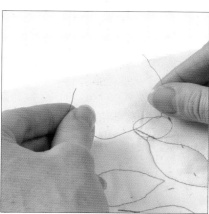

4 Finish off the threads neatly and securely at the end of every stitched line. Remove the tacking threads.

Stripes

Decide which stripes you want to contour quilt and then use "invisible" thread to work rows of zigzag stitches along and beween some of the others. Then straight stitch down your chosen stripes.

Patchwork

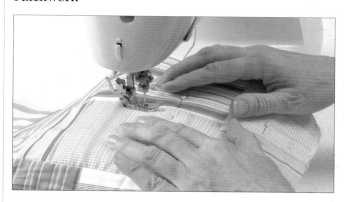

Pick out some of the shapes you want to make "stand out" and straight stitch around these. Don't stitch every pattern as the three-dimensional effect will be lost.

Quilting by hand

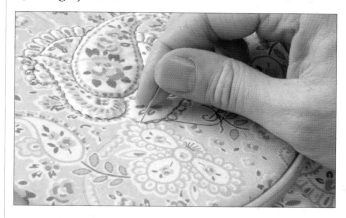

After tacking the layers together, use short, even running or back stitches to quilt along the main lines of the design. Work from the centre outwards.

CORDED QUILTING

THIS FORM OF RAISED quilting, which can be done by hand or machine, involves stitching parallel lines, about 5 mm (¼ in) apart on to a double layer of fabric to create channels into which a filling is inserted. The filling is inserted from the wrong side and afterwards, unless the motif is applied to another fabric, the quilted piece is lined to hide any filling that shows and prevent it raveling from wear.

MATERIALS AND THREADS

Corded quilting is best worked on a closely woven fabric with a sheen such as satin, silk jersey or cotton. For the backing, use a loosely woven fabric such as muslin, through which the cord can be inserted easily. Make sure the material is pre-shrunk and dye-fast. Use a contrasting coloured thread for the tacking and a matching thread for your main fabric.

MACHINE SEWING

If using a machine for corded quilting, place wrong sides facing and tack both fabrics together using tacking thread. Then stitch with matching thread following the design lines using straight stitches of a medium length. Remove tacking thread.

BASIC CORDED METHOD

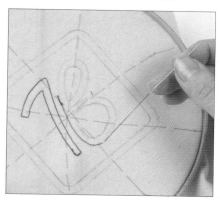

1 Transfer your design to the right side of the top fabric (see pages 190-91). Always use a hoop to ensure an even tension. With wrong sides facing and the material held in a hoop, tack the top and bottom fabric pieces together. Using neat running stitches, stitch along the lines of the design. Once fabrics are joined, remove tacking stitches and hoop .

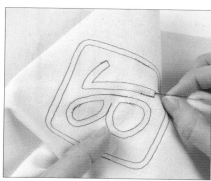

2 Thread a blunt-ended number 16 or 18 tapestry needle with a length of yarn sufficient for your design and make a small entry hole in the backing fabric.

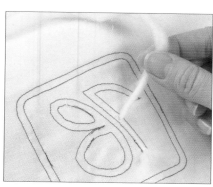

3 Work the thread through the hole and along the channels of your design, leaving a 5 mm (¼ in) tail at the opening. Bring out the needle through the backing approximately 3 cm (1¼ ins) from the opening.

4 Reinsert the needle through the same gap and continue to thread the cord through the channels, taking it out at 3 cm (1¼ in) intervals. On curves and corners, bring the needle out in the same way but leave a little loop of cord showing to prevent the fabric puckering. When finished, clip the cord, leaving a 5 mm (¼ in) tail.

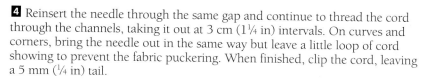

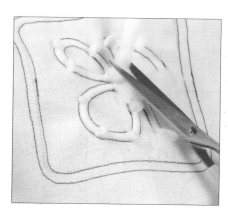

5 When channels cross, cut the cord, leaving a 5 mm (¼ in) tail. Re-insert your needle on the other side of the channel, leaving another 5 mm (¼ in) tail.

UNBACKED VARIATION

If you are going to apply a raised motif to another fabric, you don't have to work with a backing fabric. Simply transfer your design on to the wrong side of your top fabric and secure filling along the lines using a matching thread.

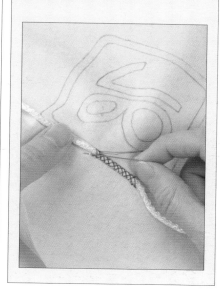

FILLING

Use a thick yarn – wool, pearl cotton or cotton cord are all suitable. Make sure it is pre-shrunk and if coloured, dye-fast.

TRAPUNTO

ANOTHER FORM OF raised quilting, trapunto involves inserting wadding or a padding of soft cotton, behind a motif in order to make it stand out from the background fabric. A crochet hook or a blunt-ended needle can be used to insert the stuffing. By varying the amount of stuffing used in each area, you can produce some highly three-dimensional effects. Trapunto can be applied to another surface, such as the box lid below, but if it is used for a stand-alone item, such as the sachet, it needs to be backed.

DESIGN SCHEMES

Trapunto can be quite complicated or extremely simple. Here, a plain heart shape is stitched and stuffed with padding and lavender to become a sweet smelling sachet. More intricate designs can be created by ganging up simple shapes. However, the technique can be used successfully for more elaborate motifs.

CREATING TRAPUNTO

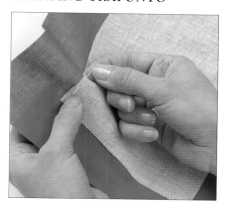

1 Mark the design onto the front of the fabric, either drawing it freehand or using one of the methods on page 191. Tack the fabric, right side facing outwards, to a lining fabric.

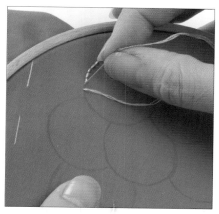

2 Place the fabric in an embroidery hoop and stitch along the outlines of your design. If hand stitching, use a firm backstitch in a strong thread to give definition to the "pockets" you will be filling.

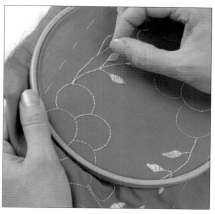

3 If you like, add additional details using embroidery such as satin stitch and stem stitch (see page 129).

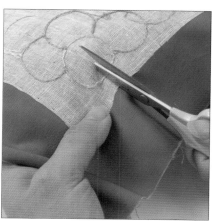

4 Make a small slit in the fabric at the back of each motif, being careful not to cut the top fabric. If you use a loosely woven backing fabric, you can pull apart the threads with a crochet hook rather than cut them.

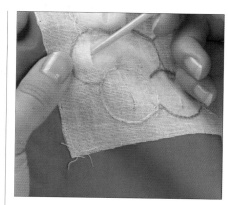

5 Insert the padding with a crochet hook or a blunt needle, taking care to position it evenly and not to overstuff the design; check the front for the effect.

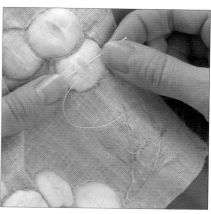

6 When finished, make overhand (see page 212) or slip stiches (see page 213) to close the slit.

ADDING A BACKING FABRIC

A backing fabric may be necessary to protect the stuffing from falling out due to wear and tear. Tack the backing, right side facing outwards to the lined piece. Then, if you like, echo the pattern of your motif with backstitching a short distance away from the padded design. Pink the fabric close to the outside stitching to prevent it raveling and to create a decorative edge.

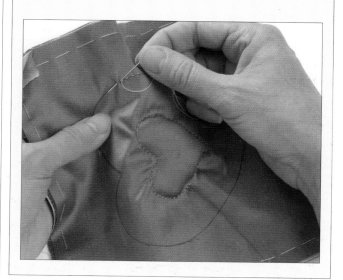

TIED QUILTING

TIED QUILTING IS a quick and simple alternative to hand or machine quilting. It is effective when making quilts for children or projects that have a thick layer of wadding. It is worked by making a series of double knots through all three layers to secure them. If the quilt is tied from the back, the ties will be virtually invisible on the front, leaving only small indentations that can form an attractive pattern of their own.

Alternatively, if you wish to make the ties a decorative feature, tie the quilt from the front so that the ends are visible, or use a contrasting colour thread to make the ties stand out from the background.

TYING THE QUILT

Ties must be spaced every 6 cm (2½ in) if you are using polyester wadding, and closer if using cotton wadding. You can use silk or cotton thread, embroidery floss, or yarn for the ties. Work with a crewel needle and a 45 to 60 cm (18 to 24 in) length of your chosen thread.

Separate ties

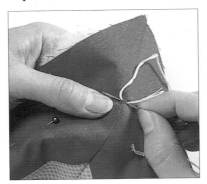

1 Assemble the quilt layers as directed on page 195. Decide on where you wish the ends of the ties to show, and work from that side of the quilt. Leaving a short end of thread, make a backstitch through all three layers.

Knotted ties on the front of a quilt can be used as decoration

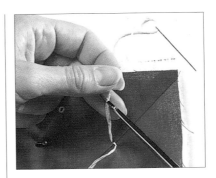

2 Make another backstitch in the same spot and cut the thread, leaving a short end.

3 Tie the ends together in a double knot. Trim the ends evenly. Continue tying knots across the quilt, spacing them evenly.

Joined ties

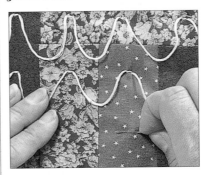

1 If the ties are going to be spaced close together, work the 2 backstitches, then go on to the next area without cutting the thread. Continue with the same length of thread until you run out.

2 Cut the thread in between the ties, then tie the ends into a double knot.

BINDING A QUILT

ADDING THE BINDING is the last step in making a quilt, and it is the finishing touch that determines the overall appearance. The edges should lie smoothly without puckers or ripples. Therefore, you should bind the quilt carefully, using binding that matches the rest of the quilt in weight and quality.

JOINING THE BINDING

Cut 4 cm (1 1/2 in) wide strips across the width of fabric on straight grain. Cut enough strips to fit around the raw edges of the quilt plus 10 cm (4 in). Sew the strips together, then press the seams to one side. Press the binding in half length-wise with wrong sides facing one another; then press one long edge to the centre crease, again with wrong sides facing. You will need room to spread out, so choose a suitable work space.

Adding the binding

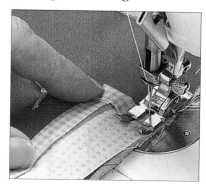

1 Place the middle of one side edge of the quilt on your sewing machine, right side up. Fold one end of binding 1 cm (1/2 in) to wrong side and place on quilt top with right sides together and raw edges even. Stitch the binding to the quilt making a 5 mm (1/4 in) seam.

2 As you approach first corner, shorten your stitch length and align binding to next edge of quilt, leaving a fold of binding that lines up with quilt edge. Stitch up to edge of fold. Stop stitching.

3 Lift the needle and the presser foot and refold the binding so that the fold is on the edge of the quilt that you have just sewn. Lower the needle exactly into the fold so that it does not catch your previous fold; lower the presser foot and continue stitching. Adjust the stitch length to normal after about 1 cm (1/2 in). Continue machine stitching to the next corner.

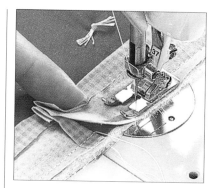

4 Sew each corner in the same way. When you reach the starting point, allow the binding to over-lap the beginning fold by 1 cm (1/2 in). Trim away any excess binding.

5 Wrap the folded pressed edge of the binding over to the back, overlapping the stitching line. Pin in place. Slip stitch the binding to the quilt back using matching thread.

6 When you reach the end of the binding strip, fold the end of the binding 1 cm (1/2 in) to the wrong side to make a neat join at the point the ends overlap.

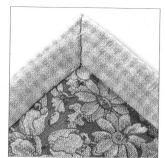

7 Use a pin to adjust the tucks at each corner into a perfect mitre. Carefully stitch the mitred corners in place.

SEWING

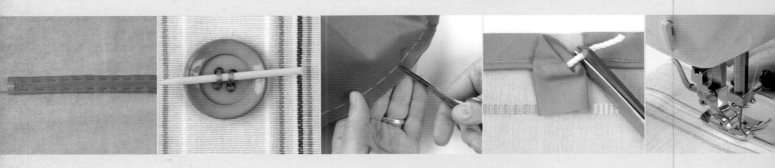

YOU'LL BE SURPRISED BY JUST HOW EASY IT IS to get started making your own beautiful and desirable household furnishings and accessories. With an entry-level sewing machine, and your choice of fabrics and threads, you can create fashionable items for every room of your home and at a fraction of the store-bought price!

Possibly what's best about creating your own home soft furnishings is that you can ensure that they fit your specific needs, that they suit your home decor, and that you can have them as soon as you'd like.

All the basics – useful equipment, essential stitches, some general techniques, and a guide to hand and machine sewing. – as well as the necessary core techniques you will need to master to give your creations that professional look are included. As well as learning essential techniques such as how to mitre corners in order to produce a flat edge, and how to put in a zip, the chapter is filled with suggestions for making your items more decorative. using trims and special techniques.

You'll find a lot of satisfaction in creating your own home furnishings and you're certain to be the envy of your non-sewing friends.

CONTENTS

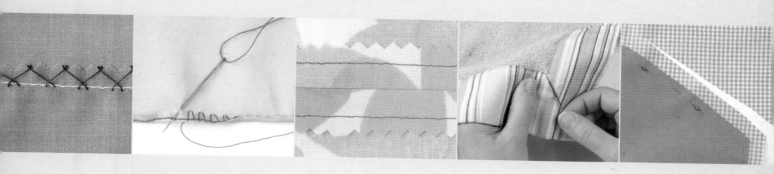

FURNISHING FABRICS

FOR A SUCCESSFUL RESULT, it's important to choose an appropriate fabric for your item. All the projects in this book are accompanied by simple advice about the type of furnishing fabric you should use. This usually takes the form of a recommendation as to the weight of fabric you need – whether it's sheer, lightweight, mediumweight or heavyweight. You won't find your choice is limited – there is a huge range of different materials on sale within these weights. Generally speaking, dressmaking fabrics are too fine for soft furnishings.

FABRIC KNOW-HOW

When buying fabric, it's worth checking with the retailer as to its suitability for your project. He or she may also be able to advise you on how much fabric to buy, especially if you have chosen a material with a repeat pattern that may need matching up.

You also will need to find out about the care of your fabric – is it washable or does it need dry cleaning? Check, too, whether a washable fabric has been pre-shrunk – and if in doubt, wash the fabric before you use it. Most fabric is well labeled with this kind of information – just make sure that you take the information away with you.

RIGHT SIDE OR WRONG SIDE?

If your fabric looks the same on both sides, it is a good idea to try to use the same side throughout your project. Although they may look the same, there may be a subtle difference to the way each side catches the light, which may be more obvious after you've finished sewing. Make a small mark in an unobtrusive place, right on the edge of each piece that you cut out, to indicate what will be the wrong side for the purposes of your project.

Fabric amounts

Most of the projects in this book give you instructions on how to make up an item to a size that suits your specific needs. Therefore, you will have to measure up before you buy your fabric, and sometimes create your own pattern. You will be shown how to do this and how to use your measurements or pattern to cut out your fabric.

Bear in mind that most furnishing fabrics are 135 to 150 cm (54 to 60 in) wide and are sold by the metre (yard). You will have to work out how many times the fabric pieces would fit across the width of your chosen fabric to determine how many metres (yards) you need. You also will need more fabric if you are trying to match a pattern across a piece. If the fabric you choose is an unusual width, sales staff can advise you as to the amount you need.

Cutting

You need first to line up edges and centre lines with the grain of the fabric (see box). If you cut across the grain, you are cutting along the bias (any diagonal direction on the fabric) and the fabric will be stretchy. If you put two pieces of fabric together, say for a cushion cover, that haven't been cut out along the grain, they will pull in different directions as you stitch and the finished cover will be distorted.

When you cut out a square or rectangle, make sure you cut along the direction of the grain. If you cut out a circle, the true diameter should line up with the direction of the grain. If you are cutting out a shaped piece, then you need to find the vertical center line and match this to the grain.

So before you cut anything out, you will need to straighten the cross-wise grain and when you buy material, make sure you buy a bit more than you need to allow for these adjustments.

Straightening the ends

Before you begin, iron the fabric to get out any creases or folds. Snip into one selvedge near the end of the fabric and pick out one or two weft (cross-wise) threads. Hold the fabric in one hand and pull at the threads with the other so the fabric gathers. Cut the threads free from the opposite selvedge, then draw them out while pushing the fabric back at the same time. Cut along this line to straighten the end of the fabric. Repeat at the other end.

Re-aligning fabric

Fold the fabric in half lengthwise. Bring the selvedges together and then check that the straightened edges line up. If any of the edges do not align correctly you need to re-align the grain. Fold the fabric in half lengthwise and pin along the straightened edges, making sure they match. Bring the selvedges together and pin. Spray or sponge the fabric with water until damp then stretch it along the bias, pulling it gently in both directions. Lay the material out on a flat surface to dry and then iron, if necessary.

If the fabric is distorted along the lengthwise edges, it may be simply that the selvedges are too tight. All you need to do is snip into the selvedges at intervals.

Cutting surface

Always lay fabric out flat, ideally on a cutting mat placed on a table. This will give you a firm surface and cutting mats often have measurements marked on them that can be helpful. Alternatively, cover a table with a blanket; the fabric will grip the blanket slightly, making it easier for you to keep the material in position.

If you are cutting out anything particularly large, you may have to work on the floor. Again, put a blanket down first – this will also serve to protect your fabric from any dirt on the floor.

SEW SMART

Grain of fabric

The selvedges are the fabric's finished edges. The lengthwise grain (warp) runs parallel to the selvedges and has little give. The crosswise grain (weft) runs perpendicular to the selvedges and has a slight give. A fabric has its maximum give when it is cut on the bias, which runs at a 45° angle to the selvedges.

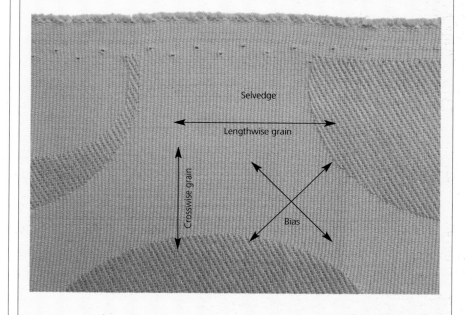

Selvedge

Lengthwise grain

Crosswise grain

Bias

EQUIPMENT

PINS, NEEDLES, SCISSORS, tape measure and threads are essential to any sewing kit. Additionally there are a number of useful items, such as thimbles, bodkins, seam rippers, and pin cushions that will make any sewing project easier to achieve. It's a good idea to keep everything together in a special box.

Pins and needles
Dressmaker's pins are most useful since they are suitable for nearly all fabrics. Those with coloured ball heads are particularly handy since they are easier to see and pick up. Most needle types come in different sizes, and are numbered accordingly. The lower the number, the thicker and shorter the needle. For most general sewing projects, use needles known as sharps. These are available in a range of different sizes to suit different fabrics. Generally speaking, the finer the fabric, the finer the needle you should use.

Thimble
This protects your fingers and is especially useful if you are working with a thick or stiff fabric, or are stitching through several layers.

Needle threader
If you experience difficulty when threading a needle, then this useful little tool is the answer. You simply insert the fine wire loop of the threader into the eye of the needle, pass the thread through the wire loop and then pull it back through the eye.

Pincushion
This is the perfect place to store your pins safely. Particularly useful are those with a wrist band, allowing you to keep pins close by while you work. Many come with a little emery bag attached. This is filled with an abrasive substance and you clean your pins and needles by pushing them inside.

Seam ripper
This is used for unpicking seams and cutting into buttonholes.

Bodkin
This is a long blunt needle-like tool with a large eye, useful for threading ribbon, tape, cord or elastic through a casing or row of eyelets. Some have two eyes or a safety-pin type closure to hold the ribbon securely.

THREADS

Different types of thread are available and you should choose a thread to match your fabric weight, colour, and purpose. Use a thread that is darker or the same colour as your fabric.

For general machine and hand sewing, general purpose cotton thread is recommended for cotton, rayon and linen fabric. Mercerised means it has a smooth and silky finish. Polyester thread should be used on light- to medium-weight synthetics.

Choose the right weight of thread for your fabric. For heavier fabrics, use a thicker thread and for fine fabrics, use a fine thread. Ticket is the term used to define the thickness of thread; the higher the "ticket" number the finer the thread.

You can buy special tacking thread but it's more economical to use the ends of reels, especially if they are distinctive colours that you are less likely to use again. Don't be tempted to use cheap thread for tacking – it will snap as you work and won't hold as firmly. Use a strong coloured thread that's visible against whatever you are making, so it's easy to pick out when you've finished.

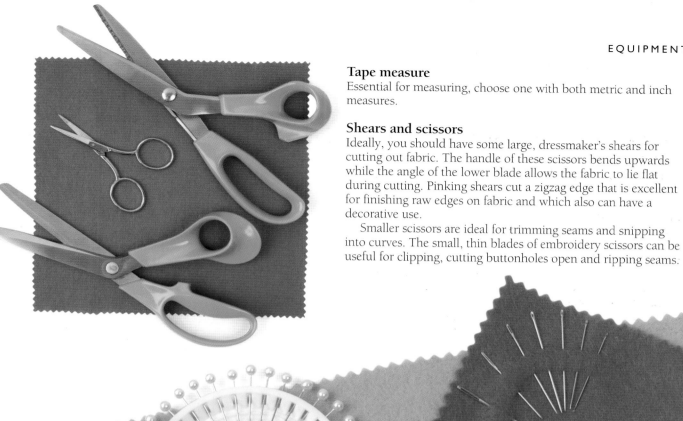

Tape measure

Essential for measuring, choose one with both metric and inch measures.

Shears and scissors

Ideally, you should have some large, dressmaker's shears for cutting out fabric. The handle of these scissors bends upwards while the angle of the lower blade allows the fabric to lie flat during cutting. Pinking shears cut a zigzag edge that is excellent for finishing raw edges on fabric and which also can have a decorative use.

Smaller scissors are ideal for trimming seams and snipping into curves. The small, thin blades of embroidery scissors can be useful for clipping, cutting buttonholes open and ripping seams.

HAND SEWING

ALTHOUGH MOST OF the sewing you do will be with a sewing machine, very few projects won't require handstitching of some kind. You may simply need to use some tacking to hold fabrics together more firmly than pins, or you might have to do some fine slipstitching to close an opening. Below are the hand stitches you are most likely to use.

THE BASIC STITCHES

Most, but not all, hand stitches are worked from right to left, although if you are left-handed you will want to reverse the working direction. Cut your thread with scissors to get a neat end that will make it easier to thread the needle.

Before you start stitching, secure the thread to the wrong side of the fabric. Tie a knot at the end of the thread; you might have to use a double or triple knot so it can't be pulled through the fabric. Alternatively, make several small stitches in one spot at the beginning of your stitching. When you finish, make a few small backstitches. If you are working a line of permanent stitching, secure the beginning and end of the thread where it won't be seen on the right side.

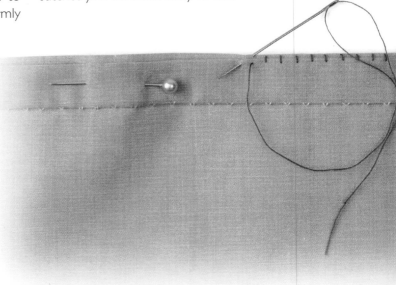

Tacking

This is used to hold together temporarily pieces of fabric before final stitching. The more firmly you want your fabric held together, the smaller and neater your stitches should be. You can also use a line of tacking – instead of a marker pen – to indicate a position on the fabric. Remove tacking stitches at the end of a project; to avoid too much repetition, the instructions for the projects in this book will not mention this. You will only find references to removing tacking when it's taken out before the end.

Running stitch

This is used for quilting, gathering, mending and tucking. It's usually a permanent stitch.

Backstitch

Use this when you want a stitch that is particularly secure. It looks like machine stitching on the right side but the stitches overlap on the wrong side. You would also use backstitch at the end of a row of hand stitching to secure the thread.

Slipstitch

This is used when you need to make hand stitches that won't be seen. You make even slipstitches when joining two folded fabrics together and uneven slipstitches when joining a folded edge to a flat surface. It's useful for hemming and when you want to stitch an opening closed after turning an item to the right side.

Overhand stitch

These small even hand stitches (pictured above) are used when joining two finished edges together, such as when adding an edging or trim With right sides together, so one edge is at the back and one at the front, insert the needle diagonally from the back to the front, picking up only a couple of threads along each edge. Pull the thread through then insert the needle directly behind the point where the thread emerges for the next stitch.

Hem stitch

Hem stitch is a slanting stitch that is stronger than slipstitch. You can see the stitches on the wrong side but they are tiny on the right. If you don't want the stitches to be seen on the fabric or the hem, use slipstitch.

Catchstitch

This looks like the herringbone stitch that's used in embroidery. It is used on a hem where the edge of the turned fabric is pinked or finished with zigzag stitch. It's worked from left to right.

Blanket stitch

Though often used as an embroidery stitch, blanket stitch is used to finish the raw edge of an unfrayable fabric, like fleece or felt, and to hold a turning in place. This stitch is worked from left to right on the right side, with the edge at the bottom.

Tacking

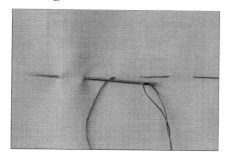

Make short even stitches – about 5 mm (¼ in) long – the same distance apart. Pass the needle in and out of the fabric several times before you pull it through.

Running stitch

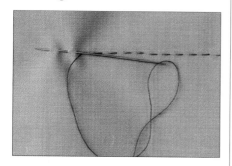

Similar to basting, but stitches are much smaller and evenly sized and spaced.

Backstitch

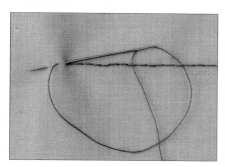

Bring the needle to the right side and insert it a half-stitch's length behind the point where the thread emerges. Bring the needle out again a half-stitch's length in front of that point; pull the thread through. For the next stitch, insert the needle where the thread emerged for the previous stitch and then bring the needle out again a half-stitch's length in front; continue. At the end, bring the needle to the front where the thread emerges.

Slipstitch

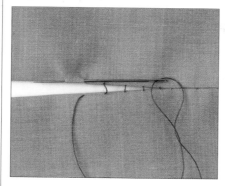

To work along two folded edges, bring the needle out through one edge and make a stitch along the fold of the opposite edge. Draw the thread through and make a stitch in the opposite edge; continue. To work along a folded edge and flat surface, bring the needle out though the folded edge and make a very small stitch in the flat fabric, catching just a few threads with the needle. Opposite this stitch, insert the needle in the fold and take a small stitch along it, bring the needle out and pull the thread through. Continue alternating between the flat surface and the folded edge.

Hem stitch

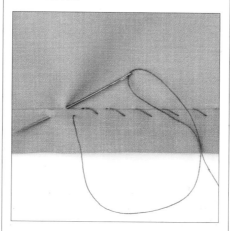

Bring the needle through to the front of the fold. Pick up one or two threads from the flat fabric and insert the needle through the folded edge at the same time. Draw the thread through; continue in this way.

Catchstitch

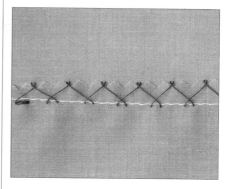

Bring the needle through the hem. Take a very small stitch in the fabric above the hem, just a little way to the right, inserting the needle from right to left and picking up only a couple of threads. Take the next stitch in the hem, just a little way to the right. Blind catchstitch is worked in the same way, but just under the edge of the hem – you hold the edge back with a finger as you work.

Blanket stitch

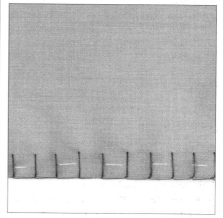

Secure the thread on the wrong side at your starting point and bring it below the edge. Insert the needle through the fabric from the right side and down toward the edge. Making sure the thread is looped behind the needle, pull in through to form the stitch on the edge. Keep the depth of the stitches and the distance between them even.

SEWING MACHINE BASICS

FOR ALL BUT the smallest of tasks, a sewing machine is essential. The most advanced, top-of-the-range models offer a huge number of different stitches – upward of 50 – and allow you to perform many functions. They are often computerised, with built-in memories where you can store your embroidery stitch designs. However, even the most basic models provide a great range of functions – you can do buttonholes, sew in zips and piping, and stitch stretch fabrics as well as working with the basic straight and zigzag stitches.

CHOOSING A MACHINE

All the projects in this book have been completed using a fairly simple, standard sewing machine and a couple of attachments. All you need is a machine that does straight and zigzag stitching, makes buttonholes, and has a zipper foot. A useful optional extra is an even-feed (or walking) foot (see page 217), especially if you make up anything that is quilted. It is worth making sure that your machine can sew heavy fabrics, as some lightweight models can't be used with the thicker upholstery materials.

All machines operate on the same principle. Basically, a sewing machine works with two threads, a top thread and a bottom thread. The bottom thread is wound around a bobbin that is inserted inside the machine, under the needle. As you sew, the needle pierces the fabric and takes the top thread down to the bobbin. The top thread loops round the bobbin and picks up the bottom thread, pulling it up into the fabric. So the two threads interlock to create the stitching.

Most sewing machines are threaded in a fairly similar way and use similar controls to adjust important features such as tension and stitch length. You will find that once you learn how to thread and use one model, you will probably be able to apply that skill to almost any other machine.

These pages are intended as a general guide only and you will find that the positioning of certain features will differ from machine to machine. You should rely on the manual for your particular model.

GUIDE TO SEWING MACHINE FEATURES

1 Stitch length/type selector – This allows you to select both the size and type of stitch. Some machines have separate stitch length and type controls, and others also have stitch width selectors for zigzag or fancy stitches.

2 Spool pin – Place your reel of thread on the spool pin before threading the machine. Some models come with an attachment to hold the reel in place.

3 Bobbin winder – This is the spool on which you place the bobbin for winding. The reel of thread is placed on the spool pin, the thread is passed through a thread guide (refer to your manual) before being wound around the bobbin a few times. The bobbin is placed on the winder and then the needle is disengaged – this is often done by simply moving a switch, or by loosening the flywheel (refer to your manual). Then, when you press the foot pedal, the bobbin will wind. Make sure the thread winds evenly on to the bobbin and always use the same thread that you are using for the top thread.

4 Handwheel – Modern electric machines are operated by means of a foot pedal. However, they still have a handwheel so you can control the needle without using the pedal. It means you can stitch slowly, if necessary, and you can raise or lower the needle as required.

5 Tension guide – The top thread passes through two discs, which exert pressure on the thread. The more pressure, the tighter the tension on the thread. Lower pressure and you'll have looser thread (see page 216).

6 Tension settings – This adjusts the tension that helps control the flow of the top thread.

7 Take-up lever – The top thread is passed through the take-up lever after being passed round the tension discs. It rises and falls with the needle: When the take-up lever is at its highest point, so is the needle.

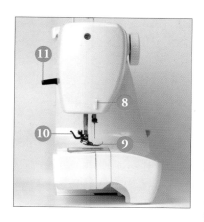

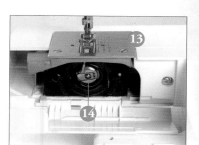

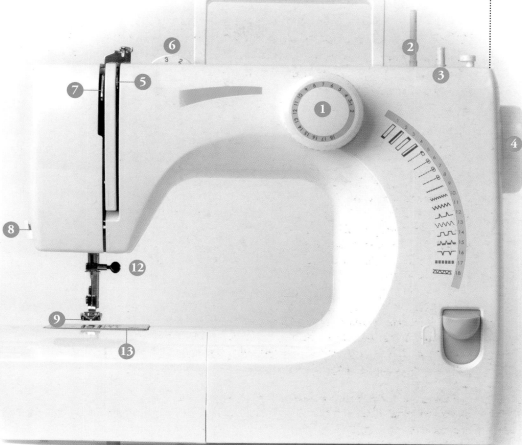

8 Thread cutter – when you've finished sewing, pull the thread over the cutter to cut it. The position of a thread cutter varies, if present, but it will be somewhere near the needle.

9 Presser foot – This presses down on the fabric to hold it in place, and works with the feed to move the fabric through as you sew. When it's lowered, it engages the tension discs, so to thread the machine, you need to have the foot raised. The foot may be changed, depending on the task (see below).

10 Presser foot clamp – This is released (or unscrewed) to remove the presser foot.

11 Presser foot lever – This lever, usually at the back of the machine, is raised or lowered to raise or lower the presser foot.

12 Needle clamp – This is released to remove the needle. When changing needles, always replace them correctly or the machine won't work. Refer to the manufacturer's manual for instructions.

13 Throat plate/feed – The throat plate lies under the needle; the feed is the metal teeth that emerge through openings in this plate. When the sewing needle goes down into the machine to pick up the bobbin thread, it passes through a hole in the throat plate. The feed works with the pressure

of the presser foot to move the fabric along and get it in the right position for each stitch.

14 Bobbin case – Once a bobbin has been wound, it goes into the bobbin case. The type of bobbin case varies. Some are located under a removable plate, beside the needle plate, and you simply drop the bobbin in place. With other models, the bobbin is held in place with a small latch or it can be accessed from the front of the machine and then removed. The bobbin is then slipped into the case and the thread passed through the relevant notches before the case is returned to the machine.

USING THE SEWING MACHINE

FIRST WIND THE thread on to the bobbin then thread the machine. Raise the presser foot then turn the handwheel so the take-up lever is in its highest position. Put a reel of thread on the spool pin. Take the thread across the machine to the first thread guide, then down to the tension guide. Take it up to the take-up lever – some of these have an eye for the thread or a simple slot. Then take the thread down toward the needle, passing it through any thread guides. Thread the needle in the direction indicated by your machine's manual. If it is not in the correct direction, the machine won't work.

Insert the bobbin in the bobbin case, following your manual's instructions, making sure there is about 15 cm (6 in) of thread emerging from the bobbin. Leave the plate or covering open so you can see the bobbin. Turn the handwheel so the needle moves down and then up again to its highest position. As the needle comes up you will see that the top thread has picked up a loop of the bottom thread. Use a pin and pull the loop through so the bottom thread is now on the outside of the machine. Close the plate or cover to conceal the bobbin.

GETTING STARTED

Sewing

Before starting your work, try out your stitching first on a scrap of the same fabric in order to get the stitch length and tension right. Choose your stitch and select a length (see page 217). Fold the scrap in half to work through two layers. Use the handwheel to lift up the needle to its highest point. Make sure the presser foot is raised. Place the fabric under the needle, with the bulk of the fabric to the left. Lower the presser foot and turn the handwheel to bring the needle down into the fabric. Make sure the tension setting is at its mid point. Press the foot pedal to start sewing. Use your hands to lightly guide the fabric through – never pull – but keep your fingers away from the needle. Stitch for a short distance.

When you've finished, raise the presser foot and turn the handwheel to raise the needle. Draw the fabric away from the machine and use the integral cutter or scissors to cut the threads free, leaving about 15 cm (6 in) of thread loose.

Finishing

To secure the thread ends at the ends so the stitches don't ravel, use the reverse stitch function on your machine. When you start stitching, position the needle just in from the beginning of your seam. Hold down the reverse and stitch back to the beginning. Release the reverse and then stitch forward to the end of your seam. Now hold down the reverse again and stitch backwards for a few stitches.

CORRECTING TENSION

If the tension is just right, the point where the top and bottom threads interlock will be midway between the two layers of fabric, and the stitching will look the same on both sides.

If, however, the bottom thread appears on the top of the fabric then the tension for the top thread is too tight. To correct this, turn the tension setting to a lower number (or toward the minus range on some machines) and then do another test. If the top thread appears on the bottom of the fabric then the tension of the top thread is too loose. Turn the tension setting to a higher number (or toward the plus range) and test again.

It is always preferable to adjust the top thread tension if the stitching is not right. While the bobbin tension can be changed on most machines, it is a fiddly job and you wouldn't want to do it every time you changed fabrics. Usually you have to tighten or loosen a small screw on the bobbin case. Refer to your manual before attempting this – and only adjust bobbin tension as a last resort.

Correct tension

The top and bottom threads should lay flat on the surfaces.

Inorrect tension

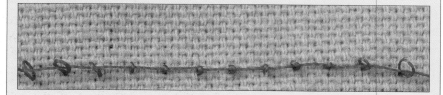

When either the top or bottom thread is too loose, you will get this result.

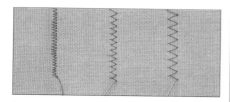

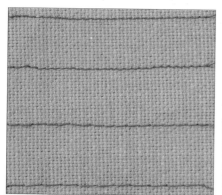

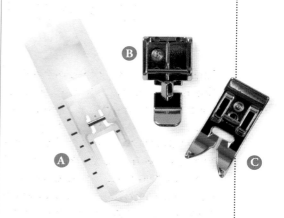

Sewing machine needles

Needles for sewing machines are made in different sizes; the lower the number the finer the needle. Commonly available sizes range from 9 to 18. Match the needle to your project; for a fine, sheer fabric, you need a fine needle, such as size 9 or 10. Needles also vary in the type of point. Most projects use regular, sharp-pointed needles, but if you're stitching a knit fabric use a ball-point needle. You also can get wedge-point needles specially designed for leather, suede or vinyls.

Sewing-machine feet

Different kinds of sewing-machine feet allow you to work on a range of projects. You can get feet that will help you to sew on beads or sequins, to do appliqué or to make ruffles. The following will be the most useful for the projects in this book.

Buttonhole foot (A) Most machines come with this attachment, which allows you work the stitching for a buttonhole in just four steps. A gauge on the foot helps you to work even buttonholes.

Straight stitch foot Your machine may use specific feet for straight and zigzag stitches so this foot can only be used for straight stitch.

Zip foot (B) Use this when you want to stitch along the side of something bulky. It's used, obviously, when

inserting zips, but also can be used to stitch piping in place, or when covering cord to make your own piping. You can fix it so the needle passes to either the right or the left of the foot, depending on your needs.

Multipurpose foot (C) Your sewing machine will probably come with one of these, which is used for straight and zigzag stitch. It can be known as a zigzag foot.

Even-feed foot This feeds layers of fabric through the machine at an even rate. It's useful for any bulky, slippery, or stretchy fabrics and for quilting, when it may be combined with a quilting guide attachment that helps you to work parallel lines.

Stitch length

Match your stitches to your fabric – use short stitches for fine fabrics and long ones for heavyweights. Generally speaking, the lower the number on your stitch length selector, the longer the stitches – although you should refer to your manual. If you use stitches that are too small, the fabric will pucker and you will find it hard to get the tension right. If the stitches are too long, they will be too loose and may pull out. Check the stitch length when you test the tension (see page 216).

MACHINE STITCHES

1 Straight stitch

The basic machine stitch, it is formed by two interlocking threads and looks the same on the front and back. The length of the stitches can be changed to suit the fabric (see Stitch length, above).

2 Topstitch

This is used on the right side of the fabric for decorative as well as functional purposes. When you've stitched two layers of fabric together and turned them to the right side, topstitching around the edges helps them lie flat. It also can give turnings a neater finish.

3 Zigzag stitch

Often worked along the raw edge of fabric, at seams, and on turnings, most machines offer this stitch. By working it close to the edge, it forms an overcast stitch.

3   1   2

SEAMS

The most basic seam is formed when you use a straight machine stitch to sew two pieces of fabric together. This plain seam is the most commonly used and is suitable for many different purposes.

ALLOWANCES

When you stitch two pieces of fabric together, the distance between your line of stitching and the edge is the seam allowance. When the seam has been finished, that area is then referred to as the allowance. The most common seam allowance is 1.5 cm (⅝ in) wide, but this can vary depending on your project. It is important to use allowances – if you aren't consistent, you will find that the pieces don't match up correctly when you are putting a project together. To stitch a plain seam, pin your fabric together and machine stitch along the edge of the fabric, keeping to the seam allowance.

If you have stitched a seam that goes around a sharp corner, you will need to trim the allowance at this point to reduce the bulk of the fabric when you turn the finished sewing to the right side. If you have stitched a curved seam you need to make small cuts in the seam to get a neat finish when turned to the right side. And if you think the raw edges of your seam are likely to unravel, you can finish them in a variety of ways.

TURNING TO THE RIGHT SIDE

If you need to leave a gap in a seam in order to turn an item to the right side, when you get to the point where you want to start the gap, stop stitching. Then stitch backward for a short interval. Draw the fabric out of the machine and cut the threads. Reposition the fabric in the sewing machine a short interval in front of where you want the seam to start again. Stitch backward to that point and then stitch forward to complete the seam.

When you've finished stitching, finish the seam as necessary and turn the item through the gap to the other side. Push a knitting needle gently into any corners to get a neater finish. Press the allowance under on both sides of the gap and then slipstitch (see page 213) it closed.

FINISHING PLAIN SEAMS

Pinked finish

This is the simplest finish for the edges of a seam. Use the pinking shears to trim along the edges of the allowance.

Pinked and stitched finish (1)

Stitch along each seam allowance 5 mm (¼ in) in from the edge. Then trim the edge with pinking shears.

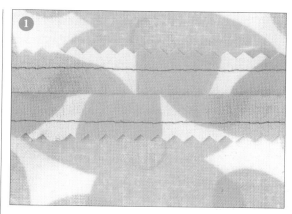

Turned and stitched finish

Turn under the edge of each seam allowance by 5 mm (¼ in) and press. Stitch along the edge of the fold.

Zigzagged edges

Set the machine to zigzag and stitch along each seam allowance, close to, but not on, the edge. Then trim close to the stitching. Sometimes you will want to stitch the seam allowance together using zigzag stitch – this reinforces the seam at the same time as neatening the edges.

Bound edges

Fold binding over each seam allowance and then secure with topstitching (see page 217).

SELF-FINISHED SEAMS

There are some seams where the raw edges are enclosed within the seam, so avoiding the need for finishing.

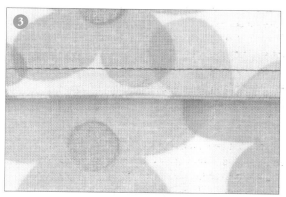

French seam (2)

Pin your fabric wrong sides together. Stitch, taking a 5 mm (¼ in) allowance. Press the seam to one side. Turn the fabric so the right sides are together and pin along the seam again, making sure the stitching is exactly on the edge. Stitch again 1 cm (½ in) from the folded edge, so the first seam is enclosed; press the seam to one side.

Mock French seam

Pin the fabric right sides together. Stitch, taking a 1.5 cm (⅝ in) allowance.. Turn in each allowance by 5 mm (¼ in) and press. Pin the turned edges together and stitch, close to the fold. Press the seam to one side.

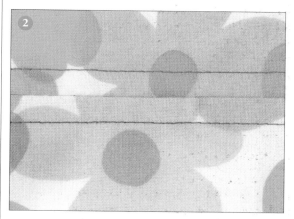

Flat fell seam

This seam (see detail on page 218) lies flat and is held in place with topstitching, that shows on the right side. Pin the fabric right sides together. Stitch taking a 1.5 cm (⅝ in) allowance. Trim one of the allowances to 5 mm (¼ in). Fold the other allowance over the trimmed one and press. Pin the allowance flat on the fabric so the trimmed seam is underneath. Topstitch through all the layers.

TOPSTITCHED SEAMS

These are a good way to hold seams flat, and so also help prevent raveling of raw edges. If you are planning on using topstitching elsewhere in your project, consider using this kind of seam.

Double topstitched (3)

Stitch a plain seam with a 1.5 cm (⅝ in) allowance and press the seam open. Topstitch 5 mm to 1 cm (¼ to ½ in) from the seam on the right side, so you are stitching through the fabric and allowance. Turn and topstitch down the other side of the seam, keeping to the same distance.

HAND FINISHING

Seams on lightweight fabrics that don't fray easily can be finished with handstitching. First, press the seam open then trim one allowance to 3 mm (⅛ in). Turn the edge of the other seam allowance under 3 mm (⅛ in) and press. Turn again, bringing it to the seamline so that it encloses the trimmed edge. Press, then hemstitch as close to the first line of stitching as possible.

HEMS

A HEM IS USED to finish the raw edges of fabric by folding it out of sight. When you are instructed to turn under a hem, you need to fold the fabric to the wrong side. If you turn under the fabric once, you make a single hem. Turn the fabric under twice and you have a double hem.

HEMS FOR DIFFERENT PURPOSES

You can hold a hem in place with stitching that is either visible or invisible. Machine stitching along a hem is the simplest way and it will be very secure. However, the stitching will be visible on the right side. Alternatively, you can use one of the variety of hand stitches that catch up only a few threads of your fabric and that are barely visible on the right side. You also can make a feature of a hem and use means of securing it in place that will serve a decorative purpose.

A hand-rolled hem should be used on very fine or sheer fabrics; a flat turned hem would show through the fabric.

A blanket-stitch hem gives a decorative edge at the same time as hemming fabric. It looks particularly good stitched with darning wool or embroidery thread on fabrics with a thick pile, such as fleece and felt, where the stitches sink into the raised surface of the fabric. As the name suggests, it is the traditional finish for the edge of blankets.

If you are hemming a square or rectangular item, such as a napkin or tablecloth, you will come to a corner. You can simply fold under one hem first, and then fold the next one over the top of the first. This will, however, be bulky since you are folding several layers of fabric into each corner. The neatest way to deal with corners is to fold them into mitres (see page 224). Since you cut away excess fabric with this method, the corners should lie flat and neat.

BASIC SINGLE HEM

In both these versions, the raw edge of the hem has been pinked and stitched (see page 239).

Machine stitched

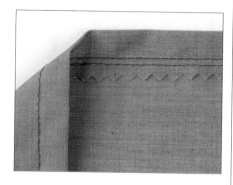

Finish the raw edge of the fabric. Turn under the edge by 1.5 cm (⅝ in) and press. Machine stitch on the wrong side, close to the first stitching.

Hand stitched

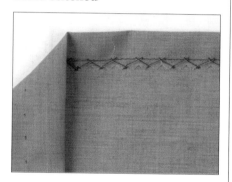

Finish and turn the edge of the fabric as above. Use catchstitch (see page 213) to sew along the edge, making your stitches in the hem just below the pinking or zigzag.

BASIC DOUBLE HEM

Machine stitched

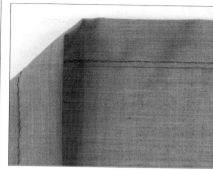

Turn under the fabric by 6 mm (⅜ in) and press. Turn it under again by 1.5 cm (⅝ in) and press again. Machine stitch on the wrong side, close to the first fold you made.

Hand stitched

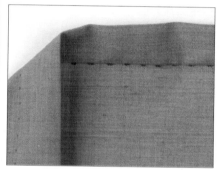

Turn under the fabric as above and pin along the hem to hold it in place. Use hem stitch or slipstitch (see page 213) along the first fold you made.

HAND ROLLED HEM

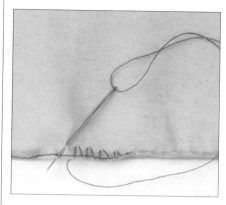

Machine stitch 6 mm (⅜ in) from the edge of the fabric, then trim the fabric close to the line of stitching. Turn under a hem so this line of stitching is close to the fold on the wrong side. Secure the thread at the right-hand side and take a small stitch in the fold, just outside the stitching. Take the next stitch in the fabric, 5 mm (¼ in) from the fold. Continue in this way until you've made about five stitches in both the fold and the fabric. Pull up the thread to roll up the hem. Continue stitching for short intervals and then pulling the thread.

BLANKET-STITCHED HEM

Turn under a single or double hem and pin it in place. Secure the thread under the hem on the right-hand side and bring the needle out on the very edge. Turn to the right side and work blanket stitch (see page 213) along the hem, making sure the vertical stitches are the same depth as the turning.

PATTERNS & SCALING

When items, such as the projects in this book, are to be made to individual measurements, you need to create your own patterns, based on your own requirements. However, when patterns are supplied, these generally must be scaled up or enlarged for use. The easiest way to do this is to use a photocopier. However, it is also possible to scale up small designs using tracing paper (see page 124).

PATTERN MAKING

You should use an inexpensive but sturdy plain paper for cutting out patterns. You may want to use the patterns again, so its important that the paper won't deteriorate with handling. However, avoid stiff paper since it will be hard to pin to the fabric without it buckling. You may have to join several pieces of paper together if the pattern dimensions exceed those of the paper. Do not use newspaper, which can leave marks on fabric.

A ruler and pencil are vital for creating many of the patterns used in this book. Use an ordinary HB pencil that doesn't smudge so as to prevent marks transferring to your fabric. It can also be useful to have a set square or protractor for getting right angles correct when drawing squares or rectangles. As you draw, make sure the line is clear enough to cut around later.

Some of patterns may have marks that need to be transferred to the fabric – these marks will help you line up the various sections of a make when putting them together. Use an erasable marker to do this.

If you are going to scale up a pattern, the easiest way is to photocopy the pieces, enlarging them to the right size (see page 223).

It's important to ensure that you position the pattern correctly on your fabric before you cut around it. You need to make sure that the pattern follows the grain of the fabric (see page 209). If you position the pattern any old how, your cut pieces will have a bias stretch and may become distorted when you come to sew them together.

When pinning the pattern to the fabric, using too many pins will cause the pattern to wrinkle, while too few will allow the pattern to move while you are cutting.

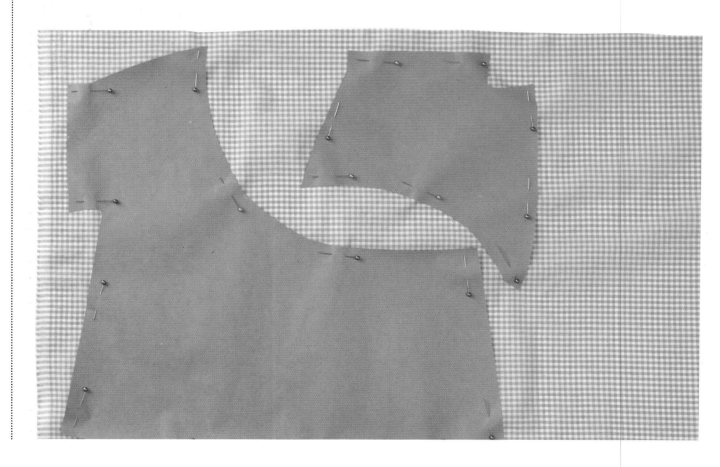

MAKING CURVES

To draw a large curve, take a length of string and attach it to the centre point of one long edge of the fabric with a pin. Tie a pen to the other end, making sure the distance between pin and pen is the required radius. Keeping the string taut, draw the curve.

You also can use a circular object, such as a plate, saucer or cup to round off an edge. If you want a large sweeping curve use a large plate. If you want a sharper, smaller curve, use a teacup.

Lay the paper out flat and place the plate in the corner you want to round off. Move the plate until its edges touch the straight edges of the paper. Draw around the curve and then cut away the unwanted paper.

USING A PATTERN

Lay your fabric out flat and place the pattern(s) on top, positioning it so as to get the most out of the available fabric. If the pattern has a straight edge, line this up with either the lengthwise or crosswise grain. If it doesn't have straight lines but is symmetrical, fold it in half and run your finger along the crease to make a prominent fold line. Place the unfolded pattern on the fabric so the fold line is roughly lined up with the grain. Pin one end of the fold line in place and measure from this to the edge of the fabric (if this is not the selvedge, make sure the edge is perfecly straight). Measure from the other end of the fold line to the selvedge and adjust the pattern so the second measurement is equal to the first.

CUTTING OUT

Pin around the outside of the pattern so it lies as flat as possible. Cut through the fabric toward the pattern. Rest one hand lightly on the pattern and cut around it. If an allowance has been included, cut close to the paper's edge. If you have to add an allowance, cut around the pattern the given measurement from the paper's edge. If you like, mark the fabric to indicate the allowance. If you have to cut out more than one piece of a pattern, either fold the fabric in half or put two layers together before you pin the pattern in place. If you are putting two layers together, make sure their grains line up with each other first. Then cut around the pattern, through both layers.

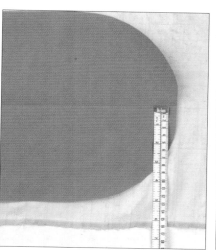

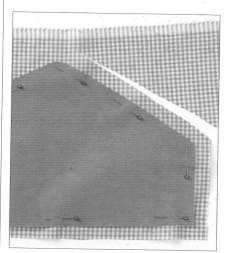

ENLARGING A DESIGN

Take the scaled-down pattern and enlarge it on a photocopier until it is the right size. For example, consider a pattern where the longest back measurement is 5 cm (2 in) while the finished pattern needs to be just over 40 cm (16 in) long. You first should photocopy the printed pattern, enlarging it by 200 percent – it will be 10 cm (4 in) long. Then take the copy and enlarge that by 200 percent – it's now 20 cm (8 in) long. Enlarge that copy again to get the final length – you will have to print it out on A3 paper at this stage. This technique can be used to scale up patterns of any size, although you may have to work out the percentage of the enlargement to get the size that you need.

MITRED CORNERS

PLAIN SQUARE AND RECTANGULAR items such as tablecloths, napkins, and placemats, look best when they have mitred corners. Mitring the corners eliminates any bulky or untidy edges and creates a neat flat finish. Mitred corners can be a decorative feature in themselves if they appear on the surface of the item as a border.

MAKING MITRES

The secret to making neat mitres is accuracy. For the best results, when you turn under your hems, make sure the depth of each turning is the same all round. These turnings will then be pressed to make sharp fold lines that act as guides for stitching. If your turnings aren't consistent, these fold lines will not line up correctly. You can make a single or double mitred hem.

For the purposes of this illustration, each turning is 2 cm (¾ in) deep, but you can use this technique for any depth of hem. Where it is not possible to have the same depth all around, refer to the box, below.

UNEQUAL SEAMS AND HEMS

Occasionally you may want to make a mitred corner where the side seams are thinner than your hem – say with curtains. In this case, both the side and bottom hems need to be double. Fold your side and bottom hems under once and press. Mark the side hems with a pin at the depth of your bottom hem then fold over the side hems from this point and press in place. Then turn the remainder of the side hem allowances to the wrong side. Pin and press firmly in place to provide a steep diagonal edge at each corner at the bottom. Finally, fold over the other half of the bottom hem, aligning the two diagonal edges of each mitred corner. Pin, press then slipstitch the joins in place and then the side and bottom hems.

DOUBLE MITRE

Use a double mitre when you want the mitres to appear on the surface of your make, as on the mats pictured opposite. For the sake of simplicity, the instructions show just one corner being mitred, though you are most likely to be working on four corners at the same time.

SINGLE MITRE

Use a single mitre when you are going to use a lining, as with curtains. If you are not going to use a lining, then make sure you finish off the edges with pinking shears or a zigzag stitch before using catchstitch. If the hems are not the same size, follow the technique outined in the box, page 224. These instructions show just one corner being mitred, though you are most likely to be working on four corners at the same time.

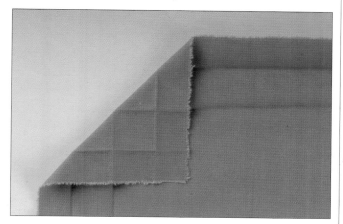

1 Turn under 2 cm (¾ in) all round and press firmly to make a sharp crease. Turn under a further 2 cm (¾ in) and press again. Unfold the hem completely. Fold in a corner so that the folds line up as shown in the picture.

1 Turn the hem allowance to the right side all round. Fold the fabric at the corner diagonally from the point formed at the edge of the fabric to the place where the edges of the hem meet; press.

2 Turn under the first hem again all round, and press. Fold back the top edge of the corner so that the point touches the outer folded edge of the fabric; press.

2 Machine stitch along the diagonal fold line. Trim the seam 5 mm (¼ in) from the stitching and at the corner, and press the seam open.

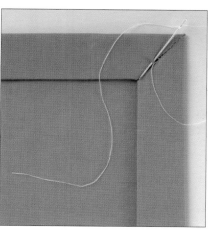

3 Turn under the second hem again all around so that the edges butt together at the corner and pin to hold in place. Slipstitch the edges together at the corner. Press and then slipstitch the hem in place.

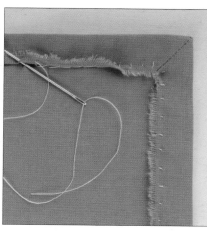

3 Turn the hem to the wrong side of the fabric and press. Catchstitch in place all around. If you like, you can pink the edges first.

BUTTONS & BUTTONHOLES

MOST SEWING MACHINES will make buttonholes and there are even some that will sew on buttons, too, though you will generally sew a button on by hand. If you have an older machine that won't do buttonholes, you can make them by hand, although it will take a little longer. For a machine-made buttonhole, you cut the hole after the stitching is completed; for a handmade one, you cut the slit first. For both types, begin by marking their position on the fabric — draw a line the length you want the hole using an erasable marker. To help you line up buttonholes evenly if you are going to make a row, baste two parallel lines along your fabric, the length of the buttonholes apart.

BUTTON TYPES

Buttons that have a loop on their undersides are known as shank buttons; those with holes in them are sew-through buttons. When you are making something with a medium- or heavyweight material, the buttons you use need to have a shank to raise them above the overlapping fabric and prevent the button pulling the underlapping fabric. If the buttons you want to use are the sew-through variety, you can create a thread shank when you stitch them in place. To sew on either type, use special buttonhole thread or your ordinary thread doubled.

MACHINE-MADE BUTTONHOLES

To make machine buttonholes, follow the instructions in your sewing machine manual, making sure you make holes big enough for your chosen buttons.

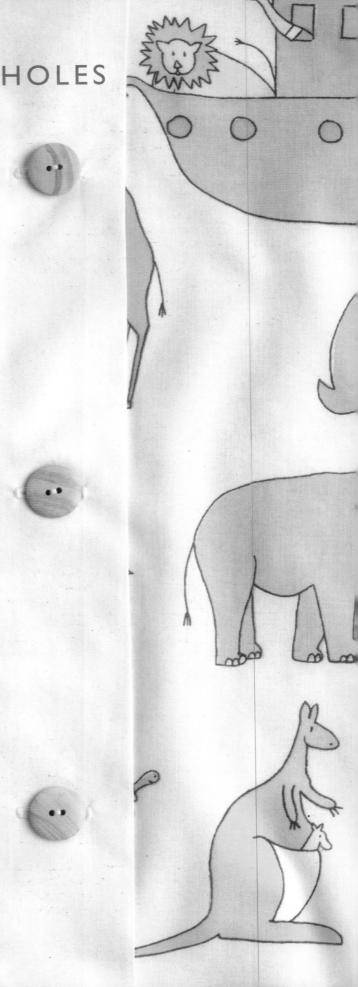

SEWING ON BUTTONS

Stitching a shank button in place

Mark the position of the button. Bring the needle through the fabric at the marked position. Pass the needle through the button's shank and then take it back into the fabric. Bring the needle out again at your starting point. Continue, making five or six small stitches through the shank. Take the needle to the wrong side and fasten off with a few small stitches.

Four-hole buttons

You can stitch between the holes in a variety of ways. One way is to stitch diagonally across the holes to form stitches that cross. A second way is to stitch between two holes and then stitch between the next two holes to form two parallel lines. A third way is to repeat the second technique between the holes at the top of the lines, to form a square.

Stitching a sew-through button

1 Mark the position of the button. Bring the needle through the fabric at the marked position. Pass the needle through one of the holes in the button. Lay a matchstick on top of the button and then pass the needle through the second hole and back into the fabric, so the thread passes over the top of the matchstick. Make five or six more stitches in this way, over the matchstick.

2 Take the needle under the button. Remove the matchstick and then lift the button. Wrap the thread around the stitches under the button a few times to form the thread shank. Take the needle through to the wrong side and fasten off with a few stitches.

MAKING BUTTONHOLES BY HAND

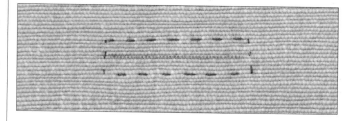

1 First work a rectangle of small running stitches around the mark, 3 mm (⅛ in) from the line on either side and lining up with the ends of the mark. Use matching thread.

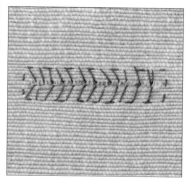

2 Cut along the marked line and to make a slit. Using matching thread, oversew the raw edges of the slit with long diagonal stitches. Keep these within the rectangle of running stitches.

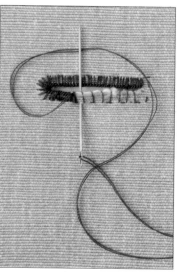

3 Work around the slit, inserting the needle just outside the rectangle of running stitches and bringing it out at the edge of the buttonhole. Loop the thread hanging from the eye of the needle from right to left under the point of the needle and draw the needle upward to knot the thread at the buttonhole edge. At the end of the buttonhole nearest the edge of whatever you are making, work the buttonhole stitches so they fan out.

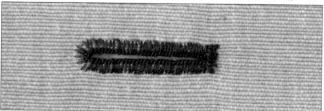

4 At the other end, work a few evenly spaced long stitches, each one the depth of the whole buttonhole. Then work neat horizontal stitches over these to create the bar at the end of the buttonhole. Take the thread through to the wrong side and fasten off.

LOOPS, TIES & TABS

PROJECTS, INCLUDING A NUMBER in this book call for fabric fastenings that are ornamental as well as practical. A bias loop is a handmade fabric tube that passes over a button to hold an opening closed. Ties are simple rectangular strips used as trimmings and to secure an item; bias loops also can be used as ties. Tabs are wider fabric strips used to hang curtains or wall hangings from a pole.

FASTENING KNOW-HOW

Bias loops emerge from a seam and are generally sewn to the edge of fabric before the seam is stitched. If you are making several bias loops, you can make one long tube and then cut it into sections for each loop. Loops should be as long as the combined diameter and depth of the button, plus 2 cm (¾ in). Multiply this loop length by the number of loops you need, and cut a bias strip of fabric (see page 234) to this length by 3 cm (1½in).

Ties and tabs also are generally sewn into the seam, so when making them, one short side can be left unfinished. However, if the tie is to be used simply as a trim, then you have to topstitch down all edges. The same is true of tabs.

Purpose-bought fastenings, such as Velcro® and snap tape (see box), can be used for invisible joins.

SNAP TAPE

If you want to use snaps on an item with a long opening you could use snap tape. This is made up of two lengths of tape with the ball parts of the snaps secured on one side and the socket parts on the other. You simply stitch the tape to either side of the opening, making sure the two parts of the snaps line up exactly.

Making bias loops

Fold your fabric in half lengthwise, right sides together, and stitch between 5 mm (¼ in) and 8 mm (⅜" in) from the fold, depending on the width of the finished loop. Trim the allowance to 5 mm (¼ in). Thread a needle with a

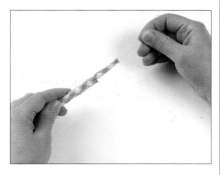

doubled length of thread, making sure this is about 7 cm (2¾ in) longer than the fabric strip. Secure at one end by taking a few stitches in the allowance. Remove the thread from the needle and then thread it into a bodkin.

Insert the bodkin into the fabric and work it along. As it pulls the thread along the tube, it turns the fabric right side out. Continue until the loop is completely turned through; cut into lengths.

Making ties and tabs

Cut strips of fabric to the required length and width remembering to add on seam allowances on all sides. If the ties or tabs are to be sewn into a seam, press in 8 mm (⅜ in) on the long edges and one short side.

1 Fold each tie in half lengthwise, wrong sides together. Pin.

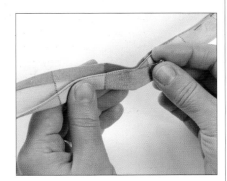

2 Topstitch along the long edges on each one, close to the edge. Topstitch across the short end. If the ties need finishing off, topstitch the other short end.

3 With tabs, fold in half lengthwise, right sides facing. Stitch both long sides together, taking a 8 mm (⅜ in) allowance. Press the seam open so it is centred on the back then stitch across one short end. Turn to right side.

VELCRO

Velcro® is made up of two pieces of tape. One of the pieces is covered with minute stiff hooks, the other with a pile of soft loops. When the two pieces are pressed together, the hooks catch in the loops and hold the tape together. Velcro® can be used for all manner of projects where you want a simple closure for an opening. It comes in different weights, ranging from the soft and lightweight, suitable for delicate fabrics, to the thick and stiff, suitable for heavyweight materials. It can be bought by length and comes in several different widths. You also can buy circles of Velcro® known as coins, which are useful when you would want only a small piece to use as an alternative to snaps. Another Velcro® product has an adhesive backing for sticking to a wall.

Sewing on Velcro®

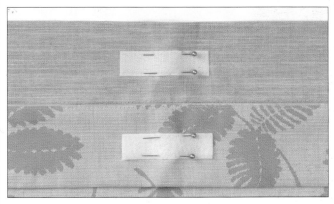

1 Cut a piece of Velcro® to the length you need and pull the two pieces apart. Mark the positions for the Velcro® on either side of your opening and then pin the pieces in place, turning under the raw ends on each. Pin the hook piece to the underlap and the loop piece to the overlap.

2 Machine or hand stitch around each piece, close to the edge. Stitch diagonally, in both directions, across large pieces of Velcro® for extra security. Remember that your stitching will be seen on the other side, so either sew the Velcro® to a lining or facing, or make a feature of the stitching and combine it with topstitched finishes.

ZIPS

INCREDIBLY PRACTICAL and because they close an opening completely, zips work particularly well on anything where you don't want the opening to gape. They are great for a wide range of household accessories and soft furnishings, such as cushion covers and bags.

CHOOSING A ZIP

The instructions on these pages are for the conventional, closed-end type of zipper that is inserted into a seam. This comes in different lengths and weights and has either metal or plastic teeth that are opened and closed with a metal or plastic slider. The teeth are bonded to fabric strips known as tapes. The tapes can be cotton, a cotton blend or synthetic.

Choose a zip appropriate for your project. Buy one where the length of the teeth is just slightly shorter than the opening. If you can't get one in the correct size, use a slightly longer one then shorten it (see below). If you can't find an exact colour match to your fabric, try to keep to the same shade and just look for one that is lighter in tone. If you are using a patterned material, match the zip to the background shade rather than any colour in the pattern. Make sure the zip is an appropriate weight – use lightweight zips with lightweight fabrics, and so on.

TAPE GUIDE

When you are using either of the methods described on page 231 and stitching around the zip on the right side of the fabric, you can use a length of masking tape as a guide. On a centred zip, use tape that's slightly wider than the slider section and cut a piece that's slightly longer than the zip. Stick it over the tacked part of the seam on the right side and stitch around the edge of the tape when you do the final stitching. On the lapped zip, use tape that's as wide as the slider and stick it along the tacked seam.

SHORTENING A ZIP

Close the zip and measure the desired lenfth from the top of the slider. Mark this by a pin, inserted in the zip tape. Set the sewing machine to a wide zigzag but with the length at zero. Stitch across the teeth at the marked point and then trim off the excess zip below the stitching.

SEWING IN A ZIP

With a centred zip, the zip is placed just under the point where the edges of the opening meet. The stitching around the zip that secures it is visible on the right side.

On a lapped zip, one of the edges of the opening overlaps the zip and conceals it. The stitching is only visible on one side of the zip.

Centred zip

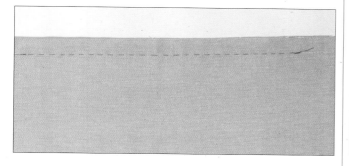

1 Put your two pieces of fabric right sides together and pin along your seam. Mark the beginning and ending of the opening and machine stitch the seam on either side of the marks. Tack across the opening using small, even stitches. Press the seam open.

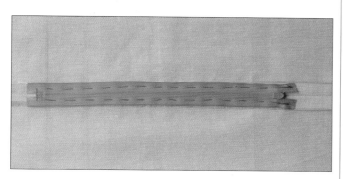

2 Pin the closed zip along the seam on the wrong side, right side down, and tack in place. Fit your sewing machine with a zip foot (see page 217).

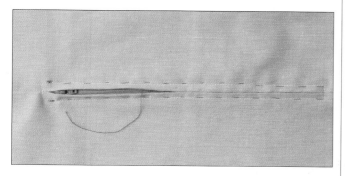

3 Stitch around the zip on the right side, as close to the zip as possible. Use an seam ripper and remove the tacking. Open the zip; when you finish the project and turn the item to the right side, you will be able to turn it through the zip opening.

Lapped zip

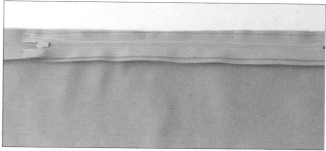

1 Prepare your two pieces of fabric as in step 1 of the centred zip. Lay them out wrong side up so the two pieces of fabric are together and one seam allowance extends above the fabric. Place the closed zip right side down along the seam and pin to the top allowance only. Using a zipper foot, machine stitch in place, close to the teeth.

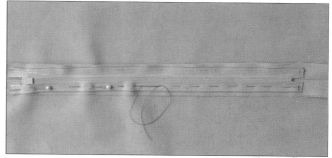

2 Lay the fabric out flat again and pin the other side of the zip to the other allowance, pinning through the tape, the allowance, and the fabric underneath; tack.

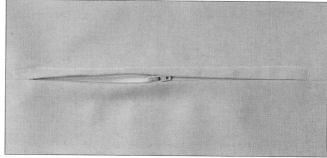

3 Turn to the right side and machine stitch around this side of the zip, where the tacking is visible, close to the zip's teeth. Unpick all the tacking and open the zip.

BIAS BINDING

BIAS BINDING IS USED instead of a hem to finish the raw edges of fabric. It's made from fabric that has been cut on the bias (see page 209) so it is very stretchy and can be eased around shaped edges. It is a neat and sturdy finish and is particularly practical where areas get a lot of use or the fabric is worn or raveled. It's also good for finishing a quilted item to avoid a bulky hem.

BOUGHT BIAS BINDING

You can buy bias binding in limited colors and widths or you can create your own (see pages 234-5). Most commercially produced bias binding is made of cotton but there are also metallic finishes and special, satin binding, which is available to finish off throws and blankets. Ready-made binding is most often sold as long strips that have their edges folded in. (Double bias binding is also available.) You simply place the binding over the edge of your fabric and topstitch once all the way around – which is the fastest method, or machine stitch one side and slipstitch (see page 213) the other side by hand – which makes the stitching invisible. You'll also need to turn the ends of the binding if you are finishing a single edge, and to join the ends if you are binding all around an item.

REINFORCED EDGING

Bias binding is often used around the pockets of aprons or tote bags to prevent the fabric tearing at the bottom when fingers push inside or when they are used to hold heavy or sharp objects. For extra security, you can use double bias binding.

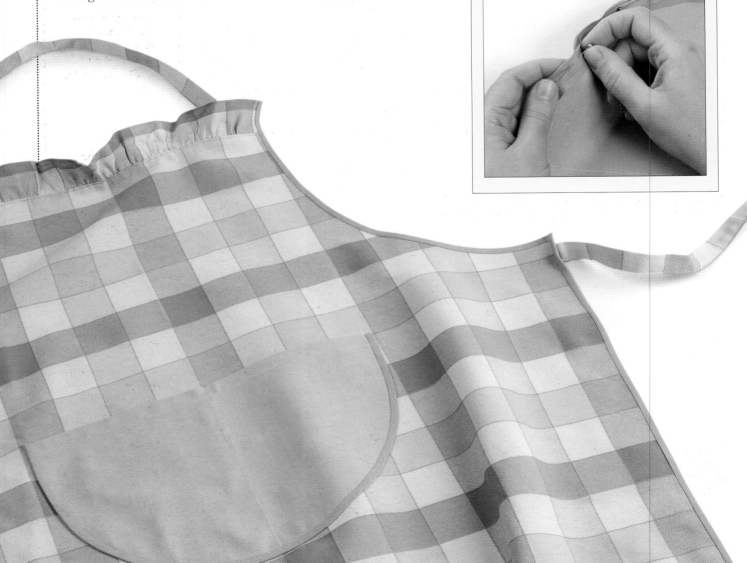

USING BOUGHT BIAS BINDING

Attaching the binding (slipstitch method)

1 Trim the seam allowance on your fabric to the same depth as the turning on the binding. Open out one turning on the binding and pin it along the edge of the fabric, right sides together and matching the raw edges. Tack and then machine stitch along the fold line.

2 Fold the binding over the fabric edge to the wrong side, so the edge of the binding is just above the machine stitching, and pin in place. Use slipstitch to stitch the folded edge of the binding to the fabric, catching up the fabric in the allowance, just above the machine stitching.

Joining the ends of the binding

Stitch the binding to the edge of the fabric, turning under the raw end at the beginning of the binding by 5 mm (¼ in), and when you get to the end, allow the binding to overlap the turned end by about 2 cm (¾ in). Fold the binding over the fabric, as before. If you like, slipstitch around the fold of the turned end.

Turning under the ends

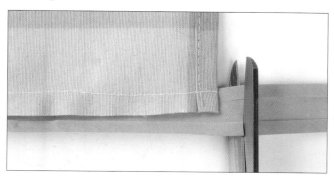

1 Stitch the binding to the fabric. Turn the fabric to the wrong side and trim the excess binding to 8 mm (⅜ in).

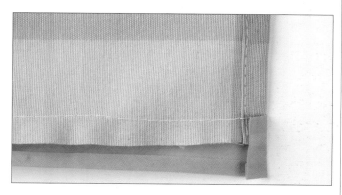

2 Fold the end of the binding over, so the fold lines up with the edge of the fabric; press. Then fold the rest of the binding to the wrong side. Use slipstitch to stitch the edge of the binding in place and along the end to secure.

Stitching binding to a corner

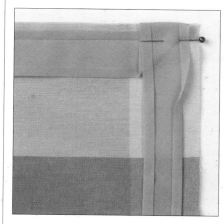

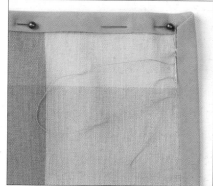

1 Stitch the edge of the binding to the first edge of the fabric as in step 1 of attaching the binding, stitching right up to the edge. Fold the binding up to form a diagonal fold at the corner, then fold it down so the edge of the binding lines up with the second edge of the fabric. Pin, baste, then stitch this edge as before.

2 Fold the binding stitched to the first edge up on the right side and then over to the wrong side.

3 Press the binding on the right side into a neat mitre at the corner. A diagonal fold will be formed in the binding.

4 Fold the binding over the second edge; you should get a neat miter at the corner on the wrong side. Slipstitch or machine stitch to hold in place.

BIAS STRIPS

HOME-MADE BIAS BINDING has several advantages: you can make it in any fabric, including the main fabric for your project, and to any width. You also can use it to cover cord and make your own piping (see page 236). A special device, known as a bias tape maker, can make short work of creating your own strips.

MAKING YOUR OWN BIAS BINDING

Although you can make binding from any fabric, closely woven light- or medium-weight fabrics will give you the best result. Make sure that whatever fabric you use, it has the same care instructions as your original fabric. For a single binding, you need to cut out strips that are four times the desired finished width. You will most likely have to join strips of your fabric together to get a long-enough length. You'll then need to stitch the binding in place. If you are finishing a single edge, you'll also need to turn the ends of the binding (see page 233) and if you are binding all around an item, you'll have to join the ends. Instructions are given below.

A BIAS TAPE MAKER

This handy device turns both edges of your bias strip simultaneously, making it ready for ironing.

Cut the end of the bias strip on the diagonal and feed it through the tape maker.

As the folded strip emerges, press.

Cutting bias strips

If you want only small amounts of binding, you can cut out individual bias strips and join them by pinning two strips right sides together with short diagonal edges matching. Stitch, taking a 5 mm (¼ in) allowance. Trim the points at the ends of the seam allowance level with edges of the strip. Or, for a longer, continuous strip, use this method.

1 Take a square or rectangle in your chosen fabric. Straighten the ends and then re-align the grain if necessary (see page 209). Fold the fabric diagonally so the straight crosswise edge is parallel to the selvedge or lengthwise-grain edge. Press the fold firmly to create an obvious crease. Unfold the fabric then draw parallel lines on either side of the crease, spaced evenly apart. Trim the fabric to make a square or rectangle.

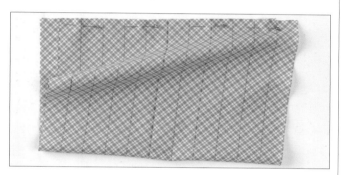

2 Bring the lengthwise-grain edges right sides together, so the cut edge of the fabric lines up with the first drawn line in from the same edge. Pin and then stitch along the seam, just inside the selvedge. Press the seam open.

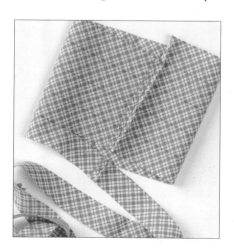

3 Trim off the points at the end of the seam allowance. Begin at one end and start cutting along the marked line. Cut continuously until you reach the end of the marked line.

Forming the binding

Use a bias tape maker to turn under the raw edges, then press the folded strip as it emerges. Alternatively, turn under each long edge of the strip by 5 mm (¼ in) and press in place.

Attaching the binding

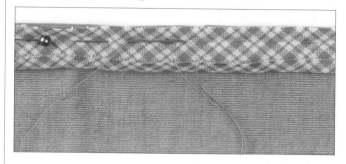

1 Trim the seam allowance on your fabric so it is the same depth as the turning on the binding. Open out one turning on the binding and pin it along the edge of the fabric, right sides together. Baste it in place, then machine stitch along the fold line, remembering to turn under the raw end at the beginning by 5 mm (¼ in).

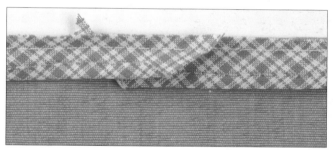

2 When you get to the end, allow the binding to overlap the turned end by about 2 cm (¾ in). Cut the end on the diagonal.

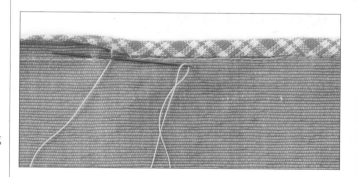

3 Fold the binding over the fabric edge to the wrong side, so the edge of the binding is just above the machine stitching, and pin in place. Slipstitch the folded edge of the binding to the fabric, catching up the fabric in the allowance, just above the machine stitching. You can slipstitch around the fold of the turned end, if you like.

PIPING

PIPING IS A POPULAR trimming that's often used on soft furnishings to give seams a firm, definite finish. It is made of a colour that either complements or contrasts with the main material and is made from a bias strip of fabric that's folded over a length of cord. Piping is sewn between two pieces of fabric so it creates a definite ridge, running along the seam.

WORKING WITH PIPING

Ready-made piping is available in a huge range of colours, fabrics and sizes but if you want piping to match your fabric, you can make your own (see below). There are several different thicknesses of cord you can buy; you could even use narrow rope if you want a really chunky piping.

On the opposite page, you will find information about how to attach piping – you use the same technique for both store-bought and home-made. Whether you are making piping or sewing it on, you need to fit a zip or piping foot to your sewing machine.

To get the width you need, measure the circumference of your cord and add on 3 cm (1¼ in). To get the length, measure along the edge of the fabric on which you want to add the piping and add on 5 cm (2 in) for overlaps.

MAKING YOUR OWN PIPING

Cut a bias strip (see page 235) to your dimensions and your cord to length. Fold the strip over the cord, with right side outermost, bringing the raw edges of the strip together. Pin and tack along the strip, close to the cord.

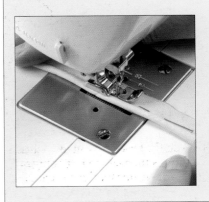

Position the strip under the zip foot so the needle is up against the cord. Machine stitch along the fabric, keeping the needle close to the cord, but avoiding stitching through the cord itself.

Sewing on piping

If you are using home-made piping, you can make it to length (see box, page 236). If you are buying piping, measure along the edge of the fabric on which you are adding the piping and add on 5 cm (2 in) for overlaps.

Joining piping

If you are applying a continuous length of piping around an object, you will have to join the ends. If you want to be absolutely certain that your piping won't ravel, you can, if you like, unpick the ends of both the old and new cords and interweave them before replacing the bias strips on both ends.

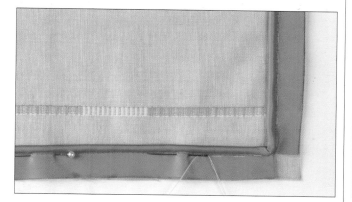

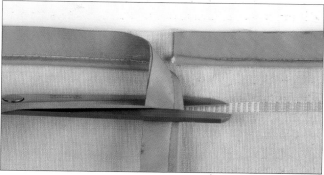

1 Pin the piping to the edge of the fabric, on the right side, and matching the raw edges of the piping to the raw edge of the fabric. Leave at least 2 cm (¾ in) of piping free at the start and finish 3 cm (1¼ in) from your starting point. Tack in place. If you're applying piping in a sharp angled corner, snip into the flat part of the piping to ease the fit.

2 Fit a zip or piping foot and machine stitch around the piping, as close to the cord as possible, leaving the 2 cm (¾ in) of piping free at the start. Finish stitching 3 cm (1¼ in) from the starting point of your stitching. Take your sewing out of the machine and finish as in joining piping, steps 2 and 3.

1 When you have finished stitching your piping (3 cm [1¼ in]) from the end), trim it so it overlaps the beginning by 2 cm (¾ in). Unpick the stitching in the piping by 2 cm (¾ in).

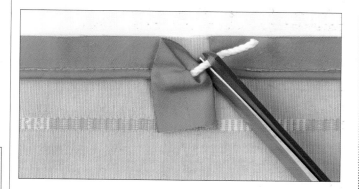

2 Roll back the fabric to reveal the cord. Trim the end so it fits flush with the beginning of the new piping.

MAKING A NEAT EDGE

To ensure a neat finish when sewing on piping, stitch close to the covered cord, following the line of stitching on the piping. When you have finished, use zigzag stitch along the raw edge of the piping and fabric. Alternatively, pink and stitch the raw edges (see page 219).

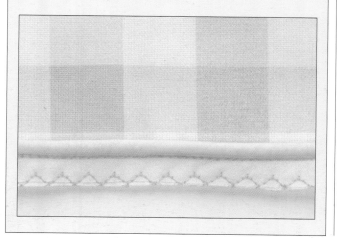

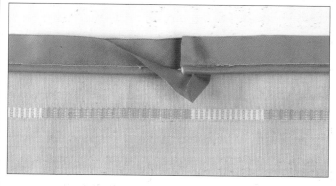

3 Turn under 8 mm (⅜ in) on the bias strip you just rolled back, then fold this piece of bias strip over the beginning of the piping. Pin in place and then resume machine stitching the piping.

USING TRIMS

HOME-SEWN PROJECTS can be given that special touch that lifts them out of the ordinary by adding a decorative trim. The simple cushion, below, for example, has been made up with two different fabrics.

A plain ribbon is stitched over the seam and a pleated ribbon is stitched at each end of the panel. Circles were cut from embroidered fabric and applied as appliqués (see page 182).

ADDING TRIMMINGS

Trims fall into two types – those that are bonded to a length of tape (the insertion tape) that is concealed inside a seam or under a turning – and flat trims. When you stitch flat trims into a seam or under a turning you conceal part of the decorative element. Therefore, flat trims are ideal for stitching over a hem or seam. Beaded and bobble trims generally come on an insertion tape, and you can also buy ready-made ruffles, where the fabric is gathered onto the insertion tape. Some lace is attached to tape, but generally lace is sold as a flat trim, as is ribbon, braid, and rickrack.

MAKING RUFFLES

Cut a fabric strip to at least double the length of the piece to which you will add it and to the desired width, remembering to add seam allowances all around, if appropriate.

Take your strip and hem one long and two short edges as required.

Run a line of tacking stitches for gathering along the remaining raw long edge, leaving a loose thread at the beginning and end. Pull on the loose ends of the tacking thread to gather the ruffle so that it fits the dimensions of the fabric you are trimming. Pin the pieces together, tack, then stitch.

Stitching a trim to a hem

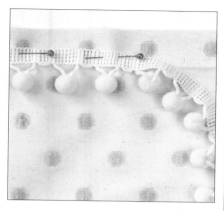

1 Turn under your hem allowance and press in place. Unfold the hem and lay out the fabric flat, right side up. Take your trim and match up the bottom edge of the insertion tape to the fold line; pin along the insertion tape; tack.

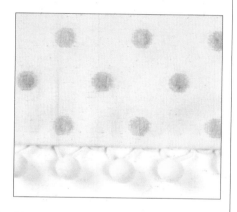

2 Turn under your hem again. Press again and pin in place. Hand or machine stitch the hem – the trim will hang below the edge of the hem.

Using a trim to cover a seam

Begin by pressing your seam open. Cut your flat trim to length and pin over the seam, turning under the ends of the trim. Secure with tacking: If the trim is narrow, make diagonal stitches, zigzagging over the trim; if it is wide, tack along either side. Machine stitch in place along each side of the trim. You also can use a strip of contrasting fabric in the same way. Simply cut to length and turn under the raw edges before tacking.

Using a trim as hemming

When adding a decorative trim to the edge of a project, you can use the stitching that secures the trim to hold a hem in place. Begin by turning under your hem and pressing it, then baste along the hem.

Lay your trim over the hem so it covers the basting, turning under the ends of the trim; pin. Stitch over the trim, making sure that you stitch through the hem. Here, rickrack has been stitched using herringbone stitch. Working from left to right, bring the needle and thread to the right side of the fabric at the bottom of the trim. Take the needle and thread across the trim and take a small stitch through the hem at the top of the trim where the curve dips down, inserting the needle from right to left. Repeat to make a stitch at the bottom of the trim. Continue in this way to the end of the trim. Using a thread that matches the trim will conceal the diagonal stitches. Choose a contrasting thread and you can make a feature of the stitching.

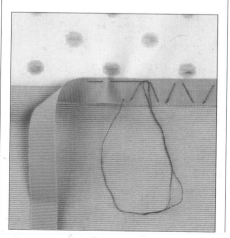

Stitching a trim in a seam

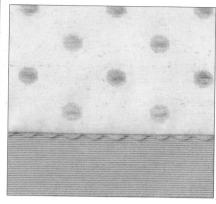

1 If using a flat trim, like rickrack, press under the allowance on one of your pieces of fabric. Unfold, then baste the trim along the allowance on the right side, so that part of the trim is above the pressed fold. Pin your pieces of fabric right sides together and stitch, making sure you take the correct allowance. Press the seam open; the trim will be between the two fabrics.

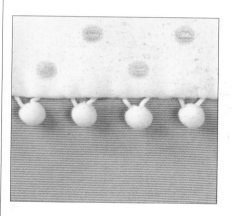

2 If using a trim with an insertion tape, press under the allowance as above. Unfold and pin the trim along the allowance, on the right side, so that the bottom edge of the insertion tape lines up with the pressed fold; tack in place. Stitch your pieces of fabric together as above; when the seam is pressed open, the trim will be sandwiched between the two fabrics.

FABRIC GLOSSARY

FABRICS ARE DEFINED by their composition – the fibres of which they are made and their construction – and the type of weave. Other defining factors are their texture and weight. The most important consideration when choosing fabrics, besides personal taste, is whether they are suitable for the use to which you want to put them. Always read the label in store before you buy.

FABRIC TYPES

Fabrics can be made of natural fibres, which can be of animal origin like wool or silk or from plants such as linen and cotton. Manmade fabrics (i.e. rayon) are those in which naturally occurring materials such as cellulose fibre, are chemically processed. Synthetic fabrics, such as polyester, are made entirely from chemicals. Natural, manmade and synthetic fibres also may be blended together in different combinations before final processing in order to create fabrics with different qualities. Adding polyester to cotton, for example, increases the cotton's lightness, strength and resistance to wrinkles. Moreover, other processes may be applied to natural materials in order to increase their useability. Cottons are often glazed to enhance their appearance and help them resist soiling and they may have minimum-iron, crease-, stain- or shrink-resistant finishes added. Wool may be pre-shrunk or treated for shrink-resistance and can be made mothproof and stain resistant.

As far as construction goes, most home furnishing fabrics are plain weaves. Patterns are printed on their surface. However some, such as Jacquard fabrics, are woven to produce textured surface effects, and both self-coloured pattern motifs and those of two or more colours.

Texture is a result of both the fibres used and the method of construction. Found in all weights, textured fabrics may have surfaces that are smooth and shiny, rough or soft, or discreet.

Barkweave
A self-coloured fabric with a rough texture similar to that of tree bark. It is generally made from cotton.

Brocade
A medium- or heavyweight fabric with a raised pattern. The patterns are often formed by metallic threads.

Broderie Anglaise
A white or pale pastel coloured lightweight cotton fabric with a lacy embroidered pattern and cut-out detail. Generally available as a trimming.

Buckram
This is usually made from cotton or jute and is used with other fabrics as stiffening. It comes in several different weights. Washing may remove some of the stiffening.

Burlap
Usually made from jute, this is a strong, coarse, and loosely woven fabric that is hardwearing and informal. It may sag when draped.

Calico
Plain-woven cotton that comes in a range of weights and qualities depending on the yarn used. Can be bought pre-shrunk or un-shrunk, and bleached and unbleached.

Cambric
A fine, plain-woven cotton or linen fabric, it usually has a glaze on the right side that adds stiffening. A down-proof form is used as a permanent inner cover for pillows and quilts.

Canvas
A heavyweight, closely woven, cotton or linen that is informal and hardwearing. Sometimes known as duck.

Chambray
A lightweight but hardwearing cotton fabric. Generally, the warp threads of this material are coloured, whereas the weft threads are white. It has a denim-like appearance and is most commonly available in shades of blue.

Chenille
A medium- to heavyweight cotton or cotton/synthetic blend with a soft pile.

Chiffon
A very sheer, plain weave fabric made in cotton, silk, or synthetic fibres.

Chintz
A plain-weave, mediumweight cotton with a glazed surface, that is usually printed with floral patterns.

Corduroy
Hardwearing, medium- to heavyweight fabric, usually cotton, with a ridged pile. The ribs can vary from very wide to narrow needlecord.

Crêpe
This is a fine, lightweight fabric, with a slightly crinkled surface, which can be made from cotton, wool, silk or synthetic fibres.

Curtain interlining
Used inside curtains to add warmth; Domette is a lightweight interlining, whereas bump is thicker.

Curtain lining
This is usually a closely woven, cotton sateen, a fabric with a slight sheen. It comes in a range of colours, though is most usually sold in white or shades of cream.

Damask
Made on a Jacquard loom so that the threads form an unraised floral or geometric design against a satin-weave ground. Similar to but finer than brocade.

Denim
A hardwearing, mediumweight cotton fabric with a twill weave. The warp threads are usually a dark blue and the weft are generally white.

Dimity
A sheer cotton that uses heavier threads to create a pattern in the weave.

Dobby weave
Any fabric where the weave produces a small, raised geometric pattern.

Dotted Swiss
A sheer cotton with a woven pattern of opaque dots.

Drill
A hardwearing, mediumweight, closely woven cotton with a twill weave.

Dupion
Medium- to heavyweight, silk or synthetic fabric with a distinctive slubbed surface on one side.

Fake fur
Synthetic fabric with fibres that simulate real fur.

Fake suede
A plain-weave cotton or synthetic fabric that has been given a slight nap on one side to resemble the texture of real suede.

Felt
A non-woven, mediumweight fabric that can be made of almost any fibre. It doesn't fray when cut.

Flannel
A soft, lightweight fabric with either a plain or twill weave. It has a slight nap and can be made with cotton, wool or synthetic fibres.

Fleece
A modern synthetic fabric with the texture of a lightweight wool fleece.

Gabardine
A light- to mediumweight, hardwearing cotton or wool with a twill weave.

Gingham
A plain-weave, light- to mediumweight checked or striped cotton or cotton/synthetic blend in two colours. The checks or stripes come in a range of sizes and shades.

Interfacing
This is used to stiffen other fabrics. You can use a fusible interfacing that is ironed on, or a sewn-on variety. Both come in a wide range of different weights.

Jacquard weave
This is any fabric where the weave produces a raised pattern (such as damask or brocade).

Jersey
A lightweight, plain-knit fabric made from wool, cotton, silk or synthetic fibres, or a blend.

Lace
An openwork, lightweight fabric in cotton or synthetic fibres. A wide range of lace trimmings is also available.

Lawn
A very fine, semi-sheer cotton or cotton blend with a smooth, even surface.

Linen
A hardwearing fabric made from the flax plant that ranges from very fine to heavyweight but with a tendency to crease.

Linen union
A mediumweight, linen and cotton blend.

Madras
A plain-weave, lightweight cotton in strongly coloured plaids, stripes or checks.

Moiré
Any fabric finished with a water-marked effect. It's generally associated with silk taffeta, but can be made with cotton or synthetic fibres. Light- to mediumweight.

Muslin
This plain-weave cotton comes in a range of weights and qualities, bleached or unbleached. The sheer, loosely woven, very lightweight muslin is the most popularly used. Swiss muslin has decorative embroidered detail.

Nap
A fabric with a nap has short fibers on the surface that have been drawn out of the yarn of the fabric.

Net
A very lightweight, sheer fabric with an open mesh, made in cotton or synthetic fibres.

Organdy
A sheer, plain-weave fabric, usually cotton, that has been stiffened slightly.

Organza
A thin, transparent silk or synthetic that is slightly stiff.

Ottoman
Medium- to heavyweight, hardwearing fabric with a horizontal rib, made from wool, cotton, silk or synthetic fibres.

Plain weave
Any fabric where the weft thread goes under one and then over one warp thread.

Percale
A lightweight cotton or cotton-blend fabric with a fine, plain weave, that's often used for bed linen.

Pile fabrics
Any fabric that resembles fur to some degree, in that it has raised fibres that obscure the basic weave of the fabric. Fake fur, terrycloth, corduroy and velvet are all pile fabrics.

Polished cotton
Any cotton with a glazed finish.

Poplin
A fabric where the weft threads are slightly heavier than the warp, giving a slight ribbed effect. It can be made from most fibre types but is most commonly found in a medium- to heavyweight cotton.

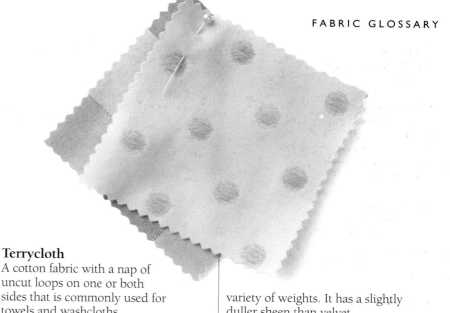

PVC coated
A polyvinyl chloride topcoat is applied to a woven or knitted fabric so that a tough, non-porous fabric is produced. This can be wiped clean.

Repp
A fabric with a ribbed effect, such as ottoman.

Sateen
A cotton fabric woven with the same type of weave used for silk or synthetic satin to create a light- to mediumweight fabric with a subtle sheen.

Satin
A silk or synthetic fabric created with a satin weave to produce a smooth and slippery fabric. It comes in a wide range of weights.

Satin weave
Any fabric where the weft threads pass over more than one and then under one warp thread, giving the fabric a lustrous sheen.

Seersucker
A mediumweight cotton or cotton blend with a crinkly texture in the weave. It is usually striped or checked.

Serge
A hardwearing, mediumweight wool, silk or synthetic fabric with a twill weave.

Shantung
A lightweight fabric with an uneven, slubbed texture. Usually silk but it can also be cotton or synthetic.

Sheeting
Plain-weave cotton, linen, or polyester/cotton mix fabric of a weight suitable for sheets and another bedlinen. Available in larger than average width and in a range of colours and patterns.

Suiting
Any fabric that could be used to make suits or coats.

Taffeta
A mediumweight, slightly shiny fabric with a crisp finish. It can be made with silk, cotton or synthetic fibres.

Terrycloth
A cotton fabric with a nap of uncut loops on one or both sides that is commonly used for towels and washcloths.

Ticking
A mediumweight drill cloth that is traditionally striped.

Tweed
A heavyweight woollen fabric with a rough texture that is usually checked or plaid.

Twill
Any fabric where the weave has created diagonal ridges on the surface of the material (such as gabardine, serge, or drill).

Union
A name give to fabrics that consist of mixed fibre in the yarn or cloth. Cotton and linen unions are robust nd hardwearing.

Velour
A warm, heavy fabric with a thick pile. Can be made of cotton, wool or synthetic fibres.

Velvet
A pile fabric made from cotton, silk, or synthetic blends – the pile may be made from one fiber while the backing is made from another. It's a medium- to heavyweight fabric.

Velveteen
A cotton pile fabric that is very similar to velvet and which comes in a variety of weights. It has a slightly duller sheen than velvet

Voile
A soft, sheer fabric made from loosely woven cotton or synthetic yarn.

Worsted
A combed wool yarn or woolen fabric that is hardwearing but has a smooth surface texture.

PROJECTS

HERE'S YOUR OPPORTUNITY TO PUT YOUR SKILLS
TO WORK. There are over fifty original projects – at least ten for
each craft – on which to practise the techniques learned. You will
find lots of items to wear, use in the home or to give as gifts.

The projects have been created by top designers – and all are
within the capabilities of novice needleworkers. Of course, you
may be able to use the pattern glossaries in the technique
sections to further personalise your item.

Some of the projects require templates, which are found at the
back of this section, and many are illustrated with step-by-step
photographs so that success is assured. Now all that's required is
for you to take up needle(s) and thread and begin creating.

CONTENTS

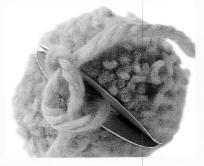

TWISTED RIB HAT

BRIM

Using main colour, cast on 40 stitches.
Work 8 rows in twisted rib: k1b, p1.
Work 8 rows st st.

SHAPE CROWN

Row 1 (RS): (K7, K3 tog) 4 times – 32 sts.
Row 2: Purl.
Row 3: (K5, K3 tog) 4 times – 24 sts.
Row 4: Purl.
Row 5: (K3, K3 tog) 4 times – 16 sts.
Row 6: Purl.
Row 7: (K1, K3 tog) 4 times – 8 sts.
Row 8: Purl.
Break yarn (leaving enough to sew up hat)
and thread through remaining sts. Pull up
tightly and secure.

FINISHING

Stitch back seam on inside. Press lightly.
Make pompom and attach to top of hat.

❖ **SIZE**
One size: To fit average head,
48 cm (19 in) circumference

❖ **MATERIALS**
Yarn Super Chunky 100% merino
wool (approx 180 m per 100 g).
1 x 100g ball. Scraps of
contrasting colour for pompom
(optional)
Needles One pair 12 mm or
size to obtain tension
Notions Tapestry needle

❖ **TENSION**
8 sts and 11 rows to 10 cm
(4 in) over stocking stitch

❖ See page 37 for knitting terms.

MAKING POMPOMS

1 Cut two cardboard circles to desired size
of finished pompom. In the centre of each
circle, cut a hole about one third of the total
diameter. Place the circles together. Wrap
the yarn as shown.

2 Continue wrapping yarn until the central
holes are completely filled. If you run out of yarn,
take a new length, continue wrapping, and leave
the ends dangling at the outer edge.

3 Cut through the yarn around the outer
edge. Ease the circles slightly apart and
wrap a length of yarn tightly around the
central strands a few times. Secure with a
firm knot. Pull off the cardboard circles. Fluff
out pompom, and trim with sharp scissors.
Use dangling threads to attach to garment.

TUBE TOP

✤ SIZES

XS, S, M, L, XL: To fit bust 81 (86, 91, 96.5, 101.5) cm (32 [34, 36, 38, 40] in).
Finished size: Bust 71 (76, 81, 86, 91) cm (28 [30, 32, 34, 36] in)

✤ MATERIALS

Yarn Brocade tape 50% cotton/40% rayon/10% nylon (approx. 144 m per 100 g).
2 (2, 2, 3, 3) x 100 g hanks
Needles One pair each 4 mm and 6 mm or size to obtain tension
Notions Tapestry needle, crochet hook

✤ TENSION

13 sts and 18 rows = 10 cm (4 in) over moss stitch

✤ See page 37 for knitting terms.

✤ See template on page 306

TWISTED CORD

The thicker the cord you want, the more strands of yarn you will need. The minimum is 4 strands. The length of the strands should be 3 times the length of the finished cord, including the tassel. Tie the strands together at one end and loop over a door handle. Then stand back and hold the yarn taut in one hand. Twist the strands towards the right until a firm twist has been obtained along the whole length of the strands. Still holding the yarn taut, remove the strands from the handle, and fold in half lengthways. Knot together the two ends about 2.5-4 cm (1-1½ in) from the end. Hold the knotted end and let the cord twist up on itself, then smooth out any irregularities. Snip the yarns at the end to form a tassel.

BACK AND FRONT

(One piece)
With 4 mm needles cast on 358 (382, 410, 434, 462) sts.

FRILLY EDGE

Row 1 (RS): K1 *k2, slip 1st st over 2nd st on RH needle, rep from * to last st, k1.
Row 2: Purl.
Row 3: Work as row 1.
Row 4: Purl – 91 (97, 104, 110, 117) sts.
Change to 6 mm needles and work in moss st (see page 00) until piece measures 25 [25, 25, 28, 28) cm 10 [10, 10, 11, 11] in) from cast on edge. Cast off.

FINISHING
SHOULDER STRAPS

Make two 38 cm (15 in) (or size to fit) twisted cords (see page 40). Attach one cord to the top edge, one end 11.5 (11.5, 11.5, 13, 13) cm (4½ [4½, 4½, 5⅛ 5⅛] in) from centre back and other end 25 (28, 30, 32, 33) cm (10 [11, 12, 12.5, 13] in) from centre back. Repeat with the other cord.

BACK FASTENINGS

Make two 60 cm (24 in) twisted cords. Sew the cords to the back above the frilly edge. Using a crochet hook, lace the straps evenly at approximately 4.5 cm (1¾ in) intervals up the centre back and tie in a bow at the top. Steam lightly.

CABLED SKI HATS

CABLE PATTERN

C4F: Slip 2 sts purlwise one at a time to cable needle (cn) and hold at front of work, k2, k2 from cn.

Row 1: *P2, k4; rep from * to last 2 sts, p2.
Row 2: *K2, p4; rep from * to last 2 sts, k2.
Row 3: *P2, C4F; rep from * to last 2 sts, p2.
Row 4: *K2, p4; rep from * to last 2 sts, k2.
Repeat rows 1 to 4.

HAT WITH FLAPS
BRIM

Using 5 mm needles, cast on 86 sts. Work 6 rows in garter st.
Change to 6.5 mm needles and work in cable pattern until work measures 18 cm (7 in) from cast-on edge ending on patt row 2.

SHAPE CROWN

Row 1: *P2tog; C4F; repeat from * to last 2 sts, p2tog – 71 sts.
Row 2: *K1, p1, p2tog, p1; repeat from * to last st, k1 – 57 sts.
Row 3: *K2tog; rep from * to last st, k1 – 29 sts.
Row 4: Purl.
Row 5: *K2tog; rep from * to last st, k1 – 15 sts.
Row 6: Purl.
Row 7: *K2tog; rep from * to last st, k1 – 8 sts.
Rows 8–11: Work in st st.
Row 12: P2tog across row. Break off yarn, thread through remaining sts and secure firmly on inside.

EAR FLAPS

Make 2.
Using 5 mm needles, cast on 2 sts.
Row 1 (RS): K2.
Row 2: Yarn over needle to make a st (yo), k2.
Row 3: Yo, k3.
Row 4: Yo, k4.
Row 5: Yo, k5.
Cont as above, making one yo at beg of every row until there are 20 sts. Work even in garter st until flap measures 18 cm (7 in) from point. Cast off. Make second flap.

FINISHING

With tapestry needle and yarn, stitch back seam on inside. Stitch ear flaps onto hat 7.5 cm (3 in) from back seam. Make 6 21.5 cm (8½ in) tassels (see below) and attach three tassels to point of each ear flap. Steam lightly.

HAT WITHOUT FLAPS
BRIM

Work as Hat with Flaps up to row 7 of crown.
Row 8: Purl.
Break off yarn; thread through remaining sts and secure firmly.

FINISHING

Make 4 21.5 cm (8½ in) tassels (see below) and attach to crown. Steam lightly.

MAKING A TASSEL

1 Wrap yarn around cardboard cut to desired length. Thread length of yarn under top loops, and tie tightly; leave one end long. Cut through yarn at lower edge.

2 Hide knot and short end of yarn under tassel strands. Wind long end tightly around strands to form a neat top. Thread needle with long end of yarn and push under binding and out through top of tassel. Trim ends if necessary.

SIZE
One size: 28 cm wide and 33 cm long (11 x 13 in)

MATERIALS
Yarn Medium weight 100% cotton denim (approx 93 m per 50 g). 4 x 50 g balls
Needles One pair each 3.25 mm and 4 mm or size to obtain tension, cable needle
Notions Tapestry needle

TENSION
20 sts and 32 rows = 10 cm (4 in) over stocking stitch using 4 mm needles

See page 37 for knitting terms.

DOUBLE CABLE STITCH
C10B: Place 5 sts on cable needle (cn) and hold at back of work, k5, k5 from cn
C10F: Place 5 sts on cn and hold at front of work, k5, k5 from cn.

BACK
With 4 mm needles cast on 56 sts.
Work in st st until piece measures 30 cm (12 in).
Change to 3.25 mm needles and work **4 rows garter st, then 2 rows st st.
Next row (eyelet row): K3 *yo, k2tog, k5; repeat from * to last 4 st, k4.
Next row: Purl.
Work 4 rows garter st.
Cast off.

FRONT
With 4 mm needles cast on 78 sts. Work 2 rows in st st.
Row 1 (RS): P13, k20, p12, k20, p13.
Row 2: K13, p20, k12, p20, k13.
Row 3: P13, C10B, C10F, p12, C10B, C10F, p13.
Row 4: K13, p20, k12, p20, k13.
Rows 5, 7, 9, 11: P13, k20, p12, k20, p13.
Rows 6, 8, 10, 12: K13, p20, k12, p20, k13.
Repeat rows 1 – 12 until piece measures 30cm (12in), ending on RS row.
Next row (WS) and continuing in pattern: *work 1, work 2 tog, work 2, work 2 tog; rep from * 11 times, work 1 – 56 sts.
Change to 3.25 mm needles and work as for Back from ** to end.

FINISHING
Block and press on WS. Using backstitch on edge of work, join 3 seams, leaving top edge open. Make a 165 cm (65 in) twisted cord (see page 247). Thread cord through the eyelets; start at the side seam, once around, then back again to finish on other side seam. Knot the ends of the cord and cut to form tassels. Secure the tassels at the bottom corners of the bag.

RIBBON-TIED CARDIGAN

BACK

Using 4 mm needles, cast on 114 (118, 126, 134, 142) sts and work in trinity st (see page 51) until piece measures 33 (33, 34, 34, 35.5) cm (13 [13, 13½, 13½, 14] in) from cast-on edge ending on WS row.

ARMHOLE SHAPING

Keeping patt correct as set, cast off 3 (3, 4, 4, 5) sts at beg of next 2 rows and then dec 1 st at both ends of the next and foll alt rows 5 (6, 8, 11, 13) times – 98 (100, 102, 104, 106) sts. Continue even in patt as set until the armhole measures 18 (18, 18, 19, 19) cm (7 [7, 7, 7½, 7½] in) ending on WS row.

SHOULDER SHAPING

Keeping patt correct as set, cast off 8 sts at the beginning of the next 4 rows and 7 sts at the beginning of the following 4 rows. Cast off remaining 38 (40, 42, 44, 46) sts.

LEFT FRONT

Using 4 mm needles, cast on 57 (59, 63, 67, 71) sts and work in trinity st until piece measures 33 (33, 34, 34, 35.5) cm (13 [13, 13½, 13½, 14] in) from cast-on edge ending on WS row.

ARMHOLE AND NECK SHAPING

*Keeping patt correct as set, cast off 3 (3, 4, 4, 5) sts at beg of next row. Work 1 row. Then dec 1 st at beg of next and foll alt rows 5 (6, 8, 11, 13) times.
*At the same time dec 1 st at centre front edge on first and then every alt row 10 (13, 16, 15, 18) times, then every 3rd row 8 (6, 4, 6, 4) times – 30 sts.
Cont as set until work measures 51 (51, 52, 53, 54.5) cm (20 [20, 20½, 21, 21½] in) ending on WS row.

SHOULDER SHAPING

Cast off 8 sts. Work 1 row. Cast off 8 sts. Work 1 row. Cast off 7 sts. Work 1 row.
Cast off rem 7 sts.

RIGHT FRONT

Work as for Left Front, reversing all shapings.

SLEEVES

Using 3 mm needles, cast on 54 (54, 58, 58, 62) sts. Work 6 rows in garter stitch. Change to 4 mm needles and work in trinity st, inc 1 st at both ends of next and every 8th row 0 (7, 0, 5, 0) times, then every 9th row 12 (8, 12, 10, 8) times, then every 10th row 2 (0, 2, 0, 6) times – 84 (86, 88, 90, 92) sts. Work even in patt as set until sleeve measures 46 (46, 46.5, 46.5, 47) cm (18 [18, 18¼, 18¼, 18½] in) from cast-on edge, ending on WS row.

❖ SIZES
XS, S, M, L, XL: To fit bust 81 (86, 91, 96.5, 101.5) cm (32 [34, 36, 38, 40] in). Finished size: 81 [86, 91, 96.5, 101.5) cm (32 [34, 36, 38, 40] in)

❖ MATERIALS
Yarn Lightweight 100% mercerized cotton (approx 105 m per 50 g). 13 (13, 14, 15, 16) x 50 g balls
Needles One pair 4 mm and one pair 3 mm or sizes to obtain tension
Notions Tapestry needle, 2 m (2¼ yds) of 2.5 cm (1 in) wide ribbon

❖ TENSION
28 sts and 32 rows = 10 cm (4 in) over trinity stitch

❖ See page 37 for knitting terms.

❖ See template on page 310

SLEEVE CAP SHAPING

Cast off 3 (3, 4, 4, 5) sts at beg of next 2 rows. Then dec 1 st at both ends of every alt row 16 (15, 17, 17, 19) times, then every row 10 (12, 10, 10, 8) times. Cast off remaining 26 (26, 26, 28, 28) sts.

LEFT FRONT BAND

Join shoulder seams. With right side of work facing, using 3 mm needles, starting at centre back neck, pick up and knit 1 st for each stitch or row to cast-off edge of cardigan. Work 5 rows in garter stitch. Cast off.

RIGHT FRONT BAND

Work as for Left Front Band starting at cast-on edge up to centre back neck.

FINISHING

Sew sleeve cap into armhole. Join side and sleeve seams in one line. Join front bands at centre back. Steam lightly. Cut ribbon in half and sew one piece onto each front at start of neck shaping.

SLOUCH SOCKS

SIZE
One size: To fit average foot, 25 cm (10 in); leg 30 cm (12 in)

MATERIALS
Yarn Super chunky hand-dyed 100% cotton chenille (100 m per 100 g skein). 2 skeins
Needles One pair 5 mm set of five 4 mm dpn or sizes to obtain tension
Notions Tapestry needle, stitch holder, stitch marker

TENSION
11 sts and 16 rows = 10 cm (4 in) over stocking stitch using 4 mm needles

See page 37 for knitting terms.

When working with random and hand-dyed yarns, disguise any difference in skein colours by using two skeins at a time. Work 2 rows from one skein and then 2 rows from the other, carrying the yarn not in use up the side of the work.

SOCKS
CUFF
With 5 mm needles cast on 26 sts loosely. Transfer the sts to 4 dpn, so that 6 sts are on the 1st, 7 sts on the 2nd, 6 sts on the 3rd and 7 sts on the 4th. Join into round, taking care not to twist the sts. Mark end of round with a marker, slipping the marker every round.
Work 5 cm (2 in) in k1, p1 rib, then work in st st (k every round, see page 76) until piece measures 24 cm (9½ in).

HEEL
*k1, k2tog; rep from * 3 more times, k1. Place these 9 sts onto holder. Work 24 rows back and forth in st st on rem 13 sts for heel. Cast off. Fold heel in half lengthways, WS together, and stitch cast off edge to form heel seam.

INSTEP
With RS facing pick up and knit 17 sts along sides of heel, place marker for beg of round, knit across 9 sts from holder — 26 sts. Divide sts evenly on 4 needles, as before, and work in st st until foot measures 18 cm (7 in), slipping the marker every round.

TOE
Rejoin yarn at marker.
Round 1: Needle 1; sl 1 k-wise, psso, k to end. Needle 2; k to last 3 sts, k2tog, k1. Needle 3; sl 1 k-wise, psso, k to end. Needle 4; K to last 3 sts, k2tog, k1.
Rounds 2, 3 and 4: Work as for Round 1. Place rem 10 sts on two needles and graft together (see page 72).

FINISHING
Steam lightly to measurements. Attach 18 cm (7 in) tassel (see page 248) to centre back of each sock.

EMBROIDERED CUSHION

FRONT

With 3.25 mm needles cast on 54 sts in Colour B and then 54 sts in Colour A – 108 sts. Work 23 cm (9 in) in st st, twisting Colours A and B around each other at centre point to avoid holes (see page 57). Swap colours so that Colour A is on top of Colour B and vice versa. Work 23 cm (9 in) in st st as before, then cast off.

BACK

(Made in 2 sections)
Section 1: (Button band)
With Colour A and 3.25 mm needles cast on 108 sts. Work 21.5 cm (8½ in) in st st. Change to 2.75 mm needles and work 2.5 cm (1 in) in twisted rib (K1b, P1). Cast off in rib.
Place markers for 5 buttons equally spaced along centre of button band.

Section 2: (Buttonhole band)
Work as for section 1 until rib measures 1 cm (½ in). Make 5 open eyelets (see page 53) as buttonholes to correspond with markers. Cont in twisted rib until buttonhole band measures 2.5 cm (1 in) and then cast off.

FINISHING

Block cushion front and back to measurements. Embroider cushion front following chart. With RS facing, join back sections 1 and 2 at side edges of twisted rib, placing buttonhole band (section 2) on top of button band (section 1). Sew cushion back and front together on inside along four seams. Press seams. Attach 5 buttons beneath buttonholes. Make 4 multicoloured pompoms (see page 246) and attach to corners. Insert cushion pad.

❖ SIZE
One size: 46 cm (18 in) square

❖ MATERIALS
Yarn 4-ply 50% merino wool/50% cotton (approx 113 m per 50 g ball). 4 x 50 g balls Colour A (navy), 1 x 50 g ball Colour B (lavender), plus small amounts of red and yellow for embroidery and pompoms
Needles One pair each 2.75 mm and 3.25 mm or size to obtain tension
Notions Tapestry needle, 5 buttons, 46 cm (18 in) square cushion pad

❖ TENSION
24 sts and 32 rows = 10 cm (4 in) over stocking stitch

❖ *See page 37 for knitting terms.*

❖ *See template on page 310*

EMBROIDERING THE CUSHION

Enlarge this template on page 310 on a photocopier by approximately 400 per cent, to the right size to fit the cushion front. Trace off the four flower shapes that make up the pattern and cut each one out. Lay each one on the cushion cover in turn, tacking around the outside of each to transfer the pattern to the cover. Following the tacking lines and using the chart as a guide, embroider the pattern. Instructions for embroidery on knitting can be found on pages 66–67.

1 *Work chain stitch around the outside of the pattern in red. Thread yellow yarn in and out of the chain stitch.*

2 *Work stem stitch around the outside of the second flower shape. Use the blue yarn over the lavender squares, and the lavender over the blue.*

3 *Work chain stitch in red round the third flower and then another line of chain stitch in yellow.*

4 *Using blue yarn, work couching around the fourth flower.*

5 *Work a cluster of bullion knots at the centre.*

6 *Make straight stitches of varying lengths, radiating out from the centre.*

7 *Fill the second flower shape with squared filling stitch. Use the blue yarn over the lavender squares, and the lavender over the blue.*

❖ SIZE

One size: To fit average hand, 19 cm (7½ in) long

❖ MATERIALS

Yarn 4-ply 100% wool (approx 148 m per 25 g).
1 x 25 g ball each Colour A, Colour B, Colour C, Colour D, Colour E
Needles Set of four 2.75 mm dpn, set of four 3.25 mm dpn or sizes to obtain tension
Notions Stitch holders, stitch marker

❖ TENSION

28 sts and 44 rows = 10 cm (4 in) over stripe pattern using 3.25 mm needles

❖ See page 37 for knitting terms.

STRIPE PATTERN (24 ROW REPEAT)

4 rounds st st (k every round) Colour B.
2 rounds garter st (k 1 round, p 1 round) Colour A.
4 rounds st st Colour C.
2 rounds garter st Colour A.
4 rounds st st Colour D.
2 rounds garter st Colour A.
4 rounds st st Colour E.
2 rounds garter st Colour A.

RIGHT GLOVE
CUFF

Using Colour A and 2.75 mm dpn, cast on 48 stitches (16 on each of three needles). Join into round, taking care not to twist the sts. Mark end of round, slipping marker every round.
Work 7.5 cm (3 in) in twisted rib (K1b, p1).
Next round: Rib 2, inc in next st, *rib 4, increase in next st, repeat from * to last 2 sts, rib 2 (60 sts).
Change to 3.25 mm dpn and work 18 rounds in stripe pattern. Continue in pattern correct as set.
**Round 19: Patt 30 sts, slip next 9 sts onto a stitch holder and leave for thumb. Cast on 9 stitches, patt to end.
Change to 2.75 mm dpn and cont in stripe pattern until hand measures 10 cm (4 in) ending on first row of garter st in Colour A.
Next round: Patt 34 sts, p2tog, patt to end – 59 sts.

FIRST FINGER

Using Colour A, 1st needle k30 sts, 2nd needle k8 sts, slip remaining 21 sts of round

and first 21 sts from 1st needle onto holder. Cast on 3 sts – 20 sts.
***Divide these 20 sts onto 3 needles.
Knit 5 rounds in Colour A, purl 1 round in Colour A. Cast off loosely.

SECOND FINGER

With palm of glove facing, slip 7 sts from holder onto needle. Using Colour A, k7, cast on 3 sts, k7, pick up and knit 3 sts from base of first finger – 20 sts.
Knit 5 rounds in Colour A, purl 1 round in Colour A. Cast off loosely.

THIRD FINGER

As second, but sts picked up from base of 2nd finger.

FOURTH FINGER

Divide remaining 14 sts onto 2 needles and using Colour A knit them. Pick up and knit up 3 sts from base of 3rd finger.
Knit 5 rounds in Colour A, purl 1 round in Colour A. Cast off loosely.

THUMB

Using 3.25 mm dpn, slip 9 sts left on holder onto needle, using 2nd needle pick up and knit 9 sts from cast on sts. Divide sts onto 3 needles.
Knit 5 rounds in Colour A, inc 4 sts evenly across first row – 22 sts. Purl 1 round in Colour A. Cast off loosely.

LEFT GLOVE

Work as for Right Glove until ** is reached.
Round 19: Patt 21 sts, slip next 9 sts onto holder for thumb, cast on 9 sts, patt to end.
Change to set of 2.75mm dpn and cont in stripe pattern until hand measures 10 cm (4 in) ending on first row of garter st in Colour A.
Next round: Patt 24 sts, p2tog, patt to end – 59 sts.

FIRST FINGER

Using Colour A, 1st needle k29 sts, 2nd needle k9 sts, slip remaining sts of round and 21 sts from 1st needle onto a st holder. Cast on 3 sts – 20 sts.
Complete glove as for Right Hand reading back of hand in place of palm and work from *** to end.

FINISHING

Weave in any loose ends. Press lightly.

BIG LOVE THROW

Use separate balls of yarn for moss st at right and left of heart motif. Use one ball of yarn for heart and weave background along behind motif.

BASIC SQUARE

For colourway 1: With Colour A cast on 51 sts. Follow graph up to row 56, working the border colour in moss st (see page 40) and the heart panel in st st. Cast off.
Make 30 squares in colourway 1 and 30 squares in colourway 2.

FINISHING

Join squares together with backstitch following chart (right) for background colour and orientation. Tidy loose ends back into own colours. Press on right side with a warm iron over a damp cloth.
Make 7 25-cm (10-in) fringe tassels (see page 248) and fasten to top and bottom of throw at outside edges and at seams of squares. Steam tassels.

❖ **SIZE**
One size: 122 cm wide and 178 cm long, (48 x 70in), excluding tassels

❖ **MATERIALS**
Yarn 4-ply 70% lambswool/26% kid mohair/4% nylon (approx 140m per 50g ball). 8 x 50g balls each Colour A and Colour C, 11 x 50g balls Colour B
Needles One pair 5 mm or size to obtain tension
Notions Tapestry needle

❖ **TENSION**
24 sts and 32 rows = 10 cm (4 in) over intarsia design

❖ See page 37 for knitting terms

❖ See template on page 312

SIZES

XS, S, M, L, XL: To fit bust 81 (86, 91, 96.5, 101.5) cm (32 [34, 36, 38, 40] in). Finished size: Bust 91 (96.5, 101.5, 106.5, 112) cm (36 [38, 40, 42, 44] in)

MATERIALS

Yarn Lightweight 100% cotton (approx 115m per 50g ball). 6 (7, 7, 8, 9) x 50g balls Colour A, 2 x 50g balls each Colours B, C & D
Needles One pair each 3.25 mm and 4 mm, one circular 3.25 mm, or size to obtain tension
Notions Tapestry needle, stitch holder

TENSION

22 sts and 26 rows = 10 cm (4 in) over intarsia and stripe patterns

✤ See page 37 for knitting terms

✤ See template on page 309

BACK

With Colour A and 3.25 mm needles cast on 100 (104, 110, 116, 122) sts. Work 6 (6, 6, 8, 8) rows moss st (see page 40). Change to 4 mm needles and, working in st st, work the last 14 (16, 1, 4, 7) sts of chart, then work all the 36 sts of chart 2 (2, 3, 3, 3) times, then work the first 14 (16, 1, 4, 7) sts. Continue in this way, repeating the 54 rows of chart until piece measures 43 cm (17 in) from cast on edge ending on WS row.

SHAPE RAGLAN ARMHOLE

Cast off 5 sts at beg of next 2 rows – 90 (94, 100, 106, 112) sts. ***Keeping patt correct as set, dec 1 st at both ends of next and every row 4 (8, 12, 16, 18) times, then every alt row 20 (18, 17, 15, 16) times – 42 (42, 42, 44, 44) sts.

SHAPE BACK NECK

Next row (RS): K2tog, k5 and turn, leaving rem sts on holder. Work each side of neck separately.
Cast off 4 sts at beg of next row.
Next row (RS): K2tog and cast off last st.
With RS facing rejoin yarn to rem sts. Cast off centre 28 (28, 28, 30, 30) sts, work to last 2 sts, k2tog. Work to match first side, reversing shapings.

FRONT

Work as for back to ***
Keeping patt correct as set, dec 1 st at both ends of next and every row 4 (8, 12, 16, 18) times, then every alt row 16 (14, 13, 11, 12) times – 50 (50, 50, 52, 52) sts.

SHAPE FRONT NECK

Next row (RS): K2tog, k17 and turn, leaving remaining sts on a holder. Work each side of neck separately.
Cast off 5 sts at beg of next row – 14 sts. Dec 1 st at neck edge on next 4 rows. At the same time dec 1 st at raglan edge on next and foll alt row – 8 sts.
Dec 1 st at both ends of next and foll 2 alt rows – 2 sts.
Next row (WS): P2 tog and cast off.
With RS facing, rejoin yarn to rem sts. Cast off centre 12 (12, 12, 14, 14) sts, work to last 2 sts, k2tog. Work to match first side, reversing shapings.

LEFT SLEEVE

With Colour A and 3.25 mm needles cast on 49 (49, 53, 53, 53) sts and work 8 rows moss st.
Change to 4 mm needles and work in st st, repeating stripe sequence to end:
4 rows Colour D, 4 rows Colour C, 4 rows Colour A.
At the same time inc 1 st at both ends of every 9th row 0 (6, 0, 0, 6) times, then every 10th row 6 (5, 0, 6, 5) times, then every 11th row 4 (0, 4, 4, 0) times, then every 12th row 0 (0, 5, 0, 0) times – 69 (71, 71, 73, 75) sts. Continue even until sleeve measures 47 cm (18½ in) from cast on edge ending with a WS row.

SHAPE RAGLAN

Cast off 5 sts at beg of next 2 rows.
Keeping patt correct as set, dec 1 st at both ends of next and every alt row 12 (15, 13, 16, 15) times, then every 3rd row 8 (6, 8, 6, 8) times – 19 sts. End with a RS row. **

SHAPE NECK

Cast off 6 sts at beg of next row, then dec 1 st at beg of foll row, rep last 2 rows once more. Work 1 row. Cast off rem 5 sts.

RIGHT SLEEVE

Work as for left sleeve to **. Work 1 row ending with a WS row.

SHAPE NECK

Cast off 6 sts at beg and dec 1 st at end of next row. Work 1 row, rep last 2 rows once more. Cast off rem 5 sts.

FINISHING

Join raglan sleeves onto back and front.

NECKBAND

With Colour A and circular needle and RS facing pick up and knit 18 sts at top of left sleeve, 36 (36, 36, 38, 38) sts at front neck, 18 sts at right sleeve and 36 (36, 36, 38, 38) sts from back neck – 108 (108, 108, 112, 112) sts. Work 6 rounds moss st. Cast off loosely in moss st.
Join sleeve seams and side seams. Steam lightly.

Using double knitting and 5 mm hook, ch 10; turn. Work in rows of tr until you have used up the whole ball of yarn. Fasten off.

FINISHING

Using needle and thread, stitch beads and patch motifs to the ends of the belt.

❖ **SIZE**
One size

❖ **MATERIALS**
Yarn Tweed-effect double knitting, 1 x 50 g ball
Hooks One 5 mm crochet hook
Notions Needle and thread, beads and other trimmings

❖ **TENSION**
10 sts and 10 rows = 6 cm (2½ in)

❖ See page 85 for crochet terms

❖ **SIZE**
One size: 45 cm (18 in) circumference, to fit average head

❖ **MATERIALS**
Yarn 4-ply cotton, 1 x 50 g ball
Hooks One 2.5 mm crochet hook
Notions 30 cm (12 in) of narrow ribbon

❖ **TENSION**
24 sts and 21 rows = 10 cm (4 in)

❖ See page 85 for crochet terms

ADDING BEADS

Stitching beads to the ends of this belt gives it extra visual interest and detail as well as adding some useful weight that will make the ends hang nicely when the belt is tied.

This belt has been made in a tweed-effect yarn that is mainly turquoise in colour, with little flecks of other colours. These shades are picked up in the beads that have been used. Fabric flowers motifs in the same colourway have been stitched along the ends.

Match your beads to your chosen yarn: they come in all shades, shapes and sizes, so you're bound to find something to suit.

BABY HAT

Using 4-ply yarn and 2.5 mm hook, proceed in exactly the same way as the adult hat, up to and including Round 12 (108 dc). Work 20 rounds in dc without shaping.
Next round: Ch 2, 7 dc, 2 dc in next dc, *8 dc, 2 dc in next dc, rep from * to end; join with a sl st to 2nd ch of first ch (120 dc).
Next round: Ch 2, 8 dc, 2 dc in next dc, *9 dc, 2 dc in next dc, rep from * to end; join with a sl st to 2nd ch of first ch (132 dc).
Next round: Ch 2, 9 dc, 2 dc in next dc, *10 dc, 2 dc in next dc), rep from * to end; join with a sl st to 2nd ch of first ch (144 dc).
Next round (picot edge): (Ch 4, sl st into same dc, sl st into next 2 dc) 48 times; fasten off.

FINISHING

Turn back brim, push ends of ribbon through from inside, between stitches, and tie in a bow.

SIZE
One size: 57 cm (22½ in) circumference, to fit average head

MATERIALS
Yarn Cotton glacé 100% cotton, 2 x 50 g balls
Hooks One 2.5 mm crochet hook

TENSION
22 sts and 22 rows = 10 cm (4 in)

See page 85 for crochet terms

ADULT HAT
Using cotton glacé and 2.5 mm hook, ch 6 and join with a sl st to form a foundation ring.

Round 1: Ch 2, 11 dc in ring, join with a sl st to 2nd ch of first ch (12 dc).

Round 2: Ch 2, 1 dc in 1st dc; *2 dc in each dc, rep from * to end; join with a sl st to 2nd ch of first ch (24 dc).

Round 3: Ch 2, 2 dc in next dc, *1 dc, 2 dc in next dc, rep from * to end; join with a sl st to 2nd ch of first ch (36 dc).

Round 4: Ch 2, 1 dc, 2 dc in next dc, *2 dc, 2 dc in next dc, rep from * to end join with a sl st to 2nd ch of first ch (48 dc).

Round 5: Ch 2, then continue in dc without shaping.

Round 6: Ch 2, 2 dc, 2 dc in next dc, *3 dc, 2 dc in next dc, rep from * to end join with a sl st to 2nd ch of first ch (60 dc).

Round 7: Ch 2, 3 dc, 2 dc in next dc, *4 dc, 2 dc in next dc, rep from * to end; join with a sl st to 2nd ch of first ch (72 dc).

Round 8: Ch 2, then continue in dc without shaping.

Round 9: Ch 2, 4 dc, 2 dc in next dc, *5 dc, 2 dc in next dc, rep from * to end join with a sl st to 2nd ch of first ch (84 dc).

Round 10: Ch 2, 5 dc, 2 dc in next dc, *6 dc, 2 dc in next dc, rep from * to end; join with a sl st to 2nd ch of first ch (96 dc).

Round 11: Ch 2, then continue in dc without shaping.

Round 12: Ch 2, 6 dc, 2 dc in next dc, *7 dc, 2 dc in next dc, rep from * to end; join with a sl st to 2nd ch of first ch (108 dc).

Round 13: Ch 2, 7 dc, 2 dc in next dc, *8 dc, 2 dc in next dc, rep from * to end; join with a sl st to 2nd ch of first ch (120 dc).

Round 14: Ch 2, then continue in dc without shaping.

Round 15: Ch 2, 8 dc, 2 dc in next dc, *9 dc, 2 dc in next dc, rep from * to end; join with a sl st to 2nd ch of first ch (132 dc).

Sides: Work 23 rounds in dc without shaping.

Shape brim: Ch 2, 9 dc, 2 dc in next dc, *10 dc, 2 dc in next dc, rep from * to end; join with a sl st to 2nd ch of first ch (144 dc).

Next round: Ch 2, 10 dc, 2 dc in next dc, *11 dc, 2 dc in next dc, rep from * to end; join with a sl st to 2nd ch of first ch (156 dc).

Next round: Ch 2, 11 dc, 2 dc in next dc, *12 dc, 2 dc in next dc, rep from * to end; join with a sl st to 2nd ch of first ch (168 dc).

Next round: Ch 2, 12 dc, 2 dc in next dc, *13 dc, 2 dc in next dc, rep from * to end; join with a sl st to 2nd ch of first ch (180 dc).

FINISHING
Pin or stitch crochet flowers to the hat for an extra flourish. See page 269 for instructions on how to make flowers.

PEEK-A-BOO CUSHION COVER

Using colour A and 5 mm hook, ch 39; turn.
Row 1: Skip 3 ch, 1 tr in each ch to end; turn.
Row 2: Ch 3, *1 tr, inserting hook between stems of next 2 sts of previous row and below all horizontal connecting threads; repeat from * to end; turn.
Next and all subsequent rows: Repeat row 2 until work measures 97 cm (38 in).

FINISHING

Lay the work flat and press lightly. Fold over 20 cm (8 in) at one end and 36 cm (14½ in) at the other end. The two short edges should overlap. Stitch the two long edges of the cushion cover together. Alternatively, work a row of dc along the long edges, through both layers, to make a decorative crocheted edge.

Divide the colour B yarn into four equal lengths and use to make four pompoms (see page 246). When finishing the pompoms, leave long ends of yarn and use these to thread through the holes in the stitches at each corner of the cushion and knot the pompoms firmly in place. Insert the pillow into the lapped opening.

❖ **SIZE**
One size: 30 cm wide and 41 cm long (12 x 16 in)

❖ **MATERIALS**
Yarn Double knitting 100% cotton, 4 x 50g balls colour A, 1 x 50 g ball colour B
Hooks One 5 mm crochet hook
Notions 30 x 41 cm (12 x 16 in) solid-colour cushion pad, cardboard (to make pompoms)

❖ **TENSION**
21 sts and 9 rows = 10 cm (4 in) over pattern

❖ See page 85 for crochet terms

SIZE
One size: 25 cm wide and 114 cm long (10 x 45 in)

MATERIALS
Yarn Double knitting 100% wool, 2 x 50 g balls colour A, 2 x 50 g balls colour B
Hooks One 4 mm crochet hook

TENSION
8 rows = 10 cm (4 in)
1 pattern repeat = 6 cm (2½ in)

See page 85 for crochet terms

Using colour A and 4mm hook, ch 283; turn.
Row 1: 1 dc into 3rd ch from hook, *5 dc, skip 3 ch, 5 dc, 3 dc into next ch, repeat from * to end but finish with 2 dc (instead of 3 dc) in last; turn.
Row 2: Ch 1, 1 dc into same st, 5 dc, skip 2 dc, 5 dc, 3 dc into next dc, rep from * to end, but finish with 2 dc.
Row 2 forms the pattern. Repeat this row throughout, working 2 rows in alternate colours (18 rows).

CHANGING THE SIZE
To make a longer scarf, simply increase the length of the foundation chain. This chain can be any length, but should be a multiple of 14, plus 1, plus 2 for the turning chain.

To make a wider scarf, simply work more rows, until you have achieved the desired width.

If you are going to increase the size of the scarf, remember that you will need additional yarn.

WORKING IN NEW COLOUR
In a piece of work like this scarf, where there are no seams, and no "right" or "wrong" side, it is important to hide yarn ends neatly or they will spoil the look of the finished piece. The colour not in use should be carried up the side of the work; to avoid a loop, twist the two coloured yarns together.

When you start a new ball of yarn, leave a 7.5 cm (3 in) tail of yarn, lay this across the top of the row to be worked, and work over and around it so it becomes trapped inside the new row of stitches. When the piece is finished, break off the yarn, leaving about 7.5 cm (3 in), and weave this neatly in and out of the stitches along the edge of the scarf. It is preferable to break the yarn, rather than cutting it, as cutting produces a blunt end which is more difficult to "hide".

STRIPED HALTER TOP

Using colour A and 3.25 mm hook, ch 4; 2 dc in 3rd ch from hook; turn (3 sts). Work in rows of dc, increasing 1 st at each end of every row, until you have 9 sts. Then join in colour B and work 2 rows, increasing 1 st at either end of both rows. Continue like this, working in stripes of 2 rows of alternate colours and increasing 1 st at the beginning and end of every row, until you have 139 sts.

Work 14 rows without shaping.

To make the bra top, work 68 sts and turn. Work in rows of dc, maintaining the striped pattern, decreasing 1 st at each end of every row, until you have 6 sts. Continue on these stitches, in main colour and without further shaping, for 96 rows, to make halter strap. Break off yarn, rejoin and work second side of bra top in the same way; break off yarn.

BORDER AND STRAPS

Join yarn to point at base of garment. Work 2 turning ch and 2 dc in same st, then 69 dc, evenly spaced, up left-hand side. Ch 84

(this is the back tie); turn. Ch 2 then work 83 dc back to start of ch. Work 19 dc up back edge. Then ch 84 (this is the second back tie); turn. Ch 2 then work 83 dc back to start of ch. Work 31 dc up left outer side of bra top. Work 95 dc along edge of halter strap and 3 dc in corner st; 5 dc along end of strap; 3 dc in corner st; 95 dc down other edge of strap. Work 31 dc down inner side of bra top, 1 dc in centre stitch, 31 dc up inner side of right bra top; continue border around second halter strap in exactly the same way as the first, dc 31 down right outer side. Make a third back tie in same way as first and second; work 19 dc down right back edge. Make a fourth tie, as before; work 70 dc down right-hand side; join with a sl st at 2nd ch of t-ch. Fasten off yarn.

❖ SIZE
One size: 45 cm (18 in) circumference, to fit average head

❖ MATERIALS
Yarn 4-ply cotton, 1 x 50 g ball
Hooks One 2.5 mm crochet hook
Notions 30 cm (12 in) of narrow ribbon

❖ TENSION
24 sts and 21 rows = 10 cm (4 in)

❖ See page 85 for crochet terms

CHANGING THE SIZE

To make the bra top slightly larger, simply work an extra row of dc all round after making up. An extra row of dc will also make the straps slightly wider.

TUBULAR TOTE

✤ **SIZE**
One size: 30 cm (12 in) long and 66 cm (26 in) around

✤ **MATERIALS**
Yarn Cotton glacé 100% cotton, 2 x 50 g balls colour A, 1 x 50 g ball colour B, 2 x 50 g balls colour C
Hook One 3 mm crochet hook

✤ **TENSION**
22 sts and 22 rows = 10 cm (4 in)

✤ See page 85 for crochet terms

Using colour A and 3 mm hook, ch 6, join with sl st in first ch to form ring.
Round 1: Ch 2, 11 dc in ring, join with a sl st to 2nd ch of ch-2 (12 dc).
Round 2: Ch 2, 1 dc in 1st dc; *2 dc in each dc, rep from * to end; join with a sl st to 2nd ch of ch-2 (24 dc).
Round 3: Ch 2, 2 dc in next dc, *1 dc, 2 dc in next dc, rep from * to end; join with a sl st to 2nd ch of ch-2 (36 dc).
Round 4: Ch 2, 1 dc, 2 dc in next dc, *2 dc, 2 dc in next dc, rep from * to end join with a sl st to 2nd ch of ch-2 (48 dc).
Round 5: Ch 2, then continue in dc without shaping.
Round 6: Ch 2, 2 dc, 2 dc in next dc, *3 dc, 2 dc in next dc, rep from * to end join with a sl st to 2nd ch of ch-2 (60 dc).
Round 7: Ch 2, 3 dc, 2 dc in next dc, *4 dc, 2 dc in next dc, rep from * to end; join with a sl st to 2nd ch of ch-2 (72 dc).
Round 8: Ch 2, then continue in dc without shaping.
Round 9: Ch 2, 4 dc, 2 dc in next dc, *5 dc, 2 dc in next dc, rep from * to end join with a sl st to 2nd ch of ch-2 (84 dc).
Round 10: Ch 2, 5 dc, 2 dc in next dc, *6 dc, 2 dc in next dc, rep from * to end; join with a sl st to 2nd ch of ch-2 (96 dc).
Round 11: Ch 2, then continue in dc without shaping.
Round 12: Ch 2, 6 dc, 2 dc in next dc, *7 dc, 2 dc in next dc, rep from * to end; join with a sl st to 2nd ch of ch-2 (108 dc).
Round 13: Ch 2, 7 dc, 2 dc in next dc, *8 dc, 2 dc in next dc, rep from * to end; join

with a sl st to 2nd ch of ch-2 (120 dc).
Round 14: Ch 2, then continue in dc without shaping.
Round 15: Ch 2, 8 dc, 2 dc in next dc, *9 dc, 2 dc in next dc, rep from * to end; join with a sl st to 2nd ch of ch-2 (132 dc).
Round 16: Ch 2, 9 dc, 2 dc in next dc, *10 dc, 2 dc in next dc, rep from * to end; join with a sl st to 2nd ch of ch-2 (144 dc).
Work 25 rounds without shaping; fasten off yarn.
Next round: Join in colour B and work 3 rounds without shaping; turn, and work 8 rounds; turn and work 10 rounds (this forms a textured stripe in the centre of the bag); fasten off yarn.
Next round: Join in colour C and work 30 rounds; do not fasten off yarn but start to make first handle: Ch 100, count 20 sts along top of bag and sl st to next st. Work back along ch, working 1 dc into each ch; sl st in dc next to 1st ch, then work back along handle again, working 1 dc in each dc of previous row; sl st to top of bag, then work 1 sl st in each of 26 sts along top edge of bag, to take you to the position

HANDLES

Make handles shorter or longer, according to your needs, or simply work one wide shoulder strap from one side of the bag to the other, if you prefer.

where you begin the 2nd handle. Work the 2nd handle in the same way as the first; fasten off yarn.

STRIPY POUCH

Worked in the round, in one piece, starting from the base.

Using the fine yarn and 1.5 mm steel hook, ch 6, join with sl st in first ch to form ring.

Round 1: Ch 2, 11 dc in ring, join with a sl st to 2nd ch of ch-2 (12 dc).

Round 2: Ch 2, 1 dc in next dc, *2 dc in next dc, rep from * to end; join with a sl st to 2nd ch of ch-2 (24 dc).

Round 3: Ch 2, 2 dc in next dc, *1 dc, 2 dc in next dc, rep from * to end; join with a sl st to 2nd ch of ch-2 (36 dc).

Round 4: Ch 2, 1 dc, 2 dc in next dc, *2 dc, 2 dc in next dc, rep from * to end; join with a sl st to 2nd ch of ch-2 (48 dc).

Round 5: Ch 2, 2 dc, 2 dc in next dc, *3 dc, 2 dc in next dc, rep from * to end; join with a sl st to 2nd ch of ch-2 (60 dc).

Round 6: Ch 2, 3 dc, 2 dc in next dc, *4 dc, 2 dc in next dc, rep from * to end; join with a sl st to 2nd ch of ch-2 (72 dc).

Round 7: Ch 2, 4 dc, 2 dc in next dc, *5 dc, 2 dc in next dc, rep from * to end; join with a sl st to 2nd ch of ch-2 (84 dc).

Work 50 rounds in dc without shaping.

Next round (eyelets): Ch 3, 1 tr in next dc, *ch 1, skip 1 dc, 2 tr, repeat from * to end, ch 1, join with a sl st to 3rd ch of ch-3.

Work 1 round of dc without shaping.

Next round (picot edge): (Ch 4, sl st into same dc, sl st into next 2 dc) 28 times; fasten off.

CORDS

Using the fine yarn and 1.5 mm steel hook, ch 100, turn and work dc all along chain to end; fasten off. Repeat to make a second cord.

FINISHING

Thread one of the cords in and out of the eyelets and join the ends. Starting on the opposite side of the bag from where the first cords emerge, thread the remaining cord through the eyelets and join the ends.

✤ **SIZE**
20 cm (8 in) long

✤ **MATERIALS**
Yarn Very fine (12-gauge) cotton, 1 x 50 g ball
Hooks One 1.5 mm steel crochet hook

✤ **TENSION**
33 sts and 30 rows = 10 cm (4 in)

See page 85 for crochet terms

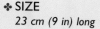

SIZE
23 cm (9 in) long

MATERIALS
Yarn 4-ply cotton, 1 x 50 g ball
Hooks One 2.5 mm crochet hook
Notions 90 beads, approximately 5 mm diameter

TENSION
24 sts and 21 rows = 10 cm (4 in)

See page 85 for crochet terms

Worked in the round, in one piece, starting from the base.

Using 4-ply cotton and 2.5 mm hook, ch 20.
Round 1: Ch 2, 18 dc along foundation ch; 3 dc in last st, then work 19 dc back along opposite side of foundation ch, 3 dc in last st, join with a sl st to 2nd ch of ch-2 (44 dc).
Round 2: Ch 2, 19 dc, 3 dc in next dc, 21 dc, 3 dc in next dc, 1 dc; join with a sl st to 2nd ch of ch-2 (48 dc).
Round 3: Ch 2, 20 dc, 3 dc in next dc, 23 dc, 3 dc in next dc, 2 dc; join with a sl st to 2nd ch of ch-2 (52 dc).
Round 4: Ch 2, 21 dc, 3 dc in next dc, 25 dc, 3 dc in next dc, 3 dc; join with a sl st to 2nd ch of ch-2 (56 dc).
Round 5: Ch 2, 22 dc, 3 dc in next dc, 27 dc, 3 dc in next dc, 4 dc; join with a sl st to 2nd ch of ch-2 (60 dc).
Work 30 rounds in dc without shaping.
Next round (increase): Ch 2, 2 dc in next dc, *1 dc, 2 dc in next dc, repeat from * to end; join with a sl st to 2nd ch of ch-2 (90 dc).

Work 5 rounds in dc without shaping.
Next round (eyelets): **Ch 4, 1 tr in next dc, *ch 1, skip 1 dc, 1 tr in next dc, repeat from * to end, 1 ch, join with a sl st to 3nd ch of ch-4.
Work 1 row of dc. Fasten off yarn.
Thread beads onto ball of yarn and rejoin yarn to edge of work.
Next round (picot edge): *Ch 2, slip one bead along yarn, close to last stitch worked, ch 2, sl st into base of picot, sl st into next 2 dc, repeat from * to end (45 times in total – i.e. 45 picots, each with a single bead) and fasten off.
Rejoin yarn to work 1 row below eyelet row, work 1 row of dc, then repeat from ** to make the second layer of the double-layered edging.

CORDS
Using 4-ply cotton and 2.5 mm hook, ch 100, turn and work dc all along chain to end; fasten off. Repeat to make a second cord.

FINISHING
Thread the cords in and out through both layers of eyelets, as in the multicoloured bag, page 262.

Note: the basket and the liner are each worked in one piece, in the round.

BASE

Using utility string and 6mm hook, ch 6, join with sl st in first ch to form ring.

Round 1: Ch 2, 11 dc in ring, join with a sl st to 2nd ch of ch-2 (12 dc).

Round 2: Ch 2, 1 dc in 1st dc; 2 dc in each dc; join with a sl st to 2nd ch of ch-2 (24 dc).

Round 3: Ch 2, 2 dc in next dc, [1 dc, 2 dc in next dc] 11 times; join with a sl st to 2nd ch of ch-2 (36 dc).

Round 4: Work 1 round in dc without shaping.

Round 5: Ch 2, 2 dc in next dc, [2 dc, 2 dc in next dc] 11 times, 1 dc; join with a sl st to 2nd ch of ch-2 (48 dc).

Round 6: Ch 2, 2 dc in next dc, [3 dc, 2 dc in next dc] 11 times, 2 dc; join with a sl st to 2nd ch of ch-2 (60 dc).

Round 7: Work 1 round in dc without shaping.

Round 8: Ch 2, 2 dc in next dc, [4 dc, 2 dc in next dc] 11 times, 3 dc; join with a sl st to 2nd ch of ch-2 (72 dc).

Round 9: Work 1 round in dc without shaping.

Round 10: Ch 2, 2 dc in next dc, [5 dc, 2 dc in next dc] 11 times, 4 dc; join with a sl st to 2nd ch of ch-2 (84 dc).

Round 11: Work 1 round in dc without shaping.

Round 12: Ch 2, 2 dc in next dc, [6 dc, 2 dc in next dc] 11 times, 5 dc; join with a sl st to 2nd ch of ch-2 (96 dc).

Round 13: Work 1 round in dc without shaping.

Round 14: Ch 2, 2 dc in next dc, [7 dc, 2 dc in next dc] 11 times, 6 dc; join with a sl st to 2nd ch of ch-2 (108 dc).

SIDES

Turn and work 14 rounds without shaping.

Next round: Ch 3, 1 dc in next dc, *ch 1 skip 1 dc, 1 dc in next dc, repeat from * to end; join with a sl st to 2nd ch of ch-3; fasten off yarn.

BORDER

Join in fabric strip; ch 2, 1 dc into 1st ch sp; *2 dc into next 1 ch sp, repeat from * to end; fasten off.

LINER

Note: As you come to the end of one fabric strip, join in another of the same or a different colour.

Using fabric strips and 7mm hook, ch 6, join with sl st in first ch to form ring.

Round 1: Ch 2, 11 dc in ring, join with a sl st to 2nd ch of ch-2 (12 dc).

Round 2: Ch 2, 1 dc in 1st dc; 2 dc in each dc; join with a sl st to 2nd ch of ch-2 (24 dc).

Round 3: Ch 2, 2 dc in next dc, [1 dc, 2 dc in next dc] 11 times; join with a sl st to 2nd ch of ch-2 (36 dc).

Round 4: Ch 2, 2 dc in next dc, [2 dc, 2 dc in next dc] 11 times, 1 dc; join with a sl st to 2nd ch of ch-2 (48 dc).

Round 5: Ch 2, 2 dc in next dc, [3 dc, 2 dc in next dc] 11 times, 2 dc; join with a sl st to 2nd ch of ch-2 (60 dc).

Round 6: Ch 2, 2 dc in next dc, [4 dc, 2 dc in next dc] 11 times, 3 dc; join with a sl st to 2nd ch of ch-2 (72 dc).

Round 7: Ch 2, 2 dc in next dc, [5 dc, 2 dc in next dc] 11 times, 4 dc; join with a sl st to 2nd ch of ch-2 (84 dc).

Round 8: Ch 2, 2 dc in next dc, [6 dc, 2 dc in next dc] 11 times, 5 dc; join with a sl st to 2nd ch of ch-2 (96 dc).

Round 9: Ch 2, 2 dc in next dc, [7 dc, 2 dc in next dc] 11 times, 6 dc; join with a sl st to 2nd ch of ch-2 (108 dc).

Round 10: Ch 2, 2 dc in next dc, [8 dc, 2 dc in next dc] 11 times, 7 dc; join with a sl st to 2nd ch of ch-2 (120 dc).

Round 11: Ch 2, 2 dc in next dc, [9 dc, 2 dc in next dc] 11 times, 8 dc; join with a sl st to 2nd ch of ch-2 (132 dc).

Round 12: Ch 2, 2 dc in next dc, [10 dc, 2 dc in next dc] 11 times, 9 dc; join with a sl st to 2nd ch of ch-2 (144 dc).

❖ **SIZE**
One size: 34 cm (13½ in) diameter, 15 cm (6 in) high

❖ **MATERIALS**
***Yarn** Utility string, about 200 m*
***Plus** One old T-shirt, cut into 1 cm (½ in) strips, see below*
***Hooks** One each 6 mm and 7 mm crochet hooks*

❖ **TENSION**
10 sts and 11 rows = 10 cm (4 in)

See page 85 for crochet terms

MAKING FABRIC STRIPS FROM OLD T-SHIRTS

This can be done so that you end up with one long, continuous strip. First cut off the T-shirt hem and discard, then, beginning at one of the side seams, start to cut around the body of the garment, 1 cm (½ in) from the raw edge. When you reach the starting point, do not cut off the strip you have made but continue cutting in a spiral around the garment until you reach the armholes, then snip off.

SIZE

One size: To fit 86-91 cm (34-36 in) bust. Finished size 94 cm (37 in) around bust and 60 cm (24 in) from shoulder to hem

MATERIALS

Yarn 4-ply 100% cotton, 3 x 50 g balls

Hook One 3 mm crochet hook

Notions 6 mm (¼ in) mother-of-pearl buttons

TENSION

12 rows = 10 cm (4 in) over shell pattern

20 sts and 7 rows = 10 cm (4 in) over yoke

See page 85 for crochet terms

LEFT CUP

Using cotton glacé and 3 mm hook, ch 36; turn.

Row 1: Ch 2, 1 dc in each ch to end; turn. Repeat this row 14 more times.

Row 16: Ch 2, 17 dc; turn. Repeat row 16, 14 more times.

You will now have an L-shaped piece, measuring 15cm (6in) on the longer edges and 7.5cm (3in) on the shorter edges. Stitch the two short edges of the 'L' together, starting at the point where they meet at a right angle.

RIGHT CUP

Make this in the same way. Opposite side will be the right side.

FINISHING

Take the left cup: Starting at beginning of original foundation ch (this is inner edge), join yarn: Ch 2, dc to end; work 90 ch, (this is the neck strap); turn. Ch 2, 89 dc back along the ch. Then work 36 dc, evenly

spaced, along the outer edge, to the outer corner; work 90 ch (this is the back strap); turn. Ch 2, 89 dc back along the ch. Then work 36 dc, evenly spaced, along the lower edge, until you reach the inner corner. Work 4 ch (to make the strap that joins the two cups), then join with a sl st to inner corner of right cup. Then work along the inner edge; work 90 ch (neck strap); turn. Ch 2, 89 dc, back along the ch. Then work 36 dc, evenly spaced, along the outer edge, to the outer corner; work 90 ch (back strap); turn. Ch 2, 89 dc back along the ch. Then work 36 dc, evenly spaced, along the lower edge, until you reach the inner corner. Work 4 dc along the joining strap. Break yarn and fasten off.

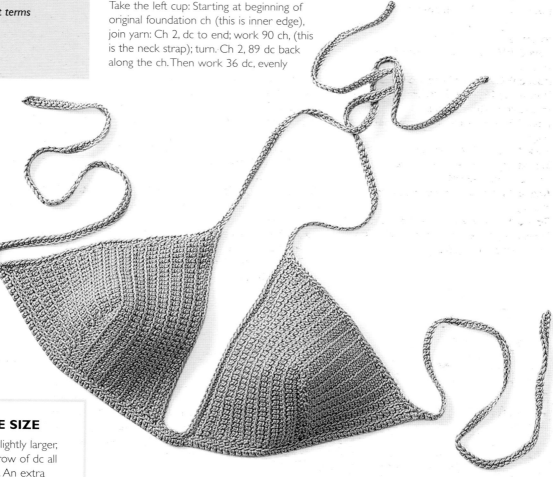

CHANGING THE SIZE

To make the bra top slightly larger, simply work an extra row of dc all round after making up. An extra row of dc will also make the straps slightly wider.

SHOULDER BAG

Using colour A and 4 mm Tunisian crochet hook, ch 45.

Row 1: Skip 1 ch, (insert hook in next ch, yrh, draw loop through ch only and keep on hook) repeat to end. Do not turn.

Row 2 (and all even rows): Yrh, draw through 1 loop, *yrh, draw through 2 loops, repeat from * until 1 loop remains on hook. Do not turn.

Row 3 (and all odd rows): Count loop on hook as first st and start in second st. *Insert hook at front and from right to left around single front vertical thread, yrh, draw through and keep on hook, repeat from * across. Do not turn.

Work a total of 98 rows. Break off yarn

GUSSET AND STRAP

Along one side of work, count in 45 rows from each end. Loop the centre 8 sts onto hook then starting with Row 2 of Tunisian simple stitch, work until you have completed 255 rows. Join with sl sts to the central 8 rows on the opposite side.

EMBROIDERY

Using the chart as a guide, stitch the design at the centre of the back and front of the bag. Use

colours B and C, as indicated on the chart, threaded into a tapestry needle. Each square on the grid corresponds to one crochet stitch. Each cross stitch (see below) is worked over four crochet stitches (two rows of two stitches). This is also the size of the gap between each cross stitch.

JOINING AND EDGING

Using colour B, work two rows of dc on the two top edges of the bag. Then, starting at one of the lower corners of the bag and matching row for row, join the edge of the strap (which will form the gusset) to the edge of the bag, with a row of dc. When you reach the top of the bag, carry on in dc along the edge of the strap until you come to the opposite top edge, then continue as before, joining the edge of the strap to the edge of the bag. Repeat for the other side of the bag.

◆ **SIZE**
One size: 17 cm (6¾ in) wide, 20 cm (8 in) long and 3.5 cm (1½ in) deep

◆ **MATERIALS**
Yarn Cotton glacé 100% cotton, 2 x 50g balls in colour A, 1 x 50 g ball contrasting colour B (for border and embroidery), small amounts of contrasting colour C (for embroidery)
Hook One 3.5 mm Tunisian crochet hook
Notions Tapestry needle

◆ **TENSION**
24 sts and 24 rows = 10 cm (4 in)

◆ See page 85 for crochet terms

MAKING CROSS STITCHES

To make a cross stitch, bring the needle out at the top left of the four stitches you are going to cover. Insert it again at bottom right. Bring the needle out again at bottom left and insert again at top right to finish the stitch. Repeat, following the chart as a guide and changing colour as indicated.

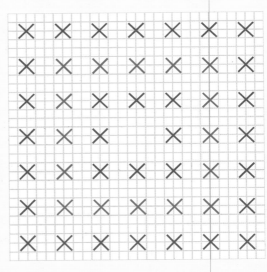

JOINING TIPS

The edge formed by this pattern is very firm and it is easy to match the ends of rows when joining. You may find it easier to pin the edge of the strap to the edge of the bag before you start to join them with a row of double crochet. Just remove each pin as you get to it.

LACY CAMISOLE

SIZE

One size: To fit 86-91cm (34-36 in) bust. Finished size 94 cm (37 in) around bust and 60 cm (24 in) from shoulder to hem

MATERIALS

Yarn 4-ply 100% cotton, 3 x 50 g balls
Hook One 3 mm crochet hook
Notions 6 mm (¼ in) mother-of-pearl buttons

TENSION

12 rows = 10 cm (4 in) over shell pattern
20 sts and 7 rows = 10 cm (4 in) over yoke

❖ See page 85 for crochet terms

Note: The camisole is worked in one piece, with the edging and straps added. The cord is worked separately and is optional.

Using 4-ply cotton and 4 mm crochet hook, make a foundation chain of 217 sts, plus 2 t-ch.

Row 1: Skip 2 ch, 2 tr in next, [skip 2 ch, 1 dc, ch 5, skip 5 ch, 1 dc, skip 2 ch, 5 tr in next] 17 times, skip 2 ch, 1 dc, ch 5, skip 5 ch, 1 dc, skip 2 ch, 3 tr in last ch; turn.
Row 2: Ch 1 (does not count as dc), 1 dc in first st, [ch 5, 1 dc in 3rd of ch-5 loop, ch 5, 1 dc in 3rd of 5 tr] 17 times, ch 5, 1 dc in 3rd of ch-5 loop, ch 5, 1 dc in 2nd of ch-2 in previous row; turn.
Row 3: [Ch 5, 1 dc in ch loop, 5 tr in dc, 1 dc in ch loop] 18 times, ch 2, 1 tr in dc; turn.
Row 4: Ch 1 (does not count as dc), 1 dc in first st, [ch 5, 1 dc in 3rd of 5 tr, ch 5, 1 dc in 3rd of ch-5 loop] 18 times; turn.
Row 5: Ch 3, 2 tr in 1st st, [1 dc in ch loop, ch 5, 1 dc in ch loop, 5 tr in dc] 17 times; 1 dc in ch loop, ch 5, 1 dc in ch loop, 3 tr in last st.

Rows 2 to 5 form the shell pattern. Repeat these rows until work measures 24 cm (9½ in).
Next row: Work 1 tr into each ch of previous row; skip each dc; 180 tr worked.
Next row: Work 1 tr into each tr of previous row.
Repeat last row 11 more times. Break off yarn.

BORDER AND STRAPS

Rejoin yarn to bottom corner of left front and work 81 dc, evenly spaced, up left front, then work 2 more dc in last st to turn corner. Work 26 dc, ch 80 (for left strap), skip 40 tr and rejoin with a sl st to next tr. Work 48 dc, ch 80 (for right strap), skip 40 tr and rejoin with a sl st to next tr. Work 26 dc. Work 2 more dc in last st to turn corner, then work 81 dc, evenly spaced, down right front; turn.
For the buttonholes: ch 2 (counts as 1st dc), [ch 2, skip 2 sts from previous row, 5 dc] 11 times, ch 2, skip 2 sts from previous row, 1 dc; work 2 more dc in last st to turn corner, then continue in dc around border to top of left edge and turn (do not work 2nd row of dc down left edge).
Next row (picot border): [Ch 4, sl st into same st, 2 dc] repeat across top, over left strap, across back, over right strap, along right top edge and down right-hand edge. Fasten off.

FINISHING

Sew buttons on left front to correspond with buttonholes.

DRAWSTRING

Make flat cord, 76 cm (30 in) long (see page 114). Weave it in and out of ch loops below bustline.

COLOURWAYS

The choice of dusky pink yarn is fresh and feminine. But you could make this pretty top in any colour – in primrose yellow for a sunny summer top, or in black yarn with contrasting red border for a really sophisticated effect.

GRANNY SQUARE VEST

Note: At beginning of every round, work ch 3 in place of 1st tr.

MAKING A GRANNY SQUARE

Using colour A and 2.5 mm hook, ch 5 and join with a sl st to form a foundation ring.

Round 1: (3 tr in ring, ch 2) 4 times; join with sl st to 3rd ch of ch-3). Break off yarn.

Round 2: Join in colour B in any ch-2 sp. [(3 tr, ch-2, 3 tr) in ch-2 sp, ch 1] 4 times. Break off yarn.

Round 3: Join in colour C in any ch-2 sp. [(3 tr, ch 2, 3 tr) in ch-2 sp, ch 1, 2 tr in ch-1 sp, ch 1] 4 times. Break off yarn.

Round 4: Join in colour D in any ch-2 sp. [(3 tr, ch 2, 3 tr) in ch-2 sp, (ch 1, 2 tr in ch-1 sp) twice, ch 1] 4 times. Break off yarn.

Make 47 more squares in this way. Using a tapestry needle and length of colour D, stitch 10 squares together in a row. Repeat this three more times then stitch the four rows together to make the body. Add two rows of four to make the straps.

FINISHING

Join in colour B at front lower right corner in ch-2 sp. Work border: (3 tr, ch 2, 3 tr) in ch-2 sp, [(ch 1, 2 tr in next sp), ch 1] 18 times, (3 tr, ch 2, 3 tr) in ch-2 sp. This forms the border for the right front (buttonhole) edge. Continue in the same manner, around the neck edge, over the right strap, across the back, over the left strap, down the left front and around the lower hem, in exactly the same way, working (3 tr, ch 2, 3 tr) in ch-2 sp at outer corners. When you get to an inner corner, skip one of the ch-2 sp (at the corner of the square motif) and simply work 2 tr in the next ch-2 sp, on the adjacent square. Work a similar border around each armhole.

Sew buttons, evenly spaced down left front edge, and aligned with holes in border on opposite edge, which act as buttonholes.

MAKING A DOG COAT

Make a matching coat for your dog — a kind of pooch poncho! Sizes will vary, according to the size of your dog, but use the one pictured as a guide. Join rows of squares to achieve the size and shape you desire, then add straps to fasten under the tummy and around the chest.

FUNKY FLOWERS

SCRAPS AND REMNANTS

As with all small-scale crochet projects, this is an ideal way to use up scraps from larger projects. Use your own colour combinations: you could make the inner and outer parts of the flower from different colours. You could also try a fancy button for the middle of your flower.

Each flower is made in two parts: An outer set of petals and a smaller centre.

OUTER PETALS

Using cotton glacé in colour A and 2 mm hook, ch 9, join with a sl st in first ch to form foundation ring.
Round 1: Ch 3, 2 tr into ring, (ch 6, sl st sideways into top of last tr, 3 tr in ring) 5 times, ch 6, sl st sideways into top of last tr, sl st in 3rd ch of ch-3.
Round 2: Sl st into first tr of previous round, (11 tr into ch-6 loop, sl st in centre tr of 3 tr group) 5 times, 11 tr into ch-6 loop, sl st to first sl st. Fasten off.

CENTRE PETALS

Make a foundation ring of 9 ch, as before, and work round 1 only; fasten off.

LEAF

Using cotton glacé in colour B and 4 mm hook, ch 10; turn.
Row 1: 1 sl st into each of first 3 ch, 1 dc into each of next 3 ch, 1 tr into each of next 3 ch, 5 dtr into last ch. Now work back down the other side of the foundation ch: 1 tr into each of next 3 ch, 1 dc into each of next 3 ch, 1 sl st into each of last 3 ch.
Row 2: 1 sl st into each of first 3 sts, 1 dc into each of next 3 sts, 1 tr into each of next 3 sts, 1 dtr into each of next 2 sts, 3 dtr into next st, 1 dtr into each of next 2 st, 1 tr into each of next 3 sts, 1 dc into each of next 3 sts, 1 sl st into each of last 3 sts. Fasten off. Make more leaves, as required.

FINISHING

Stitch the outer and centre petals together and stitch a button over the hole in the centre. Stitch a leaf or leaves to the back of the flower, attaching the pointed ends to the centre back of the flower.

1   Enlarge the template on page 306 or cut your own heart shape out of paper or card to fit in the centre of your shoes. Draw round it onto the fabric using a light coloured pen or pencil.

2   Start by sewing on a row of overlapping sequins, following the outline of the heart motif. Knot your thread and bring the needle and thread to the surface. Work a backstitch (see page 129) over the right edge of the first sequin into the eye, then bring out the needle at the left edge and through the eye of the next sequin, placed edge to edge with it. Work another backstitch through the eye of the first sequin then bring the needle out to the left of the second sequin to thread the third sequin. Continue until all the sequins are secured.

3   Stitch three larger sequins inside the heart shape, securing each with stitches threaded through the centre.

4   Fill in the remaining space with round glass beads. Thread a bead onto your thread and insert needle into the fabric close to the bead's edge before bringing needle to the surface close by to attach the next bead.

5   Finally, add a border of beads around the outside of the heart shape.

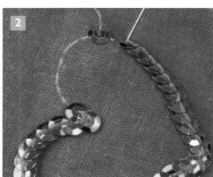

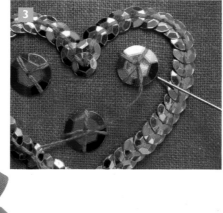

YOU WILL NEED

❖ *Pair of espadrilles*

❖ *Matching sewing thread*

❖ *Pink and red sequins*

❖ *Pink glass beads*

❖ *See template on page 306*

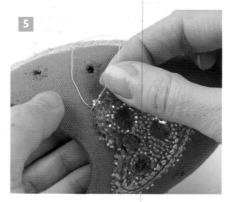

SEWING SEQUINS

In order to sew the beads and sequins in place you will need to employ a little dexterity, manoeuvring fingers and needle inside the shoe. Wear thimbles to protect your fingers and keep the design away from the tip of the toe, where it is more difficult to stitch.

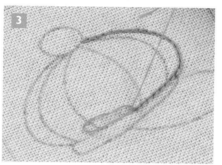

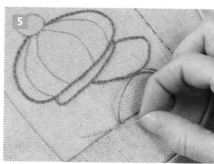

YOU WILL NEED (for each label)

❖ *Iron-on interfacing*

❖ *Hessian or other closely-woven cloth or canvas*

❖ *Embroidery floss in three contrasting colours such as blue, orange and green. Use three strands when stitching.*

❖ *Four buttons*

❖ *See template on page 307*

1 Press an 11-cm (4 ½-in) square of iron-on interfacing to the centre of a 25-cm (10-in) square of canvas on the wrong side.

2 Enlarge the design, if necessary, to your chosen size and then copy it onto tracing paper. Using a water soluble marker and the Prick and Pounce method (see page 190), transfer it to the centre of the square.

3 Fix the canvas in an embroidery hoop. Chain stitch (see page 131) the outline of the design.

4 Using two contrasting thread colours, backstitch (see page 129) the details.

5 Using the same colour thread as used for the outline, work running stitch (see page 129) along the border of the design, stitching under and over three threads of the canvas.

6 Cut out the square, leaving 16 threads along each edge of the running stitch border. Fray the threads, leaving three threads unfrayed along each edge. Sew the label to the front of the basket with a button at each corner of the running stitch border.

BOTTLE BAG

Cut two rectangles of fabric and one rectangle of lightweight buckram, each 45 × 38 cm (18 × 15 in) for the bag and lining. Cut two rectangles of fabric and one rectangle of lightweight buckram, each 15.5 × 10.5 cm (6¼ × 4¼ in), for the base.

1 Mark the centre of one fabric piece with a row of pins parallel with the short edges. Enlarge the design, as necessary, and transfer it (see page 125) to the fabric, matching the upper edges to the row of pins. Fix the material in an embroidery hoop. Couch the leaf and stalks (see page 134) in green, using one strand over six strands. To couch the thick stem, place rows of six threads side by side and stagger the holding stitches made with a single thread.

2 Using three green strands, backstitch the tendril.

3 To couch the grapes and retain their shape, bring six purple strands to the right side at the outside edge of each grape. Lay the strands along the circumference of the grape and stitch over them with one strand at 4-mm (⅛-in) intervals. Continue to the centre of the grape. Insert the six strands into the wrong side at the centre and fasten off.

Couch the large grapes with purple and the small grapes with violet.

4 Make up the bag: Tack the larger piece of buckram between the fabric pieces with the right sides facing outward. Stitch the short edges of the fabric pieces together (right sides facing) taking a 1.5-cm (⅝-in) seam allowance, forming a tube. Finish 1.5 cm (⅝ in) above the lower edge. Press the seams open; neaten with a zig-zag stitch.

5 Hand sew a 3.5-cm (1½-in) hem at the upper edge.

6 Tack the buckram base between the fabric bases with the right sides facing outward. Tack the base to the lower edge of the bag, matching the seam to one corner. Snip the lower edge of the bag at the other corners to pivot the seam. Stitch the base to the bag. Snip the seam allowance across the corners. Neaten the raw edges with zigzag stitch. Turn right side out. Press the bag from the corners of the base.

7 Make two small holes – one in each side of the bag and blanket stitch (see page 131) around the circumference. Thread through the leather cord.

YOU WILL NEED

❖ 45 cm (½ yd) medium-weight fabric

❖ Remnant lightweight buckram

❖ Embroidery floss in green, violet and purple

❖ 75 cm (1 yd) leather cord

❖ See template on page 307

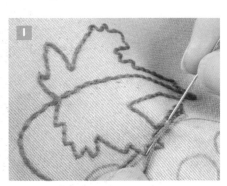

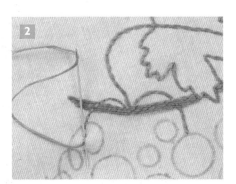

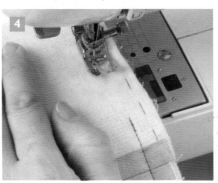

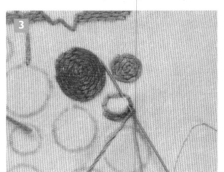

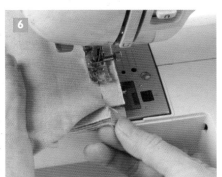

YOU WILL NEED

❖ *40 cm (16 in) white cotton fabric, at least 57 cm (23 in) wide*

❖ *Cotton thread in white, blue, red and green*

❖ *Hand towel, 55 cm (22 in) wide*

1 Cut a strip of white fabric measuring 57 × 10 cm (23 × 4 in) and six 10-cm (4-in) squares. Fold each square in half, then fold in the corners so that the short raw edges line up with the long raw edges. Press. Fold in 1 cm (½ in) all round on the long strip, then fold the strip in half lengthways. Press.

2 With white thread in the top and bottom of the machine (blue thread is used here to show up the stitching), zigzag down the centre of each triangle to hold the folded edges in place.

3 Pin the six triangles, evenly spaced, along one folded edge of the strip.

4 Fold the other edge over, pin and tack. Stitch along one short edge of the strip, then along the folded edge, and up the other short edge, about 3 mm (⅛ in) from the fold.

5 With blue thread on top, straight stitch close to the zigzag edge then stitch close to the border's top edge.

6 Change to herringbone or other patterned stitch and make a line of stitching down the centre of the border.

7 Change the top thread to red and stitch two more rows of herringbone (or your chosen stitch) either side of the line of blue, going in the opposite direction. Follow these with lines of zigzag stitch in green.

8 Press the border, then slipstitch to the edge of the towel.

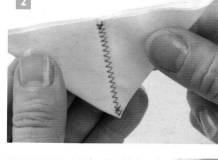
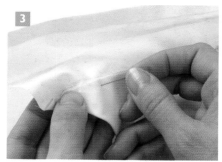

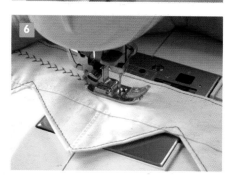

CHANGING THE SIZE

The instructions are for a border to fit a hand towel 55 cm (22 in) wide but you can easily adapt this project to fit a towel of any width. The border would also look very pretty on other items: the edge of a curtain, tablecloth or pillowcase, for example.

1 Trace a flower shape on to water soluble embroidery film and stretch the film in a hoop.

2 Thread the bobbin with violet thread and the needle with deep pink. Lower the feed dogs and remove the foot. Set the stitch length to 0 and the stitch type to straight stitch. Place the hoop under the needle and lower the needle lever. Bring the bobbin thread to the top of the work and, holding both threads in one hand, lower the needle into the fabric and make the first few stitches by turning the wheel manually. .

3 Holding the hoop lightly with both hands, proceed to stitch slowly, rotating the hoop to create overlapping spirals of stitching. Continue until you have covered the whole pattern area with an interlaced cobweb of stitches.

4 Change the top thread to turquoise and stitch another network of threads over the top of the pink. Finally, add a lighter covering of gold stitches.

5 Remove the work from the hoop and trim off excess film. Make a second flower shape in exactly the same way.

6 Plunge the work into a bowl of cold water and agitate gently until the film has completely dissolved. Tease the work into shape and dry.

7 Cut a circle of self-adhesive film 7.5 cm (3 in) in diameter and peel off the backing. Cut short lengths of ribbon and metallic cord and lay these across the adhesive film, then place this in the centre of a square of dissolving film and stretch in a small hoop.

8 Place the hoop on the sewing machine and create spirals of stitching, as before. Trim off any excess fabric, dissolve the film and dry the work. Use it to cover the button.

9 Run a gathering stitch around the centre of one of the flowers and pull up to gather slightly, then slipstitch to the edge of the button. Do the same with the second flower, reversing it to create a contrast colour.

EXCESS FILM

When cutting away excess film, do not discard it, as it can be used for other projects. Even the tiniest scraps can be useful for mending tears that may appear in the fabric while stitching.

YOU WILL NEED

❖ Water-soluble embroidery film

❖ Medium and small embroidery hoops

❖ Rayon machine embroidery thread in violet, deep pink and turquoise

❖ Gold metallic machine embroidery thread

❖ 3.8 cm (1½ in) self-covering button

❖ Self-adhesive water-soluble embroidery film

❖ Scraps of pink narrow ribbon and metallic cord

❖ See template on page 313

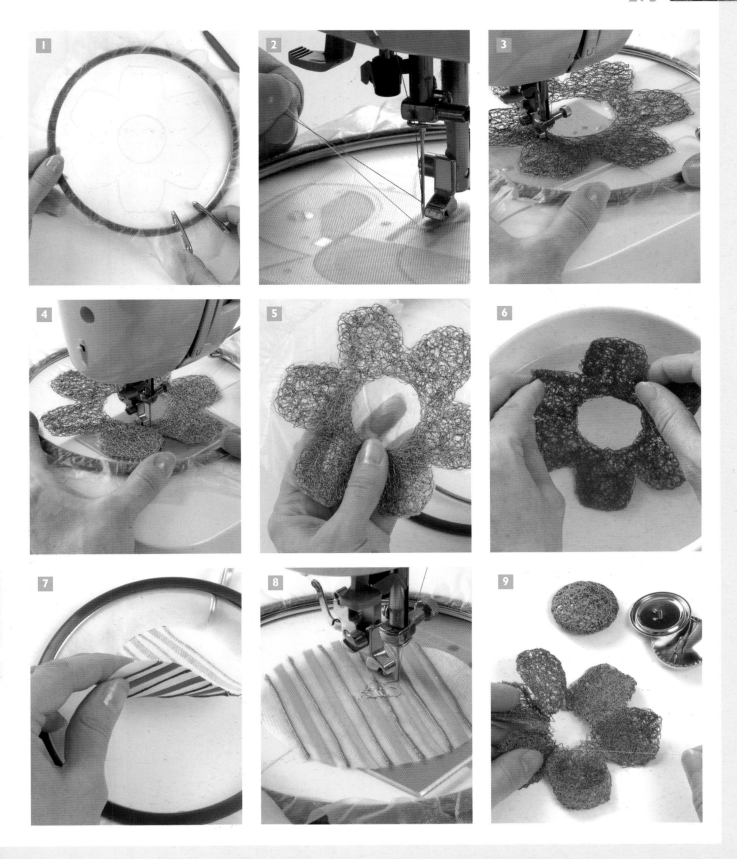

RECIPE BOOK COVER

1 Trace the motifs. On the reverse of the tracing, go over the lines using the transfer pencil, then position it on the fabric, to correspond with the centre of the front cover. Transfer using a hot iron, according to the manufacturer's instructions.

2 Using a hoop and two strands of embroidery thread in your needle, embroider the flowers. Use stem stitch in green for the stems and satin stitch in yellow and violet for the centres and petals.

3 For the bases of the cupcakes, stitch rows of satin stitch between the marked lines, altering the direction of each row of stitches. For large areas, such as the strawberries, stitch using long-and-short satin stitch.

4 When all the motifs have been stitched, add little stars in yellow thread by making five straight stitches radiating from a single point. Scatter French knots in several colours, over the background.

5 Press the work carefully on the reverse, placing a folded towel underneath to prevent the embroidery from becoming flattened. Press under 3 cm (1¼ in) all round and hand- or machine stitch 6 mm (¼ in) from the folded edges. Fold under a further 4 cm (1½ in) on the two long edges, then fold in 8 cm (3¼ in) at both sides.

6 Slipstitch the corners to create two narrow pockets for the covers of the book to slip inside. Trim any loose threads.

YOU WILL NEED

❖ 66 x 45 cm (26½ x 18 in) piece washable **woven check fabric**

❖ *Iron-on transfer pencil*

❖ *Six-stranded embroidery floss in sugar pink, yellow, primrose, violet, beige, white and red*

❖ *Crewel needle*

❖ *Sewing thread to match fabric*

❖ *See template on page 313*

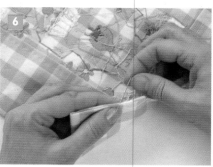

EASY CLEANING

Using washable fabric means the slip cover can easily be removed and hand laundered should it become stained.

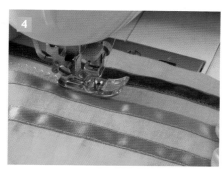

YOU WILL NEED

✤ Three lengths of 1 cm (¹/₂ in) ribbon, 1 velvet and 2 satin, each slightly longer than the circumference of the skirt

✤ Matching sewing thread

✤ Contrasting sewing thread

✤ Scraps of lightweight fabric and iron-on interfacing

✤ See template on page 311

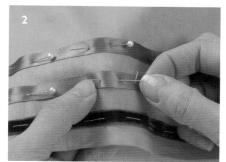

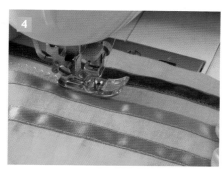

1 Pin the first ribbon in place about 2.5 cm (1 in) from the lower edge of the skirt. Pin two more lengths of ribbon in a similar way, spacing them evenly apart.

2 Tack all three lengths in place.

3 With matching thread, stitch along both edges of the first ribbon, using a medium straight stitch. Stitch the other two ribbons in the same way, with matching thread as needed.

4 Add lines of feather stitching between the ribbons in a contrasting colour to the skirt. You could vary the stitches using herringbone or zigzag, depending on your sewing machine (see pages 158-9), or the number of lines used.

5 Finish with a line of decorative stitching above the top ribbon.

6 Trace the flower motif onto a scrap of fabric. Iron on interfacing to back and stiffen the fabric. Using a close zigzag stitch and contrasting thread, stitch around the edge of the flower. Place a small circle of a contrasting fabric in the centre and close zigzag around this. Stitch radiating lines out from the central circle. When finished, cut around the design, close to the stitching. Make a second flower motif.

7 Pin the motif in place, using it to cover the joins in the ends of the ribbons. Slipstitch round the edge to secure. Pin the second motif in position at a different point around the bottom; slipstitch in place over the ribbons.

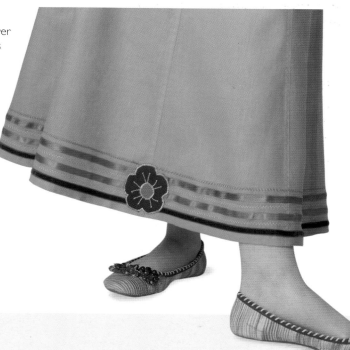

BEADED EVENING WRAP

1 Use clusters of three beads to highlight areas of the design. Then stitch bead clusters of another colour in the centre of each flower. Beginning at the central cluster and radiating out along the center of each petal, couch lines of five beads of another colour.

2 Place the beaded fabric and plain fabric right sides together. Pin and machine stitch down the two long sides, about 1 cm (½ in) from the edges. Turn right sides out.

3 Fold under 1 cm (½ in) on each of the short open ends; pin.

4 Tack around the entire circumference of each end, about 10 mm (⅜ in) away from the edge.

5 Carefully insert the beaded fringe between the tacked edges. Slipstitch the folded edges of the fabric to the braid on both sides, allowing a little of the braid to show at the edge.

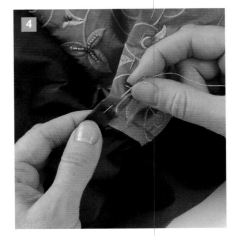

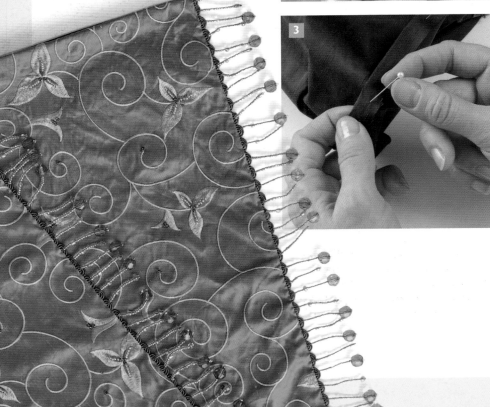

YOU WILL NEED

❖ 1.8 m (2 yds) turquoise blue embroidered silk fabric, any standard width

❖ (1.8 m (2 yds) of dark blue silk fabric, any standard width

❖ Glass beads of two contrasting shades

❖ Beaded braid to tone with fabric, twice the length of the fabric width

YOU WILL NEED

- ❖ *135 cm (1½ yds) panne velvet, 30 cm (12 in) wide*
- ❖ *135 cm (1½ yds) satin, 30 cm (12 in) wide*
- ❖ *Silk embroidery floss in three different colours*
- ❖ *Embroidery needle*
- ❖ *Tacking thread*
- ❖ *Matching sewing thread*
- ❖ *Knitting needle, if necessary*

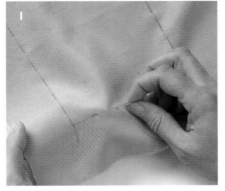

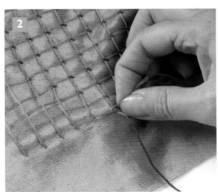

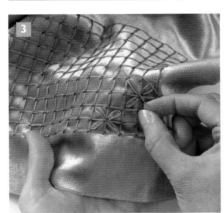

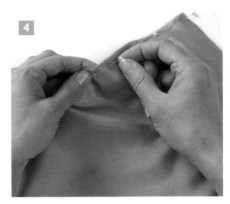

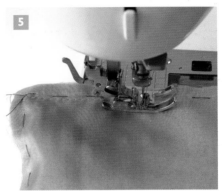

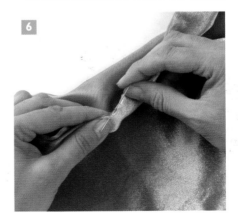

1 Take your length of velvet and decide on how deep you want the panel of embroidery at each end; use tacking or pins to mark the areas and make sure you leave allowances of 2.5 cm (1 in) round the raw edges.

2 Using six strands of colour A, work the horizontal and vertical stiches of an open lattice pattern across the marked area (see page 135) at one end of the velvet. Change to colour B and, using six strands, work the couching stitches that secure the lattice in place.

3 Change to colour C and using four strands, work a series of detached chain stitches across the lattice work to make a flower pattern. You can position these at regular intervals or create a more random design as wished.

4 Repeat steps 2 and 3 at the other end of the velvet. Remove any tacking stitches. Put the velvet and satin right sides together, matching raw edges. Pin and then tack all round.

5 Machine stitch around the edges, leaving a 20 cm (8 in) gap at the centre of one long side. Make sure you don't stitch over your embroidery. Snip across the allowance at the corners to reduce the bulk of the fabric. Turn the scarf to the right side through the gap.

Use a knitting needle to gently push the fabric into the corners, if necessary.

6 If the care instructions for your fabric allow, press lightly along the seams, covering your embroidery work with a cloth before you begin, and turning under the allowances at the gap. If your fabrics cannot by ironed, then lightly crease the seams between your fingertips. Slipstitch the gap closed to finish.

TISSUE PAPER

When working with very slippery fabrics such as satin, silk, and silk velvets, it is a good idea to place a sheet of tissue paper between the layers to keep them from sliding away from each other. Stitch through all the layers and pull the tissue away afterwards.

SMOCKED BANGLE BAG

1 Turn under each long edge of the fabric by 5 mm (¼ in); press. Turn under each edge again by 1 cm (½ in); press and pin. Machine- or handstitch each hem in place.

2 Lay out the fabric flat so that the short edges are at the top and bottom. Mark your first row of dots 12.5 cm (5 in) down from the top edge. Position the first and last dots in the row 1 cm (½ in) from the turned edge and make the dots 8 mm (⅜ in) apart. Make five more identical rows below the first one so that the rows are 1 cm (½ in) apart. Turn the fabric through 180 degrees and repeat the process.

3 Gather up the fabric in both panels as described on page 142. Then use two strands embroidery floss to work smocking stitch across the panels. Here, each panel is made up of five rows of honeycomb stitch (see page 143) but you could use a different stitch if preferred.

4 Finish off and press the smocked fabric (see page 144). Fold the fabric in half widthwise, right sides together and matching up the panels of smocking; press lightly along the fold. Pin the sides together as far as the smocking panels and then slipstitch the seams together.

5 Lay the bag out flat and place one of the bangles at the top, so the edge of the bangle is just above the top edge of the smocking. Fold the fabric over the bangle so that the bangle is enclosed and pin in place – you will have to gather up the fabric to fit. Trim the excess fabric to within 1.5 cm (⅝ in) of the pins. Remove the pins and bangle and trim the other side of the bag to match.

6 Turn under each top edge of the bag by 1.5 cm (⅝ in); press and stitch in place. Then turn one top edge over one bangle and tack to secure, gathering up the fabric as you go to fit. Handstitch the turning in place. Repeat to attach the other bangle to the other side. Turn the bag to the right side.

YOU WILL NEED

❖ Silk fabric 80 x 31.25 cm (32 x 12½ in)

❖ Dressmakers pencil, card and ruler for marking up the fabric

❖ Tacking thread

❖ Embroidery floss

❖ Two 10 cm (4 in) diameter bamboo rings

FINISHING TOUCH

Why not jazz up this bag with two beaded tassels? Simply insert at the corners before you stitch up the sides in step 4.

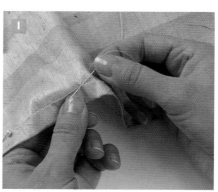

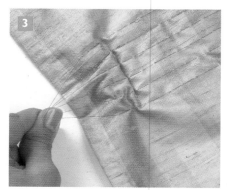

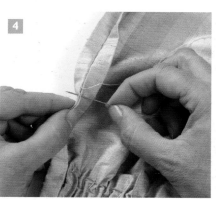

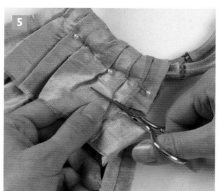

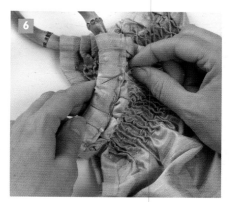

YOU WILL NEED

❖ 70 cm (¾ yd) lightweight cotton fabric, 90 cm (36 in) wide, for the foundation fabric

❖ 20 cm (8 in) lengths of six plain and patterned cotton fabrics, each 90 cm (36 in) wide

❖ 3m (3⅓ yd) satin ribbon, 5 cm (2 in) wide

❖ See template on page 311

Cut a 30 cm (12 in) wide strip of lightweight cotton for the foundation fabric. Set the remaining foundation fabric aside. Cut patches in various straight edged shapes from the six assorted fabrics.

1 Working across the piece, arrange the patches on the foundation fabric, overlapping the edges by 6 to 8 mm (¼ to ⅜ in). Pin and tack in place.

2 Stitch the patches to the foundation fabric 3 mm (⅛ in) inside the raw edges.

3 Set the sewing machine to a close zig-zag stitch about 6 mm (¼ in) wide. Stitch over the straight stitches on the patches using contrasting machine embroidery thread. When you reach a corner, lift the presser foot with the needle in the fabric at the outside edge of the zig-zagging. Pivot the fabric so that the work is now facing the new direction and continue. Pull all the thread ends to the wrong side.

4 Pin the remaining foundation fabric and patchworked fabric together with right sides facing. Trim the fabrics to a 26.5-cm (10½-in) wide strip. Refer to the cutting diagram to cut 8 pennants. Stitch the foundation fabric and patchworked fabric pennants together along the slanted edges. Clip the corners, turn right side out and press.

5 Tack the raw top edges of pennants together. Press the ribbon lengthwise in half with the wrong sides facing then open out flat. Starting 45 cm (18 in) from one end of the ribbon, pin the pennants to the wrong

side of the ribbon 10 cm (4 in) apart, matching the raw edges to the fold.

6 Refold the ribbon and tack the long edges together, enclosing the top of the pennants. Stitch close to the long edges with a straight stitch.

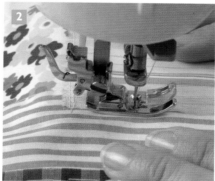

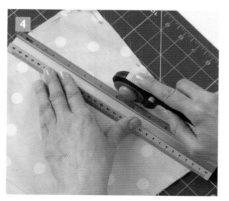

BOUDOIR PILLOW

Cut out two pieces of fabric 35 × 45 cm (14 × 18 ins) – this is the front panel on which you will create your design. Cut out another piece of fabric 35 × 65 cm (14 × 26 ins) for the back panel. Fold the back panel into thirds widthwise and press. Cut along one of the folds to produce two pieces – the larger one should be twice the size of the smaller. Mark the cut edges with pins.

1 Enlarge the motif as necessary and transfer it (see pages 190-91) to the wrong side of the front piece of your fabric.

2 Tack the backing piece to the front and then stitch along both sides of the marked lines on the design to create channels 6 mm (¼ in) apart.

3 Insert the cord as directed on page 201. Carefully slipstitch a lining to the backing piece to cover the cording.

4 Now take your two back pieces and turn under each of marked edges 6 mm (¼ in), then 4 cm (1½ in) and press. Pin and topstitch both hems in place.

5 Pin the back pieces to the front, right sides together, matching raw edges and making sure the hemmed edges overlap. Stitch round the sides, 1.5 cm (⅝ in) in from the edge. Stitch a 2nd line of stitching just inside the first at the side where the back panels overlap, for extra strength. Snip across each corner to reduce the bulk and make a neater finish.

6 Finish the raw edges with zigzag stitch to neaten and prevent fraying. Turn the cushion cover to the right side through the opening and press, being careful not to flatten the crown. Carefully stitch all around the case, 1 1/2 ins (4 cm) in from the edge through all fabric layers, to create a flange. Insert the cushion form.

YOU WILL NEED

❖ *90 cm (1 yd) fabric*

❖ *Remnant for lining*

❖ *Rectangular cushion form 30 × 40 cm (12 × 16 ins)*

❖ *Matching thread*

❖ *Filling*

❖ *See template on page 307*

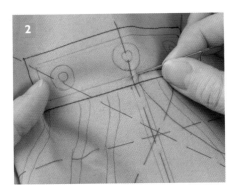

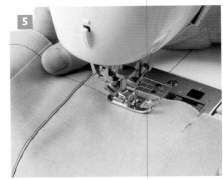

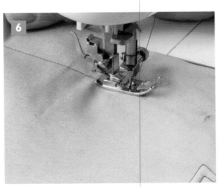

PATCHWORK APRON

YOU WILL NEED

Fabric apron

❖ *30 cm (⅓ yd) fabric in colour A, 90 cm (36 in) wide*

❖ *10 cm (⅛ yd) fabric in colours B and C, each 90 cm (36 in) wide*

❖ *20 cm (¼ yd) lining fabric 150 cm (60 in) wide*

❖ *1 m 70 cm (2 yds) bias binding*

❖ *Bonding web*

❖ *Erasable marker*

❖ *See template on page 308*

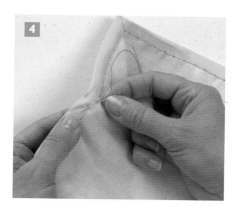

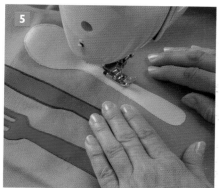

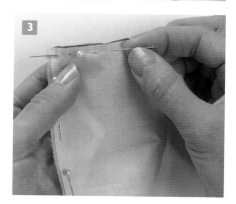

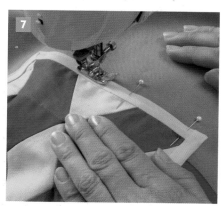

If necessary, unpick any pockets on the apron and discard them.

1 Use the template to cut six diamonds each from fabrics A, B and C. Cut four of the C fabric diamonds in half along the solid line and two diamonds in half along the broken lines. Cut one A fabric diamond and one B fabric diamond in half along the broken lines.

2 Refer to the photo to position the patches right sides up. Stitch the patches together to make the pocket (see the setting in technique on page 177).

3 Trim the raw edges of the pocket level. Cut the lining fabric to the size of the pocket and pin and tack the lining to the pocket.

4 Bind the side and bottom edges of the pocket with ready-made bias binding (see page 205); slipstitch in place on the underside of the pocket. Stitch bias binding to the upper straight edge of the pocket, having 1.5 cm (⅝ in) of the binding extending beyond the ends of the bound edges. Turn in the ends and slipstitch in place.

5 Using the templates, enlarged as necessary, cut out the knife, fork and spoon from your fabrics. Attach to the apron with

bonding web following manufacturer's instructions. Zigzag stitch around each item with matching thread.

6 Carefully pin the patchwork pocket to the apron.

7 Topstitch using matching thread along the side and bottom edges, just inside the bias binding.

PET CUSHION

From fabric A, cut out four 17-cm (7-in) squares. From fabric B, cut out four 16.5-cm (6½-in) squares for the front, one 62.5 cm (25 in) square for the back and two 62.5 × 40 cm (25 × 16 in) rectangles for the back panels. Cut out four 23.8-cm (9½") squares of fabric C. Cut the B and C squares diagonally into halves.
Note: Stitch the seams making 1.5 cm (⅝ in) seam allowance and stitch the seams with right sides facing.

1 To make one block, stitch the long edge of four B triangles to each edge of square A. Press the seams toward the B triangles.

2 Stitch the long edge of four C triangles to one edge of the stitched B triangles. Press the seams toward the C triangles.

3 Make up three more blocks in the same way. Join the blocks together to form a large square for the cushion front.

4 Turn under 5 mm (¼ in) then 4 cm (1½ in) on one long edge of each back panel and press in place to form a hem. Stitch close to the inner pressed edges.

5 Pin the back panels to the front with right sides facing, matching the raw edges and overlapping the hems at the centre. Stitch the outer edges. Stitch again just inside the first stitching for extra strength.

6 Clip the corners and trim off excess seam allowance. Turn right side out and insert the cushion pad.

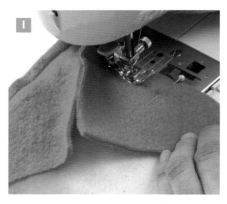

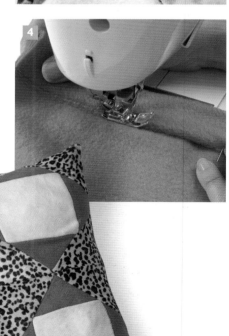

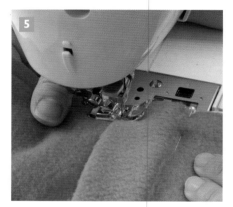

YOU WILL NEED

❖ 1 m 20 cm (1¼ yds) fabric B, 90 cm (36 in) wide

❖ 20 cm (¼ yd) fabric A, 90 cm (36 in) wide

❖ 50 cm (⅔ yd) fabric C, 90 cm (36 in) wide

❖ 60 cm (24 in) square cushion pad

❖ See template on page 313

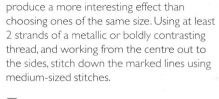

QUILTED CLUTCH BAG

YOU WILL NEED

✤ *50 cm (½ yd) striped silk fabric*

✤ *50 cm (1½ yds) wadding*

✤ *50 cm (½ yd) silk lining*

✤ *Metallic or strongly contrasting thread*

✤ *Notions: snap, button and ribbon*

1 Cut a rectangle, approximately 43 x 29 cm (17¼ x 11½ in) from your fabric, wadding and lining. Trim diagonally both corners on one short end.

2 Sandwich the fabric between the batting and the lining and stitch all three fabrics together, making a 1.5 cm (⅝ in) seam allowance. Leave a large gap along one short edge. Trim seam edges.

3 Turn the bag inside out so the striped fabric is at the front. Slip stitch the gap closed then press the seams flat.

4 Make several lines of horizontal tackng stitches using a contrasting coloured thread to hold the fabric layers together.

5 Mark the stripes you will want to emphasise. Stripes of different widths will produce a more interesting effect than choosing ones of the same size. Using at least 2 strands of a metallic or boldly contrasting thread, and working from the centre out to the sides, stitch down the marked lines using medium-sized stitches.

6 Fold up the short, straight edge approximately 15 cm (6 in) and stitch both sides close to the edges to create the bag. Sew the ball part of the snap to the top of the bag – in the centre of the back. Sew the socket of the snap in the middle of the bottom of the bag – about 7.5 cm (3 in) up from the bottom.

7 Secure the button on top of the snap on the front of the fabric and top with a small ribbon bow.

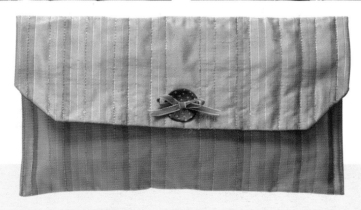

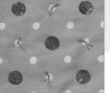

PICNIC BASKET COVER

Cut a rectangle of paper to the same length and width of your basket.

1 Tape the paper to the top of the basket with masking tape. Cut slits in the paper around the handles so that the paper lays flat. On the paper, draw a smoothly curved edge around the handles. Draw any curves on the basket's circumference, at the corners for example.

2 Remove the paper and cut along the curved lines. Draw around the cut paper on another piece to make the final pattern. Add 5.5 cm (2¼ in) to the outer edges and 1 cm (½ in) to the handle cut-outs.

3 Cut out the pattern. Use the pattern to cut the cover, wadding and lining.

4 Place the wadding between the fabric and lining and tack. With right sides facing, pin 1 cm (½ in) wide bias binding to the handle cut-outs. Stitch the binding, using 5 mm (¼ in) seam allowance. Trim away the wadding in the seam allowance. Clip the curves. Press the binding to the underside and slipstitch in place to the lining. Topstitch close to the handle cut-outs.

5 With right sides facing, stitch 2 cm (¾ in) wide bias binding to the outer edges of the basket cover with the binding extending 1 cm

(½ in) beyond the handle cut-outs and making 1 cm (½ in) seam allowance. Trim away the wadding in the seam allowance. Clip the curves and trim the seam allowance to 5 mm (¼ in). Turn under the extending ends of the binding and handsew to the binding.

6 Turn the binding to the underside. To make the drawstring channel, pin the binding to the lining, folding any fullness at the corners in small pleats.

7 Tack close to the inner edge of the binding. On the right side, topstitch close to the outer edges of the cover and along the tacking. Remove the tacking.

8 Thread a crewel needle with a double length of six strands of embroidery floss. Make a tie at the centre of the cover (see page 204), threading on a button before tying the threads on top. Arrange the remaining buttons equally around the centrebutton and tie them to the cover. Scatter additional floss ties among them.

9 Cut the ribbon in half. Thread each piece through a channel using a bodkin. Slip the cover over the basket and tie the ribbons in a bow below the handles.

YOU WILL NEED

For a basket 40 x 32 cm (15½ x 12½ in)

❖ *Fabric, wadding and lining: 50 cm (⅔ yd) of any width fabric*

❖ *50 cm (⅔ yd) bias binding, 1 cm (½ in) wide*

❖ *1 m 70 cm (2 yds) bias binding, 2 cm (¾ in) wide*

❖ *7 3-cm (1¼-in) diameter buttons*

❖ *Stranded cotton embroidery floss*

❖ *Crewel embroidery needle*

❖ *2 m 80 cm (3¼ yds) striped ribbon, 1.5 cm (⅝ in) wide*

❖ *Bodkin*

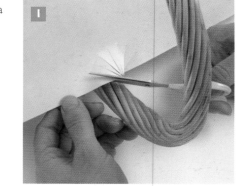

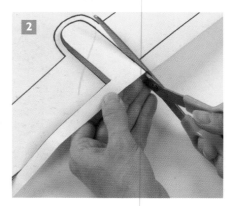

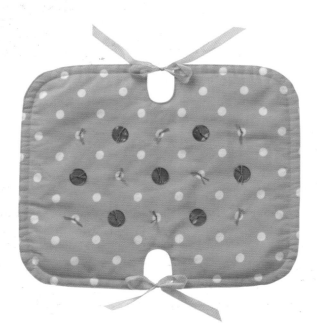

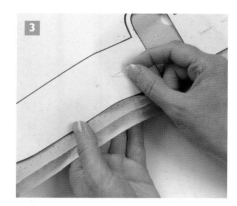

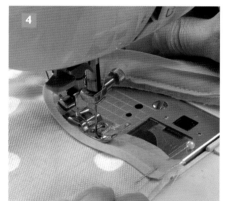

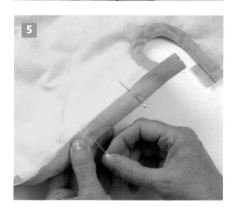

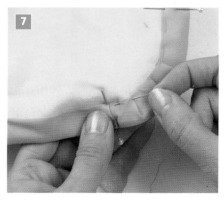

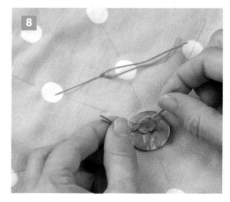

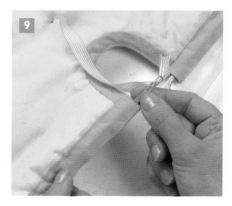

From fabric A, cut out two rectangles 43 × 16 cm (17 × 6 ¼ in) for bands and one rectangle 43 × 87 cm (17× 34¾ in) for the lining. From fabric B, cut out two rectangles 43 × 16 cm 17 × 6 ¼ in) for bands. From fabric C, cut out one rectangle (43 × 35 cm (17 × 13 ½ in) for bands and base.

Note: use 1.5 cm (⅝ in) allowance for all seams.

1 Stitch band A to band B along the long edges. Repeat with another A and B. Press the seams toward A.

2 Stitch band C to bands B along the long edge. Press the seams toward B.

3 Enlarge the seagull template and use to cut out shape from turquoise fabric. Place motif left of centre on the front; pin in place. Turn edge under 5 cm (¼ in) and using 2 strands of floss, secure with small neat stitches near the edge. Add the button.

4 With right sides facing and matching side edges, stitch side seams of front and back. Press the seams open.

5 Mark along the fold at the base of the shopper with pins. Match the pins to one side seam with the right sides facing. Pin at right angles across the seam, 5 cm (2 in) from the end of the seam. Stitch as pinned. Trim the seam to seam allowance. Repeat on the other side seam to form the shopper's base.

6 Fold lining lengthwise in half. Stitch down both sides. Finish bottom as in step 5 above. With wrong side facing out, place in bag. Turn under the tops of the lining and bag by 1.5 cm (⅝ in) and top stitch close to the edge on the front .

7 Fix the metal eyelets to the bag, 12 cm (4¾ in) in from the side seams. Thread the cord through and make double knots under the eyelets.

YOU WILL NEED

❖ 40 cm (½ yd) plain fabric A, 90 cm (36 in) wide

❖ 20 cm (¼ yd) denim fabric B, 90 cm (36 in) wide

❖ 40 cm (½ yd) striped fabric C, 90 cm (36 in) wide

❖ 20 cm (8 in) square fabric in turquoise for motif

❖ Four 1.5 cm (⅝ in) metal eyelets

❖ 1 m 30 cm (2 yds) cord, 2.5 cm (1 in) wide

❖ Stranded cotton embroidery floss

❖ Small button

❖ See template on page 310

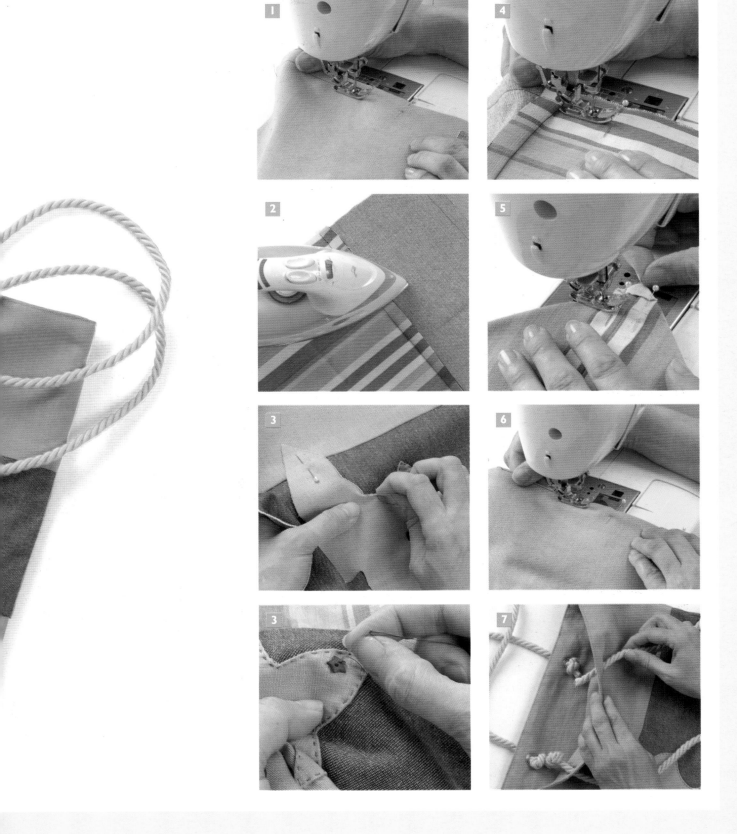

QUILTED BELT

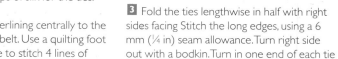

1 Enlarge the template to suit and cut 2 silk pieces and 1 interlining piece. Cut 6 38 × 2.5-cm (15 × 1-in) bias strips of silk for the ties.

2 Pin and tack the interlining centrally to the wrong side of one silk belt. Use a quilting foot on the sewing machine to stitch 4 lines of quilting 1.5 cm (⅝ in) apart along the

length of the belt, starting and finishing 1.5 cm (⅝ in) from the short edges.

3 Fold the ties lengthwise in half with right sides facing Stitch the long edges, using a 6 mm (¼ in) seam allowance. Turn right side out with a bodkin. Turn in one end of each tie and slipstitch the ends together.

4 Pin the raw end of one tie centrally to the ends of the quilted belt. Pin a tie above and below the centre tie 6 mm (¼ in) apart. Tack in place.

5 With right sides facing, pin and stitch the belts together using a 1.5-cm (⅝ in) seam allowance, leaving an opening in the lower edge. Clip the seam allowance across the corners. Trim the interlining in the seam allowance close to the seam. Trim and clip the seam allowances. Turn the belt right side out. Slipstitch the opening closed, Press the belt.

6 Roughly cut out nine large motifs and nine small motifs from the printed fabric. Apply the motifs to scraps of the silk dupion with bonding web. Zig-zag along the edges of the motifs with coordinating sewing thread.

7 Arrange the small motifs on the large ones and place in groups of three on the belt. Sew in place with small stitches over the zig-zagging. Sew clusters of eight beads to some of the smaller motifs.

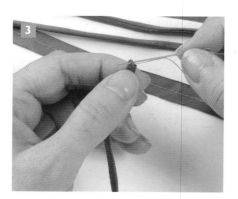

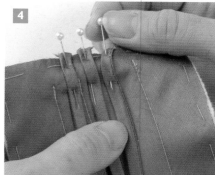

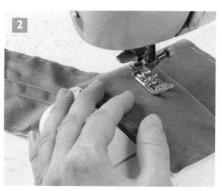

YOU WILL NEED

❖ 15 cm (6 in) square lace fabric

❖ Erasable marker

❖ 6.5 cm (2½ in) ribbon, 3 mm (⅛ in) wide

❖ Sharp, pointed embroidery scissors

❖ Blunt-ended scissors

❖ Sequins, optional

❖ See template on page 306

1 Draw the butterfly on the top with an erasable marker. Pin and tack the lace smoothly to the fabric. If the lace is too dense to see through, the butterfly can be drawn on the lace instead of the camisole. Stitch along the outline and centre of the butterfly using short, straight stitches. Remove the tacking.

2 Set the sewing machine to a close zig-zag stitch about 3 mm (⅛ in) wide. Stitch over the straight stitches of the outline, guiding the fabric around the curves. When you reach a corner, lift the presser foot with the needle in the fabric at the inside edge of the zigzagging. Pivot the top so the work is now facing the new direction and continue.

3 Pull the thread ends to the back of the work. Thread the ends onto a needle and insert the needle through the zigzag stitches for about 2 cm (¾ in) to secure. Cut off the excess thread.

4 With a sharp pair of embroidery scissors, trim the lace around the motif close to the stitches. Adjust the stitch width on your machine to about 2 mm (¹⁄₁₆ in) wide. Zig-zag stitch along the antenna. When complete,

work the thread ends through the zigzag stitches on the wrong side as before.

5 At each end of the ribbon, press under 8 mm (⅜ in). Tack the ribbon along the centre of the butterfly to create the body. Adjust the stitch width to 1 mm (¹⁄₂₀ in) wide. Zigzag stitch along the centre of the ribbon. Work the thread ends through the zigzag stitches on the wrong side as before.

6 Carefully cut away the fabric from beneath the lace butterfly with a pair of blunt ended scissors.

7 Some some sequins to the motif and scatter the rest close by on the top itself.

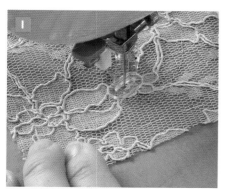

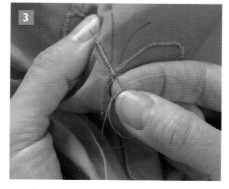

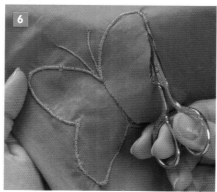

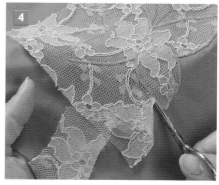

BABY'S QUILTED COVERLET

Cut out two rectangles of fabric and one rectangle wadding, each 100 × 70 cm (40 × 28 in). Round off the corners on each piece; to do this, place a saucer at the corner and draw round the curved edge. Use the template to create the cloud shapes out of scrap paper, enlarging or reducing it as necessary. You will need about nine clouds, 16 × 10 cm (6½ × 4 in) to 18 × 12 cm (7 × 4¾ in).

1 Arrange the clouds on one fabric piece at least 6 cm (2½ in) away from the outer edges. Pin the clouds in place and then draw around them with an erasable marker. Remove the clouds.

2 Sandwich the wadding between the two fabric pieces, so the right sides of the fabric face outward. Pin the layers together then, to hold the pieces together, make diagonal rows of tacking (by hand or machine) across the coverlet, starting at the centre and working outward.

3 Using matching quilting thread, make small running stitches along the outlines of the clouds. When finished, remove the tacking threads and erase any marks.

4 Trim the raw edges evenly. Using slipstitch, apply the binding all round the edge of the coverlet.

YOU WILL NEED

❖ *1.5 m (1½ yds) light blue brushed cotton fabric, 112 cm (44 in) wide*

❖ *90 cm (1 yd) 2 oz wadding*

❖ *43.4 m (4 yds) bias binding, 2.5 cm (1 in) wide*

❖ *Erasable marker*

❖ *Even-feed foot*

❖ *See template on page 308*

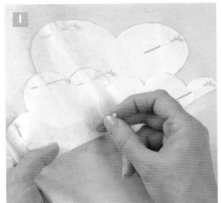

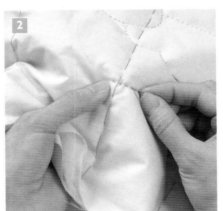

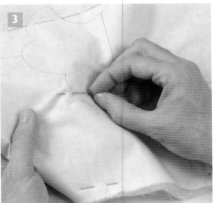

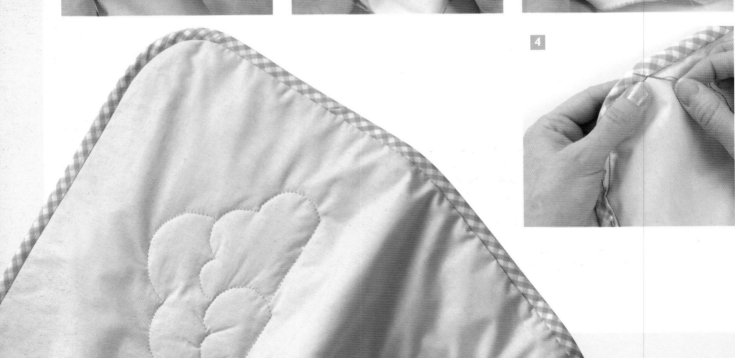

SIMPLE CUSHION

YOU WILL NEED

❧ *Fabric – for amount see right*

❧ *Square cushion form*

❧ *Matching thread*

Measure your cushion form and cut out one piece of fabric to the same size; this is for the front panel. For the back panel, cut out a piece of fabric that is 20 cm (8 in) longer. Fold this into thirds widthwise and press. Cut along one of the folds to produce 2 pieces – the larger should be twice the size of the smaller. Mark the cut edges with pins.

1 Turn under each of the two marked edges, 5 mm (¼ in), then 4 cm (1½ in); press. Pin and topstitch both hems in place.

2 Pin the back pieces to the front, right sides together, matching raw edges and making sure that the hemmed edges overlap. Stitch around the sides, taking a 1.5 cm (⅝ in) seam allowance. Stitch a second line of stitching just inside the first, at the side where the back panels overlap, for extra strength.

3 Snip across each corner to reduce the bulk and make a neater finish.

4 Finish the raw edges with zigzag stitch to neaten and prevent fraying. Turn the cushion cover to the right side through the opening and press. Insert the cushion form.

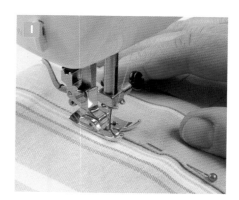

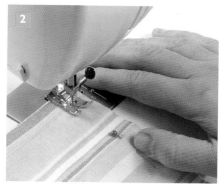

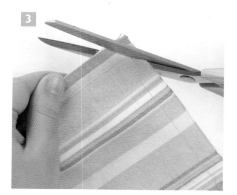

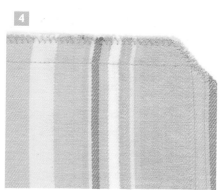

FABRIC CHOICE

If you plan to sit directly on the cushion then it's best to choose a mediumweight fabric. But if you're making scatter cushions for your bed or sofa, you also could use a lighter weight material. Alternatively, if you've got a heavyweight piece of fabric that you particularly want to make into a cushion cover, then use this for the front panel and a lighter material for the back panels. This cover is removable and so can be cleaned separately from the cushion form; if your cushion is going to get a lot of wear, then pick a washable fabric.

Once you have mastered the basic technique, you could add piping, tassels, or fringing before making up the final cover.

TAB-TOP CURTAIN

First, you need to decide what length you want your finished curtain to be and then you can measure up to work out how much fabric you will need. Measure 12 cm (4½ in) down from your curtain pole; then measure down from this point to where you want the curtain to end to find the curtain length. Add on 28.5 cm (11¼ in) for turnings and facings for the cut length.

Measure the width of your pole and multiply this by one and a half to find the curtain width. If you are making a pair of curtains, divide this by two to find the width of each one. Divide the curtain width by the width of your fabric. Round this up to find how many widths of fabric you need. Multiply this figure by the cut length to work out how much material you will need for the curtains. You will also need extra for the tabs: 30 cm (12 in) of 140 cm (54 in) wide fabric is enough for 8 tabs, so increase the amount of fabric as necessary.

YOU WILL NEED

❖ Fabric

❖ Tacking and matching thread

Before you begin, you may need to join widths of fabric to get the correct curtain width. If you are using plain fabric then simply cut enough pieces to the required length and stitch together, taking 1.5 cm (⅝ in) allowances. If you are using a patterned fabric, make sure you cut your lengths to allow for joining the pattern. This also applies if you are making two curtains, as you will want the pattern to line up when the curtains are hung.

You also will need to cut a backing panel for each curtain you are making; this should be the same width as the curtain by 11 cm

(4¼ in) high. Again, you may need to join widths of fabric.

Each finished tab is 7.5 cm (3 in) wide; work out how many tabs you can fit across your curtain width, allowing for 15-23 cm (6-9 in) between each one. You will need to cut this many pieces of tab fabric, each one 17 x 27 cm (6¾ x 10¾ in). The instructions given here are for making one curtain, you simply repeat the method, where appropriate, for two or more.

SHEER FABRICS

Tab-top curtains work well in sheer fabrics but you must take care to make your seams and turnings as neat as possible since they will show through to the right side. Use flat-fell seams (see page 219) and rolled hems (see page 220).

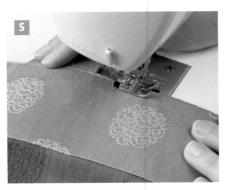

1 Fold each tab in half lengthwise, right sides together, and stitch the long edges together, taking a 1 cm (½ in) allowance. Press each seam open then turn each tab to the right side. Press each one so the seam is centred on one side of the tab.

2 Turn under 1 cm (½ in) on both side edges of each curtain piece; press. Turn under the sides again by 1.5 cm (⅝ in); press. Topstitch along each side. Turn under 8 cm (3¾ in) along the bottom edges; press. Turn under the hem by the same amount again; press. Topstitch the hem in place.

3 Fold each tab in half widthwise, wrong sides together. Pin a tab to each top corner of the curtain, matching raw edges and making sure the outer edges of the tabs line up with the sides of the curtain. Tack in place. Pin the remaining tabs across the top of the curtain, matching raw edges and spacing them evenly across the width; tack.

4 Pin the backing panel to the top of the curtain, right sides together, so the curtain is centred on the panel. Stitch across the top of the curtain, taking a 1.5 cm (⅝ in) allowance. Fold the backing over to the wrong side of the curtain; press.

5 Turn under the sides of the backing so they match up with the sides of the curtain; press. Turn under the bottom of the backing by 1.5 cm (⅝ in); press. Pin to the curtain then topstitch round all the edges of the backing panel where it attaches to the curtain.

DUFFEL BAG

Cut out a 28 cm (11¼ in) diameter circle from the main fabric. Cut out a rectangle of main fabric, 63 × 88 cm (25 × 34¾ in).

1 If you are going to use appliqué motifs, lay out the fabric and mark five evenly spaced positions with lines of tacking.

2 Cut out animal shapes from the contrast fabric, leaving an ample allowance around the drawn line. Pin and tack to main fabric then machine stitch in place following the drawn line. Using a small pair of sharp scissors, trim away the allowance, close to the machine stitching. Select a zigzag stitch where the stitches will be close together and sew around the shape, covering the raw edges. Alternatively, use the iron-on method described in the box, below.

3 Fold the fabric in half to bring the shorter edges right sides together; pin. Mark a position along the pinned seam 8 cm (⅜ in) from the top. Make another mark 4 cm (1½ in) below this mark. Stitch along the seam up to the first mark. Start stitching again at the second mark, then continue to the end of the seam (creating the gap through which to thread the cord). Press the seam open.

4 Turn under 1.5 cm (⅝ in) around the top; press. Turn under again 7 cm (2¾ in); press and pin. Topstitch around the edge of the hem, 1 cm (½ in) in from the fold. Topstitch all around again, 5 mm (¼ in) from the first line of stitching. Topstitch all around the top of the turning, 1.5 cm (⅝ in) in from the pressed edge. Topstitch again, 1 cm (½ in) in from the pressed edge.

5 Pin the body of the bag and the circular base right sides together. Tack around the edge, snipping into the straight edge of the bag to fit. Machine stitch all round, taking a 1.5 cm (⅝ in) allowance. Neaten the raw edges with zigzag stitch and turn the bag to the right side.

6 Using a threader or large safety pin, thread the cord through the casing. Knot the two ends together.

YOU WILL NEED

❖ *Main fabric – for amount see left*

❖ *Small amount of contrasting fabric for appliqué (optional)*

❖ *Cord, 160 cm (63 in) long*

❖ *Tacking and matching thread*

❖ *Threader or safety pin*

❖ *See template on page 311*

BONDING WEB

Iron-on adhesive is a useful way to fix appliqué shapes to your main fabric. Draw your shape onto the paper backing. Cut roughly round the shape and then place, paper-side up onto your appliqué fabric. Iron over the adhesive, following manufacturer's instructions. Allow to cool, then cut round your drawn line. Peel off the backing paper and position the shape, adhesive-side down, on the main fabric. Iron to fix then oversew the edges of the shape.

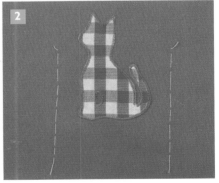

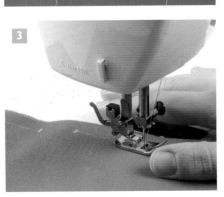

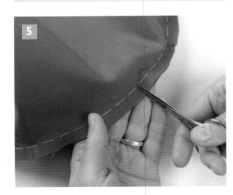

YOU WILL NEED

❖ *Main fabric, 1 m (1yd)*

❖ *Contrasting fabric or webbing*

❖ *Tacking and matching thread*

❖ *Fabric scraps*

❖ *Ribbon scraps*

❖ *See template on page 313*

Cut out 2 rectangles 41 × 47 cm (16¼ × 18½ in) from the main fabric for the front and back. Cut a 13 × 135 cm (5⅛ × 54 in) strip from the main fabric for the gusset. Cut 2 strips of contrasting fabric, each 10 cm × 1.2 m (4 in × 1½ yds), for the straps. Cut a pocket measuring 20 × 25 cm (8 × 10 in). You will also need two 20 cm (8 in) lengths of ribbon.

1 Stitch one piece of ribbon about 5 cm (2 in) up from the bottom edge of the pocket. Cut fabric scraps into shapes for the appliqué and apply to the pocket using iron-on adhesive (see page 296). Zigzag stitch around the shapes for a decorative border.

2 Turn under a double 1.5 cm (⅝ in) hem on one short edge of the front and back pieces. Press and pin. Machine stitch in place close to the edge. Place the pocket centrally on the front of the front fabric piece with bottom edges lined up. Pin and tack in place.

3 Take the straps and fold each one in half lengthwise, right sides together. Stitch, taking a 1 cm (½ in) allowance, then trim seam and corners. Turn right sides out and press flat, with the seam in the centre on one side.

4 Place one strap onto the front of the bag, covering the raw edges of the pocket and with the outer edges 8 cm (3 in) from the side edges of the front. The ends of the straps should line up with the bottom edge of the bag. Pin and tack.

5 Topstitch in place beginning at the bottom end. When you get to the top of the bag, continue topstitching across the strap until you reach the opposite edge, then continue down the other side to the bottom. Attach the other strap to the back in the same way, positioning it the same distance from the side edges.

6 Turn under a double 1.5 cm (⅝ in) hem on both short edges of the gusset; pin, press, and stitch. Pin one long edge of the gusset round the raw edges of the bag front, right sides together. You will need to snip into the lower corners of the gusset to fit. Stitch taking a 1.5 cm (⅝ in) allowance. Repeat to stitch the gusset to the back piece. Finish the raw edges with zigzag stitch. Turn the bag to the right side.

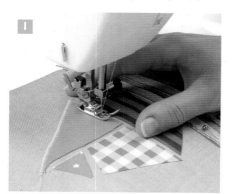

BEACH ROLL

1 Cut four pieces of batting, each 30 × 85 cm (12 × 38½ in), for the padded section. Put the four pieces together and tack loosely together to hold. Position the batting at one end of the towelling fabric 7.5 cm (3 in) down from the top edge and 7.5 cm (3 in) from either side. Secure to the towelling with a few large, loose tacking stitches.

2 Cut two lengths of main fabric, each 4 × 115 cm (1½ × 45 in) for the ties. Make the ties, finishing off both ends (see page 229).

3 Now mark the positions for the ties. Using a pin and on the right side, mark a point 32.5 cm (13 in) from one long edge of the fabric and 44 cm (17¼ in) down from the top edge. Repeat on the opposite side of the fabric so you have two positions marked at one end of the fabric.

4 Fold one tie in half and press to make an obvious fold mark. Pin this tie to the fabric through this fold at one of the marked positions and then stitch in place along the fold line. Repeat with the other tie to stitch it in place.

5 Turn under 1.5 cm (⅝ in) around the edge of the fabric; press in place. Lay out the fabric flat, wrong side up, with the ties at the bottom. Centre the towelling on top so the padded section is at the top of the fabric, with the wadding on the underside. Fold the edges of the fabric up and over the edges of the toweling, folding the fabric into mitres at the corners. Pin in place and trim away any excess fabric at the corners.

6 Press and then topstitch all around the pinned edge of the fabric, making sure that you don't stitch through the ties. Then topstitch across the width of the towelling, just below the edge of the padding – starting and finishing your stitching at the edge of the fabric border. Slipstitch the seams (see page 219) at the corners by hand.

7 Cut a length of main fabric 4 × 104 cm (1½ × 41 in) and make into a tie, finishing off both ends (see page 229). Stitch one end 17 cm (6¾ in) in from the outside edge and 16 cm (6½ in) from the bottom edge, stitching though the main fabric. Stitch the other end the same distance in from the opposite edge and up from the bottom.

YOU WILL NEED

❖ *Main fabric 115 × 165 cm (45 × 65 in), plus extra for the ties and shoulder strap ties (see steps 2 and 7 left)*

❖ *Towelling, 100 × 150 cm (40 × 60 in)*

❖ *1 m (1 yd) wadding, 2 cm (¾ in) thick*

OVEN MITTS

YOU WILL NEED

❖ *Main fabric – for amount see below*

❖ *Contrasting fabric – for amount see below*

❖ *Curtain interlining – for amount see below*

❖ *Bias binding, 2.5 m (2¾ yds)*

❖ *Paper, pencil and small plate*

❖ *Erasable marker*

Cut out a piece of paper 18 × 25 cm (7 × 10 in). Round off two of the corners on one short side (see page 223). Trim away the paper around the curve. Use the paper pattern to cut out four pieces of main fabric and two pieces of interlining. Cut out one rectangle of main fabric 18 × 80 cm (7 × 31½ in). Cut a piece of contrasting fabric and piece of interlining the same size. Use

the pattern as a guide to round off the corners on both rectangles of fabric and the interlining. Cut one 12 cm (4¾ in) and 2 18-cm (7-in) lengths of bias binding. Cut one 196 cm (77¼ in) length of binding.

1 Take one of the long pieces of fabric and, using an erasable marker, mark the desired quilting lines on the right side. Do the same on two of the smaller pieces of fabric. Take the two long pieces of fabric and the interlining and sandwich the interlining between the fabric so the right sides of the fabric are outermost; pin. Repeat with the smaller pieces. Tack the pieces together, working from the centre outward.

2 Stitch along the marked lines on the longer piece. Tack the smaller pieces of fabric and interlining together and then stitch along the quilting lines.

3 Take the shortest length of bias binding and fold in half lengthwise, wrong sides together. Stitch to join the two edges together. Fold the longest of the fabric pieces in half widthwise to find the centre point and mark it on one edge with a pin on the main-

fabric side. Take one end of the stitched length of binding and pin it to the edge of the fabric to the right of the marker pin, so the raw edges match and the stitching on the binding is next to the pin. Repeat with the other end of the binding to pin it to the left of the marker pin. Tack across the ends.

4 Take one 18-cm (7-in) length of bias binding and use to bind the straight edge of one of the small pieces of fabric, using the slipstitch method (see page 233). Repeat with the second small fabric piece.

5 Pin one of the small pieces of fabric at each end of the longer piece, on the contrasting fabric side and tack to secure the edges.

6 Use the remaining length of binding to bind all around the edge of the oven mitt, trimming any excess binding to 2 cm (¾ in) before overlapping the ends (see page 229).

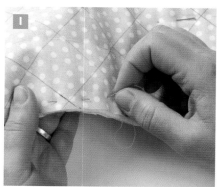

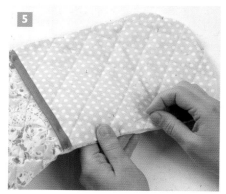

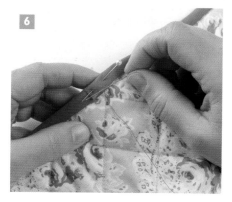

EYELET CURTAINS

For this kind of curtain you need to begin by cutting the right length of eyelet tape. Multiply the length of your curtain pole by one and a half to find the curtain width. If you are making two curtains, halve this to find the width of each one. Cut your curtain tape to this measurement plus 4 cm (1½ in). You need the holes in the tape to be evenly spaced so you may need to cut the tape slightly longer – if you do, measure the tape and use this as the curtain width measurement.

Measure from your curtain pole to the point where you want the curtain to end; add on 9.5 cm (4 in) to get the curtain length. Add on 15 cm (6 in) for turnings to find the cut length. Divide the curtain width by the width of your fabric. Round this up to find how many widths of fabric you need. Multiply this figure by the cut length to work out how much material you will need for the curtains.

YOU WILL NEED

❖ Main fabric, to calculate the amount you need, see left

❖ Contrasting fabric, 19 cm (7½ in) x the curtain width

❖ Eyelet tape, to calculate the amount you need, see left

❖ Matching and tacking thread

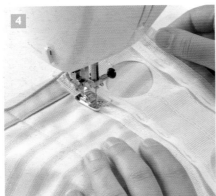

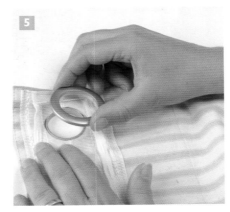

EYELET TAPE

Eyelet tape is similar to curtain tape but has holes along its length at regular intervals. Cords run along the top and bottom of the tape – these are gathered up when the curtain has been made to draw it into folds. Some tapes also feature coloured markers and sewing lines that act as guides when you are stitching. Once the tape has been sewn to the top of the curtain, the fabric you can see behind the holes is cut away and the eyelet rings pressed in place – these cover the raw edges of the fabric. The rings should be removed before the curtains are cleaned, but they are easily levered apart with a small screwdriver.

You may need to join widths of fabric to get your curtain width. Cut your lengths of fabric as required and stitch them together.

1 Turn under 1 cm (½ in) on both side edges; press. Turn under the sides again by the same amount; press. Topstitch each turning in place. Turn under 1.5 cm (⅝ in) along the bottom edge; press and then topstitch in place.

2 Pin the border to the curtain top, the right side of the border to the wrong side of the curtain, and so the curtain is centred on the border. Stitch across the top of the curtain taking a 1.5 cm (⅝ in) allowance.

3 Fold the border to the right side of the curtain; press. Turn under the sides of the border so they match up with the sides of the curtain; press. Turn under the bottom of the border by 1.5 cm (⅝ in); press. Pin the border to the curtain then topstitch all round the border, close to the edges.

4 Position the eyelet tape across the top of the curtain, on the wrong side, so that the tape is positioned just below the topstitching that runs along the top of the border. Following the manufacturer's instructions, pin the tape in place, turning the ends under at the curtain edges. Stitch along the bottom and top of the eyelet tape, making sure you stitch in the same direction along each edge. Stitch over the ends of the tape. Take care not to stitch over the gathering cords.

5 Use a pair of small scissors and cut away the fabric at the eyelet holes, making sure you cut through both layers of fabric. Following the manufacturer's instructions, fix the eyelets over the holes.

6 Hang the curtain on your pole. Tie the gathering cords together at one end. Pull on the other end until the curtain is the width you require; tie the loose ends together and tuck out of sight. Turn up the bottom edge of the curtain until it is the required length; pin. Take the curtain down and hem the bottom edge before re-hanging.

Before you begin to make your shade you will need to prepare a batten from which the shade will hang. This is simply screwed to the wall or window frame above the window. You need to decide how far you want the shade to extend on either side – this will be the length of the batten. Mark the position where you want to fix the batten and measure down from this to where you want the shade to end – this will be the finished length of your shade.

    Two screws should be enough to secure the batten for a narrow window, but a wider span may require more. The screws need to be long enough to go through the 2.5-cm (1-in) width of the batten and into the wall or window frame. The shade is secured to the batten with stick-and-sew Velcro®; the adhesive side of the product is applied to the batten after you've fixed it to the wall.

YOU WILL NEED

+ *Main fabric, cut to your required measurements*

+ *Lining fabric, enough for your required measurements plus extra for the ties*

+ *Fixing batten – 5 x 2.5 cm (2 x 1 in) cut to your required length*

+ *Stick-and-sew Velcro® – the same length as the fixing batten*

+ *Suitable screws and tools*

VELCRO®

If you can't get stick-and-sew Velcro® use ordinary Velcro®. Separate it into its two parts. Apply a suitable adhesive to the wrong side of the stiffer part. Press onto the batten. Using a staple gun, staple through the strip at both ends and at intervals along the length.

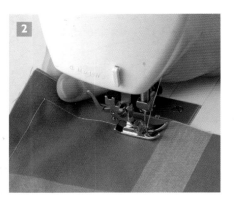

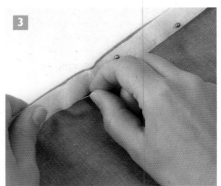

Work out the desired length of your shade
and add on 3 cm (1¼ in) for allowances.
Measure the width of your batten and add
on 4 cm (1½ in) for allowances and a little
extra to overlap the batten at the top. Cut
out a piece of main fabric to these
dimensions. Cut out a piece of lining fabric
the same size. For the ties, take the desired
length of the shade and double this; add on
3 cm (1¼ in) for allowances for the length.
The finished ties are 5 cm (2 in) wide, so
cut the strips 3 cm (1¼ in) wider – 8 cm
(3¼ in). Cut 2 strips of lining fabric the
same size.

1 Fold each tie in half lengthwise, right sides
together. Stitch the long edges of each, leaving
a 15 cm (6 in) gap in the centre. Press the
seams open, so they are centred. Cut
diagonally across each end and then stitch.
Turn to the right side and press again;
slipstitch the opening closed.

2 Pin the main fabric and lining fabric right
sides together. Stitch around the sides and
bottom edge, taking a 1.5 cm (⅝ in)
allowance. Snip across the corners then turn
to the right side; press.

3 Turn under the top edge by 1.5 cm (⅝ in)
and press. Pin the appropriate part of the
Velcro® to the top edge, on the lined side,
ensuring that you cover the raw edge of the
fabric. Stitch along both sides of the Velcro®
close to the edge to secure.

4 Stitch across the bottom of the shade, 4
cm (1½ in) above the bottom edge, to make
a channel for the flat batten. Unpick the side
seam at one end of the channel and then slip
the batten in. Slipstitch the unpicked end
closed.

5 Fix the 5 × 2.5 cm (2 × 1 in) batten above
the window in its desired position but don't
tighten the screws completely; the batten
should stand out a little way from the wall.
Slip the ties over the batten so they hang
down with the ends level. Tighten the fixing
screws. Lift up the ties and apply the adhesive
side of the Velcro® to the batten. Press the
Velcro® strip on the shade onto the batten.
Roll the shade up and knot the ties to hold.

First make a pattern for the top and base of the cushion. Cut out a rectangle of paper 78 × 53 cm (31 × 21 in). Round off the corners (see page 223) to make an oval shape. Using the pattern, cut out two pieces of main fabric for the top and base. Measure around the outside edge of the pattern and then cut out a strip of fabric this measurement plus 3 × 26 cm (1¼ × 10¼ in) for the side.

You will also need a number of different pieces of fabric for the appliqué circles that decorate the side of the cushion. Cut the pieces roughly to size, using circular objects in different sizes – such as cups and saucers – as templates, but don't cut into circles yet; this is done after the iron-on adhesive is applied (see step 1).

1 Cut out pieces of iron-on adhesive, each one a bit bigger than the circle you will be cutting out. Iron these onto the wrong side of the contrasting fabrics you are using for decoration (see page 296). Place your chosen circular objects on the paper backing and draw around to make the circles. Cut out each circle.

2 Peel off the paper backing of each circle and iron onto the side fabric, one by one. Set your sewing machine to a narrow zigzag stitch and oversew the edges of each appliqué circle.

3 Fold the side strip in half widthwise, right sides together and pin along the short edges. Machine stitch along the seam for 4 cm (1½ in) at the beginning and the end of the seam; the gap left in the seam is for adding the filling later.

4 Pin the side strip to the top piece of fabric, centring the seam on one of the longer edges of the oval. Stitch together, taking a 1.5 cm (⅝ in) allowance.

5 Snip into the allowance at the curves. Repeat step 4 to stitch the side to the base piece of fabric and snip the curves.

6 Turn the cushion to the right side and pour in the polybeads (see box below). Only put in enough to two-thirds fill the cushion. Slipstitch the gap in the side seam closed using small stitches so the opening is firmly secured.

YOU WILL NEED

* Main fabric, 2.5 m (2¾ yds), 140 cm (54 in) wide

* Small pieces of contrasting fabrics, enough to decorate the side of the cushion

* Iron-on adhesive

* Polybead filling – a 90 cm³ (3ft³) bag

* Matching and tacking threads

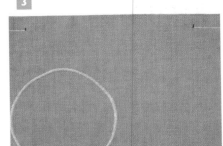

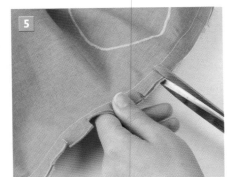

POLYBEADS

Polybeads can be quite tricky to work with – when you handle them, static electricity will cause them to stick to your skin and clothing. The best way to ensure that they get through the gap you've left in the side seam and into the cushion is to construct a funnel apparatus out of paper. Simply take a piece of paper and roll it up into a cone, making sure that there is a large enough hole at the bottom and that your cone fits into the gap in the side seam; secure the paper with sticky tape. To avoid handling the polybeads, scoop them up with a jug and then pour them into the cone.

YOU WILL NEED

❖ *Fabric – for amount see step 1 or 4*

❖ *Bolster form*

❖ *Tacking and matching thread*

❖ *Ribbon or cord – about 1¼ m (1½ yds) for the ribbon-tied cover*

❖ *Shirring elastic – about 1 m (1¼ yds) for the elastic cover*

❖ *Threader or safety pin for the elastic cover*

CORD TIE

For a more decorative touch, you can thread cord rather than elastic through the casing and secure with a decorative bow. To clean the cover, untie the bow and ease open the cord (or elastic) to remove the bolster form.

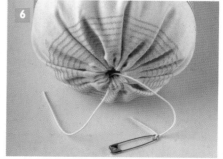

Ribbon-tied ends

1 Measure the length and diameter of your bolster form and then add on 82 cm (32¼ in) to give you the length of your fabric. Measure the circumference of your bolster form, adding on 3 cm (1¼ in) for turnings, to get the width. Cut out a rectangle of fabric to these measurements.

2 Fold your fabric in half lengthwise, right sides facing, and pin along the long edges. Stitch 1.5 cm (⅝ in) in from the edge. Press the seam open.

3 Turn under a 1 cm (½ in) hem at both ends and press. Turn under an 20 cm (8 in) hem and press again. Pin and slipstitch all

around the hem. Turn the cover to the right side and insert the bolster form. Tie the ends closed with ribbon.

Elastic ends

4 Measure the length and diameter of your bolster; add these together then add on 6 cm (2¼ in). Fold your fabric in half lengthwise, right sides facing, so the long sides match. Pin and stitch the seam, starting 3 cm (1¼ in) in and finishing 3 cm (1¼ in) before the end. Press the seam open.

5 Turn fabric under 1 cm (½ in) then 2 cm (¾ in) at both ends of the cover and press. Topstitch around the hems, to make the casings for the elastic. Turn the cover to the right side.

6 Slip the bolster form into the cover. Using a threader or safety pin, thread elastic through the casing at both ends. Use the elastic to pull the openings shut. Tie the ends of the elastic together tightly and trim. Work the elastic around inside the casing to hide the ends.

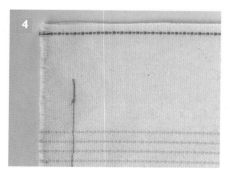

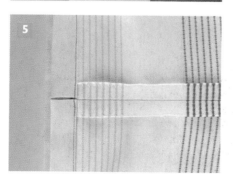

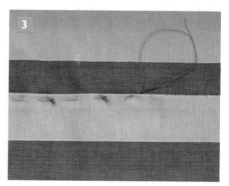

p.270

BEADED ESPADRILLES

p.247

TUBE TOP

71 (76, 81, 86, 91) cm 28½ [32½, 34½, 36½] ins

25 (25, 25, 28, 28) cm 10 [10, 10, 11¼, 11¼] ins

p.291

BUTTERFLY TOP

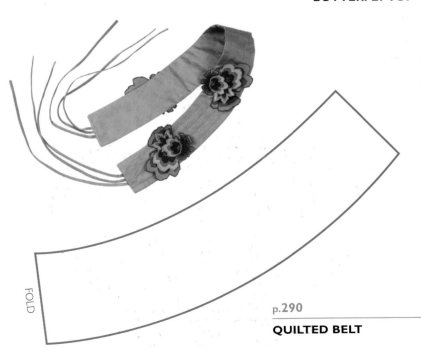

FOLD

p.290

QUILTED BELT

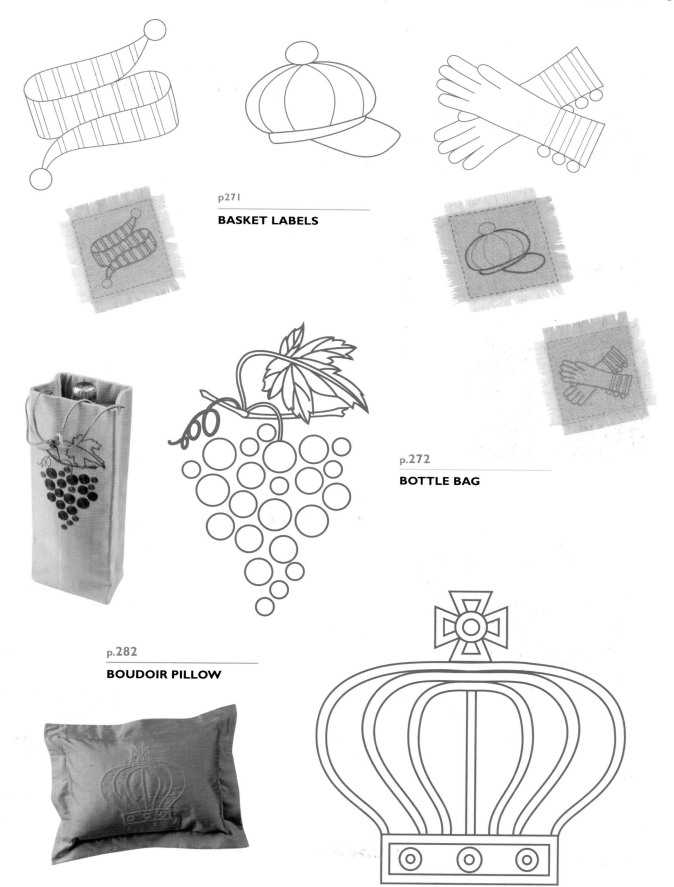

p271

BASKET LABELS

p.272

BOTTLE BAG

p.282

BOUDOIR PILLOW

p.283

PATCHWORK APRON

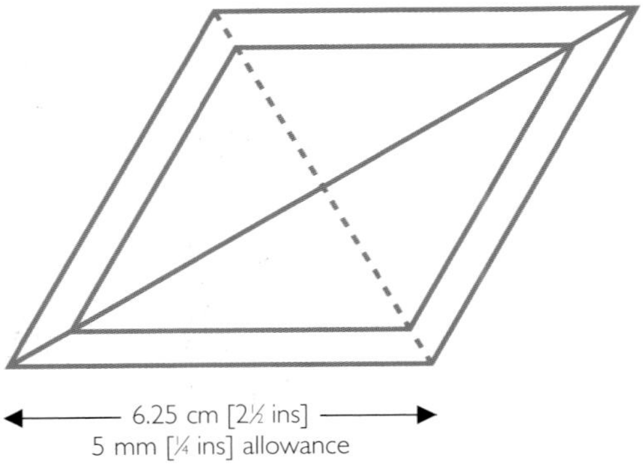

6.25 cm [2½ ins]
5 mm [¼ ins] allowance

21.25 cm [8½ ins]

p.292

BABY'S QUILTED COVERLET

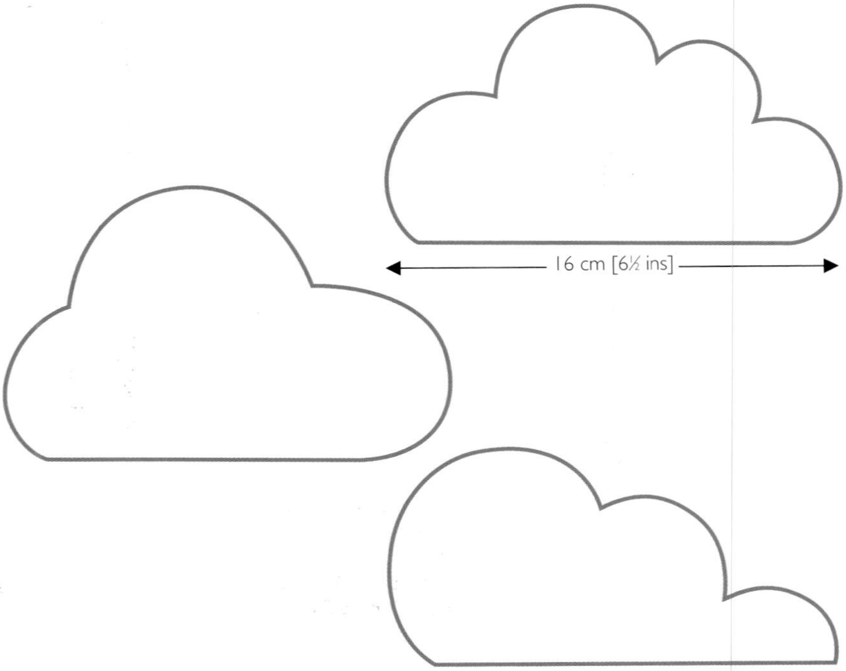

16 cm [6½ ins]

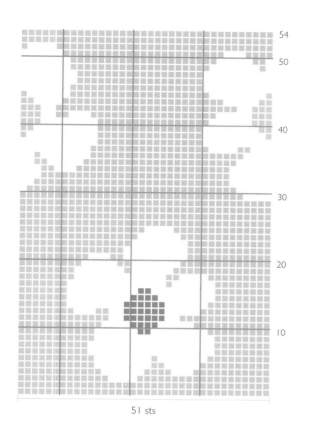

54
50

40

30

20

10

51 sts

p.255

DAISY TUNIC

16.5 (16.5, 16.5, 18, 18) cm
6½ [6½, 6½, 7, 7] ins

18 (18, 19, 19, 20) cm
7 [7, 7½, 7½, 8] ins

60 (60, 61.5, 61.5, 63.5) cm 24 [24, 24¼, 24¼, 25] ins

57 (57, 58, 58, 59.5) cm 22½ [22½, 23, 23, 23½] ins

43 cm [17 ins]

46 (48, 51, 21, 22) cm
8 [8, 8½, 8½, 8½] ins

32 (32.5, 33, 33.5, 34) cm
12½ [13¾, 13, 13¼, 13½] ins

47 cm [18½ ins]

68.5 (68.5, 70, 70, 71) cm 27 [27, 27½, 27½, 28] ins

20 (20, 21.5, 21.5, 21.5) cm
8 [8, 8½, 8½, 8½] ins

BLUE   LAVENDER

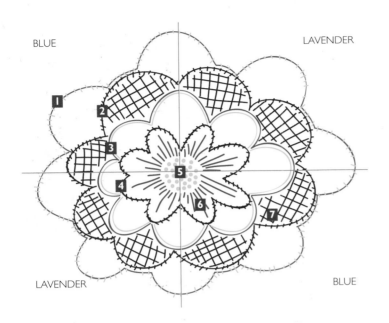

1
2
3
5
4
6
7

LAVENDER   BLUE

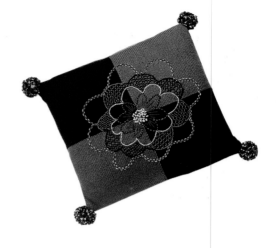

p.252

EMBROIDERED CUSHION

p.250

RIBBON-TIED CARDIGAN

35.5 (36, 36, 37.5, 38) cm [14, 14¼, 14½, 14¾, 15 ins]
14 (14.5, 15, 16, 16.5) cm
5½ [5¾, 6, 6¼, 6½] ins

18 (18,18, 19, 19) cm
7 [7, 7, 7½, 7½] ins

33 (33, 34, 34, 35.5) cm
13 [13, 13½, 13½, 14] ins

53 (53, 55, 56, 57) cm 21 [21, 21½, 22, 22½] ins

41 (43, 46, 48, 51) cm
16 [17, 18, 19, 20] ins

30 (31, 32, 32.5, 33) cm
12 [12¼, 12½, 12¾, 13] ins

14 (14, 14.5, 14.5, 15) cm
5½ [5½, 5¾, 5¾, 6] ins

46 (46, 46.5, 46.5, 47) cm
18 [18 ,18¼, 18¼,18½] ins

59.5 (59.5, 60, 60, 60.5) cm
23 [23½, 24, 24, 24½] ins

20 (20, 20.5, 20.5, 23) cm
8 [8, 8¼, 8½, 9] ins

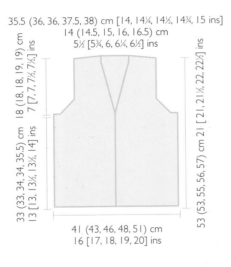

15 cm [6 ins]
5 mm [¼ ins] allowance

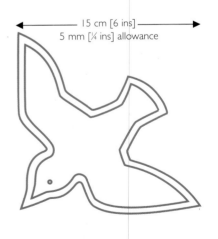

p.288

PATCHWORK SHOPPER

p.296

DUFFEL BAG

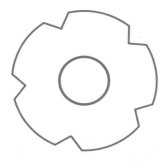

p.277

RIBBON BORDERED SKIRT

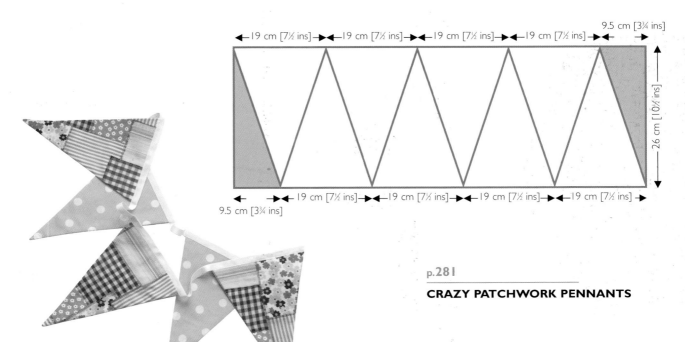

9.5 cm [3¾ ins]

←19 cm [7½ ins]→ ←19 cm [7½ ins]→ ←19 cm [7½ ins]→ ←19 cm [7½ ins]→

26 cm [10½ ins]

←19 cm [7½ ins]→ ←19 cm [7½ ins]→ ←19 cm [7½ ins]→ ←19 cm [7½ ins]→

9.5 cm [3¾ ins]

p.281

CRAZY PATCHWORK PENNANTS

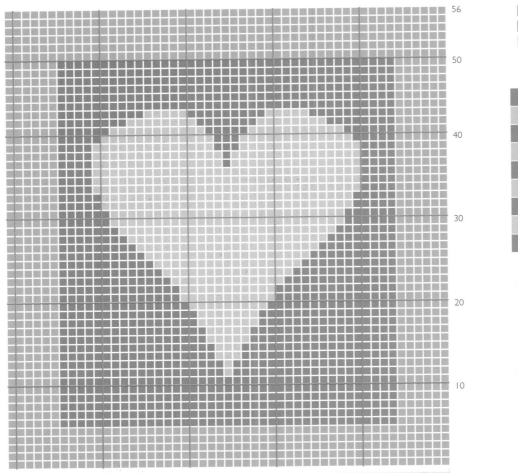

Colour A
Colour B
Colour C

56
50
40
30
20
10

•51 sts

	Colourway 1
Border	A
Background	B
Heart	C

	Colourway 2
Border	B
Background	C
Heart	A

p.254

BIG LOVE THROW

p.276

RECIPE BOOK COVER

p.297

APPLIQUED TOTE BAG

p.284

PET CUSHION

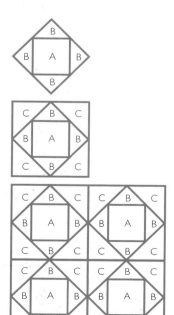

p.274

EMBROIDERED CORSAGE

YARNS USED

Some yarns have been discontinued and are marked with an *. A suggested replacement is given below.

Twisted rib hat
Rowan Big Wool
Colour A Smitten Kitten #003*
Smudge #019
Colour B Whoosh #014

Tube top
Colinette Giotto
Fresco #147

Cabled ski hats
Hat with flaps:
Rowan Pure Wool DK
Ultramarine #009

No Flaps:
Fuchsia #887*
Dahlia 042

Cotton cable backpack
Rowan Denim
Tennessee #231

Ribbon-tied cardigan
Jaeger Albany
Peony #274*
Rowan 4 ply cotton
Cheeky #133

Slouch socks
Colinette Fandango
Ischia #131

Embroidered cushion
Rowan Wool Cotton
Colour A French navy #909
Colour B August #953*
Bilberry #969
Colour C Rich #911
Colour D Citron #901

Stripy fingerless gloves
Rowan Yorkshire Tweed 4 ply
Colour A Whiskers #283*
Colour B Foxy #275*
Colour C Sugar #723*
Colour D Turkish #722*
Colour E Temptation #725*

Rowan Scottish Tweed 4 ply
Colour A Midnight #00023
Colour B Thistle #00016
Colour C Lavender #00005
Colour D Claret #00013
Colour E Porridge #00024

Big love throw
Rowan Kid Classic
Colour A Pinched #819 *
Sherbet dip #850
Colour B Juicy #827*
Cherry red #847
Colour C Cherish #833*
Tea rose #854

Daisy tunic
Rowan Cotton Glacé
Colour A Pier #809
Colour B Hyacinth #787
Colour C Tickle #811
Colour D Bleached #726

Simple sash belt
Rowan Summer Tweed
Exotic #512

Bucket hats
Adult hat:
Rowan Cotton Glacé
Sunny #802*
Butter #795

Baby hat:
Rowan 4-ply Cotton
Cheeky #133

Peek-a-boo cushion cover
Rowan Handknit Double Knitting Cotton
Colour A Chime #204
Colour B Flame #254

Zigzag scarf
Debbie Bliss Merino Double Knitting
Colour A #605
Colour B #607

Striped halter top
Rowan Lurex Shimmer
Colour A Minty #337
Colour B Bedazzled #338

Tubular tote
Rowan Cotton Glacé
Colour A Sky #749
Colour B Splendour #810*
Maritime #817
Colour C Bleached #726

Stripy pouch
12-gauge cotton yarn, dyed to shade required

Beaded bag
Rowan 4-ply Cotton
Ripple #121

Pet basket with liner
Utility string

Bikini top
Rowan Cotton Glacé Pier #809

Shoulder bag
Rowan Cotton Glacé
Colour A Zeal #813*
Buttercup #825
Colour B Mystic #808*
Mocha choc #816
Colour C Shoot #814

Lacy camisole
Rowan 4-ply Cotton
Orchid #120

Granny square vest
Rowan 4-ply Cotton
Colour A Zest #134*
Honeydew #140
Colour B Cheeky #133
Colour C Fennel #135
Rowan Cotton Glacé
Colour D Splendour #810*
Maritime #817

Funky flowers
Rowan Cotton Glacé
Colour A Tickle #811
Colour B Shoot #814

Rowan/Jaeger (UK)
Green Lane Mill
Holmfirth
West Yorkshire HD9 2DX
Tel 01484 681881
www.knitrowan.com
mail@knitrowan.com

Colinette Yarns (UK)
Banwy Workshops
Llanfair Caereinion
Powys SY21 0SG
Tel 01938 810128
www.colinette.com

KNITTING

CROCHET

EMBROIDERY

SEWING

ACKNOWLEDGEMENTS

Carroll & Brown would like to thank Clare Watson of Coats Crafts UK for her help with this project

Photography
All original photography by Jules Selmes and Roger Dixon. Log cabin quilt, page 181, four quilts, page 204, by Buck Miller.

Templates
Amanda Williams

Knitting
Projects designed and made by Sasha Kagan. Knitters: Audur Norris, Teresa Schiff, and Denise Robertson. Knitwear detail, page 37, Tony Davey. Aran sweater, page 42, from Kilkeel Knitting Mills Ltd. Colour motifs, page 62-4 by Sasha Kagan.

Crochet
Crochet contributors: Sylvia Cosh and James Walters. Crochet projects designed and made by Susie Johns. Crochet worker, Pat Rhodes.

Embroidery
Embroidery text by Susie Johns, Caroline Smith, Claire Slack , Deborah Gonet, Moyra McNeill, Jean Hodges and Jan Eaton. Projects designed and created by Gwen Diamond, Lorraine Diamond, Sam Beresford, Hazel Arnott, Susie Johns and Cheryl Owen. Samplers, page 133, by Terry Meinke, The Scarlet Letter, and Ruth Ann Russell. Antique embroideries pages 126-7, loaned by Meg Andrews.

Patchwork & Quilting
Patchwork text copyright © Linda Seward. Additional quilting text by Cheryl Owen. Projects designed and made by Cheryl Owen, Gwen Diamond, Susie Johns. Patchwork and quilting worked by Lynne Edwards, Judy Hammersla, Monica Milne, and Gwen Diamond. Log Cabin quilt, page 181, quilted by Helen Manzanares. Strawberries quilt, page 182, from the permanent collection of the Museum of American Folk Art (gift of Phyllis Haders). Quilts page 194 (top left), Maggie Potter; (top right), Constance Finlayson; (bottom left), Mary Jo McCabe; (bottom right), Frances V. Dunn. Quilted leaf, page 192, designed by Paul Doe.

Sewing
Sewing text Caroline Smith. Projects designed and made by Gwen Diamond, Cheryl Owen and Caroline Smith.